DIALOGUE WITH EUROPE, DIALOGUE WITH THE PAST

DIALOGUE WITH EUROPE, DIALOGUE WITH THE PAST

COLONIAL NAHUA AND QUECHUA ELITES IN THEIR OWN WORDS

Edited by

JUSTYNA OLKO, JOHN SULLIVAN, AND JAN SZEMIŃSKI

UNIVERSITY PRESS OF COLORADO

Louisville

Published by University Press of Colorado
245 Century Circle, Suite 202
Louisville, Colorado 80027

Printed in the United States of America

The University Press of Colorado is a proud member of
the Association of University Presses.

The University Press of Colorado is a cooperative publishing enterprise supported, in part, by Adams State University, Colorado State University, Fort Lewis College, Metropolitan State University of Denver, Regis University, University of Colorado, University of Northern Colorado, Utah State University, and Western State Colorado University.

∞ This paper meets the requirements of the ANSI/NISO Z39.48-1992 (Permanence of Paper).

ISBN: 978-1-60732-832-2 (cloth)
ISBN: 978-1-60732-833-9 (pbk.)
ISBN: 978-1-60732-834-6 (ebook)
DOI: https://doi.org/10.5876/9781607328346

Library of Congress Cataloging-in-Publication Data

Names: Olko, Justyna, editor. | Sullivan, John, 1956– editor. | Szeminski, Jan, editor.
Title: Dialogue with Europe, dialogue with the past : colonial Nahua and Quechua elites in their own words / edited by Justyna Olko, John Sullivan and Jan Szeminski.
Description: Boulder : University Press of Colorado, [2018] | Includes bibliographical references and index.
Identifiers: LCCN 2018045831| ISBN 9781607328322 (cloth) | ISBN 9781607328339 (pbk.) | ISBN 9781607328346 (ebook)
Subjects: LCSH: Mexico—History—Spanish colony, 1540–1810—Sources. | Peru—History—Conquest, 1522–1548—Sources. | Nahuas—Mexico—History—Sources. | Quechua Indians—Peru—History—Sources. | Nahuatl language—Texts. | Quechua language—Texts. | Spanish language—Texts. | Elite (Social sciences)—Mexico—History. | Elite (Social sciences)—Peru—History.
Classification: LCC F1219 .D4595 2018 | DDC 972/.02—dc23
LC record available at https://lccn.loc.gov/2018045831

The University Press of Colorado gratefully acknowledges the generous support of the University of Warsaw toward the publication of this book.

The research leading to these results has received funding from the European Research Council under the European Union's Seventh Framework Program (FP7/2007–2013)/ERC grant agreement no. 312795.

Cover photograph: Contemporary ritual offering on the floor of the colonial church in Huahquechula (the former Nahua state of Cuauhquechollan), Puebla, © Justyna Olko.

In loving memory of Jim Lockhart (1933–2014)

Contents

PETITIONS AND LETTERS

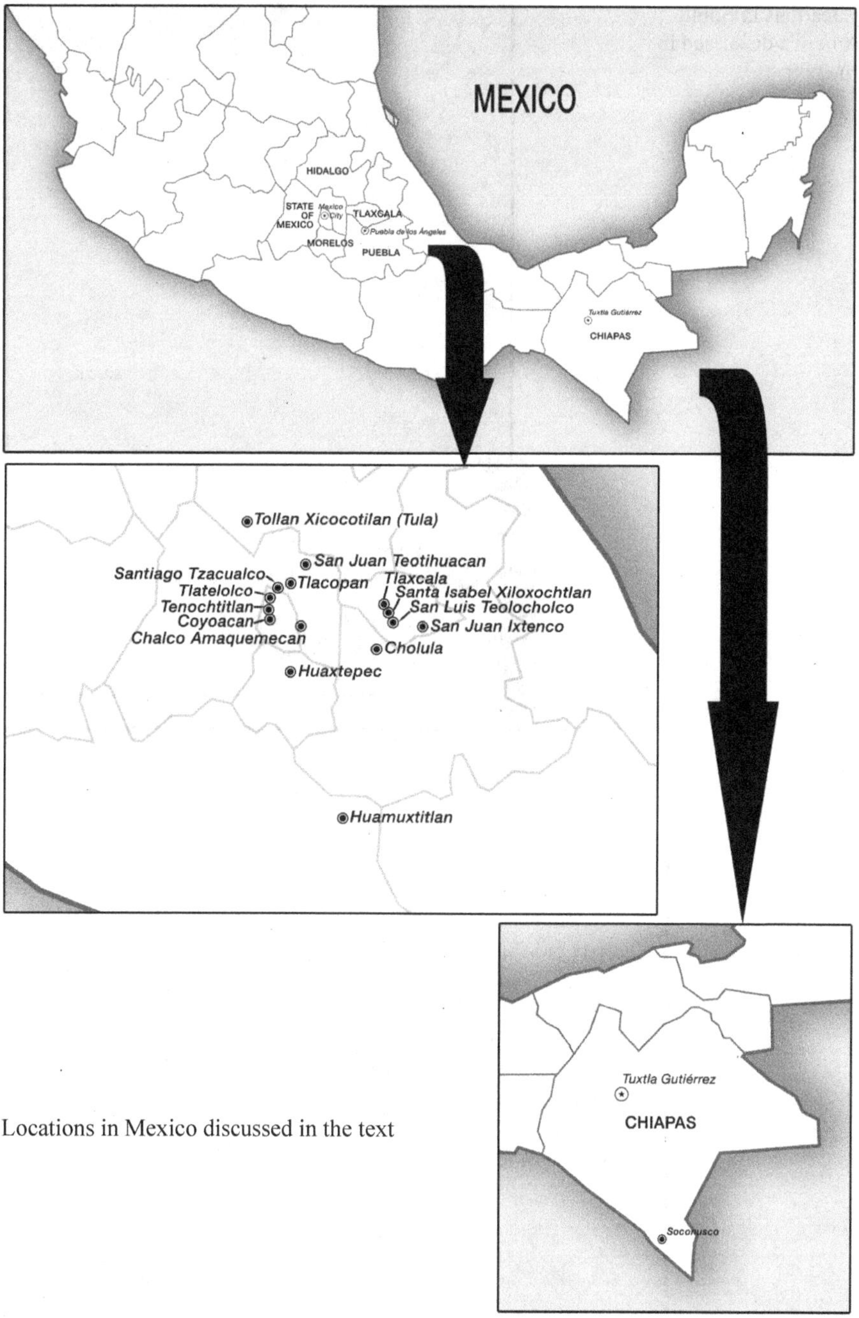

Locations in Mexico discussed in the text

Locations in South America discussed in the text

DIALOGUE WITH EUROPE, DIALOGUE WITH THE PAST

Introduction[1]

Justyna Olko and Jan Szemiński

Over the years, indigenous elites under Spanish rule have been both acknowledged and ignored by historians, anthropologists, and linguists. No one contests the fact that these people existed; however, their own voices are rarely heard and still have a rather limited impact on the modern readings of their history. Today, as a result of the slow but systematic development of research on indigenous sources, focusing first on the ways that those who were supposedly conquered in Mexico and Peru imagined the conquest itself and their own role in it, and subsequently on how they dealt with its consequences, it has become increasingly obvious that the Spanish Empire Over the Sea was not constructed only by the brave conquerors,

1 The research on indigenous elites was supported by a grant from the National Science Center (decision DEC-2011/01/B/HS3/02185, 2011–2014). The study was further developed and significantly extended—in terms of the content, the research questions, and the scope of the sources included—in the years 2015–2017 with funding from the European Research Council under the European Union's Seventh Framework Programme (FP7/2007–2013/ERC grant agreement n° 312795). As part of this project it embraced the phenomena of cross-cultural transfer between indigenous and European cultures, with special focus on language as well as culture contact and change, as reflected in Nahuatl and Quechua. Jan Szemiński's participation was also supported by the Hebrew University of Jerusalem. John Sullivan's participation was supported in part by the Universidad Autónoma de Zacatecas.

DOI: 10.5876/9781607328346.c000a

but also, to a very large extent, by local indigenous elites.[2] Simultaneously subjects and officials of the Crown, it was they who truly carried out the daily governance of the entire Amerindian population where it survived in New Spain and most parts of the Viceroyalty of Peru. Without the service and collaboration of these members of the dynasties of former kings, lords, and other indigenous leaders, Spanish administrators, and conquerors, who had neither the knowledge nor the ability to govern a local population—initially of tens of millions but crashing later to only several million—would not have succeeded. They were too few. However, it is clear from indigenous documents that native elites looked at this process, as well as their position, roles, goals, and advantages in it, in a much different way than was perceived by the Spaniards and, later, the historians who relied exclusively on Spanish sources.

These processes were obviously also directly influenced by the Crown's strategies and the attitudes of its representatives. The conquerors wanted native Americans alive and economically productive. In Haiti (Hispaniola, Española, Santo Domingo), the Spaniards had already discovered that they desperately needed the cooperation of the local leaders, called *caciques* in the Taino language. Without them they would not get food, much less gold, women, or other precious goods. This initial experience must have had lasting impact, because the word *cacique* became the general name for all indigenous leaders in the Spanish empire, from California and Florida to Chile and Buenos Aires, from Navajos and Seminoles in the north to Mapuches and Tehuelches in the south. Indigenous elites, however, were not composed of only *caciques* and their families. Administration in native states and chiefdoms was much more complex because local rulers relied on various kinds of functionaries to administer their own possessions, organize and supervise the

---

2 Pioneering research on indigenous Mesoamerican elites studied from the perspective of their own sources was carried out by Reyes García 1988a, 1988b; Lockhart 1991, 1992; Haskett 1986; Horn 1991; Restall 1995; Doesburg 2002; Terraciano 2002; Wood 2003; Pizzigoni 2007; Chuchiak 2010; Rojas 2012; Townsend 2016; Melton-Villanueva 2016, and others. More recently, there has been important research in colonial and modern Mesoamerican studies focusing on native intellectuals, studied through both indigenous and Spanish sources (e.g., Tavárez 2013; McDonough 2014; Villella 2016). In Andean studies the first texts on indigenous elites appeared in the nineteenth century, motivated by the Great Rebellion of 1780–1783 and other supposed precursors of the wars of independence (Lewin 1967; Rowe 1955). The *indigenista* movement in the twentieth century provoked new research (Rowe 2003), which slowly generated a new perspective on native elites (for example Estenssoro Fuchs 2003; Pärssinen Kiviharju 2004, 2010; Husson 2005; Curatola, Petrocchi, and de la Puente Luna 2013; Gonzales 2014; Ramos and Yannakakis 2014; Adorno and Boserup 2015).

work of their subjects, and collect their taxes. Thus all local states in Mexico and Guatemala had their *calpixqueh* (administrators) and scribes, while all local officials in the Inca empire had their *khipu kamayuqs*, specialists in knot notations for keeping track of statistics, calendars, properties, and histories. These are not exhaustive: native elites needed many more types of specialists, including artisans, agronomists, and engineers. On the other hand, the kings of Castile and Leon, both of whose kingdoms rather than Spain as a whole shared rights to the American possessions, recognized Amerindian elites as nobility. This was extremely important to native noblemen because it meant that, solely because of their birth status, they were exempt from head tax and could not be obliged to participate in forced labor, as were all other indigenous subjects. For this reason, the numbers of local nobility quickly swelled. Everyone sought to be included, just as did those Spaniards in America who cited Asturias, inhabited exclusively by *hidalgos*, as their place of origin.

From the arrival of the Spaniards in 1492 until about 1700, new illnesses from the Old World, the destruction of economic infrastructure, wars, forced labor, and hunger drastically reduced the Amerindian population in all of the Spanish domains, with the most extreme estimates suggesting as much as a 90 percent reduction (Cook 1998; Crosby 1972: 44–56; 1994: 97–106; Nutini and Isaac 2009: 33).[3] It is estimated that the indigenous population in central Mexico (from the Isthmus of Tehuantepec in the south to Nueva Galicia in the north) was reduced from ca. 25 million in 1518 to ca. 1.9 million in 1585 and only 0.75 million in 1622 (Borah 1983: 26). This catastrophe forced the new rulers to take special administrative and organizational measures in order to protect the interests, both of the empire—taxes and forced labor—and the colonists, who wanted to build large *latifundia* and needed a ready work force. Thus in the mid-sixteenth century Spanish administrators were already beginning to resettle the indigenous population into bigger, centralized villages and towns, in order to facilitate political control, tax collection, forced labor administration, and Christianization. After all, even though the Spanish Empire needed local indigenous people, it wanted them as Catholic Christians and not as heathens. In the new settlements, which always had land assigned both to the town as a whole and to each family in particular, a new type of administration, modeled after Castilian municipal government, was to prevail. One of its objectives was to diminish the influence of local rulers;

3 It is estimated that the demographic recovery of the indigenous population got underway in New Spain around 1650, but in the Andes the process began a bit later, near the beginning of the eighteenth century.

however, the process developed differently in each region. In the empire as a whole, local Amerindian elites managed to take over most or all municipal administrative functions, thus adding influence to the power they already had from precolonial times. But after all, it was power over a diminishing native population, and Amerindian administrators had no jurisdiction over non-indigenous people, except in cases when they possessed slaves, imported from Africa by the Spaniards.

Native ways of representing colonial reality through their own writings and documentary production have already made their way into the modern scholarly world through a number of anthologies, some of them editions of indigenous sources with English or Spanish translations, accompanied by both extensive and abbreviated studies and commentaries.[4] Building and expanding on this important tradition, the present book is a critical, commented anthology of indigenous-authored texts, including the Nahua, Quechua, and Spanish originals. As such, it is a first attempt to bring together native testimonies from two different areas of Spanish expansion in the Americas in order to compare these geographically and culturally distant realities of indigenous elites in the colonial period.[5] Our intention is not to comprehensively present and describe

4 Editions of Nahuatl documents hold an especially prominent and in many ways pioneering place in this vein of scholarship. While the following list is certainly not exhaustive, publications of original Nahua documents along with modern translations and critical commentaries/studies go back to 1976 and have continued to appear until recently: Anderson, Berdan, and Lockhart 1976; Karttunen and Lockhart 1976; Cline and León-Portilla 1984; Karttunen and Lockhart 1987; Reyes García 1988b, 2001; Lockhart 1991; Lockhart 1992; Cline 1993; Zapata y Mendoza [Reyes García and Martínez Baracs] 1995; Dakin and Lutz 1996; Schwaller and Sell 1999; Burkhart 2001; Sullivan 2007; Pizzigoni 2007; Townsend 2010; Melton-Villanueva 2014, 2017, among others. A separate, large group of publications includes editions of the so-called primary sources in Nahuatl (e.g., Sahaguntine corpus, works by Chimalpahin, *Cantares mexicanos*). An anthology of documents in Spanish dealing with indigenous elites was published by Pérez-Rocha and Tena (2000); an extensively commented anthology published by Restall and Asselbers (2007) contains the translation into English of Spanish and native documents (without the originals) related to the different stages and experiences of the conquest; similarly, the anthology edited by Restall, Sousa, and Terraciano (2005) provides only English translations of documents originally in Nahuatl and Yucatec Maya, representing different genres of colonial writing. Some publications contain transcriptions and Spanish colonial *trasuntos* of original native documents with no modern translations (Luis Reyes García et al. 1996; Rojas Rabiela et al. 1999). Andean examples include Salomon and Urioste 1991; Pärssinen and Kiviharju 2004, 2010; Husson 2001; Gonzales 2014.

5 A certain precedent is no doubt established by the collective book edited by Kellogg and Restall (1998) that deals with native testaments of colonial Mesoamerica and the Andes. Sample wills accompany the chapters of the book; although a number of Nahuatl documents are included, the Andean sample contains testaments written in Spanish.

native elites in these two essential macroregions of the Spanish Empire Over the Sea. Our objectives are much more modest. First, we wish to demonstrate that they existed as independent actors in colonial society, as well as agents of social change and indigenous sustainability in colonial times. We know, of course, that indigenous elites survived the Wars of Independence; however, both the armed conflicts and independence itself changed their situation and eroded their existence as a separate social group. Second, we want to show the elites through documents they themselves produced or caused to be produced, giving as much priority as possible to indigenous ways of expression, perspectives, and concepts. Elites were particularly influential in the Nahua area of Mexico and in the former Inca empire. The Mexican elites, who had paper and hieroglyphic writing before the conquest, quickly produced documents written in Nahuatl with the Latin alphabet. The Andean elites' writing systems did not resemble anything the Spaniards brought with them. After the conquest they continued using their traditional knot-records; they used three-dimensional hieroglyphics in Quechua and Aymara for Catholic prayers; and later they produced texts using the Latin alphabet in Spanish and, exceptionally, in Quechua. Written Quechua was used more by Catholic missionaries than by indigenous people themselves.

Our choice of documents is not entirely and exhaustively representative for the topic. This would indeed require many volumes. Thus, although our intention is to showcase the important and varied colonial genres of indigenous writing, the documents we have selected reveal only some, but by no means all, of the realities, needs, strategies, behaviors, and attitudes associated with the lives of the elites. Likewise, we do not presume to have collected a corpus of documents that speaks for all the elites, because it is impossible to define them strictly and establish borders that set them apart from other social actors. It is evident in the sample presented here that many groups in indigenous society had access to writing (through notaries) and used it to defend and promote their needs and interests. As we show, indicators such as the material base, degree of wealth, and social position form a kind of continuum: defining boundaries between "elites" and "non-elites" is an inherently problematic endeavor. Perhaps elites can be best understood not only as nobility but also as active groups within local communities enjoying varying shades of status.

We do, however, wish to present and discuss the characteristics of specific genres of documents. Each document in this anthology is transcribed exactly as it appears in the manuscript or in the colonial printed document, rendering as faithfully as possible, all abbreviations, marginal notes, signs, numbers, measures, and so on. Each is translated to English from Nahuatl,

Spanish, or Quechua, and accompanied by a commentary and footnotes, and a collective glossary of recurrent expressions from Spanish, Nahuatl, and Quechua appears at the end of this volume. The original documents have been identified, transcribed, translated, and studied by the authors of each particular section and, with some exceptions, are published here for the first time.[6] Accompanying each document, a study comments on the content of the document, its historical and cultural context, as well as the reasons it was composed in the first place—highlighting the identities, roles, strategies, and actions linked to indigenous elites and other members of local communities. The characteristics of a specific genre, along with literary and orthographic conventions, are also discussed. We give special attention to the language of the documents: on the one hand, we focus on the survival of preconquest concepts, and on the other hand we examine the contact-induced changes in language that simultaneously accompany, result from, and contribute to more general and varied types of cross-cultural transfer and cultural change. The contributors to the volume comment extensively on the mutual influences between Spanish and Nahuatl, or Spanish and Quechua, showing that in many cases a scholar studying a text written by an indigenous person in Spanish may not be able to understand its form or content completely if he or she cannot interpret it from the perspective of the writer's first language.

So, for whom is this book? Students and researchers interested in indigenous colonial societies in the Spanish Empire will discover in its pages the persistent existence and the blurred boundaries of Amerindian elites, the sources that need to be mustered and the problems that should be addressed in order to study them, and the need to explore such elites in each region with the careful and multifaceted analyses of their own sources. To these objectives we add the overarching imperative to compare and contrast indigenous elites in the empire as a whole; this will allow us to demonstrate that the imperial sociopolitical group known as *caciques* was an artificial generalization created by Castilian administrators, bureaucrats, and modern historians and existed on paper only. We want to embrace different members of local elites, at different levels of the social hierarchy; we want to compare the *apus* (Andean lords) and their servants with the Mexican *tlahtohqueh* and *pipiltin* (rulers and nobles, respectively) and their modes of organization under the rule of the viceroys of New Spain and Peru. We will leave the *caciques* in peace on the Caribbean Islands.

6 Information regarding the previous publication of a given document appears in a footnote in its respective study.

Nahua and Quechua Elites of the Colonial Period

Continuity and Change in a Cross-Cultural Context

Justyna Olko and Jan Szemiński

OUR APPROACH TO THE TOPIC

The indigenous nobility of colonial America has gained a substantial space in scholarly pursuits, much more than other sectors of indigenous society. Engagement with the topic has no doubt been complex: researchers have used both sources written by the colonizers and by the colonialized, who employed the colonial language to tell the story of their peoples and themselves. There has also been considerable interest in directly exploring the native perspective through indigenous documents in religious, literary, and mundane genres (e.g., León-Portilla 1959; Reyes García 1988a; Burkhart 1989, 2001; Haskett 1991, 2005; Horn 1997; Lockhart 1991, 1992; Schroeder 1991; Kellogg 1995; Terraciano 2002; Estenssoro Fuchs 2003; Pärssinen Kiviharju 2004, 2010; Husson 2005; Pizzigoni 2007, 2012; Townsend 2010, 2016; Hosselkus 2011; Curatola, Petrocchi, and de la Puente Luna 2013; Wood 2013; Gonzales 2014; Ramos and Yannakakis 2014; Adorno and Boserup 2015; Medrano, Kellogg, and Davidson 2016, among others). This approach, however, has only rarely highlighted the status or specific voices of other non-elite social groups (Offner 1984: 138–147, 163–174; Lockhart 1991: 66–74; 96–101, 110–117; Hicks 1999). In Mexico and in Peru, research on indigenous perspectives, based on indigenous sources, began with the works of such scholars as Miguel León-Portilla (1959), Luis Reyes García (e.g., 1972, 1988a, 1988b, 1996, 2001) and José María Arguedas (1956). Later, this kind of research was

DOI: 10.5876/9781607328346.c000b

continued and amplified with new topics and new sources in Latin America and beyond. An important methodological framework for this venture has been provided by the so-called New Philology, an important vein in modern North American ethnohistorical research emphasizing the study of the past through indigenous sources written in indigenous languages (Restall 2003; Lockhart 2007). While space has been given to indigenous voices of the past, there have been virtually no attempts to traverse the geographical boundaries of two key areas of the Spanish colonial empire, the Mesoamerican and Andean worlds, despite the existence of numerous parallels and variations of responses to basically similar experiences.[7] As we intend to show, the two perspectives are mutually enriching and enlightening. This book is a collective search, employing diverse research tools and disciplinary perspectives, into the past reality of the purportedly "colonized" indigenous people through their own voices and expressions. In approaching the fragments of microhistories perpetuated in alphabetic script by indigenous actors who struggled to do so on their own terms, we attempt to bring to the surface the contexts, the circumstances, and the very processes of creation of those testimonies, as well as the language that constitutes them, language that both shaped and was shaped by the reality and the situations we are now attempting to reconstruct. Thus, our work may also be viewed as a scholarly endeavor that seeks to delve, as much as possible, into the ontological perspective of the indigenous people who participated in and fashioned the reality of the past.

In our effort to sidestep the preconceived criteria of modern scholarship and embrace the broad spectrum of indigenous voices, we propose a wide, contextual definition of indigenous "elites." This is by no means limited to the prehispanic rules (not themselves always precise or rigid) of membership in the noble class, nor to their transformation during the colonial period based on Spanish principles. Sources coming from the Nahua world lead us to understand that thinking in terms of elites versus non-elites is not compatible with the intermediate, fluent, dynamic categories that were an inherent part of the native social hierarchy. The fluidity of Nahua social dynamics was reflected in the preconquest category, which included the *cuauhpipiltin* 'quasi-nobles' and the *cuauhtlahtohqueh* 'quasi-rulers' (Tomicki 2003: 241–258), who could

7 An exception is Lockhart's study (1997) focusing on the impact of Spanish on Nahuatl, Yucatec Maya, and Quechua, to which we refer in the latter part of this chapter, as well as the already-mentioned collective book on native testaments of colonial Mesoamerica and the Andes (Kellogg and Restall 1998).

rise high, especially in the military ranking in the Aztec empire. However, it was this very category that benefited from the political opportunities emerging during and immediately after the conquest when political turmoil and shifting alliances with Spaniards eliminated many "legitimate" candidates for rulership (as was the case in Tenochtitlan); Cortés himself elevated loyal indigenous collaborators from outside both the ruling dynasty and even the nobility, strictly defined, to the rank of "governors." Another category was that of the *teixhuihuan* 'grandchildren of someone,' situated at a certain genealogical or generational distance from their high-ranking noble progenitors; often they were impoverished members of the elite class who merged with the commoners. As is evident in the case of the famous native annalist from Chalco Amaquemecan, Don Domingo de San Antón Muñón Chimalpahin Quauhtlehuanitzin, having local rulers among one's grandparents as well as contemporary high-ranking family members did not guarantee recognition as a member of the aristocracy (Schroeder 1991: 8–13). The already-fluid nature of social categories in the indigenous world was further enhanced by the colonial situation and its legal duality, situating individual struggles for political and social advancement between the two traditions and legal systems: indigenous and Spanish. The latter, taking into account both peninsular patterns and New World opportunities, was far from being a closed system either: accession to the noble class was easier in the sixteenth century than ever before and it was closely linked to economic success (Lockhart and Schwartz 1983: 4–5). Besides, indigenous social hierarchy and its roles were constantly evolving throughout the colonial system. This was especially the case toward the later colonial period when the highest nobility often became somewhat disassociated from indigenous communities and was linked more to the Spanish and *mestizo* culture (Lockhart 1992: 134, 320). As early as in the seventeenth century, the Tlaxcalan annalist, Don Juan Buenaventura Zapata y Mendoza, attested to this ongoing sociopolitical change as he complained that people of commoner origin as well as *mestizos* gained political prominence, usurping and eroding the traditional position of the noble class as "entrusted representatives of the indigenous community" (Townsend 2016: 200–201). For this reason, we have also decided to provide space in this volume for other members of indigenous society whose voices were recorded and who, rather than pertaining to the hereditary nobility, strictly speaking, apparently belonged to the "middle" or "upper commoner" class or, in some cases, may have been commoners of varying but usually good economic status (Documents 2–6, 8, 9, 15, 17). Among the participants in the documents we also have a probable representative of the above-mentioned lower noble class of *teixhuihuan*, which merged with the commoners over the course of the colonial period (Document 4).

The fluid boundaries between lower groups of native nobility and the "middle class" were further weakened by the dynamics of colonial adaptations, institutions, and ongoing negotiations, especially given the lack of rigidity in the Spanish system of social ranking. Therefore, it is imperative that any scholarly endeavor addressing topics related to indigenous elites in colonial times embrace the long-term—in fact, permanent—reality of culture contact, along with its associated translations, dialogues, and transfers, and consider as well the adaptations and transformations of the native systems. While attempting to approach parallel (though intertwined) colonial realities ruled by different ontologies, we should also envision a middle ground (White 1991), a common zone of developments, communication, exchange, and (mis) understanding between the two cultures and groups of agents who shaped their own local worlds. Looking at the documents as holistically as possible, we aim to grasp the microrealities and ontologies they represent (Anderson 2015), and by doing so, aspire to understand the broader context and patterns of the cultural, sociopolitical, and economic lives as well as the cross-cultural entanglements of their actors. We believe that giving priority to indigenous voices and focusing on their agency in numerous facets of the early colonial worlds constitutes a step toward the decolonization of colonial history.

LEGAL STATUS IN THE SPANISH EMPIRE: THE DUALITY OF LAW

After their first experience in the colonization of the Caribbean, Spaniards already had an initial set of laws, institutions, and procedures to deal with indigenous people and the resources they produced. Some of those institutions, such as the *encomienda*,[8] and certain forms of economic enterprises were to a great extent directly implemented on the mainland. However, there were also important differences between the two settings that forced the colonizers to develop new strategies to deal with much more complex sociopolitical and economic structures extending over vast areas that, above all, were characterized by an unparalleled number of indigenous populations, both in Mesoamerica and in the Andes. They soon realized that they could not replace the native system of rule; rather, they inserted it within a subtle imperial structure, efficient enough to ensure economic gains.

---

8 See the glossary.

When the Spaniards arrived in Central Mexico, a highly multiethnic area dominated by speakers of the Nahuatl language, and—on the political level—by the Aztec empire,[9] they faced a highly complex micro- and macrolevel sociopolitical organization and administrative apparatus, and well as mechanisms of interregional communication, trade, and exchange. Although the conceptual framework and detailed operational rules of native sociopolitical and administrative organization were not entirely clear to them, even after decades of interactions—the Spaniards tended to impose their own criteria and concepts on the local reality—they became aware that they had to deal efficiently with local rulers and leaders. The Nahuas' ethnic states, called *altepetl,* varied in size, rank, and ethnic composition (some were strongly multiethnic). The members of a given *altepetl* had rights over certain territories, which could be their property or tribute areas (e.g. Berdan 1996, 2006, 2007; Berdan and Smith 1996, 2003; Smith 2005, 2008). Such an entity could either have sovereign status or be subordinated to other local or regional states (or empires, as in the case of the Aztec empire), which claimed tribute from them. The *altepetl* had a "cellular structure": it was composed of constituent parts that were complementary and symmetrical, preserving a certain degree of autonomy and operating on a rotational basis (Lockhart 1992: 14–25); some of its essential features continued after Mexican independence (Melton-Villanueva 2016: 150–152). The transition period in the sixteenth century was characterized by general confusion, due in great part to the fact that each group, Spanish as well as indigenous people, possessed deficient knowledge about the other. Given this situation, and despite the Spanish presence, native elites strove to keep their key structures and legitimization mechanisms intact. A good example of how they did this is contained in the pictorial document *Painting of the Idols of the Temple of Huitzilopochtli, Mexico Tenochtitlan, 1539–1540* (Document 1, this volume), which reveals how rulers and nobles of many *altepetl,* bound by strong kinship ties, collaborated to protect the sacred bundle of their preeconquest patron god, Huitzilopochtli. The bundle was believed to contain the spiritual force crucial to the legitimacy of power in Tenochtitlan; it probably served the same function for the indigenous colonial ruler of Tenochtitlan, Don Diego Huanitzin (Castañeda de la Paz, Document 1).

When they initiated their rule, Spaniards usually dealt directly with particular *altepetl*—and especially, with their rulers or collaborating political leaders,

9 The term *empire* also crops up in sixteenth-century sources to designate the Triple Alliance of Tenochtitlan, Tetzcoco, and Tlacopan, called *excan tlahtoloyan* 'triple place of rule' in the original Nahuatl terminology.

often elevating them to the rank of Spanish-nominated governors—because they did not have any other practical choice. The *altepetl* became the base for establishing Spanish administration and municipal structures, at least in the areas with a dense native population, such as Tlaxcala. Thus, while not abolishing indigenous divisions, entities, and power structures, Spaniards often ignored or misunderstood the internal divisions and topography of a specific *altepetl*, urging the indigenous authorities to found a *cabecera*, or head town, in low-lying, flat areas located within or neighboring the territory of the original *altepetl* (Lockhart 1992: 14–30). However, one should ponder the true extent and genuine interest of the Spaniards in this centralization policy. Peninsular cities were themselves strongly integrated with the surrounding territory; both a good portion of their citizens' property and a considerable percentage of the general population were in fact situated outside the city walls (Lockhart and Schwartz 1983: 3). In many cases, such as Tlaxcala, this reorganization did not imply a forced abandonment of the original sections of the complex *altepetl* (which continued to thrive on several hills surrounding the river valley where the colonial town was established); rather their gradual degradation as seats of institutionalized life began once key institutions had been established in the central, low-lying area where the colonial town was founded (Gibson 1967: 125–134; Martínez Baracs 2008: 135–148). Later on, in the second half of the sixteenth century, this policy led to forced *congregaciones* (congregations or resettlements), the traumatic impact of which was stronger in those communities for whom the experience of the Spanish conquest had been often indirect or remote. In huge urbanized zones, such as Mexico-Tenochtitlan, organizational duality was maintained, with the parallel existence of indigenous and Spanish municipal structures and organizations. Newly founded centers for European populations, such as the town of Puebla de los Ángeles, could replicate Spanish patterns much more closely.

The Spanish government in early New Spain was headed by the viceroy and included the members of the high court, or Real Audiencia, as well as the judicial/administrative officers in charge of larger districts, usually encompassing several *altepetl* (*corregidores de indios*, assigned to specific jurisdictional units called *corregimientos*). By creating a certain organizational duality derived from their reliance on native organization, the Spaniards in fact contributed to the continuity of precontact entities in the colonial times (Gibson 1964: 63–74; Lockhart 1992: 28–29; Horn 1997: 19). As a result of this double organizational system, the institution of *cacique y gobernador* ('native ruler and [municipal] governor') became a typical feature of the indigenous political landscape in the early and mid-colonial period (Gibson

1964: 158–167). This figure simultaneously embodied the local, innate legitimacy (and economic base) of rule based on inheritance, and the newly introduced municipal order where the performance of office and its associated power derived from Spanish law and organizational principles (Olko 2011: 458–466; 2014: 272–275). This duality regarding the sources of legitimacy is clearly visible in the nomenclature employed in the 1560 document from Tlaxcala related to land litigation (Document 3). The judge presiding over the case is referred to as *muy noble señor alcalde ordinario* 'very noble lord, ordinary judge', whereas the claimant, holding the same municipal office but not acting in his capacity as a judge, is introduced with the native title of *pilli* 'noble', a noble citizen of the *altepetl*. Thus, the criteria for referencing one system of rank or the other appears to have been contextual, depending on the role assumed by an indigenous noble in a given situation.

Strong continuity with the indigenous past in New Spain was possible because the representatives of the Crown, at least in the early colonial times, pragmatically respected preexisting political-territorial units when attempting to transplant the most important peninsular institutional forms and legal frameworks. Certain aspects of the latter, such as the rotational nature of municipal offices, were, at least during the first phase of colonial rule, destined to fail, and became strongly readjusted to indigenous norms, customs, and laws. Native law was never officially recognized as a parallel system to that of Spain, although the Spaniards showed some interest in documenting preconquest regulations. However, local customs and laws (when not constituting a direct contradiction to those Spanish norms that were being implemented on a local level) continued to be practiced, especially given the fact that local community members were acting as the town council's first-instance judges. Colonial appellation courts such as the central *audiencia* located in Mexico-Tenochtitlan recognized the validity both of testimonies given in Nahuatl and of indigenous pictorial documents.

When the Spaniards entered the Andean area and discovered the Inca empire, they already had a well-formed policy regarding how to organize conquered lands. Earlier experiences had demonstrated the need for indigenous representatives to serve as intermediaries between a Spanish administrator and the local population. As in New Spain, the Spaniards referred to them all with the Taino word *cacique*, ignoring their specific traditional social or political status. The Catholic monarchs recognized the *caciques* as legitimate representatives of the local population, but with two stipulations: they should have the right to rule according to local custom and law; and they should be good Catholics, or at least agree to become Catholics, since it was understood that conversion took time. This policy created parallel legal systems in all the lands where native populations persisted: the laws of Castile, according to the practice of the Burgos chancellery, and local laws, provided they did not conflict with Burgos law or the Castilian version of the Catholic faith. Spanish law recognized indigenous elites as nobility, and while Spanish authorities tried to limit their numbers, noble families made every effort to include as many people as possible in the list of local noblemen, because this registry exempted a man and his family from the head tax and obligatory work for the Spaniards.

While most local issues were dealt with by local judicial instances, many appeals were directed to the *audiencia* courts presided over by the viceroy. Both he and the Spanish king were important referents in the hierarchy of power for the local nobility. The viceroys of New Spain play a special role in Nahuatl documents, especially those from the late colonial period (Wood 1991: 178, 181–186). On the other hand, in the early colonial period, native petitions are sometimes addressed directly to the viceroy and the Spanish king himself. In the present volume, the nobles from Soconusco appeal directly to King Philip II (Document 26), and the recipient of the complaint from Huamuxtitlan is most probably the viceroy, in his capacity as the president of the Royal Court (Document 28). It is possible that in the eyes of the natives, the authority of the viceroy, who resided in the city of Mexico-Tenochtitlan, was enhanced by an association with the *huei tlahtoani* ('great speaker', the supreme ruler] of the Aztec empire, who resided in preconquest Tenochtitlan. In Peru, the Inca rulers based in Vilcabamba between 1536–1572, who resisted Spanish power and planned to reconquer their former domain, were recognized as Inca kings by all the indigenous nobility and also by the Spanish authorities, including the viceroy of Peru residing in Lima. However, after the Spanish conquest of Vilcabamba and the public execution of the last Inca king in Cuzco in 1572, the viceroy in Lima was treated not only as a representative of the king in Madrid, but also as a representative of the Spanish king occupying the Inca king's place and functions. Native nobility in Peru believed that the king in Madrid was the king of Peru, a substitute for the Inca king at "the present time." Local elites managed to stay organized in local multilayered hierarchies, the top tier of which was usually occupied by the Spanish governor of the province, titled *corregidor* in the majority of cases. At least until the mid-seventeenth century, the descendants of Inca kings were at the top of the hierarchy of power; below them were various levels of provincial and local indigenous nobles, carefully claiming and safeguarding their privileges and rights in the *audiencias*. However, despite acknowledging the authority of the Spanish system, they always considered that the source of their legitimacy lay in the appointments and functions granted to their ancestors by the Inca kings. In the Spanish courts they could not use the most important Andean argument for validating their station, namely, that they were direct descendants of the ancestors who, at the beckoning of the Creator's envoy, had emerged from a place as a male-female couple (Szemiński 1997, 2016). Interestingly enough, colonial authorities also recognized this source of legitimacy, at least to a certain extent. In the instructions for the confession of *kurakas* it was important to determine if a respondent inherited his *curacazgo* legally, or if he acquired it as a result of a *llulla ñinakuy* ('unfair claim'). Thus, the position of a *kuraka* confessant was only considered legitimate if his father or grandfather was a *kuraka* himself before the Spanish conquest (Haimovich, Document 34, this volume).

LOCAL ORGANIZATION

It was on the local level that preconquest organization had the biggest chances for survival and indeed it was able to preserve many of its key elements through much of the colonial period (and some continuities can still be found in native communities today). A crucial figure in the local political landscape, both before and after the conquest, was the head of an *altepetl* and a rulership (*tlahtohcayotl*) bearing the title of a *tlahtoani* ('the speaker'). The constituent parts of a complex, decentralized *altepetl* were ruled by separate *tlahtohqueh,* who both collaborated and competed in local political struggles. Sometimes they headed distinct ethnic groups acting as rival factions (Reyes García 1988; Lockhart 1992: 18–21). With the introduction of Spanish institutions, a specific *altepetl* could first become an *encomienda*, and then a parish and municipality; although it usually deviated from the prototype, the intention was that it embody the peninsular organizational concept of a *cabecera,* or head town (Lockhart 1992: 29). However, some of the largest and most densely populated indigenous areas were assigned to the Crown right from the beginning because of their considerable size and wealth and were soon put under the supervision of *corregidores de indios* (Lockhart and Schwartz 1983: 106). The *altepetl,* then, continued as the base of native municipal government, conflating the peninsular model of *cabildos* or town councils and indigenous organizational models. Just as before the conquest, they also served as centers for tribute collection and administration of collective labor. The degree of assimilation of the *cabildo* model depended on its adjustment to the traditional structure of native sociopolitical units; for example, establishing a strict correspondence between the number of *cabildo* members and the constituent parts that made up the internal structure of an *altepetl*. Such adjustments could also relate to the dynamics of internal hierarchy. For instance, the rotational execution of the office of governor in Chalco Amaquemecan strictly followed the preconquest pattern: in 1563 the office began to rotate among the rulers of the five *tlayacatl*, the constituent parts of this originally complex *altepetl* (Schroeder 1991: 187).

In the first decades after the conquest—and also in the cases of some *altepetl* in the seventeenth century and beyond (e.g. Horn 1997: 55)—a *tlahtoani* was appointed to the office of the *cabildo* chief, or governor. Quite naturally then, in the very first phase of the colonial period, it was not uncommon for the function of the *gobernador* to precede the creation of additional municipal offices: these seats were occupied by native *tlahtohqueh*, often for life, thus stymieing Spanish efforts to keep them rotational (Gibson 1960: 188; Lockhart 1992: 30–32). However, in their attempts at the end of the sixteenth century to weaken the dominant position of the local hereditary nobility, and especially where local conflicts or legal problems came to the surface, officials of the Crown began to appoint nobles from one *altepetl* to assume control over the municipal government of another. These indigenous functionaries were known as *jueces gobernadores* and performed their duties for a specific period of time. Municipal organization in early New Spain also provided spaces for other high-ranking members of the Nahua nobility. They competed for two important offices: the *alcaldes* focused, albeit not exclusively, on judicial issues and acted as first-instance judges, and the *regidores* were councilmen responsible for the operation of the *cabildo* as well as the management and organization of public labor. Both corresponded with the main divisions of the *altepetl* and its major lineages, representing specific units of the indigenous sociopolitical organization, and their number was usually determined according to this structure. In this context, a clear relationship between preconquest and postconquest offices is revealed by the adoption of old titles, such as *teuctlahtohqueh*, referring to *calpolli* heads and judges, for colonial *alcaldes*. Among lower-ranking municipal officeholders were at least one or two notaries or *escribanos*—drawing on the position and prestige of preconquest scribes/painters or *amatlahcuilohqueh*—provincial lieutenants (*tenientes*), constables (*alguaciles* or *topilehqueh*, 'staff holders'), and stewards (*mayordomos*). A quite remarkable characteristic of Nahua municipal organization was that most, if not all, posts came to be reserved for members of the noble class (Lockhart 1990: 100; 1992: 36–43; Horn 1997: 57).

Within the provinces of the Inca empire, the conquerors encountered a very complicated, multitiered administration. Governors and other nominees of the imperial administration who resided in the capitals of the big imperial provinces lost their power and functions with the fall of the empire. The same, it seems, happened with lower-level imperial agents. Each Inca province was composed of one or more Andean states conquered by the Incas. The Incas preserved local elites, whose members were subordinated to an Inca governor, and they continued to administer their state and preside over the local noble hierarchy. With the Spanish conquest, the Inca governor was substituted for by a Spanish governor, later called a *corregidor*, or temporarily by a Spanish *encomendero*. Local elites continued exercising their functions, but here again, the Spaniards did not take into account their traditional status within the nobility: they called all of them *caciques*, or sometimes used a name taken from Quechua, *kuraka*, which originally simply meant elder, alderman, or chief of a local group. For the first two generations after 1532 the local noble hierarchy remained in place. As in Inca times and indeed before, two lords stood at the head of a local state, constituted by an ethnic group, each with jurisdiction over a part of the population, which they represented before any external entity, such as a Spanish governor. Subordinated to them were the chiefs, also usually two in each subdivision, and under them, administrators of each ceremonial center, imagined ideally by the Inca as composed of a hundred families, divided into lineages. The number of levels depended on the area and the population. In some provinces the hierarchies survived until the end of the eighteenth century, but in a few they remain to this day, even if the representation is exercised only by coopted leaders and not by noble families.

The depopulation caused by European epidemics, the destruction of agricultural infrastructure, war, terror, and obligatory work (*mita*) destroyed some segments of local groups completely, and some partially. Under the rule of the Viceroy Don Francisco de Toledo (1569–1581) the policy of *reducciones* was implemented. It consisted of constructing large villages populated by natives expelled from their lands in order to facilitate taxation, Christianization, and labor organization. This astute policy left the Spanish administration with land to be distributed among Spaniards. New villages were to have an administrative apparatus modeled on the Spanish municipality. The new organizational model was largely fictitious, since the *caciques* maintained their rights and administered their groups even after resettlement. In other words, the *caciques* carried out the political functions in municipal administration. Higher offices at the level of the province or in its subdivisions also survived reforms, at least until the Great Rebellion of the 1780s (Glave 1999; Rostworowski and Morris 1999; Saignes 1999; Spalding 1999).

The source of importance of the Andean lords and chiefs under Spanish rule was the same as under the Inca: their knowledge. A professional, well-educated Andean administrator knew how many people resided in his jurisdiction, and what workforce they represented. He had knowledge of the complicated agricultural system of the Andes: he knew what was cultivated and in what area; and he was versed with regard to the different agricultural cycles that existed at different altitudes. Thus he planned the workforce distribution according to pertinent necessities and possibilities. He was aided in his job by *khipu kamayuqs* and by specialists in farming at different altitudes. He always knew how many working days were needed for agricultural or non-agricultural activities. These aptitudes enabled him to organize the production necessary to pay the Spanish head tax, although it was a head tax only in theory. In practice it was a contribution calculated for each village, town, and sometimes province, in *pesos*, work, and products, at least during the first two centuries of colonial rule (Szemiński, research in progress).

NEGOTIATING THE ECONOMIC BASE OF EXISTENCE

The Spanish conquest and colonization set off profound changes in the traditional economy of indigenous states and communities. Numerous and simultaneously operating factors contributed to the partial erosion of the preconquest economy and the gradual formation of the colonial base of existence: epidemics and the resulting depopulation; excessive tribute requirements and forced labor (e.g., in silver mines); forced resettlements (*congregaciones, reducciones*); the disintegration of preconquest tribute networks and long-distance exchange networks; the introduction of new crops, domesticated animals, and production modes; and gradually increasing pressure on indigenous land-holdings and urbanization. The Spaniards who brought about change in the economy of the colonies were agricultural entrepreneurs, cattle breeders, and merchants focusing either on local or overseas networks. They often made use of colonial institutions such as the *encomienda*. However, as the colonial period progressed, they also acquired indigenous land and came to rely on the native workforce and other direct economic interactions with local populations in the multiple contact zones with primarily indigenous but gradually "mesticizing" communities (Lockhart and Schwartz 1983: 6, 15–16, 122–130). Following the deadly epidemics of 1545–1548, the Spanish Crown instituted in 1550 a new labor recruitment mechanism called *repartimiento*. As the Spaniards' main source of compulsory indigenous labor, it was used among other things for construction projects in urban zones until 1632 (Gibson 1964: 220–235; Nutini and Isaac 2009: 41).

All of these processes affected the Nahua world although in some places, such as the more isolated areas, they had less real impact up through the latter portion of the colonial period. But in general, indigenous nobility and other entrepreneurial individuals in native society clearly demonstrated their capacity to readjust and benefit from the new economic and political reality. Members of the noble class availed themselves of the Spanish Crown's formal recognition of their status and rights, which some of them claimed back to preconquest times (Documents 22, 23, 25). The right to patrimonial lands and tribute was crucial for maintaining a privileged position. During the initial period of the first generation of the *encomienda*, when Spanish *encomenderos* received tribute through the mediation of local rulers, the latter would sometimes increase demands upon tribute-payers, and hand over only a portion of the yield to the Spaniards (Gibson 1964: 196–197). In fact, this strategy could have had its precedent under the tribute obligations to the Triple Alliance (Smith 2003, 2005).

The power of the Nahua nobility under colonial rule was strengthed by some factors and weakened by others. On the one hand, its members supervised tribute collection for the Spanish authorities, received tribute and labor from their subjects and crops from lands worked by dependent laborers, and maintained traditional networks of elite relationships, including strategic marriage alliances, some of them interregional. On the other hand, it is unquestionable that the native population as a whole was heavily affected by the deadly recurring waves of epidemics, with taxation demands becoming difficult to meet in view of the huge population loss. For this reason, the economic base of the traditional elites, including the *tlahtohqueh* themselves, weakened continuously throughout the sixteenth century (Gibson 1960: 180; 1964: 197; Horn 1997: 53–54; Nutini and Isaac 2009: 42). This situation was to a certain degree counterbalanced by new economical strategies and entrepreneurial initiatives undertaken by many members of the native nobility (Spores 1993: 97–98): they bred livestock (cattle, sheep, horses), organized workshops (*obrajes*) for textile production, and engaged in mining, sugar and salt production, and the wood trade, with most of these activities depending on the successful borrowing and implementation of Spanish modes of production and economic activities (Rojas 2010: 243–260). Members of the middle class were also active agents in these economic enterprises. Cases of the survival and adaptation of preconquest merchant groups and commercial networks are documented in early colonial Coyoacan and Huexotzinco (Lockhart 1992:

192–193; Horn 1997: 202–207), but the picture is far from complete. Trade and exchange no doubt flourished on a more local level. The market economy was highly developed and well-organized both in indigenous communities and Spanish towns such as Puebla, where native vendors were important providers of goods (Lockhart 1992: 189–191). Local producers and merchants benefited from Spanish demand for specific goods and from individual ties to Spaniards residing in the area (Horn 1997: 205–206). New economic activities also began to flourish in the hands of entrepreneurial indigenous women, such as those who produced alcoholic beverages in colonial Peru while maintaining and benefiting from close connections to local nobility (Document 15).

Traces of non-agricultural economic activities in the indigenous textual records are unfortunately scarce. The documents included in this anthology clearly focus on land as the principal source of income, as well as the object of economic transactions, claims, and inheritance disputes. After the conquest, the rulers and other members of the nobility held exclusive property derived from the preconquest *pillalli* ('nobles' land'), *tlahtohcatlalli* ('royal land'), or *tecpantlalli* ('palace land'). However, most of the tribute-paying community members held parcels of land assigned to them under the supervision of the community, formerly within the *calpolli* organization. This land could be sold, evidence of the fact that preconquest land-holding patterns were evolving in colonial times, especially since the Spanish model was based on a more individualized concept of ownership (Lockhart 1992: 174–175). The disputable distinction between patrimonial lands/real estate and community land was often the source of intercommunity conflict, as in the case of the violent legal battle in Tula between the community and Don Pedro Tlacahuepan (Document 24). In general, issues related to land rights are the primary concern expressed in indigenous records.

Another major theme linked to the economic status and prosperity of elites are complaints against excessive taxation. In stark contrast to individual legal cases, the *altepetl* elites, and especially the highest municipal officials, position themselves as a group when they are involved in struggles against excessive tribute demands, economic abuses of their communities by the Crown or individual Spaniards, or, as in the case of the 1557 Tula document (Document 24), an abusive member of the local elite. Similarly, the people from Huamuxtitlan (Document 28) accuse local authorities of demanding excessive tax duties from the indigenous populations and of withholding part of the money due to the Crown for themselves. The latter practice, which has also been documented in provinces of the Aztec empire, may have been one of the reasons for the increase in community tribute obligations in colonial times.

An essential argument in land struggles was the demonstration of a preconquest precedent for the use and care of the parcel(s) in question. While the two parties involved in the 1558 Tlatelolco litigation (Document 2) employ slightly different legal strategies, both are based on the concept of "keeping the land." The claimants argued that they had kept the land ever since its purchase three years "after the Marqués [Cortés] arrived"; however, their opponent accused them of attempting to deprive him of patrimonial land acquired by his ancestors long before the conquest, during the rule of the king Ahuitzotl. The rights to land are usually expressed by the verb *piya*, which does more in native documents than merely refer to the Spanish concept of "possession" expressed by the verb *tener*. Its semantic field embraced long-lasting possession, an uninterrupted chain of inheritance or documented sale, and the actual use and maintenance of the land. Therefore, strategies for claiming land ownership in colonial times were based on demonstrating long-lasting possession and an uninterrupted chain of inheritance going back either to pre-Spanish times or to a legal act of purchase already under colonial law. However, from the point of view of the judges presiding over the case, one aspect was of special importance: they wanted to know who had been actively tilling the land over the past several years. It is no surprise then that this topic figured importantly in the strategies of both parties, each of whom attempted to prove their involvement in the agricultural activities carried out on the land in question. Even more discrepancies related to the Spanish legal concept of land ownership come to the surface in the transitional period of the second half of the sixteenth century. One of them was linked to the land-tenure system of the *teccalli*/*tecpan*, or 'lordly houses,' whose members could not freely distribute or sell the fields that they held. This refers both to the nobles living in a specific "lordly house" and to the dependents working on the assigned fields (Document 4). Authorization from the leaders of the *teccalli* was needed for any land reassignments or transactions. This conflict between two conceptual spheres—native corporate landholding and Spanish private property—faded as the institution of the *teccalli* disintegrated toward the latter portion of the colonial period, while local rulers and nobles became increasingly interested in documenting and defending their "patrimonial" lands.

Indigenous elites in the Andes faced similar challenges as their local economy became more tied to the Spanish system. In preconquest times the Inca exacted work from his subjects, while the Catholic monarchs taxed their subjects in money or in goods, but less with work. Andean elites did not and could not tax their subjects in the Spanish way, because in the traditional local economy it was impossible to calculate the amount of production and what portions of this should be destined, on the one hand, to a peasant family for its own survival, and on the other hand, to tribute. So in the Andean system, the product of a peasant household's labor was not taxed. Rather, the peasant owed his lords work, during which the lord had to provide him with food and everything else needed to ensure his survival during the period of forced labor. This included respect (in the form of coca leaves and corn beer), food, tools, materials, and a place to work. If any of these elements was lacking, the peasant was not obliged to work. Thus, in everyday Andean life the leaders had to carefully plan how to organize tribute work according to agricultural cycles, weather conditions, the needs of the subjects, and the exigencies of the state. The *kuraka* knew how to achieve this (Murra 1983), so when the Spaniards asked for money or products, the *kurakas* organized the direct production of goods for the Spaniards, or sold these goods in the markets of Spanish towns and cities, in exchange for money to pay taxes. Labor tribute was much more burdensome under the Spaniards than under the Inca, since the Spanish authorities never supplied food, tools, materials, or tokens of respect to the worker, and usually never paid for the work as required by law. So the *kurakas* found themselves in a difficult position: in order to retain their prestige and continue to exercise their functions, they had to satisfy the demands of both the Spanish and their own subjects. The solution was to organize additional production, participate in the market, learn Spanish law, and do everything else that would help them to keep their status, such as defending the lands of their group against the Spaniards and later leasing or selling the same lands to them. They even organized their own separate system for the production of goods, which could either be sold, or used to help their subjects (Trelles Arestegui 1982). The law aided them to some extent, since the *encomenderos*, first, and later the *corregidores*, were permitted to enter into contact with indigenous people only through a native intermediary, the *cacique*. Of course there were cases when the *kuraka* changed sides and helped the Spaniards to steal from the natives (Varón Gabai 1980; León Gómez 2002). Not unlike some of their peers in Mexico, many of them became landowners, built their own haciendas, and joined the creole aristocracies, keeping their status until the agrarian reforms of the twentieth century. Other members of noble lineages took over bureaucratic functions in *reducciones*. The documents mention indigenous notaries who wrote in Spanish, and whose archives contain contracts between economically active and relatively rich members of native elites, or between them and other social groups. Solid research is still needed on this topic (Puente Luna 2016).

Thus, while in the colonial period most indigenous communities remained economically self-sufficient—the situation being markedly different in large towns with considerable Spanish populations—this did not preclude their members' involvement in economic relationships with Spaniards, including land sale transactions, trade, and participation in Spanish economic enterprises. And in the latter part of the colonial period, the Spanish sector (*república de españoles*)—embracing creoles, *mestizos*, many native people who had separated themselves from their original communities, as well as a constant flow of immigrants from Europe—was becoming an increasingly major economic force in non-agricultural production and exchange, even if still outnumbered by the indigenous population.

SYMBOLS OF STATUS AND LEGITIMIZATION OF POWER

In order to ensure their cultural, political, and economic survival and success, the colonial descendants of the preconquest indigenous nobility needed to develop diversified strategies in their relations both with their native subjects and with the representative of the Spanish Crown. There is no question that postconquest nobles in Mesoamerica and in the Andes gradually and to a certain degree became hispanicized; however, on the level of both material and spiritual culture, traditional preconquest referents remained the principal source of their legitimacy in dealings both with their communities and with the external powers. A complex set of elements provided the basis for legitimization: traditional royal ideology and the symbolic roles played by the ruler; external attributes, dress, and other symbols of rank; residences and lifestyle; and a huge body of local and interregional connections, as well as the specific traditional roles they played in their communities, such as official political and religious celebrations or sponsored festivities.

The code of dress was an important part of the legitimization process. In Central Mexico the change in dress customs took place within the first several decades of contact. This was especially true among the elites who were exposed to some form of communication with Spaniards, and it mirrored the quick adoption of numerous elements of Spanish material culture, such as different kinds of tools. New components of costume included trousers, shirts, shoes, and hats, which usually merged with local items. In the case of more hispanicized individuals, and especially toward the latter portion of the colonial period, the replacement of indigenous garments could have been more radical. In addition to accepting foreign clothing as their daily attire, the indigenous nobility was strongly attracted to other foreign status markers, such as horses and European weapons, although the *ordenanzas reales* issued in 1529 and 1531 prohibited their use among the members of native society (Olko 2014a: 335–340). Despite this, numerous indigenous nobles were quite successful in gaining access to these symbols of status through special permissions, in some cases since the very time of the conquest. The number of licenses granted throughout the early colonial period attests to the scale of this phenomenon (Rojas 2010: 263–268).

These trends notwithstanding, there is substantial evidence that traditional status items and insignia, as well as elements of preconquest elite dress, remained important sources of legitimacy during the entire colonial period (Olko 2014a: 340–354). Nahua lords and nobles, as evidenced by early colonial pictorial documents such as the *Codex Cuetlaxcohuapan* or the *Matrícula de Huexotzinco,* continued to wear the traditional *tilmahtli* cape over Spanish shirts and, sometimes, trousers. While this confirms the early but not yet widespread use of European garments among the native elites, it is also important to mention that that they continued to wear important local prehispanic status markers, such as the *xiuhhuitzolli* turquoise diadems or twisted headbands. The indigenous allies of the Spaniards in later conquest campaigns carried out to the north and south of Central Mexico would retain traditional battle suits and insignia. In fact, there is a large body of native texts that reveals the survival of traditional status symbols throughout the early and middle colonial period in a variety of contexts. A good source of our knowledge on this point are indigenous testaments, not only attesting to the possession of certain objects, but also shedding light on their continued production and how they were passed from generation to generation, especially in association with the families of hereditary rulers or nobles with a preconquest dynastic background. The items include capes with traditional prestigious designs, a huge variety of pieces of jewelry precisely identified through their prehispanic Nahuatl terms, precious feathers, fans, hair binders, shields, and war costumes and insignia. These were all key attributes of rank before the Spanish conquest, and they continued to appear afterwards in direct relation to the native concept of power and its inheritance. As we learn from the will of Don Miguel Alejandrino, the governor and *tlahtoani* of Tullantzinco, dated 1577, such ancestral objects were not only still manufactured in colonial times for the purposes of the native nobility, but also continued to be called *tlahtohcatlatquitl* 'royal accoutrements' of the local *tlahtoani,* whose duty was to protect his people (Olko 2014a: 344–345). Traditional status markers, especially garments, often figure in women's wills, as is the case of María Toztecayatl from Tlaxcala (Document 13), who bequeathed three embroidered skirts (*tlamachcueitl*) and three shifts (*huipilli*) to her daughters. The value of two of the skirts was set at eight *pesos* and four *tomines*, a third was set at three *pesos*, while the price of each shift was five *pesos*. This was a significant amount of money for items of clothing.

It is difficult to estimate to what extent traditional status symbols, especially those associated with royal or lordly power, remained in everyday use, for example in the proceedings of an indigenous *cabildo*. Best documented is their continued appearance in secular and religious festivities and ceremonies, including both local events and huge spectacles with indigenous participation called "royal festivities" (*fiestas reales*), organized both in New Spain and in the Andes usually under Spanish supervision. They continued to be used toward the end of the colonial period, even increasing in refinement and exuberance, and retaining the strong component of the display of indigenous cultures with elements pointing back to their preconquest roots (Curcio-Nagy 2004). Equally spectacular were religious celebrations and mock battles, like those associated with the cult of the Virgin of Guadalupe in the seventeenth and eighteenth centuries. These feasts, where native insignia were used and proudly displayed, had numerous equivalents on the local level in indigenous communities. The direct evidence of such celebrations from Tlaxcala contained in the seventeenth-century annalistic records of Zapata y Mendoza, gives us some idea of the local sociopolitical importance, symbolism, and ramifications of such events. They included the participation of the *tlahtohqueh* of the four constituent *altepetl*, adorned with traditional insignia of power, who reconfirmed in their processual movement the old internal structure of the complex *altepetl,* acting both as members of the colonial governmental system and holders of the authority and customs derived from their preconquest past.

Strategies for legitimacy in the Andean world were not much different. A colonial Andean nobleman was easy to recognize. When executing his duties he sat on a *tiyana* stool, symbol of his office. He wore, at least in ceremonial situations, an Inca tunic (*unku*) adorned with *t'uqapu* signs, whose meanings are not clear. He had adornments and, especially in Cuzco, a ceremonial headdress, and would go about with an image of the solar disc hanging from a chain on his chest, a colonial invention. He would drink corn beer ceremonially, always using two large beer cups decorated with family scenes and Inca history and mythology (Martínez Cereceda 1995). As in the Nahua world, when these articles were bequethed to heirs, both within the realms of the nobility proper, and people of the "middle class" broadly conceived, they were considered valuable personal objects. Such was the case of Martín

Rimanga, who according to his 1607 will (Document 17) was the owner of a painted shirt or tunic of prestigious and symbolic value, as well as two *akilla,* silver vessels of prehispanic origin used in traditional rituals. Similarly, Catalina Carguay Chumbi, whose status between the nobility proper and the well-off middle class is not quite clear, possessed, according to her testament made in 1608 (Document 16), numerous traditional status markers, including traditional clothing (e.g., *lliklla,* or shawl, and *anaku*, or blouse), a silver *tupu* pin and a pair of decorated wooden vessels known as *qiru*. In her 1649 will (Document 20), Doña Juana Flores, who was unquestionably a member of the noble class, bequeathed two shawls or *lliklla*s, attributes of native noblewomen, to the brotherhood of Our Lady of Copacabana, perhaps to serve as an adornment for a holy picture or sculpture. Doña Juana could easily afford such a gesture, since she owned multiple items of woven clothing of preconquest origin and other objects of prestige, such as the metal pins or *tupus,* which she distributed among her godchildren.

An Andean lord had to exhibit external markers of status, but he also had to exemplify the manners of a nobleman, and his biggest problem was showing generosity. A normal Andean should exchange work, services, and goods equally and symmetrically, but a nobleman should be generous and give more than the expected equivalent. For this he had to have goods produced in his own household by his dependents and retainers at his disposal. But all this was not enough, for he needed to know how to organize work in such a way that every member, every family in the group he ruled over, would have enough to eat. He had to supply families that were not economically productive with workers, and supply food from community stores to families that lacked it. And he was responsible for organizing the financing of the church, assuring the payment of taxes, providing support for the authorities, and sending people to furnish the Spaniards with forced labor. He needed to know to whom to give a bribe, and how much should be given. And he availed himself of the aid of other professionals, Andean priests included. He also had to adore the forefathers, meaning the gods, in order to be recognized as a legitimate *kuraka* by his subjects. At the same time he had to be a good Catholic in the eyes of the Spanish administration. This situation exists to this day, with local village authorities usually having to fulfill cult obligations both according to the *costumbre* (local religion) and according to the Catholic Church.

In 1545 Cristóbal Paullo Inca, at that moment the head of the Incas in Cuzco, a city which under Spanish rule bore the title of *Cabeza de estos reinos* 'Capital of These Kingdoms', received the designation of *Alférez Real de los Incas* 'Royal Ensign-Bearer Inca' from the Spanish king. Later on other descendants of the Inca Wayna Qhapaq received the same title. By 1572 the royal Inca lineages in Cuzco, organized in twelve *casas* 'houses', represented the Inca nobility. Beginning in 1595 each of them had two members in the Cabildo de los Indios Nobles, the town council of the noble Indians in Cuzco, who elected the Royal Ensign Bearer. The *alférez* paraded together with other members of the noble corporation and with the Spanish Cuzco authorities during the feasts of Santiago Mayor (James the Greater, patron saint of Spain and Spanish Cuzco) (Amado 2002). The institution functioned until the independence of Peru. It was the most prestigious symbol of Inca nobility, who displayed traditional Inca costumes, with some Spanish additions, like Brabant lace. By the end of the eighteenth century many Andean nobles managed to change their official status to Spaniards, but conserved their Andean names as an additional source of prestige.

VIEWS OF THE CONQUEST

Indigenous views of the Spanish conquest have claimed an important place in modern ethnohistorical research over the last fifty years. They have come to the surface through the thick layers of the "European story" of this part of the worlds' history, constructed through sources written in Spanish, mainly by Europeans themselves. The turn toward a native perspective of these events began in Mexico with Miguel León-Portilla's (1959) *Visión de los vencidos*, followed by works of Juan José Vega (1963) in Peru and of Nathan Wachtel (1971) in France. This line of research was further developed by North American revisionist New Conquest History that goes back to the 1990s and was no doubt also inspired by the methods and areas of interest of the New Philology. Reaching into indigenous memories and stories of events, and emphasizing multiple accounts and multiple actors of different ethnic backgrounds, this vein of scholarship has revealed highly nuanced, subjective, discursive, and negotiable stories of the conquest, highlighting not only indigenous historical agency, but also perceptions and understandings of this aspect of colonial reality (e.g., Restall 2003; Wood 1998, 2003; Restall and Asselbergs 2007; Schroeder 2010a; Restall 2012; Matthew and Oudijk 2014; Restall and Oudijk 2014). The development of conquest historiography for the Andes does not follow quite the same road taken by the Central Mexican paradigms. It was influenced by the fact that organized Inca resistance in the Andes lasted from 1536 to 1572. During that time two kings and two courts vied for rule over the Inca subjects: one in Cuzco, under the Spanish protectorate, and the other in Vilcabamba, organizing war and anti-Spanish propaganda. Although the viceroy Don Francisco de Toledo finally destroyed both centers, thirty-six years of resistance along with other factors led to the widespread conviction that one day the Inca should come back to resume his rule. This belief appeared in ceremonies, dances, poetry, and Andean theatre. It even inspired eighteenth-century rebellions. In the nineteenth century, Peruvian and Bolivian historiography began to paint the Incas of Vilcabamba as the precursors of rebellions against Spaniards and for independence, and of all insurrections against republican governments in the nineteenth and twentieth centuries. It was clear to Andean historians that Andean elites had taken part on both sides of the conflict. Recent studies focus more on political strategies developed in the sixteenth century by the Andeans themselves: Spanish rule, Inca rule under the Spanish protectorate, Inca independent rule, and the new state in the jungle far from the Spaniards (e.g., Guillen Guillen 1981; Lamana 2001, 2008; Estenssoro Fuchs 2005; Roy 2013).

The views of the conquest found in Nahua writings tell us perhaps more about the identity and strategies of their authors and their communities than about the events themselves. Although the picture is complex, two major attitudes stand out in early colonial testimonies. The sources linked to the elite of imperial Tenochtitlan, and especially Book 12 of the *Florentine Codex* compiled by fray Bernardino de Sahagún, transmit a dramatic picture of the defense of Tenochtitlan against the assault of the Spaniards and their allies. They describe the extreme conditions in which the indigenous population of the imperial capital, deprived of fresh water and food resources, heroically resisted the Spanish conquest. They proudly relate their achievements, including detailed accounts of capturing the enemies and their horses and then having them sacrificed in the traditional manner. It is clear that for the indigenous authors, these accounts were a source of pride: they never attempted to conceal the Mexica role in resisting their contemporary overlords. Thus, while other *altepetl* highlighted their achievements as Spanish allies in order to negotiate reduced tribute obligations or other privileges from the Crown in the decades following the conquest (Documents 23, 25), this was never a strategy of the elites of Mexico Tenochtitlan, who preferred to resort to purely legal arguments (Restall, Sousa, and Terraciano 2005: 64). It is interesting to contrast the Mexica account of the conquest with the parallel vision of their direct neighbors, the Tlatelolcans, who shared living on the same island within the broader confines of the imperial capital. In 1483, their independent *altepetl* was subjugated to Tenochtitlan, which left them with strong resentment, still vivid in colonial times. The early colonial Nahuatl account of the

Anales de Tlatelolco does not differ from Mexican testimonies in conveying a proud picture of heroic struggle against invaders and emphasizing the remarkable achievements of indigenous warriors. However, while extolling its own people, it contains strong charges against the Mexica, who first defended their part of the island, but in view of the enemy's advances, were forced to abandon their city and seek refuge in Tlatelolco. The Tlatelolcans accuse them of cowardly behavior, shameful even for their women; in fact they even interpret the tactical innovations of the Mexica commanders as cowardice, such as hiding the rank of the military leaders in order to avoid being recognized by the assailants. The emphasis on ethnic discord and differences rather than alliance against the conquerors, clearly demonstrates a very localized sense of identity grounded in a specific *altepetl* rather than any broader sense of indigenous solidarity (Restall, Sousa, and Terraciano 2005: 26).

Quite a different view emerges from the documents produced by the Spanish allies, including all those who claimed this role in the past. Thus, in their 1563 letter to the king of Spain, indigenous nobles from the *altepetl* of Xochimilco, which initially resisted Cortés in his conquest of the Valley of Mexico, claim to have provided critical support to the Spaniards during the siege of Tenochtitlan, much more decisive, in fact, than that of the Tlaxcalans, the principal allies of the Spanish. Similarly, the nobility of Huexotzinco, in their missive to the king in 1560, claim the status of loyal allies of the Crown and supporters of Christianity, contrary to their Tlaxcalan neighbors, whom they charge with inconspicuously continuing their idolatrous practices. The Tlaxcalans themselves claimed merits as military allies of the Spaniards in a number of documents, including a manuscript held in the Benson Latin American Collection and the famous *Lienzo de Tlaxcala*, both of which persuasively employ nuanced responses to colonization and engaged memories of recent history in order to challenge contemporary Spanish politics (Kranz 2007). Such merits linked to participation in the conquest were used to support claims of these *altepetl* to the kind of tribute exemptions and autonomy enjoyed by Tlaxcala, or reductions in tax obligations. However, on an ideological and political level, the indigenous allies of the Spaniards saw themselves as *indios conquistadores* ('indigenous conquerors'; Matthew and Oudijk 2014), real agents and winners in the history of the conquest. Reinterpretations and visions of native participation in the conquest, such as those conveyed by different versions of the *Mapa de Cuauhtlantzinco,* in which local elites figure as principal allies of the Spaniards and advocators of Christianity, continued well into the late colonial period (Wood 2003). A slightly different picture emerges in a large group of late colonial Nahüatl manuscripts called *títulos primordiales*, titles to land often consciously archaized in order to pass for sixteenth-century documents. Contrary to early colonial accounts, the arrival of the Spaniards and the foundation of colonial towns constituted a "new beginning" for specific communities, while the theme of the conquest itself was either omitted or only briefly referenced. Scarce are documents that mention military confrontation with the oppressors (Wood 1998: 179–186). Similarly, references to the conquest in early and mid-colonial native annals are not very numerous; those that exist are not recounted in great detail, and are usually reduced to the most basic facts.

On the local level, the arrival of the Spaniards was no doubt a less traumatic event than epidemics or forced resettlements. In fact, in the eyes of the communities there wasn't much difference initially between subjugation to the Aztec empire and subjugation to the Spanish Crown: tribute was negotiated and owed to a remote, external center of power, whereas local matters were left in the hands of the indigenous elite. The difference only began to be apparent where Christianization efforts were intensified and supported by inquisitional proceedings. In Mesoamerican terms, a military conquest was the expression of the prevalence of a patron deity of a victorious group: therefore it was quite natural to accept the foreign god among the local cults, which remained otherwise unaltered. This has been a universal indigenous strategy toward the Christian God(s), which initially not only posed no danger to local religious traditions, but even seemed to fit the conceptual framework quite well, as was the case of the *Virgen de la conquista*, worshiped among traditional gods by Tlaxcalan leaders and allies of Spaniards. Eventually, the famous Acxotecatl, holder of the image reportedly presented to him by Cortés himself, was accused of idolatry and burned at the stake. Similar persecutions targeted unwary indigenous communities as soon as the friars became more conscious of the attitudes and practices in collaborating communities, purportedly baptized and successfully converted to the Catholic faith (Lopes Don 2010; Olko and Brylak 2018).

From the Andean perspective, the Spanish conquest was a calamity that needed an explanation. Local elites took advantage of the chaos produced by the wars of conquest to free themselves from Inca rule, and in many places they aided the Spaniards. In other places they fought for the Incas, and lost the war together with their rulers when the imperial stores ran out, and the Inca could no longer give his soldiers what they needed and had the right to receive. Already in the decade of the sixties local aristocracies understood that they and their subjects had lost, but the calamity had to be explained. Andean culture was and continues to be very open to new knowledge and new techniques. Very quickly the Andeans developed a theory according to which the Incas (and all the members of their society) had engaged in wrongdoing, such as the war between Ataw Wallpa Inqa and Waskhar Inqa, and were reaping the effects of their previous lack of knowledge, since they had not known about Jesus Christ, iron, writing, horses, and so on. Because of these failings, the Inca God or gods did not help them during the conquest; for this reason, the Andean elites, headed by the Incas, had lost power. This explanation was consistent with the Inca theory that history developed in sequences of three periods: an epoch of founders, followed by an epoch of disorganized barbarians, and concluding with an epoch of ordered society governed by the Inca. We lack the data needed to determine how many such sequences were imagined for the world, from its beginning to its definite conclusion; however, by the end of the sixteenth and the beginning of the seventeenth century, some members of the elite envisioned an Inca king ruling the next epoch. The real problem lay in determining who he would be. Some members of the elite thought that the Spanish king, once he began to rule well, should become an Inca. Others believed that the Spaniards would lose their legitimacy because of the crimes they committed, and that a Catholic Inca king would return to rule, even though the quality and properties of his Catholicism probably would not be recognized by Rome (Szemiński 1993; Husson 2001). In 1780, when Don José Gabriel Thupa Amaro Ynga proclaimed himself the Inca king of Peru, Inca nobility in the city of Cuzco was drafted into the troops that were sent against the rebel. Years later, a surviving participant of the battle of Sangarará (November 18, 1780) asked the Spanish authorities for copies of documents confirming that he was an Inca nobleman or new documents reafirming so. He said that he had lost the trunk, which contained his documents, during the battle of Sanagarará. When going to war one should bring arms, and not papers to confirm one's nobility. Obviously he wanted the new Inca to confirm his privileges, but the Inca lost the war (Escalante and Valderrama 2013).

The native nobility had to use their knowledge of the past, the Inca past and even the pre-Inca past, in order to stay in power. They had to know and they did know from which specific place their divine pair of ancestors had sprung from the underworld, and they celebrated all the rites necessary to sustain their noble identity and status. At the same time, in order to be *kurakas*, they had to demonstrate to the Spaniards that they were good Catholics. So not only was the memory of the Inca and of the conquest preserved, it was also used as leverage in conflicts for power or land, because inheritance deriving from Inca times was always more beneficial than that originating in Spanish times. Even the Spanish *audiencia* in Lima or in Chuquisaca had to judge if the right to a piece of land given to a group by the Inca was better-founded than the right of inheritance bestowed by ancestors-gods who had emerged from the underworld, hidden under the affirmation "from the time before the Incas." Since Spanish law and society theoretically recognized Inca and Andean colonial nobility as equal to any Spanish nobility, the noble families kept their papers, legitimized their sons and other descendants, requested confirmations of their privileges, and received them.

CHALLENGING EUROPE: CROSS-CULTURAL DIALOGUES AND INDIGENOUS TRADITION WITHIN A CHRISTIAN VISION OF THE WORLD

Cross-cultural dialogue with the Old World tradition is a vast, complex, and heterogeneous theme in indigenous writing as it develops across the colonial era, although it is especially intense in the sixteenth and seventeenth centuries. Different members of indigenous society engaged in this broad topic in different ways and on different levels. Perhaps the most salient distinction was between indigenous intellectuals—for whom Europe was an epistemological challenge—and members of traditional communities, who had to deal with cross-cultural encounters and Christianization in their daily reality, often through common-sense strategies and experience, and often as part of a deeper process of translation and adaptation of the foreign into local categories. Both the intellectual and the pragmatic perspectives (the latter often linked to renegotiations of sociopolitical and economic status and autonomy) were in fact driven by complex mechanisms of negotiations, transformations, and replications of the Nahua cultural core in the conditions of contact (Madajczak and Olko 2015).

The intellectual attitude, broadly speaking, embraced attempts to combine indigenous and European historical traditions in meaningful ways. A good example here are the ideas developed by the native chronicler Chimalpahin, living between the world of his *altepetl* Chalco Amecamecan and its traditions, and the Christian world of Mexico Tenochtitlan, where he worked in a local church and had access to the rich flow of knowledge about the Old World. For Chimalpahin, syncing the two worlds is part of a broader and more comprehensive intellectual enterprise. An important component in his construction of world history in Nahuatl is the identification of noteworthy Greeks and Romans as "pagans" or "idolaters" (*tlateotocaniḥ*; Chimalpahin 2003, I: 30; II: 18), which he links to his own ancestors through the use of the term *tlateotocani*. He thus creates an unquestionable parallel between the two worlds, which also becomes the instrument for reevaluation of the indigenous past. He openly states that the *huehuetqueh* 'the old ones' or *huehuetqueh chichimecah* 'old/ancient Chichimecs' descended from the first human generation of the Old World (Chimalpahin 2003, I: 28). Thus, the roots of the inhabitants of America go back to the biblical tradition, to "our first father Adam and our first mother Eva" (*achto totatzin Adán yuan yn achto tonantzin Eva*; Chimalpahin 2003, I: 38). In accordance with this vision, Chimalpahin also traces the ancestry of ancient Chichimecs to one of the sons of Noah (Chimalpahin 2003, I: 314). This idea of a shared, common history is reinforced by Chimalpahin's numerous attempts to synchronize biblical and Christian history with the native historical tradition: for example he dates the settlement of his ancestors eighteen years after the death of Christ (Chimalpahin 2003, I: 312). However, he rejects the hypothesis that the Chichimecs descend from Jews dispersed after the destruction of Jerusalem, because according to his calculations, based on Nahua historical tradition, his ancestors settled in Central Mexico before these events, so the native historical chronology plays an important role in his reasoning. This indigenous intellectual does not merely create links that help him explain the place of his ancestors in world history, but he goes on to negotiate their special status in reference to the Old World. Following the account by Enrique Martinez, *Reportorio* (Schroeder 2010b: 115), he claims that the New World exceeds any other continent, even if Europe is currently the most important one (Chimalpahin 2003, I: 64–65, 68–70).

We will not find similar intellectual discourse in mundane sources created in Nahua communities; however, more subtle strategies of challenging European tradition or even culturally subordinating it to the indigenous cultural interpretation are to be found in native attempts to translate and transfer elements of the Christian tradition to local audiences. This has a clear counterpart in the social reality and in the ongoing adaptation and reinterpretation of Christian concepts and rituals in indigenous communities, but it is also salient in indigenous ecclesiastical literary production. Cross-cultural translation of the Christian tradition into Nahuatl writings reveals numerous ways in which European religious concepts became indigenized, transformed, enhanced, or even corrected in order to increase their understandability for Nahua recipients and their compliance with Nahua ontology. This prolific textual production in fact abounds with culturally engaged transpositions of diverse features and dimensions of the Catholic tradition (e.g., Burkhart 1989, 2001; Christensen 2010). One of the earliest preserved testimonies of this kind is the 1548 *Doctrina Christiana* compiled by Dominican friars (Document 31). It reveals the nuances of the creation (and attempts at imposition!) of new religious terminology in the native language. This enterprise must have involved a huge degree of collaboration between friars and their indigenous collaborators, who both struggled hard to fit and translate culturally alien concepts into Nahuatl without resorting to lexical borrowings, which would have been even more enigmatic to the native audience. This enterprise involved a tremendous amount of experimentation, the results of which were often ambiguous. Not less ambiguous were the attempts of the Nahuas to pass for knowledgeable Christians. Two fragments of a seventeenth-century will from the Valley of Mexico reveal this desire to appear orthodox by resorting to formulas designed to fill in possible gaps in doctrinal knowledge: *ihua in ixquich quimoneltoquitia tonantzin santa iglecia Romana* 'and [I believe] in everything that our mother, the Holy Roman Church, believes', and *ma quimohuiquili in canpa quimohuiquilis quimoyeyamaquilis* 'may he take [my soul] where he will take it to give it a home' (Sullivan, Document 18). In most cases, however, religious matters were dealt with on a very practical level, especially when testators considered that spiritual matters were apparently of equal, if not greater, importance than the destiny and management of their private property. Thus, a rich nobleman in Coyoacan wanted to make sure his burial place would be secured inside the main church, that the bells both in the church and in the hospital would be rung during his funeral, that singers and music would accompany his corpse, that candles would be lit along the path of his funeral procession, and that there would be a sufficient number of masses said for his soul. To secure these requests, he made considerable donations to the church and friars, expecting them to deal with the legal issues surrounding a part of the donation, a parcel that had been illegally taken and tilled by other people (Document 14). Similar bequests were made in other wills from Mexico and the Andes, both by noble testators and by relatively rich members of the "middle class" (Documents 16, 17, 21).

There is no direct testimony left by learned Andeans that precolonial elites ever managed to have direct intellectual contact with Spanish thinkers of the sixteenth century. However, indirect evidence of a few cases of such contact does exist both in Spanish texts dealing with the customs and history of the natives and in Spanish protocols of information given by Andean specialists. The reasons for this lack of evidence are obvious. Andean ways of recording and transmitting information were much stranger, from the Spanish perspective, than Mesoamerican writing. According to Andean traditions, one could receive information only if one was entitled to it. The Spaniards were usually considered not entitled. So we have only one case in which a Spanish priest managed to speak with some Inca sages about religion (Molina 1575?), and another case in which Inca cartographers in Cuzco produced a clay map of a valley, and a Spanish notary wrote down all the information read from the map by the Inca specialists (de la Peña 1970). Some notaries' records in Spanish contain readings of knot records. We do not have, however, Andean records in the original form, nor in the Latin alphabet. After all, local sages had no reason to speak with the barbarians who destroyed everything and did not understand Andean government, economy, or science. However, just as in Central Mexico where Christianization was first directed at indigenous rulers and nobles (and they were exemplarily persecuted for idolatrous practices; Lopes Don 2010), Andean elites were the principal target for enhanced religious instruction. Since the *kurakas* had real power over indigenous commoners, special tactics of confession were applied in their case (Documents 34, 35). And although systematic indoctrination first targeted the Andean elites, with time it expanded to include the entire native population under Spanish rule. New parishes covered the entire population.

After all, the Spanish gods turned out to be stronger than their Andean counterparts. The followers of the first movements against Spanish domination, such as Taki Unquy in the years 1565–1572, expected that a united front of all Andean gods should defeat the Spanish God and saints (Millones 1990). They did not. New Andean Catholic intellectuals made efforts to reconcile the traditional image of the world with the new one, taught by the clergy. If the Spaniards were right and their image of the world was the true one, one had to find a way to connect Spanish and Andean worldviews. First, one needed to explain where the Spaniards had come from. Since they did not exist in this world under the Sun, and had come from the West, maintaining that they were envoys of God and the King of Spain, the obvious conclusion was that they had come from the underworld. Such understanding corresponded well with the Andean image of the Creator God, contained inside the world. Once this was accepted, it became easier to associate other persons spoken about by the Spaniards with Andean entities: for example, Andean gods who taught the correct way of life were identified with the Christian apostles (Guaman Poma 1615?: 92[92]–94[94]; Pachacuti Yamqui Salcamaygua s. a. 3v–6v, 43v).[10]

---

10 Guaman Poma de Ayala's pages have two sets of numeration: one from the original manuscript; another from the (Copenhagen) Royal Library's online edition. Pacha Cuti yamqui Salca Maygua's manuscript is not dated, hence s.a. = sine anno, without year.

Once a cosmology was in place, it had to be ordered chronologically. The natives became descendants of Adam and Eve and of Noah. Since, according to Spanish teaching, the modern world began with the coming of Jesus, Andean elites concluded that Jesus and the first Inca appeared at the same time, one over there, in the other world, in the underworld, and the Inca here, in our world. At that moment the Inca's commandments and the Ten Commandments became associated, although not completely, because the latter do not contain a prohibition of laziness, a sin in Andean eyes equal to stealing, lying, or killing. Andean tradition survived, and the Inca became the future savior of the natives, because Jesus saved non-natives (Szemiński 1993b). How did these ideas influence the daily life and ritual practices of ordinary people? Evidence coming from native testaments is suggestive. Doña Juana Flores (Document 20) says:

> '[*Al margen izquierdo*: Pussose la ofrenda] Yten tengo una obeja de Castilla con su cordero en poder de Lorenso Quispi, mi compadre, el de Tarma, mando que se trayga para poner en mi sepultura para la ofrenda" [3v].
>
> [*on the left margin:* The offering was given.] Also, I have a sheep with its lamb in the custody of Lorenso Quispi, my *compadre*, the one from Tarma. I order it brought and put in my grave as an offering.'

Animal offerings are not very common in the post-Tridentine Catholic Church. In this case, the sheep and its lamb were sacrificed on Doña Juana Flores's grave. We should ask first, why was a sheep used and not a *llama*, and second, why was it put in the grave and not eaten? In ordinary offerings, the gods get a portion, but the participants in the ceremony eat most of the meat. The offering was carried out, without any doubt, so that Doña Juana Flores would be accompanied in the grave by her sheep and lamb. The executor of the will fulfilled her wish. How then was the afterworld imagined among the Ambar elite, if not among all inhabitants of the region? It was not a traditional Andean underworld, if one needed a sheep and not a *llama*. But it was not a Catholic underworld either, if one did require the company, in this case, of a sheep. Did the deceased prefer a sheep as an indicator of her elite status? There is ample evidence to support the idea that the world ruled by Jesus and the Spaniards was seen by Andeans as a world ruled by a god of the underworld and by the living dead, who instead of staying in the underworld had managed to get to Peru. So perhaps a sheep was a better offering to these underworld inhabitants than a *llama*. The conclusion is that members of the elite, such as Doña Juana Flores, were not quite as good Christians, from a European point of view, as they pretended to be.

INDIGENOUS WRITING

The writing tradition that the Europeans proudly brought to the New World was nothing new to Mesoamerican peoples, including the Nahuas. The situation in the Andean area, where entirely different traditions of creating records were used, was markedly distinct and this seems to have had important implications for indigenous approaches toward literacy in the colonial times. In the case of the Nahuas, their preconquest tradition of manuscripts, filled with glyphic records and imagery, no doubt helped them to adopt alphabetic writing quickly; they were the first indigenous group in the New World to do so, and proceeded to use it prolifically for their own purposes. These developments were accelerated by a joint enterprise in the 1530s (if not earlier), involving friars and native nobles who worked together in the major centers of original Franciscan instruction—Mexico Tenochtitlan and Tlatelolco—to adapt the orthographic conventions of the Roman alphabet to Nahuatl. The number of freshly trained native scribes and notaries quickly expanded in the 1540s, as did different genres of writing in Nahuatl. This first generation later trained other professionals in specific *altepetl*, probably without further participation of the friars. By the third quarter of the sixteenth century at least one notary performed his duties within all municipal governments and provided services for individuals in even smaller towns (Lockhart 1992: 330–331).

Contrary to the friars' efforts to standardize Nahuatl orthography, the main concern of native scribes and authors was to reproduce actual speech, including phonetic features that changed as a consequence of interactions with neighboring sounds, which often transcended word boundaries. Thus, even if the conventions employed by the native authors of the earliest known and surviving corpus of alphabetic texts in Nahuatl, the Cuernavaca-region census records of the late 1530s and/or early 1540s, no doubt derived from those developed by friars, the Nahua writers modified them in their own ways. The priority given to the phonetic characteristics of speech is quite salient in these documents, and we can see the same tendency in the corpus of texts presented in this anthology. The level of adherence to more standardized conventions differs among notaries, while irregularities and idiosyncrasies usually increase in the smaller, peripheral localities. In general, indigenous writing became more regionalized and locally unstandardized beginning in the late seventeenth century, perhaps reflecting a decreasing involvement in Nahuatl textual production on the part of the native elites, who were switching to communication in Spanish (Lockhart 1991: 122–134; Pizzigoni 2007: 35–39).

Another consequence of the native scribes' inclination toward recording oral characteristics of speech was the fact that their writings included numerous elements of dialogue, as well as elegant and polite orations in different textual genres, all of which deeply transformed their Spanish prototypes or counterparts. In general, indigenous writing in Nahuatl can be divided into several major categories and subcategories. Thus, we can differentiate between literary genres (poems, orations, plays, and "ethnographic accounts" compiled by friars), historical writing (accounts and annals), ecclesiastical texts (canonical texts created under the supervision of friars such as catechisms, prayers, confession manuals, and sermons, as well as those created by the Nahuas themselves, such as confraternity materials, translations of devotional materials, and lives of saints), and a broad category of "mundane" documents (wills, legal proceedings, censuses, bills of sale, economic documents, private letters, petitions, city council minutes, etc.).

Present in most of these genres is the oral component, as well as a strong transformation or adaptation of Spanish sources. Part of this complex writing tradition includes the extensive Nahuatl texts compiled by fray Bernardino de Sahagún with the fundamental help of his native aides, probably their factual authors. These pioneering "ethnographic" manuscripts, known as the *Primeros Memoriales* and the *Florentine Codex*, can be considered true "native encyclopedias." Despite being based on European models of organizing and classifying knowledge, their content reflects many preconquest forms of expression. Part of this compilation contains traditional songs and speeches, also surviving in other manuscripts, such as the *Cantares Mexicanos* or the *Bancroft Dialogues,* which transmit many elements of prehispanic oral tradition. Another genre that merges indigenous and European concepts includes the numerous Nahuatl plays composed by diverse authors. Their Old World characters are strongly "indigenized" and put in the context of native sociopolitical organization and customs.

Nahuatl ecclesiastical writings, which comprise another large group of texts, are represented in this volume by an excerpt from the Dominican *Doctrina* (Document 31). These works were produced under Spanish ecclesiastical auspices to meet the goals of religious instruction, and as such, they follow European prototypes quite strongly. It is difficult to assess the factual contribution of native assistants in creating the numerous catechisms, prayers, and confessionaries signed by Spanish priests, but it must have been considerable, even if in most cases anonymous or hidden. This seems even more probable in view of the fact that the texts contain numerous elements of preconquest orality and the elegant language of the indigenous nobility. Although many friars advocated for the creation of doctrinal materials in Nahuatl, not all ecclesiastics were convinced that Christianity could be adequately explained and transmitted in a native language. Such a doubt was expressed by the First Mexican Provincial Council in 1555 and in subsequent statements concerned about securing control over the process of translating religious materials into local languages (Christensen 2012: 693). Quite understandably then, Spanish friars avoided giving adequate credits, if any at all, to their indigenous collaborators (Burkhart 1989: 25; Sell 1993: 81). Many "unofficial" devotional texts were in fact created by Nahua authors themselves for native audiences, probably with little or no supervision by friars or priests. Orality and preconquest forms of expression, in the form of dialogues, speeches, and metaphoric figures, are also very much salient in the historical records structured as annals and called *xiuhpohualli* 'year counts'. This important tradition originated in preconquest glyphic and pictorial records. In early colonial times it quickly switched to the alphabetic register, but the pictorial component survived in some of the annals until the end of the sixteenth century. The authors of Nahua annals were very concerned with the postconquest history of their *altepetl*. They wrote from an "engaged" point of view and with a very local bias, though at times demonstrating considerable interest in external events. Even in the latter part of the colonial period, in moments of crises, upheaval, or imminent threat, indigenous people continued to give expression to their oral histories in documents produced to buttress their rights and claims, both before the local audience and in colonial courts (Wood 1989; Townsend 2016: 219).

We can learn even more about native forms of expression, family and religious life, attitudes, practices, and strategies when looking at mundane documents. They tell us a great deal about the daily concerns, motivations, and activities of the Nahua people. It would be very misleading to suggest that they were merely formulaic texts based on Spanish legal prototypes. Indeed, some genres were closely patterned on Spanish models, but, as we can see in the present anthology, they acquired a strongly indigenous flavor. For example, petitions and letters, widely represented in this book, while revealing some European impact, are built upon the traditional Nahuatl conventions of formal and elevated speech. This characteristic of elegant speech was present even in the Nahuatl periphery as the petitions from Amacatlan in Chiapas and from the northern town of Coatlan de Puertos Abajo clearly show (Documents 26, 30). The oral character of the 1557 Letter of the Municipal Council of Tollan Xicocotitlan, Mexico (Document 24), is particularly interesting: the long list of signatories appears in the first person, emphasizing their direct involvement and agency as authors of the legal statement. Orality also surfaces in such mundane documents as a land sale transaction from Tlaxcala, which in addition to the direct testimonies of vendors and buyers, includes fragments of conversations (Document 6), or in an account, also from Tlaxcala, of the commissioning of a holy image (Document 32). Sometimes however, legal formulas of Spanish origin translated into Nahuatl prevail over local features. This is the case in a 1612 land sale, whose reliance on the Spanish model is due perhaps to the high price of the parcel being sold and to the participation of members of the highest Tlaxcalan nobility (Document 7).

Numerous elements of orality, dramatization, and spontaneity are also to be found in native wills. It is clear that not only the forms of individual expression but also the roles of witnesses deviated from the Spanish model, emphasizing their function in affirming the legitimacy of the will on behalf of the community (Lockhart 1992: 364–371). In contrast to the model conveyed in fray Alonso de Molina's manual, witnesses sometimes received bequests, while women, unlike under Spanish law, acted as equal witnesses along with men (Cline 1998: 21). The main period for the production of Nahuatl testaments began in the sixteenth and concluded by the end of the eighteenth century; however in some places, such as the Valley of Toluca and Tlaxcala, this practice survived well into the nineteenth century, as the Nahuas continued to attest to their organization, community practices, and rituals (Melton-Villanueva 2012, 2016). Despite revealing, on the one hand, some affinities with formulaic Spanish patterns, and on the other hand, the tendencies of local notaries to convey more individualized, idiosyncratic messages, these wills exhibit an abundance of Nahua cultural particularities. They also attest to the individual strategies employed by the members of Nahua communities to secure and protect their legacies after death: "they utilized testaments to help their souls attain heaven, to ensure that lordships survived and flourished, to protect family landholdings—in short, to promote a diverse array of personal interests" (Hosselkus 2011: 49–51). The strong tradition of orality and the tendency to reflect the actual multivoiced process of creation of the legal document survive in indigenous wills and related documents at least until the late colonial period. For example, in an inheritance resolution of 1758 from San Juan Ixtenco, Tlaxcala (Document 11), the voice switches from the authorities to the sick mother of the heiress to the heiress herself and then back to the deputy governor of the town. He addresses the participants in the inheritance case as *topilhuan* 'our children', drawing on old, preconquest conceptual terminology in which a ruler addresses his subjects as his "children," passing his words and wisdom on to them (Madajczak 2015). The resulting fluidity in a constantly changing order of speakers gives us a good idea of the nature and sequence of the colorful procedure for confirming the right to land in an eighteenth-century indigenous community.

The picture in the Andean world is quite different. At the time of the conquest, the Incas and their subjects used at least four systems used to preserve and transmit information, each serving a different purpose. The most famous is the *khipu*, knot records. Each *khipu* consisted of a principal string to which lesser strings were attached. There are a few hundred *khipus* preserved in museum collections. We can read the numbers registered with knots, but we do not understand the colors or the special kinds of knots. During the sixteenth-century, the *audiencia* and the Spanish colonial functionaries recognized *khipus* as legal documents that needed to be translated into Spanish. Thus, in colonial archives translations of some *khipus* have been preserved. Martti Pärssinen and Jukka Kiviharju (2004, 2010) together published two volumes of such translations. They include statistical reports organized by things and years, but also documentation of lineages and of rulers' stories of conquests. So it seems that not only statistics were preserved in the *khipu,* which was undoubtedly used by the Inca administration, and later by local officials under Spanish rule. Moreover, the *khipu* was used by confessants in church, in order not to forget sins, which were so different from Andean sins (Urton 2003). Some *khipus* are thought to codify text, and not only numbers, since the *khipus* included place names and group names, sequences of events, and names of the objects to which the numbers referred.

A second Andean system for transmitting information is mentioned in the sources from sixteenth-century Cuzco. It consisted of wooden tables on which the story of each Inca king was painted, including the names of his relatives and the lands he conquered. The archive was located in the Puqin Kancha temple in Cuzco. We have one translation of one of the tables, containing proper names and verbs, preserved by Cristóbal de Molina el Cuzqueño (Cristóbal de Molina el Cuzqueño 1575?: 1r–2v); however, none of these tables exists today. Similar tables describing young couples and their relatives are known to have existed in several twentieth-century villages of Peru and Bolivia, but they did not seem to contain a writing system.

Sixteenth- and twentieth-century researchers describe a third system (Acosta 1979 [1590]: 291; Sánchez and Sanzetenea 2000), a type of hieroglyphic writing that the Spaniards did not recognize as such. Fashioned on a base made of clay in the form of a circle, it contained little stones with symbols and sometimes also clay figures and other things, which were ordered in a spiral from the edge to the center. In the nineteenth century, the use of such "pizzas" and similar forms had evolved into figurative writing on parchment or paper, the content of which was limited to Catholic prayers and teachings, exactly as in Acosta's description. Today there are a number of local variants of this writing system, both in Quechua and in Aymara (Ibarra Grasso 1953). In 1988 the Catholic priest Juan Miranda M. published *Catecismo: Diuswan Munanakuypi kawsanapaj* in Sucre with the church censor's permission. The text is in Quechua hieroglyphics and in Latin-alphabet Quechua.

A fourth system is represented by rows of rectangular, mostly abstract signs present on late Inca and colonial textiles and on *qiru,* wooden cups used for libations, which are frequently mentioned in colonial testaments. The signs called *t'uqapu* (perhaps translated to Spanish as mysteries) do not occur in accidental order, as shown by Ziółkowski, Arabas, and Szemiński (2008). The sequences probably described linage titles, dignitaries, and stories, but this is still only a hypothesis.

Thus, Andean systems did not become associated with Spanish alphabetic writing. The result was that the Andeans learned to write in Spanish, and very rarely applied the alphabet to their native tongues. Most written and printed texts in Quechua and Aymara (and exceptionally in other Andean languages) were produced by the clergy for religious use. Very few administrative documents in Quechua or Aymara resembling Nahua protocols are known to exist. Some secular writing in Quechua is suggested by the tradition of local theatre troupes that presented the *Ataw Wallpap p'uchukakuyninpa wankan*, usually translated to Spanish as *The Tragedy of Ataw Wallpa's End*, and performed in many regions, normally in Quechua. Comparison of the play's versions suggests that perhaps from the first half of the seventeenth century some groups used paper notebooks to preserve the text (Husson 2001).

Local Andean elites used paper and writing for administrative purposes, but in Spanish (Puente Luna 2016). Oral tradition survived to some extent in Quechua and Aymara, but the Spanish and church administration destroyed nearly all institutions in which it was practiced and preserved: ancestors' mummies and their cult, and ancient gods and the songs of their deeds, were illegal. Of course, in the archives of noble families and notaries, any kind of written documents can appear. In any case, the Latin alphabet did not displace the Andean recording systems by itself: this was accomplished by a combination of the Spanish language and the Latin alphabet. Although some Quechua and Aymara texts were written with Spanish orthography, in general, attempts to adapt the Latin alphabet to Andean languages were few and did not attain wider use.

Finally, in both Mesoamerica and the Andes local Catholic priests produced books titled *Doctrina Cristiana*, or *Ritual formulario*, or *Confesionario*. The majority of them were written after the Council of Trent (1545–1563) and followed its recommendations. The authors used Spanish models but adapted them to local conditions. A comparison of the Spanish texts can only illustrate the differences of opinion among their Spanish authors. The Quechua texts, however, differ from their Spanish models, because they had to be adjusted to the knowledge possessed by the people who were being confessed; the same can be said for the *Doctrinas* written in Nahuatl. Nevertheless, a comparison of questions addressed to *caciques* (whatever that means in such a case) of each area reveals a very important difference (Molina 1569: 41v–45r, 48v–63r; Pérez Bocanegra 1631: 268–272, 277–280, 304–309, 317–320). Both the Nahua and the Quechua elites extorted goods, work, sex, and land from their dependents; however, the Andeans exacted work, more than goods, and gave protection to Andean priests and people accused of Catholic sins, who from the Andean perspective were innocent. In fact, a comparison of texts written in Quechua and Nahuatl yields fruitful insights regarding local ethics before and after the Spanish conquest, as well as its evolution over the time. But that is another story.

NATIVE AGENCY IN THE DOCUMENTS

Common to all the indigenous texts gathered in the present anthology are different forms—some more conspicuous, some more veiled—of native agency. They embrace different roles in the colonial reality: management of local power relationships; processes of inheritance and family affairs; religious matters and economic issues; influence on community life through exertion of pressures or claims directed to the Spanish Crown and its representatives; contributions to the processes of cross-cultural translation; and, finally, engagement in dialogues with Christianity and different components of indigenous and European traditions, including the creation of resources for an indigenous audience. There has been much discussion on the overt and covert aspects of agency manifest in languages and linked to its performative and encoding functions (e.g., Duranti 2001: 266–275). Indeed, some of the texts presented here have strong performative functions; others, however, reveal how indigenous agents—and especially "elites" on the individual and collective levels—took on active roles in daily sociopolitical reality. Thus, these testimonies show different degrees of control over available resources, as well as the abilities needed to mobilize them in accordance with the concept of agency. Agency here is understood as "the synthetic quality of the social fabric, actualizing itself in praxis" and "the capacity of society to activate itself for self-transcendence," which distinguishes active society from passive society and manifests action in both individual and collective agents (Sztompka 1991: 122, 126–128).

Many of the developments revealed by the documents are related to questions concerning intercommunity political struggles. In the colorful 1624 case of Xiloxochtlan in Tlaxcala (Document 29), residents of two *altepetl,* Santa Isabel Xiloxochtlan and San Luis Teolocholco, joined forces against a local *fiscal* 'church official', the chief constable, and the nobles of San Francisco Topoyanco, who were mistreating them. These citizens turned to the viceroy in Mexico City to report the mistreatment and managed to have the *fiscal* deposed. However, his successor only increased the harassment and thirty residents of the two towns were publicly arrested and put into jail, an event referred to in the petition with the word *neixcuitilli* 'public spectacle'. This humiliating act spurred the residents of the affected towns to file a petition to the local authority demanding release of the prisoners and punishment of the responsible officials. Another good example is the petition signed by numerous members of the nobility of Tula Xicocotitlan and directed to the town's hereditary ruler (Document 24). The joint alliance of local elites was a driving force here in the defense of communal lands against private, patrimonial property, a conflict that was no doubt fed by the early colonial ambiguity regarding the classification of indigenous land tenure within the Spanish legal framework. However, the resolution of this dispute lay outside the local legal system and required an appeal to the central *audiencia* court. Similarly, the petitions from Soconusco and Jalisco illustrate that the internal affairs and well-being of indigenous communities were directly linked to external decisions and power relationships: both cases exemplify the efforts of local elites to make authoritative decisions concerning the priests assigned to their towns. In order to achieve this political goal, local actors revealed the abuses of the colonial system and presented themselves as committed and knowledgeable Christians. The persuasive power of the documents' indigenous actors is often masterfully enhanced by the use of rhetorical devices drawing on both prehispanic and Christian traditions and resources, an example being the skillful comparison of oppressed native people to the people of Israel under Egyptian slavery (Document 30). These forms of agency sometimes involved, as was probably the case in the Soconusco communities, alliances with specific groups of Spaniards, including mendicant friars (Document 26). Sometimes, however, local elites acted against forms of exploitation and abuse committed by their own community members belonging to the high nobility or by functionaries in the Spanish municipal system (Documents 24, 28).

Andean examples of agency are more modest in this respect, no doubt due in part to the restricted roles that alphabetic writing played in native communities in that area, when compared with the Nahuas: the content of available documentary sources is different and focuses on slightly distinct aspects of colonial reality and the role of local actors in it. Testaments reveal the coexistence of Spanish and Andean technologies and objects, from robes to agricultural tools to technology for brewing corn beer. At the same time the documents show that the Andeans tried to rework their own image of the world so that it would include Spaniards and Spanish gods. We have mentioned the example of the woman who orders a sheep to be sacrificed on her tomb during the ceremony of her burial (Document 20). We have also discussed a bequest of *qiru* ceremonial cups employed in Andean religious ceremonies. Confessors' questions for the *kurakas* reveal important information about the duties of local elites and how they fulfilled them, including their responsibilities regarding the communities that they headed, the requirements imposed on them by the colonial Spanish administration (Document 34), and their Andean religious duties with respect to the ancestors and gods. On the other hand, the questions that confessors were supposed to ask indigenous notaries reveal the latter's complicated role in the local community as individuals who, while depending on recognition from the Spanish administration, the church administration, and the local people, used their position to become rich and important (Document 35). It is fascinating to discover cases in which a notary could advise a testator to leave nothing for his or her soul. It would be tempting to conclude that the notary and the testator, both Catholics, did not care for their souls. But the published wills reveal that the testators very much did.

While many forms of agency are subtle and not immediately obvious, a careful look at the corpus presented here unveils its numerous modalities, all strongly linked to existing (and evolving in colonial times) sociopolitical structures and cultural needs. We can clearly distinguish between the agency of individual actors—including persons equipped with certain power, offices, or spheres of influence and "common people" in their ordinary, everyday activities—from collective agents, such as *cabildo* members or other groups representing a specific community. However, the documents also often reveal an "agency continuum" extending from the personal involvement of individual actors to larger collective actions of groups of individuals of different sizes and configurations; from persons and officials involved in the execution of a will, to specific political factions or wider representations of a community in legal procedures, complaints, or petitions. In the latter case, individual agents receive their capacity to act only through involvement in or the acknowledgment of a collectivity.

THE LANGUAGE OF THE DOCUMENTS: COMMUNICATION, TRANSLATION, AND CONTACT-INDUCED CHANGE

The documents included in the present anthology offer numerous insights into the phenomena of cross-cultural communication, translation, and contact-induced change, reflected in the language in which they are composed: Nahuatl, Quechua, and Spanish. In the case of Nahuatl, seminal research on language contact and change in the colonial period was conducted by Frances Karttunen and James Lockhart (1976), who compiled the first listing of Spanish loanwords, documenting their chronological appearance and phonetic adaptations. They also outlined a model containing three main periods of contact-induced change in Nahuatl. This approach was later developed by Lockhart (1992) who significantly broadened the content of the phases, correlating them with general sociocultural change under European impact. His major achievement has been to show convincingly how linguistic phenomena are one of the most sensitive indicators of the nature and trajectory of cross-cultural transfer between the two cultures.

During Stage 1 of Lockhart's model, which extended from the Spanish conquest to ca. 1540–1550, Nahuatl remained almost unaffected by Spanish because its speakers drew on their own linguistic resources to describe everything new from Europe, resorting to neologisms or extensions of meaning. Stage 2, dating approximately from the mid-sixteenth to the mid-seventeenth century, was characterized by widespread borrowing of Spanish nouns, whereas the language underwent few changes in terms of morphology, syntax, and phonology. In Stage 3, which according to Lockhart began in the mid-seventeenth century and has continued to the present day in those communities where Nahuatl is still spoken, more profound changes occurred. They include the borrowing of verbs and particles, the adoption of plural forms for inanimate nouns, the incorporation of phonemes missing earlier in Nahuatl, as well as an abundance of calques. These introductions were no longer motivated solely by new objects and concepts, but rather by linguistic differences between the two interacting languages, Nahuatl and Spanish. Lockhart also proposed a Stage 4, partly overlapping with Stage 3, and referring to the use of a heavily Nahuatlized version of Spanish.

Our documentary sample and the studies of specific documents contained in this volume basically confirm the general outline of contact-induced change in Nahuatl proposed by Lockhart for the colonial period, albeit with certain important modifications. Although there are strong indicators that similar patterns of contact-induced change in Nahuatl are found in different regions, the timing of specific local developments is much more diversified than in the general, unifying model. Broader patterns of change are indeed attested in geographically separated regions with different degrees of exposure to cross-cultural contact, but our sample implies that this picture is far from being uniform. Spanish loanwords are attested in pre-1550 documents, although they are few in number. And certain features, identified with specific stages (such as the creation of neologisms) in fact overlap with other stages and continue to the present day. However, the nature and depth of contact-induced change in modern Nahuatl goes much beyond the characteristics of Stage 3 proposed by Lockhart, embracing a profound transformation of the language's typological profile and including substitutive borrowing. Therefore, the modern phase of the development of Nahuatl should be considered a different stage (which would be Stage 4 in our proposal), markedly distinct from the late-colonial Stage 3. However, as argued below, the first signs of typological change occur already in the early and mid-colonial period, calling for a revised understanding of Stages 2 and 3.

What is emerging from the study of a broad range of Nahuatl documents, including the texts contained in the present volume, is a complex, varied, and dynamic picture of language change. The microregional trajectories of this process are reflected in its local variants, and attest to varying degrees of exposure to Spanish as well as the cultural strategies of native speakers. Contact-induced change is also manifest in multilingual settings, where Nahuatl served as the language of official communication: this is the case of the documents from Ixtenco (Tlaxcala) and Amacatlan (Soconusco, Chiapas). Generally, loanwords from Spanish are widely attested in the documents: all are adapted phonologically, although this may not always be reflected in their spelling, and some have undergone morphological changes. They represent the assimilation of specialized terminology associated with European material and spiritual culture as well as with legal, administrative, and economic spheres of life. Thus, typical religious borrowings include *Dios* 'God', *misa* 'mass', or *clerigo* 'secular priest'. Sometimes there are more specialized terms, such as *extrema unción* 'extreme unction', and combinations of native terminology with Spanish loanwords: *tlahtoani obispo* 'ruler bishop' or *teopixqui merçenario* 'Mercedarian priest'. Common for legal and administrative terminology are *justicia* 'justice' or 'officer of justice', *alcalde* 'municipal judge', *regidor* 'councilman', or *cabildo* 'municipal council'. Such terms as *salinas* 'salt mine' or *salinero* 'salt mine worker' illustrate the involvement of local communities in economic enterprises patronized or controlled by Spaniards.

Already in the sixteenth century, some Spanish nouns began to be verbalized in Nahuatl. A case in point is the omnipresent reflexive verb *firmatia* 'to sign'.

It is derived from the Spanish noun *firma* 'signature', to which is added first the Nahuatl verbing suffix *-ti*, meaning 'to have', and then the causative suffix *-a*. The borrowing of verbs is also well attested in our sample documents. A good example is *espolear*, which is converted into a Nahuatl transitive verb using one of the language's standard procedures for doing so (Document 30). *Espolear* is actually incorporated in Nahuatl as an unattested noun, *espoliar*, meaning in this case, 'something spurred'; it then receives the inceptive verbing suffix *-ihui*, forming an unattested verb *espoliarihui* 'to become a spurred thing'; finally, *-ihui* is replaced by the causative suffix *-oa*, producing *espoliaroa* 'to use spurs on an animal or a person,' literally, 'to cause something to be spurred'. Sometimes attested language forms provide evidence of essential steps in language evolution, bridging traditional, sixteenth-century forms and usages in modern Nahuatl. A good example comes for the petition of the residents of Santa Isabel Xiloxochtlan and San Luis Teolocholco (Tlaxcala, 1624, Document 29) that contains the sentence *õpa otimohuicaque mexico otimotlayhtlanito* 'we went to Mexico in order to make a request'. Literally, it reads, 'there we went to Mexico, we went in order to make a request'. In fact, the verbal construction *otimohuicaqueh* 'we went [reverential form]', is entirely redundant since *ompa mexico otimotlaihtlanitoh* already expresses the act of going to Mexico, for it means 'we went to Mexico in order to make a request'. However, similar constructions in Spanish are based on the usage of two separate verbs and the equivalent of this phrase would be *fuimos a Mexico para hacer una solicitud*. This usage is clearly an antecedent of a common construction in today's Tlaxcalan Nahuatl based on the direct calquing of the grammatical structure of Spanish. Thus, it is common to say *tiyohueh titequitihueh*, literally, 'we go, we go to work', instead of just *titequititihueh* 'we go (in order) to work', because again, the Spanish equivalent is an expression consisting of two separate verbs, *vamos a trabajar*. The discovery of such long-term trends and patterns of language change is only possible by tracing microphenomena in the same region across long periods of time. Other phenomena that precede usages common for modern Nahuatl include the numeral *ce* 'one', taking on the function of the Spanish indefinite article *ce escripturah* 'a document' (Document 10).

Another surprising feature revealed in the documentary sample presented here is the pluralization of inanimate nouns. In preconquest Nahuatl, nouns of this kind are only pluralized with the help of numeral classifiers. According to Lockhart, pluralized inanimate native nouns began to appear only in Stage 3 (Lockhart 1992: 312). However, several documents from Tlaxcala contradict this view: in the land sale document dated 1612 (Document 7) we find *tlapancaltin yetetl* 'three flat-roof houses'. Here, the inanimate noun *calli* is pluralized, but it is still accompanied by the numeral classifier *tetl*, which is traditionally used only with singular nouns. Similarly, we can see *nauhtetl y͡ tlapācaltin* 'four flat-roofed houses' in the 1600 copy of a 1576 will (Document 13). While we could suspect that this unusually early presence of *tlapalcaltin* is due to changes made to the testament during the copying process, our potential doubts are resolved by a 1560 lawsuit text (Document 30) that contains the following sentence: *oncan icalhua maniah yvan ocan icuezcōhuā maniah* 'there were located his houses and there were located his granaries'. This example is particularly interesting because not only the noun *calli* is pluralized but also the verb *mani* 'for something to lie in a circumscribed space', of which *calli* is the subject. We could perhaps argue that the word *calli* was an exception to the pattern and its pluralization represents a minor preconquest usage, typical for the region. However, the 1560 document also contains the word *cuezcomatl* 'granary', likewise pluralized, and the 1576/1600 will (Document 13) features *yetetl huipiltin* 'three shifts', in which the inanimate *huipilli* is pluralized despite preserving the traditional numeral classifier for inanimate nouns. Perhaps this new use of pluralization can be attributed to the notary Francisco de San Matías who made a copy of the testament in 1600. He also employs innovative forms alongside traditional ones in a 1596 document: in *nahui teohcali* 'four churches', the noun *teocalli* is not pluralized; but in *omoteneuhque nahui teohcaltin* 'four churches mentioned', both *teocalli* and the accompanying verb *omoteneuhqueh* are pluralized (AHET Caja 73, exp. 3, fol. 4r). A later instance of this complex transition is found in the 1706 document (Document 10) where the possessed, inanimate *xahcalli* 'hut' is pluralized in *noxahcaltzitzihuan macuilli* 'my five small huts', but the numeral remains in the singular form. These examples reveal a surprisingly early change in language structure modeled on Spanish, challenging the characteristics and timing of the stages originally proposed by Lockhart. The gradual disappearance of numeral classifiers and the category of animacy, marked by an increasing pattern of pluralization of inanimate nouns, begins already in the sixteenth century and becomes more widespread in the seventeenth century—in fact, it is well attested in the corpus of Tlaxcalan colonial documents since 1560. However, despite the longevity of this process, the disappearance of animacy as a grammatical category and the pluralization of inanimates is still in transition in modern Nahuatl variants, including Tlaxcalan and Huastecan Nahuatl (Olko 2018).

Another structural modification can be found in a 1695 land sale contract from Cholula (Document 9). In traditional Nahuatl, the particle *auh* always occurs in an utterance-initial position. It signals the beginning of a new clause, often indicating a change in topic, and is sometimes translated as 'and' or 'but'. In this document, however, it turns out to be a lexical-structural calque of the Spanish *y* 'and', working as a conjunction instead of the word *ihuan* traditionally used for this function: *Antonio gerero* ***auh*** *[i]namic ytoCa Señora Jusepa maria BillaloBos* 'Antonio Guerrero **and** his wife named Lady Josepa Maria Villalobos'.

When we bring Nahua and Quechua texts together, questions arise regarding the similarities and differences in their trajectories of change under the impact of Spanish. Again, the only comparison of contact-induced change in these two languages to date was done by James Lockhart (1998). When he studied the 1600 manuscript of Huarochiri, he found an extensive use of Spanish loanwords whenever the text referred to the events and practices of the contemporary (i.e., postconquest) period. Lockhart concluded that the Quechua corpus of the colonial period showed clear evidence of only the later stages of linguistic change, when lexical borrowings and calques from Spanish became pervasive, and that the earliest stage, featuring the more moderate or almost null influence of the donor language, remained unattested in indigenous Quechua writing. However, in his observations, Lockhart did not consider other substantial parts of the Quechua colonial corpus, such as ecclesiastical literature and dictionaries. Written or compiled by Spanish-speaking clerics, this part of the corpus reveals more information about the life of indigenous people in the early colonial period and thus may touch upon subjects missing from a collection of the preconquest Andean oral tradition, such as the manuscript of Huarochiri. The *Ritual formulario* by Juan Pérez Bocanegra can partly fill this gap: the author describes many everyday situations from colonial social life, and in the course of these descriptions he makes references to multiple objects, concepts, and practices introduced to the Andes by Europeans. It is there where we can find the types of neologisms that were given by Lockhart as examples of the first stage of the contact between Nahuatl and Spanish (Lockhart 1992: 263–284; Haimovich 2018).

The majority of these Quechua neologisms are encountered in parts of the *Ritual formulario* that are not included in the present anthology (Haimovich 2016); however, at least one example from Document 35 ("Confession of Indigenous Notaries") can be discussed here. The word *çamachina* corresponds to *posa* 'a stopping place in a procession' in the analogous Spanish text. *Posa* was made several times during a Catholic funeral, when the procession stopped and the priest, who led it, said prayers, which everyone else repeated after him (Chavez Hayhoe 1991: 15). The form *çamachina*, literally 'what makes someone rest' or 'where someone can rest', does not appear in any of the colonial dictionaries preceding the *Ritual formulario*. This indicates that even if such a form existed before the conquest, it could hardly have been stable. In the context of a funeral, *çamachina* refers only to the external aspect of the ceremony. From this perspective, it can be compared to the Nahuatl term for the rite of confirmation, *tzonilpia* 'to tie one's head (hair)' (Lockhart 1992: 269). This word also only conveys a superficial perception of the sacrament and does not say anything about its true meaning, a view characteristic of neophytes.

We also find some noteworthy semantic changes in the Quechua vocabulary of social hierarchy, as in the case of *apu*. In preconquest times, the term was associated with members of the high nobility who had blood ties to the Inca family, while in the "Confession of *Kurakas*" (Document 34), a hundred years after the conquest, it had come to mean a high official in the colonial administration. We could actually situate this change within the first stage of language contact, if we could demonstrate that the use of *apu* for representatives of colonial authority originated among native speakers and was not employed by the colonial administration itself; the possibility cannot be excluded. According to Pedro Pizarro, in 1533 Atahuallpa himself titled Francisco Pizarro *apu* (Pizarro 1978: 34).

In the sample of the Quechua corpus included in this anthology, loanwords from Spanish undoubtedly constitute the largest part of the phenomena of language contact in quantitative terms. More intricate examples of the hybridization of Spanish roots and Quechua suffixes can be found, as in the case of *casaracunca*, which means 'engagement' and is composed of the verb *casarakuy*, from the Spanish *casarse* 'to marry' and the Quechua reflexive suffix *ku*. It is worth mentioning that Pérez Bocanegra clearly sought to employ all the richness of the Quechua lexicon and morphological inventory in his work and probably used borrowings only when an analogue in the native language could not be achieved or when the Quechua word had been completely replaced by a Spanish loanword that was in daily use.

Some of the sample Andean documents contained in the present volume are in Spanish, including a fragment of a text dealing with Inca history composed by one nobleman for another, and several wills of Andean nobles. These texts do not differ much in terms of phonetics or grammar. However, the vocabulary of the chronicler's fragment is distinct from that of the wills. These testaments, written in Spanish, contain Spanish words with Andean referents: for example, *sause* [sauce] '*wayaw*' (*Salix humboldtiana*), *lana de la tierra* 'alpaca wool', *camiseta pintada nuevo*, probably an embroidered *unku* or *kusma*, and *frixoles de la tierra*, meaning *p'urutu* or *pallar* (*Phaseolus lunatus*). Of course, they also contain many Quechua words with a Quechua meaning and without any translation to Spanish: for instance, *lampa* 'shovel' (this word is easy to understand, since the word is still in use today in Andean Spanish). However, it is much more difficult to understand *guauya. Wawya,* in a local dialect, could mean to 'air' or 'a winnowing'. So an instrument called *wawya* could have been a fan, or a tool for cleaning grain in the wind. All this suggests that the anticipated readers of these documents written in Spanish were expected to know Quechua well. It would seem then that they were created for use by members of the local indigenous elite.

On the other hand, some examples reveal a very complicated attitude toward language. If the documents' readers were supposed to have known Quechua, why were complicated neologistic expressions like *lana de la tierra* used in the testaments instead of "alpaca wool," or *frejoles de la tierra* instead of *pallar*. The Spanish phrases had to have been invented in order to explain these new objects, *paqu millma*, "alpaca wool," and *pallar*, to Spaniards who did not know Quechua. The Andeans did not need such an explanation, so why did they employ it? Another example complicates things further. *Mates de madera pintada* is a Spanish expression that does not make much sense, since it means a 'gourd' or 'gourd bowls made of painted wood'. *Mati* is a Quechua word signifying 'gourd' (*Lagenaria siceraria*) or a 'container made of a gourd'. There are and were many kinds of such gourds in use, usually decorated. So gourds made of painted wood could not have existed. However, under the Spanish king's rule, and after the Spaniards had stolen the gold and silver mugs used previously in the most important ceremonies, the Andean nobility had large and small ceremonial wooden mugs, called *qiru*, for drinking corn beer. They always came in pairs, and were decorated with scenes and sequences of signs. Research has been done on these adornments, but they are not yet well understood. If *mates de madera pintada* was used to explain to a Spaniard what *qiru* meant in Quechua, then it was explained *ignotum per ignotum*. Nor did the expression say much to Quechua speakers, since it was in Spanish. Therefore *mates de madera pintada* could have been a local invention used to name *qiru* in Spanish. If this is indeed the case, we can infer that all other Quechua words used in the testaments were treated by the local Spanish speakers as Spanish words. On the other hand, we need to consider the possibility that a pseudo-Spanish name of such complexity was actually being used in a much more important context. Some Spaniards, especially the clergy, would have already known that the *qiru* mugs were not used in

Christian and Catholic ceremonies proper, nor directed to the Spanish God and saints; rather, they were only employed in ceremonies directed to Andean gods. Further evidence contained in the testaments is suggestive, such as the previously discussed case of the ritual sheep offering described in the will of Doña Juana Flores (Document 20). In this context the unambiguous Spanish name for sheep, *obeja de Castilla* 'Castilian sheep', is used rather than *oveja de la tierra*, or *llama*. Summing up, the Andean documents presented here show some Quechua or Aymara influence on Spanish texts: the impact is more pronounced in narrative texts (Document 33) and in wills than in official ecclesiastical documents (Documents 34, 35). In the examples of confessor's questions in Quechua, only some very complicated religious words were left in Spanish, while the syntax and all the expressions describing local people were well translated to Quechua. This can be attributed to Juan Pérez Bocanegra's effort to produce a text that would be well understood by Quechua penitents.

Documents written in Spanish use Spanish words to describe family members: for example: *tío* 'uncle'. *Tío* in Colonial Quechua corresponds to two different words: *yaya*, and *kaka*. If translated into English, *yaya* refers to one's father, father's brother, or any father's cousin up to the fourth generation, whereas *kaka* refers to one's mother's brother, wife's father, or brothers-in-law. So who exactly was the *tío*? The example indicates that two ways of describing reality influenced the meanings in both languages, and this was as true during the colonial period as it is today.

The Spanish texts from this volume that are produced in the Andes contain some forms that are frequently used in modern Andean Spanish and do not conform with the codified norms of the Spanish language in either Spain or Peru.[11] We do not comment on cases for which there are only single attestations; rather we discuss more-widespread phenomena, including gender and number agreement, vowel substitution, use of pronouns and reflexives, and a case of the impact of Quechua worldview on morphosyntax.

In four documents authored by indigenous Peruvians, there are nineteen occurrences of the lack of gender agreement between noun and adjective: for example, *vna yegua coxa castaño* (Document 20). There are also twenty-two occurrences of the lack of number agreement: between noun and adjective or determiner, as in *de su mismo bienes* (Document 16), or between noun and verb, as in *dos tembladeras de plata que pesara ambas, doçe onsas* (Document 20). On some occasions verbal forms also do not agree in number, for example

11 We would like to acknowledge the participation of Gregory Haimovich in writing and revising this section.

*nombro por mi albaçea y testamentario a agustin capcha a quien rruego para que lo aç**eten** y execute* (Document 20). The problem with gender agreement is obviously caused by the absence of grammatical gender in Quechua and Aymara languages. Also, in these languages the adjective precedes the noun and does not acquire the plural ending if the noun has it. All this stands in opposition to the situation in Spanish, where adjectives agree with nouns in both gender and number. Furthermore, in Quechua the plural marker is not obligatory for a verb in the third person, especially if the plurality of an agent has already been mentioned or can be understood from the context. This explains the emergence of pairs like *aç**eten** y execute* in the Spanish text.

There are many indications of the influence of Quechua or Aymara phonology on written Spanish. Since both Quechua and Aymara distinguish between only three vowels, [a]/[i]/[u], the vowel oppositions [i]/[e] and [u]/[o], existing in Spanish, were often overlooked by scribes, as can be seen from the following examples: *açituni* [*aceituni*], *auturidad* [*autoridad*], *cochillos* [*cuchillos*], *cubre* [cobre], *dezen* [*dicen*], *escodilla* [*escudilla*], *Jobon* [*jubón*], *lestadas* [*listadas*], *tegerita* [*tijerita*], *tornasul* [*tornasol*], *viui* [*vive*]. Quechua has a case suffix *-(k)ta* with a broad range of functions: it can mark a direct object, an indirect object, and the adverbial form of adjective. There are a number of prepositions in Spanish that can be used in situations where Quechua employs only *-(k)ta*. With transitive verbs, direct objects do not require any preposition if they are inanimate; if an object is animate or indirect, the preposition *a* is employed. This distinction is sometimes missing from the Spanish texts included in this volume. For example, in the phrase from the testament of doña Juana Flores (Document 20), *entregose Agustin, su marido* 'it was turned over to Agustin, her husband', there should have been an *a* before *Agustin*, which is an animate indirect object in this case. The opposite case can be found in the testament of Catalina Carguay Chumbi (Document 16): *digo . . . a que nos cassamos tres años a esta parte* 'I state . . . that . . . It has been more or less three years to date since we were married'. The author marks the complementary cause with *a*, which contradicts the rules of the Spanish language, but correlates with how subordination is expressed in Quechua, namely by nominalized verbal forms with *-(k)ta*, so that in such a case in Quechua we would expect *casara(ku)-sqa-y-ku-**kta** ñinim* 'I say that we have been married . . . ,' where *-sqa-* is a nominalizer and *-y-ku-* is a possessive marker of first person plural exclusive.

There are more intricate cases that refer us not only to grammatical dissimilarities but also to the difference between the European and Andean worldviews. Such is, for example, the expression *creyendo como creo el misterio* 'believing, as I do, in the mystery' (Document 15), which would include a preposition *en* in the conventional Spanish, *creo* ***en*** *el misterio*. This phrase corresponds to the evidence of the difficulties experienced by the first missionaries in the Andes, when they tried to explain to the indigenous people the concept of belief *in* God, while the neophytes continued saying *creo Dios* instead of *creo* ***en*** *Dios* (Estenssoro-Fuchs 1998: 117). Another phenomenon is the occurrence of the reflexive particle *se* in situations where the verb syntactically and semantically must be transitive and not reflexive: *y* ***se*** *paguen La limosna acostumbrada* 'and that the customary alms be paid' or ***se*** *me asienten mi nombre* 'my name be registered' (Document 16). These cases were probably caused by an identification of the Spanish *se* with the Quechua verbal suffix *-ku-*, which can mean reflexivity but can also have other functions, such as an indication of courtesy or interest of the agent (Cusihuaman 1976: 212).

A more profound search would likely reveal more linguistic phenomena that are now well established in Andean Spanish. The examples shown here imply that the formation of this variety of Spanish across the lands of the Inca Empire began quite early, no later than the second half of the sixteenth century.

COMPARISONS AND CONCLUSIONS

The sample of documents presented here, modest although it is, reveals both parallelisms and differences in the colonial adaptations and strategies of indigenous elites in Nahua Mesoamerica and the Andes. Common points include no doubt the wide range and flexibility of adaptations to the new sociopolitical, cultural, and economic reality in which the successful survival of preconquest elites—as well as the prosperity of new elites emerging in the colonial context—depended to a large extent on the skillful combination of local and external sources of legitimacy. This is reflected in double role or identity playing, embracing both dynastic rights and new offices introduced by the Spanish Crown. Common to both areas, though probably more salient in the Andes, is the role of local rulers, who carried their prehispanic functions as protectors and stabilizers of the community into the colonial period, acting on its behalf and assuming responsibility for its prosperity. A common goal of Nahua and Quechua elites seems to have been the pursuit of a balanced power relationship within the colonial system that would assure stable cultural and sociopolitical reproduction of local communities and their successful dealings with the external world. Therefore, the forms of indigenous agency revealed by the documents are not only individual but usually collective, be that on the level of families, corporate groups, municipal officials, or entire communities. Similarities between the two major areas of Spanish colonization in the Americas can also be detected in the religious sphere, where the new faith and its cults were molded into local ritual concepts and worldview, to a more or less visible extent. We are not talking about any form of religious "syncretism" but rather the active "reworking" of foreign concepts into the local framework and religious practices, sometimes highlighting apparent "points of coincidence."

As for sociopolitical organization, similar forms and solutions were introduced by the Crown in both regions, but with different results. In the Nahua world, Spanish municipal organization easily merged with the local patterns of rule of the *altepetl*, quickly transforming the *cabildo* into an integral feature of local indigenous organization, administered entirely by local elites. Developments in the Andes, however, were somewhat different. Spanish municipal organization imposed in the *reducciones*, or new villages, took the form of a hierarchy of titles and functions usually occupied by local noblemen. The functionaries were not elected but selected and coopted by those who concluded their formal period in office. Since the *kurakas* retained their functions of organizing work assignments, as well as collecting and paying taxes, the new municipal authorities could not and did not rule in the way Spanish reformers of local administration imagined. The *kuraka*, a local nobleman, constituted the first judicial instance, to whom a complaintant could recur; the second judicial instance was the Spanish *corregidor*, and the third was the *audiencia* in Lima, Chuquisaca (Charcas, La Plata, today Sucre), or Quito. In Nahua towns, local elites also controlled the municipal government, and the role of the dynastic *tlahtohqueh* was often similar to that of the *kurakas*. However, municipal organization seems to have been more strongly adjusted or molded into the preconquest internal structure and hierarchy of the *altepetl*, leaving space for internal political competition, struggles, and power sharing among elites representing either different units or noble families that formed alliances and competed among themselves. When internal problems became insurmountable, Spanish authorities would send in an external interim governor, called a *juez gobernador* or *juez de residencia*.[12]

12 In the Andes they were two different functionaries. The *juez de residencia* judged Spanish officials, such as the *corregidores*, when they finished their time in office. The *juez gobernador* could be any Spanish governor, while the indigenous governor was called a *cacique gobernador*.

Colonial litigation involving indigenous people was carried out very differently in the Andean and the Nahua areas. In the former, court proceedings for non-natives were recorded in detail in Spanish, while in the case of natives they were only summarized in Spanish: testimony provided by witnesses was heard orally but never put into the record. Nahuatl, on the other hand, was actually used in court: legal documentation was, at least partly, produced in Nahuatl, including when Spaniards were involved in litigation, for example as an accused party. This essential difference is seen even on a more private level. In the Andes, the use of testaments, composed predominantly in Spanish, was limited to more important people. As confessors' questions show, in native municipalities there were local notaries (*escribanos del pueblo*) who wrote down all the administrative procedures and testaments in Spanish. Their status was better than that of the commoners, since they were exempt from both head tax and obligatory work service. The testaments they wrote pertained to members of the elite (if a woman who produced corn beer at home for sale can be considered a member of the elite). In Nahua communities, testaments tended to be both dictated and written down in Nahuatl. And the testators belonged to different social groups: from the high to the low nobility, as well as members of the "middle class" and commoners who had some wealth or goods to bequeath.

There are also important differences between Nahua and Andean texts with respect to the levels of usage of alphabetic writing. The Nahuas grasped it very quickly as a practical tool and employed it prolifically for their own purposes during the colonial era. It is clear from the documents presented here that it was also used, albeit through notaries, by wide sectors of local communities, including the lower nobility, the middle class, and even ordinary commoners, to defend their rights and economic affairs in the colonial legal system. In Peru, writing in indigenous languages is very scarce and exceptional in comparison to Spanish. And the use of alphabetic writing by actual members of native communities was even more limited. The reasons are complex, but the main cause seems to have been the very important differences in the preconquest traditions of recording information employed by Mesoamerican and Andean peoples. Hieroglyphic writing and books were in common usage among the precolonial Nahuas, and the same system was employed in reference to different aspects of life and social functions. In Peru, one type of notation was used for recording the sacred history of the kings (painted tables), another for the administration of goods and work (*khipu*), and yet another for prayers (circular stones or clay "pizzas"). Since those most commonly used were of a three-dimensional character, and not two-dimensional, as were hieroglyphs and the

Latin alphabet, the Spaniards did not recognize Andean recordings as writing, and the Andeans had the same problem conceptualizing writing on paper.

In practice, texts in Andean general languages—Quechua and Aymara, rarely others—were produced by the clergy for church use, such as prayers, sermons, and confessors' questionnaires. Some Quechua texts written in Spanish orthography do appear toward the end of the sixteenth century, but they are exceptional: one collection of myths (Salomon and Urioste 1991), a few letters, some poems, and, beginning in the late seventeenth century, theatrical pieces produced by Creole elites. The clergy and the representatives of the Spanish administration resisted the use of Quechua as a written language in everyday life: they preferred Spanish. Native administrators used traditional *khipu* and probably other systems for their own needs, in most places at least until the middle of the seventeenth century, and in some places until the end of the nineteenth century. Local indigenous administration functioned orally, while paper documentation was needed only in procedures involving contact with the Spanish administration. All this does not explain, however, why native elites in the Andes did not adopt alphabetic writing for use in everyday life. The Incas had imposed Quechua (already used as a *lingua franca*) as the language of imperial administration, and had organized its instruction to the elites. The Spaniards did the same: they organized schools for indigenous noble children. In such schools the future administrators learned Spanish and instruction was in Spanish. Even today the noble Inca families in Cuzco take care to teach their children Spanish before Quechua. The association of nobility with Spanish has a long history in the Andes: in the second half of the eighteenth century the word *Spanish* meant nobleman, and the word *Indian* meant peasant. The situation in Mexico, despite some similarities, was different. Nahuatl was used in Mesoamerica as the *lingua franca* of the Aztec empire, and had probably attained this status long before. This role continued after the Spanish conquest, when Nahuatl thrived as the language of Christianization and administration (Schwaller 2012). In Peru the imperial languages were Quechua and Aymara, and they also become the linguistic vehicles of Christianization. However, they were not the languages of viceregal administration nor did they ever become written languages at the level of local communities.

The different approaches to alphabetic writing characterizing the two areas have considerable consequences for the content of colonial documents and their roles in sociopolitical realities. Forms and genres imposed by Spanish bureaucracy on native elites might have been similar in Mesoamerica and the Andes, but structural similarity did not always entail similar contents: a more detailed comparative analysis reveals strong differences, as well as a rich diversity of local strategies and cross-cultural attitudes. The vast multiplicity of voices, rendered in their complex cultural, social, political, and linguistic contexts, is probably the most significant characteristic of the present volume. Independently of the cultural differences that exist between the Nahua and Quechua worlds, these voices reveal how textual production and its associated speech acts simultaneously shaped and were shaped by daily realities and practices. Allowing these voices to speak on their own terms—that is, from their own ontological perspectives—is an ongoing scholarly challenge.

DOCUMENTS AND STUDIES

LEGAL PROCEEDINGS

DOCUMENT 1

Painting of the Idols of the Temple of Huitzilopochtli, Mexico Tenochtitlan, 1539–1540

Strategies to Safeguard Legitimacy[1]

María Castañeda de la Paz

Sacred bundles—*tlaquimilolli* in Nahuatl—were one of the main objects of veneration in Mesoamerican religion. These bundles made of cloth, *amate* paper, or reed mat boxes contained a number of objects representing different deities and were the focus of great devotion.[2] However, beyond this reverence, the divine force that resided in the bundles was what legitimated the foundation of many Mesoamerican polities and their rulers' authority. This latter aspect explains why, at the height of the conquest, the Central Mexican nobles hurriedly saved the sacred bundles that were at risk of being destroyed by the Spaniards. It is this issue that is discussed in the present study. Due to the existence of an important document, known as the *Painting of the idols of the temple of Huitzilopochtli*, presented in one of the interrogations led by fray Juan de Zumárraga between 1536 and 1540, we can go in depth into a poorly

1 Archivo General de la Nación (AGN), Inquisición, vol. 37, exp. 3. I would like to thank Michael Swanton for his help with the translation of the original text from Spanish to English.

2 Various authors have analyzed, to a greater or lesser degree, the Mesoamerican sacred bundles. Among these studies are those of Olivier (1995, 2007, 2010) and the recent MA thesis by Correa Valdivia (2014) for central Mexico. Anders et al. (1993: 210–215) discuss the ceremonies related to the opening of the sacred bundle in the *Codex Borgia*; Hermann (2008) deals with the bundles of the Mixteca; Ayala (2002) considers the bundles of the Maya region; and Oudijk (2000: 161–169) provides evidence about Zapotec bundles.

DOI: 10.5876/9781607328346.c001

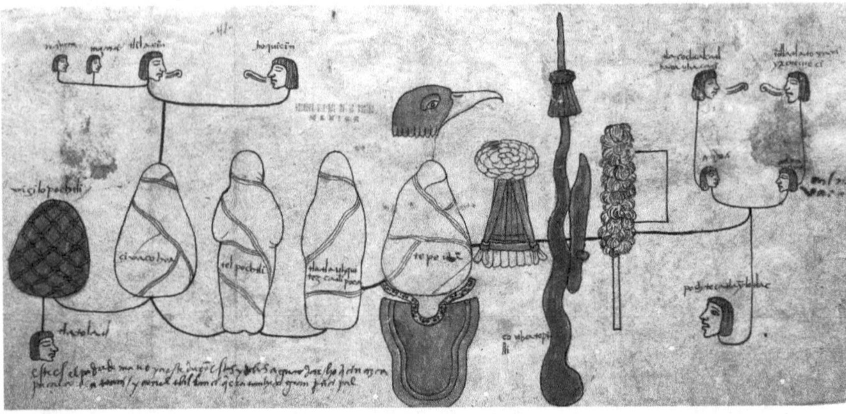

FIGURE 1.1. Painting of the idols of the temple of Huitzilopochtli (photograph of the original, Archivo General de la Nación, Mapoteca no. 4848, Mexico)

documented period of Tenochca history and explain the strategy and rationale behind the action of some of members of its royal house.[3]

The pictorial we know today as the *Painting of the idols of the temple of Huitzilopochtli* was painted in color on *amate* paper (figures 1.1, 1.2). At some point during the years 1539 and 1540, it was presented as evidence against various persons accused of hiding several sacred bundles, including the bundle of Huitzilopochtli from the *Templo Mayor* at Tenochtitlan. This explains why these sacred bundles and several associated ritual objects are the main focus of the pictorial. A series of small heads represent the accused. Volutes denoting their speech accompany some of the heads. Contrary to its traditional prehispanic style, the painter chose not to paint onomastic glyphs to identify these people, but rather employed a series of alphabetic glosses.

3 The records of the trial and the painting are kept in the AGN, Inquisición, vol. 37, exp. 3. However, the pictorial, painted on *amate* paper, was separated from the file and is kept in the Mapoteca with the catalogue number 4.848. The records have been published in 1912 and 2002 (*Proceso de indios, idólatras y hechiceros*). Nutall (1911), Padden (1967), Greenleaf (1988: 75–77), and León Rivera (1997) have made brief studies and commentaries on the trial. Lopes Don (2010) offers a more recent study of the case, identifying and contextualizing the personages who appear in the alphabetic text and in the pictorial. I should say here that in 2009 I also carried out research on this topic and submitted it for publication in the same year, before Lopes Don's book came out. Due to complications in the editorial process, my work was first published four years later (Castañeda de la Paz 2013a) and then again in another publication (Castañeda de la Paz 2015). The nature of this anthology notwithstanding (the editors asked for a short study and commentary on the original document), I reviewed the work of Lopes Don and made several references to it. However, because I concur with some of this researcher's points of analysis, the study I present here can well be considered complementary to Lopes Don's work.

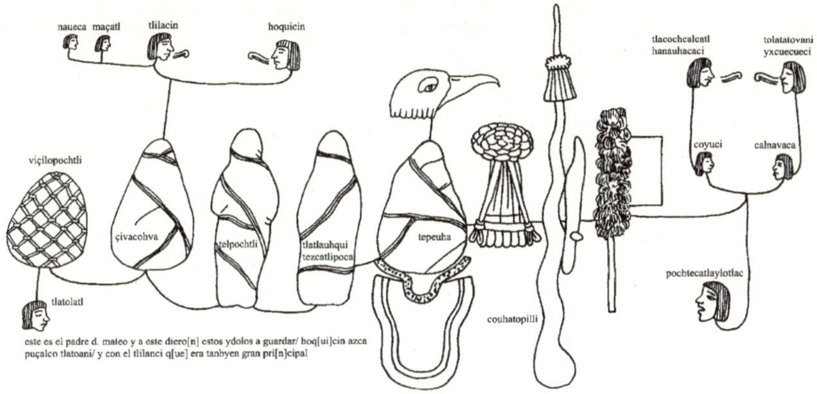

FIGURE 1.2. Painting of the idols of the temple of Huitzilopochtli (drawing by Michel Oudijk)

This choice surely reflects the fact that the painting was to be presented before the Spanish authorities, which also explains why the only text that appears in the work is in Spanish, not Nahuatl.

Some heads are larger than others, a technique used to highlight the relative importance of the figures portrayed. And all of the figures, except one, are drawn with their eyes closed, indicating that when the document was made the individuals represented had already died. The only person with open eyes is Miguel Tlaylotlac, or "Pochteca Tlaylotlac," as he is identified by a gloss. We can conclude then that he was the only person alive at the time of the trial. The size of his head clearly indicates that, as the principal defendant, he was the central person in the painting.

Two other important figures accused of hiding the sacred bundles are Ixcuecuechtzin and Oquiztzin. The gloss identifies Oquiztzin ("hoquicin"), Lord of Azcapotzalco, a fact corroborated by several witnesses. However, none of these deponents affirmed that he specifically governed the Mexicapan *parcialidad* of the city; rather they simply refer to Azcapotzalco.[4]

4 Molina (2001: fol. 4r) translated the word *altepetl* as 'pueblo' (town), although beyond that simple description, today we can indicate that the *altepetl* was a sovereign territory in which lived a multiethnic population. Given the complexity of the internal organization of the *altepetl*, authors like Lockhart (1992: 14–28) established two clearly defined categories: the simple *altepetl* and the complex *altepetl*. The territorial divisions of the first were known as *tlahxillacalli*, while the latter were constituted by two or more simple *altepetl*, called *parcialidades* by the Spaniards, which in turn were divided into *tlahxillacalli*.

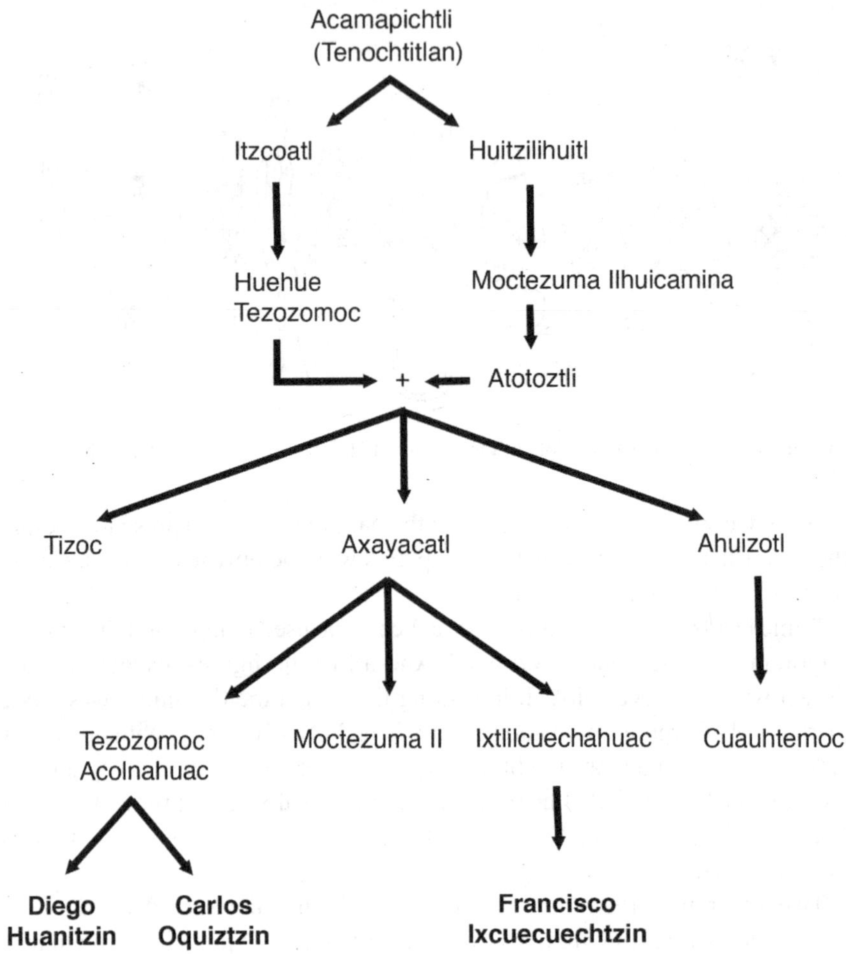

FIGURE 1.3. Itzcoatl's lineage in Tenochtitlan and Azcapotzalco-Mexicapan

That particular *altepetl* had been divided into two dynastic moieties in the aftermath of Itzcoatl's conquest of Azcapotzalco in 1428; one half was Tepanecapan, which was still governed by a Tepanec lineage, while the other half was Mexicapan, where Itzcoatl placed his son as governor, thus imposing a Tenochtitlan lineage (figure 1.3).[5] When the Spaniards arrived,

5 Regarding the history of Azcapotzalco, see Castañeda de la Paz (2013a: 40–48, 73–77, 148–153, 208–213, 322–327; 2013b).

a member of the Tenochtitlan lineage was still governing Azcapotzalco-Mexicapan; namely, a grandson of Axayacatl, who later adopted the name Don Carlos Oquiztzin.

The other individual was Don Francisco Ixcuecuechtzin, also a grandson of Axayacatl, who at the time of the conquest held the position of *tlahtoani* of Tula. This leads us to conclude that when the Spaniards arrived some of the *altepetl* in Central Mexico were governed by lords who shared close kinship ties and were, to a greater or lesser degree, members of the royal house of Tenochtitlan. This explains why together they had to decide what to do with the sacred bundles.

As mentioned above, the bundles are painted in close association with several ritual objects. All of the objects are white, except for the first one, which is purple and wrapped in some kind of net. Normally, in order to distinguish the deity to which each *tlaquimilolli* referred, an image of the divinity, or of an object closely related to it, was reproduced on the bundle itself. However, in this case—except for the bundle that corresponds to 'Tepeuha'—they bear only glosses, which allow us to identify each of them. Thus, we are able to determine that the purple one represents Huitzilopochtli, while the others corresponded to Cihuacoatl, Telpochtli, Tlatlauhqui, and Tepeuha, or Tepehua. Clearly, the most important bundle was the one that pertained to Huitzilopochtli, the patron god of the Tenochcas. We should not confuse the bird that appears on Tepehua's bundle with a hummingbird, which was a manifestation of Huitzilopochtli.[6] On one side of Tepehua's bundle we see a set of ritual objects painted in conjunction with the bundles that includes a fan, a staff shaped like a serpent, called *coatopilli*, and a flag with the upper part of its pole decorated with feathers.

The judicial process against Miguel Tlaylotlac began when Mateos, an indigenous painter from Mexico Tenochtitlan, accused him before the bishop,

6 Here my opinion differs from that by Lopes Don (2010: 113–115, 128). The name *Tepeuha* or *Tepehua* is best translated as 'mountain possessor', or 'the Lord of the Mountain', which explains its association with the *tetehuitl* seen in the image, that is the slip of paper stained with *ulli* that was used during rituals of the cult of the mountains to plead for rain. Apparently, the represented bird is also related to this ritual context. According to Alejandro de Ávila, director of the Ethnobotanical Garden of Oaxaca and the ornithologist Manuel Grosselet, it is a Veracruz or Mexican partridge, a species that, like the one in the pictorial, has a patch of red skin around its eyes and green feathers on its neck (personal communication, October 2012). Peasants in the Sierra de Zongolica say that the sound of this bird announces the rains (Aguilar Rodríguez 2000: 4), which would explain its association with this particular bundle.

fray Juan de Zumárraga, of hiding several bundles in his house so that they would not fall into the hands of the Spaniards. In the trial Mateo (not to be confused with the painter Mateos) and his brother Pedro were called to testify. They were sons of a "privado"[7] of Moctezuma Xocoyotzin called Tlatolatl (or Atolatl), a member of Moctezuma Xocoyotzin's retinue. They testified that Tlatolatl was not just any ordinary priest, but that he was responsible for guarding and securing Huitzilopochtli's bundle. Seeing how the Spaniards were quickly overrunning Tenochtitlan and Tlatelolco, Tlatolatl decided to take Huitzilopochtli's bundle from the city so it would not be captured and burned by the conquerors. He chose to take it to Azcapotzalco, specifically to the home of Oquiztzin (*Procesos de indios* 2002: 116, 118). However, Oquiztzin later returned it to Mateo (Tlatolatl´s son), together with other bundles, a fact confirmed by a gloss in the codex: "this is Mateo's father and with him [indicating Mateo], Oquiztzin, *tlahtoani* of Azcapucalco, and Tlillantzin, who was also a great principal, left these idols to be guarded."

The decision to leave all the bundles with Tlatolatl was made in 1524, the year in which Hernán Cortés took many lords and governors from Central Mexico (together with their entourage of principals) to Guatemala and Honduras (the Hibueras expedition). This turn of events left Tlatolatl no other choice than to keep the bundles hidden in Azcapotzalco-Mexicapan for a whole year and maintain the associated cult. That is why the image of Tlilantzin is facing Oquiztzin (figures 1.1–1.2); and the accompanying volutes indicate that the words emerging from their mouths concern the decision about what to do with the bundles. It is especially important to note that the painter included proof that Tlatolatl was the guardian of Huizilopochtli's bundle, while his counterpart in Azcapotzalco, Tlilantzin, was entrusted with all the others. This helps us understand why only Tlatoatl is joined to the Tenochca deity, while a separate line unites Tlilantzin to the other gods. However, the fact that all of the bundles are interconnected indicates that when Tlilantzin and Oquiztzin left for Hibueras, they were all left in Tlatolatl's custody, as is also corroborated in testimony (*Proceso de indios* 2002: 116, 118).

Mateo seems to confirm that the other four bundles, or "idols," were not from Tenochtitlan, for he was surprised by their presence: "the aforementioned Lord *cacique* of Azcapotzalco and a principal of his, called Tlilantzin, gave to the witness's father four other idols for safekeeping [. . .]. This

7 A *privado* is a person who has the close acquaintance and favor of a lord (*Diccionario de autoridades*, Vol. 3, 2012: 386).

witness and his brother, named Pedro, said to themselves: 'From whence have these lords brought these idols?'"[8]

Initially, one may assume that these four bundles belonged to Azcapotzalco but, as I show below, all the evidence indicates that the Lords of Azcapotzalco only received them for safekeeping. Behind Tlilantzin there are two heads that, due to their small size, must represent people of a lower rank. The glosses inform us that they are called *Maçal* 'Deer' and *Naueca* '4 Wind'. Again, from Mateo and Pedro's testimony we know that Nauhecatl was an old nobleman (*principal*) who was in charge of things related with Tlilantzin and the person responsible for the *parcialidad* of Azcapotzalco-Mexicapan when Cortés took the ruler and his *privado* with him to the Hibueras (*Procesos de indios* 2002: 116–118). It seems, thus, that the religious matters were in the hands of Tlatolatl.

Upon receiving news that the *tlahtoani* and his companion had died, it was he who decided to keep the bundles hidden in Azcapotzalco-Mexicapan and wait for "the lords" to reach a decision about what to do with them. The "lords" referred to are the rulers of Mexico (allusion to Tenochtitlan) and Tula, who are represented on the other side of the painting. In Tenochtitlan, this would be a man called Nanahuatzin,[9] because Cuauhtemoc, together with the lords of Azcapotzalco, had gone with Cortés. In the case of Tula, it is Ixcuecuechtzin (or Don Francisco Ixcuecuechtzin), whom I mentioned at the beginning of the essay. The small heads below them represent the messengers that each ruler sent to Azcapotzalco to retrieve the bundles. Hence, we can conclude that one or more of the bundles pertained to Tula, though I cannot explain why its ruler had it sent to Azcapotzalco-Mexicapan.[10]

Thanks to the testimony of the witnesses we know that when the messengers arrived at Azcapotzalco, Tlatolatl—who had been entrusted with the

8 "que el dicho Señor cacique de Escapuzalco y un principal suyo, que se dice Tlilanci, que dieron á su padre de este testigo á guardar otros cuatro ídolos [. . .] este testigo y un hermano suyo que se dice Pedro decían entre sí: "¿de dónde han traído estos Señores estos ídolos?" (*Proceso de indios* 2002: 116).

9 Nanahua of Nanahuatzin is a well-established name. For this reason, I don't believe that we are dealing with Anahuacaca, as Padden (1970: 257) suggests and Lopes Don (2010: 117) reiterates, because the lineage of Cuauhtemoc was not the one that possessed the rights to govern in Tenochtitlan (Castañeda de la Paz 2013a: 177–181).

10 Thanks to another judicial case, we know that the deity Tlatlauhqui (or the Red Tezcatlipoca) was from Tula, because the priest who lived with Don Pedro Tlacahuepan, or Don Pedro Moctezuma, *cacique* and governor de Tula, was the one who had him in his custody (*Proceso de indios* 2002: 180–181).

bundles—had died, and that his sons, Pedro and Mateo, were now in charge of guarding them. Therefore, they were the ones who had turned the bundles over to these messengers so that they could be transferred to Miguel Tlaylotlac's house (*Procesos de indios* 2002: 117–119). This explains why Tlaylotlac appears in the pictorial with a line that joins him to the envoys sent by the Lords of Tula and Tenochtitlan and to the bundles they delivered.

Moving the bundles from Azcapotzalco to Tenochtitlan without raising suspicions must have involved quite an operation. It is said that the task was accomplished by five bearers, or *tamemeh*, each one carrying a bundle that was deposited at the home of Miguel Tlaylotlac, who then took charge of the cult, though he kept them covered with mats (*petates*) to hide them from view (*Procesos de indios* 2002: 117–119). Unfortunately, at this point in the story everything becomes confused and full of contradictions, as each man sought to absolve himself of the responsibility for the *tlaquimilolli*. It is said that Mateo and Pedro, who remained in Azcapotzalco, were visited again by envoys who tried to ascertain where the bundles were being held, for it seems they were no longer in Miguel Tlaylotlac's house. In his defense, Miguel argued that the bundles had only been there for ten days, when the same men who had left them returned and took them away, but without telling him what their destination was (*Procesos de indios* 2002: 119–120). Some witnesses maintained that the bundles could be found close to Tula, where they had been taken by certain "prophets" from Tenochtitlan. This seems to be a reference to the court of the principal lords—ancient priests—that formed part of Don Diego Huanitzin's entourage (*Procesos de indios* 2002: 123–124). Huanitzin was none other than Oquiztzin's brother and Lord of Ehecatepec, who in 1539—the year the investigation began—became Lord of Tenochtitlan (figure 1.3). There is no evidence that he was called to testify, and he does not appear among the witnesses. Nothing more has ever been discovered about these sacred bundles.

The analysis of this document allows us to probe a little deeper into the actions of the nobility of central Mexico during the poorly documented period shortly after the Spanish conquest. We can see how the rulers of many *altepetl* were bound by close kinship ties and maintained constant contact. Also, we learn that of all the bundles represented in the painting, only Huitzilopochtli's belonged to Tenochtitlan, while the others seem to have been from Tula. If Huitzilopochtli's bundle contained the divine force that legitimated the foundation of Tenochtitlan and its rulers, then it is logical to think that, in order to prevent it from being burned, the main priest of Tenochtitlan would have transferred it to Azcapotzalco-Mexicapan, which was, after all, an extension of the Tenochca capital. This same logic would suggest that in 1539 or 1540, Don Diego Huanitzin would have had the bundle, since that was the year in which Viceroy Mendoza named him the first indigenous colonial ruler of Tenochtitlan.

DOCUMENT 2

Land Litigation, Tlatelolco, Mexico, 1558[1]

JULIA MADAJCZAK

[Fol. 11r]

informaçion de bernaldino + ~~yx~~ .q. pablo sobre trràs
+

En la çiudad de mexico cenpovali ôce meztli de noviembre . 1558 anos nezque. y moteyspaviya. ypapa tlali ŷtoca bernardino ag~~yx~~ cozcaquauh yva yveltiuh Juana teycuih . quinamiqui pablo viznavatl· y bernardino yvā yn iveltiuh . chaneque amaxac sancta maria . coceptio povi auh pablo – viznavatl· chane· tolpetlac quitoque· ŷ bernadino yva in iveltiuh techcuiliya · ŷ totlal. ŷ pablo viznavatl . ŷ ya ysquich cavitl· mochipa tictopieliya · ya cenpovalxivitl· ôcastoli ypa oxivitl· ŷ ticpiya . auh çā tlalcovali yevatl · quicouhtiya . ce tlacatl . noveltivatzin ytoca catca magdalena teyacapa ce quimili quachtli in ipatiuh[2]

The questioning of Bernardino [and?] Pablo about lands.
+

In the city of Mexico, on the twenty-first of the month of November of the year 1558, a person named Bernardino Cozcaquauh along with his sister[3] Juana Teicuh appeared to make a complaint about land against Pablo Huitznahuatl. Bernardino and his sister are citizens in Amaxac, which belongs to Santa María Concepción and Pablo Huitznahuatl is a citizen in Tolpetlac. Bernardino and his sister declared, "Pablo Huitznahuatl is taking our land, which we have had this whole time, from us. We have always had it for thirty-seven years. And it is purchased land that a lady, my late sister, named Magdalena Tiacapan, went and bought. Its price was a load of [= twenty] tribute cloaks.

1 AGN, Tierras, vol. 17, parte 2a, exp. 4, ff. 11r–14r. The transcription of the document was previously published in Reyes García 1996: 74–82.

2 This phrase is written above *ya qin ya matlacxivitl.*

3 I think *–hueltiuh* means 'sister' rather than 'elder sister' here. Magdalena (see below) is a *–hueltiuh* of Bernardino and he is later described as her *–ach* 'elder brother'. *–Hueltiuh* sometimes serves to describe sisters regardless of relative age in other texts, too.

 DOI: 10.5876/9781607328346.c002

ya qin ya matlacxivitl· onavi yn omomiquili auh y ya nepa mochipa oticnepapiyaya. y quicouh tlali y noveltivatzin ya qui oyuh ya yexivitl· maxitico marques y quicovili ytoca. acsotecatl · ôpa chane y tolpetlac Auh y yevatl · ŷ pablo viznavatl[4] · ya qui ya macuilxitl· yn ocopevalti ŷ ya quimotlaltiya amo quitova novevetlal. ça quimotequimiltiya . auh ynic tocôcauhque çâ nimococovaya y ya chiquacexivitl· auh y ya macuilxihuitl ·niquelimiquizquiya . ça ôpa nechvaltocac auh y ya matlacxivitl ŷ ya castolxivitl. y ya cenpovalxivitl · ŷ ya ômatlactli y ya ôcastoli mochipa tictopieliya. mochipa tiqueliqui mochipa ôcā titlachiqui yn ôpa tolpetlac auh yn axcâ çā tlapic y techaviliznequi ȳ pablo· viznavatl · ayc oticauhque ·mochipa tictopieliya .

Fourteen years ago she died, but before then we had together been keeping the land that my sister had bought three years after the Marqués arrived; she purchased it from one named Acxotecatl who was a citizen in Tolpetlac. And five years ago this Pablo Huitznahuatl began to occupy it; he didn't say, 'It is my patrimonial land,' but he was paying tribute from the field. And we temporarily[5] abandoned it because six years ago I was sick. And five years ago I wanted to cultivate it, but he expelled me from there. For ten years, fifteen years, twenty years, thirty years, and thirty-five years we have always been in charge of it, we have always cultivated it, we have always collected *maguey* sap in Tolpetlac. Now Pablo Huitznahuatl wants to quarrel with us about it on false grounds. We never abandoned it, we always kept it."

y[6] miguel · diez chane · tlocalpa sancta maria . coceptio ya yepovalxivitl y nemi Jurame oquimomaquili ŷ Juez ynic vel tlatolmelavaz quito y testico ya neli melavac y niquitova y notlatol amo niztlacati y yevatl · in civatzintli catca ytoca · magdalenā teyacapa ôpa valeva y tlocalpa ça nicâ monamictica. y tlatilolco · auh ynic nocomati ca tivevetque ca techixpatito · yva oc cequitin vevetque conitquitiya. octzintli nima ya · quimilviya ca nicâ catquí achitzin octzintli ōpa ovala y tolpetlac onicmocovi tlaltzintli ôpa yc amoyolotzin melava[7] yc namechnopialtiya · ma quemaniya

Miguel Diaz, a citizen in Tlocalpan Santa María Concepción, is sixty years old. He took an oath before the judge that he would certainly say the truth. The witness said, "The statement that I am making is true and correct, I am not lying. This late woman named Magdalena Tiacapan came from Tlocalpan, she had married here in Tlatelolco. The reason I know this is that she went to present the matter to us and some other elders; she took *pulque*. Then she said to them, 'Here is a little *pulque* that came from Tolpetlac, where I bought for myself a piece of land. You are informed about it and I entrust it to you, lest sometime

4 There is an annotation in the left-hand margin. The beginning is illegible, but one can make out *axotecal*, probably referring to the person, *Acxotecatl Nahualatl*, mentioned in the manuscript.

5 The use of the directional *-on-*, meaning 'to do something quickly or temporarily', is not found in the older grammars, but it is amply attested in modern variants of Nahuatl.

6 On the left margin, there is a mark that resembles *t°*. In another context, this could be an abbreviation for either *tomín* or *totecuiyo*. Here I do not know what it means.

7 This is the first time I have seen the analyzed, intransitive form of the verb *yolmelahua* 'to inform someone'.

[Fol. 11v] mocuepti yn iyollo yn onicovili ytoca acsotecatl · ôpa chane· y tolpetlac ylhuiloc ŷ testico tleyn ic mocouh quito . ŷ testico aº quiteneuh ỹtlein ic mocovh ylhuiloc ỹ testico y ya matlacxivitl ỹ ya castolxivitl ayc quipiya . ŷ tlali quito ŷ testico . ca mochipa ôcan niquita. yni yach ŷ magdalena ytoca bernardino ôca elimiqui tlachiqui mochipa yevatl quipiya . ỹ tlali yuh ticmati ytlalcoval . ya ysq'ch i nicmati ynic quineltili yn itlatol . quitlali ymachiyo · +

in the future, the person named Acxotecatl, a citizen in Tolpetlac, from whom I bought it, change his mind.'" It was said to the witness, "What was it bought with?" The witness said, "She did not mention what it was bought with." It was said to the witness, "Did they[8] ever hold the land ten or fifteen years ago?" The witness said, "I have always seen the elder brother of Magdalena named Bernardino cultivating, collecting *maguey* sap there. He has always kept the land. This is how we know it is his purchased land. This is all I know." To confirm his statement, he set down his sign. +

v pedro cali chane · maria magdalena tequixquipa ya yepovali · ôcastolxivitl· y nemi Jurameto · quimomaquili ỹ Juez ynic vel tlatolmelavaz quito ŷ testico ya neli melavac y niquitova amo niztlacati· camo yvevetlal ŷ çivatzintli catca yn iveltiuh bernardino ca ytlalcoval ỹ quicouh ya quī oyuh yexivitl. topevaloque auh in quicovili ytoca . acsotecatl navalatl · ôpa ycha .ŷ tolpetlac auh ini quicouh cenquimili ỹ quachtli auh yniqu itech cavalotevac ŷ bernardino ce onemi yconeçin ỹ çivatzıntli yuh tlanavatita yn oc ce nemi yn iconeçin yvā yevatl · quipiliz y bernardino yva oc ce yveltiuh omextin auh yn iuh nicmati aço quimopieliya y ya nauhxivitl. ŷ ya oxivitl. canel ytlalcovaltzin mochipa quipiya · ôcan tlachiqui[9]· ya ysq̂ch y nicmati ynic quineltili quitlali ymachiyo · +

Pedro Calli, a citizen in María Magdalena Tequixquipan, is seventy-five years old. He took an oath before the judge that he would certainly tell the truth. The witness said, "What I say is true and correct, I am not lying. It is not the patrimonial land of the deceased woman, the sister of Bernardino, for it is her purchased land which she bought three years after we had been conquered. The one from whom she bought it was named Acxotecatl Nahualatl, his home was in Tolpetlac. She bought it for twenty tribute cloaks. The reason why it was left with Bernardino when she died, was that one of her children, a girl, was still alive. [Magdalena] ordered that as long as one of her children were still alive, both Bernardino and another sister of his would keep it for [the child]. As far as I know, perhaps he had it four years ago, two years ago, because it was his bought land that he always held, collecting *maguey* sap there. This is all I know." He confirmed it by placing his sign. +

8 I have chosen to interpret *quipiya* as 'they hold [the land]', although the fact that Nahua notaries almost never wrote the final plural *h* makes it impossible to determine whether the subject is *he*, *she*, or *they*.

9 The *ch* is written over a *v*.

v mĩn tochtli chane amaxac sancta maria ·coceptiõ ya yepovalxivitl · y nemi Jurameto quimomaquili y Juez ynic vel tlatolmelavaz quito · ỳ testicv ya neli melavac y niquitova amo niztlacati ya neli quimocovi yn itoca magdalenā teyacapa auh ỹ quicouh ya cenpovalxivitl · ôcastoli ypa oxivitl· ŷ quicovili ytoca acsotecatl· navalatl· ôpa chane ŷ tolpetlac auh yni quicouh quachtli cenquimili ylhuiloc ŷ testico cuix mispa ỹ quicouh . quito · y` testico[10] yn iquac quicouh vevechivaya · yn iyoquichvi catca .auh techixpati yn iquac quicovh · yvh tlanavatita ·oc onemi ce yconetzin amo nicã nemi veca monemitiya . çã opoliuh .auh ytech tlacavali yn itla ŷ bernardino quipieliya . auh ỹ bernardino mochipa quipiya · ŷ tlali ya quĩ ya yexivitl. yn ôcā ontlachic ya ysq̂ch y nicmati ynic quineltili yn itlatol. quitlali ymachiyo +

Martín Tochtli is a citizen in Amaxac Santa María Concepción, he is sixty years old. He took an oath before the judge that he would certainly declare the truth. The witness said, "What I say is true and correct, I am not lying. The one named Magdalena Tiacapan truly bought it. She bought it thirty-seven years ago. She bought it from the one named Acxotecatl Nahualatl, a citizen in Tolpetlac. And she bought it for twenty tribute cloaks." It was said to the witness, "Did she buy it in your presence?" The witness said, "At the time she bought it, her late husband was serving as an elder. She presented [the matter] to us [the body of elders] when she bought it. Before dying she ordered that she had one living child who did not live here, she lived far away, but she had disappeared. And [the land] was left with her uncle Bernardino, who kept it for her. Bernardino has always kept the land. Three years ago he collected *maguey* sap there. This is all that I know." He confirmed his words by placing his sign. +

[Fol. 12r]

v domĩgõ. sochitl· chane· atenātitech sancta maria coceptiõ povĩ ya yepovalxivitl. y nemi Jurameto · oquimomaquili ỹ Juez quito y testico ya neli melavac y niquitova amo niztlacatí ỳ tlali yn ipa moteylhuiya . ỳ tlali ynic vel nocomati ya cenpovalxivitl ·ôcastoli ypa oxivitl· ỹ quicouh ỳ tlali yn ôpa tolpetlac yevatl quicouh ytoca magdalenã teyacapa auh in iquac quicouh quimispati ŷ tetavā auh y nevatl· niquĩcactica . auh ini quicouh ce quimili y quachtli yevatl · quicovili yn acsotecatl navalatl · auh ŷ çovatzintli ayamo vecauh yn omomiquili ya quĩ yquac yn cocoliztli omochiuh ·yuh tlanavatita . yconeçin ce quicauhtiya ·

Domingo Xochitl is a citizen of Atenantitech, which belongs to Santa María Concepción. He is sixty years old. He took an oath before the judge. The witness said, "What I say is true and correct, I am not lying. As for the land about which the complaint is brought, I know well that thirty-seven years ago the person named Magdalena Tiacapan bought the land in Tolpetlac. When she bought it, she presented [the matter] to the elders[11] and I was listening to them. She bought it from Acxotecatl Nahualatl. The woman died not long ago, just when the epidemic broke out. She declared upon dying that she was leaving a child

10 The *s* is written over another letter.

11 Two words are used for 'elders' in this manuscript: *tetahhuan* and *huehuetqueh.*

auh ytech tlacavali yn itla ŷ bernardino · auh in bernardino ca mochipa quipiya ŷ tlali ya qui ya yexivitl · y no hôcâ ôtlachic ŷ bernardino mochipa quipia y tlali canel. ymac ôcôcauhtevac yn iveltiuatzin oca çan ivi y nocomati ynic quineltili yn itlatol quitlali ymachiyo. +

behind. [The land] was entrusted to [the child's] uncle Bernardino. And Bernardino has always kept the land. Three years ago he also collected *maguey* sap there. Bernardino has always kept the land because his sister left it in his hands before she died. This, then, is all I know. He confirmed his words by placing his sign. +

lucas grª [*signature*]

Lucas García [*signature*]

Nispa mochiuh feliciano de niça [*signature*]

It was done in my presence, Feliciano de Niza. [*signature*]

[Fol. 13r]

\+

v pablo viznavatl · quito y yevatl · y notlal · y nechcuiliznequi ŷ bernardino ca vel novevetlal · quimacevaco y nocolvā yepcovatzin chicopachmani ynin ya napovalxitl y mimique yepcovatzin chicopachmani auh ynin ya ypa quipixtivi ŷ tlali auh y nococol ytoca socotlaquatzin y miqui ya napovalxivitl · ypa avitzotzin auh ynin oquipixta auh y nota · ya cenpovalxivitl . yn omiqui oquipixta .auh yn axca ya nevatl · mochipa ya nicpiya ŷ tlali auh yn iquac peuhqui ŷ tlatoli ya neli yn ôpa tlachic ŷ bernardino · ça nechtlacavalti ỳ allde miguel · damiyā quito ma tlachiqui ma ça pesos tlamatiz auh in quichic centecpatli y metl· auh y nevatl. mochipa nicpiya. mochipa ôcā nipisca . ayc nicava cecexivitl. çā tlapic y nechcuiliznequi ỳ bernardino / .

\+

Pablo Huitznahuatl said, "This is my land, which Bernardino wants to take away from me. Truly, this is my patrimonial land. My ancestors, Epcoatzin and Chicopachmani, came to acquire it. It has already been eighty years since Epcoatzin and Chicopachmani died. In those times they were continuously holding the land. And my grandfather named Xocotlaquatzin died eighty years ago, in the times of Ahuitzotzin. He continued holding it. And my father, who died twenty years ago, continued holding it. Now it is me, I have always held the land. When the lawsuit began, Bernardino indeed collected *maguey* sap there, but he expelled me. The *alcalde* Miguel Damián said, 'Let [Bernardino] collect *maguey* sap, only a few *pesos* are being earned.' And he collected sap from a row of twenty *magueyes*. As for myself, I have always held it, I have always harvested there, every year, I have never left it. Bernardino wants to take it away from me on false grounds."

v pedro tolcuiltecatl · chane · tolpetlac[12] ya yepovalxivitl · y nemi Jurameto.

Pedro Tocuiltecatl is a citizen of Tolpetlac. He is sixty years old. He took

12 *O* and *c* were written over the final illegible letter of this word.

quimomaquili ȳ Juez inic vel tlatolmelavaz quito y testico · ya neli Pedro Tocuiltecatl is a citizen of melavac y niquitova y notlatol yn ipāpa tlali ynic motlatoleviya y yevatl · y pablo vitznavatl· yn itatzin ocatca ca mochipa oquitlatlauhtiyaya ȳ totava ŷ quemaniyâ ytilma y quimacaya . yni quitlayliyaya y totava mochipa oniquitac yn ita y vitznavatl ytoca catca , · auh yn oc uel tevatin ça no yvi ya mochipa cecexivitl. y techtlaqueva y pablo y vitznavatl ca mochipa quimopieliya . ylhuiloc y testico yn axca y` tlatoleva yn itoca bernardino cuix ica . otiquitac ma ōcā elimiqui manoço ye tlachiqui quito ŷ testico ayyc oniquitac ça mochipa yevatl . ŷ pablo ôcan tiquita ya ysq̂ch y nicmati ynic quineltili yn itlatol. quitlali ymachiyo. +

an oath before the judge that he would certainly say the truth. The witness said, "The statement that I am making concerning the land in regard to which Pablo Huitznahuatl is falsely accused, is true and correct. His late father was always making requests to our fathers, sometimes he gave them cloaks. Our fathers were working this land for him. I always saw the father of Huitznahuatl, whose name was Xiuhnel. Continuing this practice, Pablo Huitznahuatl has always, every year, hired us. He has always held [the land]." It was said to the witness, "And now, regarding the one who brings the suit, named Bernardino, have you even seen him there cultivating or collecting *maguey* sap?" The witness said, "I have never seen him, but we have always seen Pablo there. This is everything that I know." To confirm his statement, he set down his sign. +

v agustin tecpanecatl · chane ne · tolpetlac ya yepovalxivitl y nemi Jurameto quimomaquili y Juez ynic vel [Fol. 13v] otlatolmelauhqui[13] ỳ testico ya neli melavac y niquitova · amo niztlacati y yevatl. yn ita catca y vitznavatl ytoca xiuhnel · y miqui ya cenpovalxivitl· auh y nepa ca ça mochipa oquipiyaya · auh yn iquac omic y xiuhnel nima ymac côcauhtevac ytoca Juā de sanctiago oquipiyaya ŷ tlali auh yn iquac omic ŷ Juā de sanctiago. nima ymac ocôcauhtevac yn axcā pablo vitznavatl .ya matlacxiuhtica y quipiya. yquac yn omic yn iachcauh ylhuiloc ỳ testico y bernardino cuix ma yca ôpa otiquitac ma yelimiqui anoço pixca ·

Agustín Tecpanecatl is a citizen there in Tolpetlac, he is sixty years old. The witness took an oath before the judge, with which he really declared the truth. "The statement I am making is true and correct, I am not lying. The late father of Huitznahuatl, named Xiuhnel, died twenty years ago. Until then, he had always held [the land]. When Xiuhnel died, he left it in the care of the one named Juan de Santiago—he was holding the land. When Juan de Santiago died, he left it in the care of Pablo Huitznahuatl, [who has it] now. He has held it for ten years, since his elder brother died." It was said to the witness, "Have you ever seen Bernardino around

13 The final *-qui* of *otlahtolmelauhqui* 'he told the truth' is either an older conjugation of class 2 verbs in the preterite, or it is the first syllable of *quihtoh* '[the witness] said', the second syllable of which was omitted by the notary. Under the latter option, *quihtoh* would begin the following sentence.

ça mochipa quimopieliya . ŷ pablo vitznavatl ya ysq̂ch y nicmati ynic quineltili yn itlatol quitlali yn imachiyo . +

there, even cultivating or harvesting?" He said, "Never. Pablo Huitznahuatl has always been holding it. This is everything I know." To confirm his statement, he set down his sign. +

v franco. çovaylacatz chane · tolpetlac ya yepovalxivitl · y nemi Jurameto oquimomaquili ŷ Juez ynic otlatolmelauh quito ŷ testico ya neli melavac y niquitova yn iquac ayamo valauh y marquez mochipa yevatl · quipiyaya y xiuhneltzin in ita viznavatl· auh in iquac omiqui y xiuhnel nima ymac concauhtevac Juâ sopanatl[14] · auh yn iquac omic y sopanatl· nima ya yevatl· y Juâ de sanctiago oquipilyaya ŷ tlali auh in iquac omic ŷ de sanctiago ymac ocôcauhtevac yn axca vitznavatl ya matlacxiuhtica y quipiya y vitznavatl y tlali ylhuiloc y testico cuix ica ôcā otiquitac y bernardino ma ôca elimiqui anoço ye toca anoço pixca . quito ŷ testico · ayc oniquitac ça mochipa yevatl oniquitac ŷ vitznavatl ya ysq̂ch y nicmati yni quineltili yn itlatol. quitlali ymachiyo . +

Francisco Çohuailacatz is a citizen of Tolpetlac, he is sixty years old. He took an oath before the judge, with which he declared the truth. The witness said, "What I am saying is true and correct. Xiuhneltzin, the father of Huitznahuatl, always held [the land] in the times before the coming of the Marquis. When Xiuhnel died, he left it in the care of Juan Xopanatl. After Xopanatl died, Juan de Santiago was holding the land. When de Santiago died, he left it in the hands of Huitznahuatl, [who has it] now. Huitznahuatl has held the land for ten years." It was said to the witness, "Have you seen Bernardino around there, even cultivating or sowing or harvesting there?" The witness said, "I have never seen him, but I have always seen Huitznahuatl. This is everything I know." To confirm his statement, he set down his sign. +

v pablo gr.ª chane tolpetlac ya ôpovalxivitl . y nemi Jurameto oquimomaquili ŷ Juez inic vel tlatolmelavaz quito ŷ testico amo ôca oninenca . ôpa onineca . chicuihnauhtla atenco auh yn ôca onivala ya qui ya cenpovalxivitl· ypa nauhxivitl· auh in iquac nivala . y tlali [Fol. 14r] ypa mahua yn axca quichiva . Juā de sanctiago. auh in iquac omic y de sanctiago. ymac ocôcauhtevac ŷ pablo vitznavatl auh yn omiqui de sanctiago ya chicoxivitl. auh ya chicoxiuhtica . y quipiya · y tlali y vitznavatl. ylhuiloc ŷ testico cuix ica ôcan otiquitac ŷ bernardino yn ineva

Pablo García is a citizen of Tolpetlac, he is forty years old. He took an oath before the judge to really declare the truth. The witness said, "I did not live there before, I lived in Chiconauhtlan Atenco. I came from there twenty-four years ago. When I came, Juan de Santiago worked the land that they argue over today. When de Santiago died, he left it in the hands of Pablo Huitznahuatl. De Santiago died seven years ago. And for seven years Huitznahuatl has held the land." It was said to the witness, "Have you seen Bernardino around there arguing with Pablo over cultivating or sowing there?"

14 The initial *s* of *Sopanatl* was written over another letter, possibly a *d*.

monamiqui ẏ pablo y͡ma ôcā elimiqui anoçoe[15] toca . quito y͡testico ayc ma ôca oniquitac ma çano niztlacatiz ynic quineltili yn itlatol. quitlali ymachiyo +	The witness said, "Never. I have never seen him there, nor will I lie." To confirm his statement, he set down his sign. +
lucas gr[a] [*signature*]	Lucas García [*signature*]
nispa mochiuh feliciano de niça [*signature*]	It was done in my presence, Feliciano de Niça. [*signature*]

Almost from the beginning of the colonial period, the indigenous people of New Spain engaged in lawsuits, and one of the main concerns they were bringing before the courts were property rights. Their adversaries were often Spaniards, which is fairly understandable under the circumstances of the conquest and the subsequent redistribution of land to the conquerors. However, the natives were equally often calling on the colonial authorities to resolve the disputes over real estate that they had with each other. In the early colonial period, the stage for such disputes provided by the Spanish courts was more than convenient. Both sides of the conflict and their witnesses testified in Nahuatl, and the statements were carefully recorded by indigenous notaries. The parties often presented written or painted documents and these were taken into account as important evidence. Traditional legal procedures, including those from before the conquest, were considered viable and judgments often rested on indigenous customs regarding ownership (Kellogg 1995: 30). This general attitude of the courts did not, however, imply their total flexibility towards the Nahuas. What is apparent in the surviving lawsuits is, on the one hand, a mixture of Spanish and indigenous conceptions of law and property rights, and on the other hand, the strategies employed by litigants in order not only to win the case but also to maintain or elevate their status within colonial society.

In 1558, a suit was brought before the judge in Tlatelolco over a piece of land located in Tolpetlac, a dependency of Tlatelolco (Lockhart 1992: 154). Each of the disputing parties presented a different history of the possession of the lot, supported by testimonies of several witnesses. Bernardino Cozcacuauh and his sister Juana Teiuhc claimed that, thirty-seven years earlier, in the insecure times of the conquest, the land had been bought by their sister, Magdalena Tiacapan, in exchange for a load of twenty tribute cloaks. The fact that the

15 It is difficult to determine whether the *e* at the end of *ahnozo* 'or' is the particle *ye* 'already', the third person personal pronoun *yeh*, which can serve as an anchor for particle strings, or if it actually begins the following word. In the latter case, it would be the combining form of *etl* 'beans', and *etoca* would be 'he is planting beans'.

land had been legally purchased was confirmed by elderly witnesses: Miguel Díaz and Martín Tochtli, both sixty years old, who, together with Magdalena's husband, had been, at that time, serving as *huehuetqueh* 'the elders', described also with the term *tetahhuan* 'the fathers of people'. These terms, misleadingly bringing to mind men of advanced age, apparently were not associated with age, because at the time of the conquest both Miguel Díaz and Martín Tochtli must have been in their twenties. *Huehuetqueh* may have referred to the role of "elders" as the keepers of an *altepetl*'s tradition and integrity. *Tetahhuan*, on the other hand, is a term that comes up in other colonial sources in reference to both the "town's elders" (e.g. Anderson, Berdan, Lockhart 1976: 126–128; Pizzigoni 2007: 241) and the "elders" within households (e.g. Sahagún 1950–1969, XII: 25). This suggests that the term may be derived from the status of a married man with children, a concept that would not be in conflict with the relatively young age of Miguel Díaz and Martín Tochtli.

As the former "elders" testified, the land had been purchased according to the custom observed on such occasions. Magdalena invited them to drink *pulque* and she pronounced the appropriate formulas, entrusting the purchased land to the elders and thus securing her rights in case the seller ever changed his mind. A similar pattern is to be found in a 1583 document from San Miguel Tocuillan in which a woman named Ana, having acquired a houselot, invites the local elders for a drink and acknowledges before them that her land is still under the charge of the community (Lockhart 1991: 74). This custom can most likely be traced back to preconquest times and arises from the *calpolli*, a community or neighborhood within the *altepetl* that exercised control over individual landholdings. One of the traditional roles of the elders was to keep record of all the land remaining under the custody of the *calpolli*. Before any transaction or redistribution could take place, the group of *tlahxillacalehqueh* (either elders or citizens in general) assembled and inquiries were made to make sure that no one had prior rights to the piece of land in question (Lockhart 1992: 148).

According to Bernardino Cozcacuauh, his sister Magdalena died sixteen years after having completed the transaction. She was a victim of one of the many epidemics that were constantly breaking out in the early colonial period. Her rightful heir was apparently her only living child, a daughter, who, by that time, must have already been an adult. However, she had moved away and, as Martín Tochtli put it, "disappeared." This explains why the land was entrusted to Magdalena's siblings, so that they would take care of it for their niece. As Sahaguntine manuscripts suggest, such was the traditional role of uncles who not only acted as substitute parents for their orphaned nephews and nieces, but, just as importantly, guarded the property bequeathed to them until their coming of age (Sahagún 1950–1969, X: 3). The adult ward of Bernardino and Juana apparently never showed up, because in 1558 they were claiming the property as their own.

The adversary of Bernardino and Juana, named Pablo Huitznahuatl, came up with an entirely different story. He claimed that the land was his patrimonial land (*nohuehuehtlal*), tracing its ownership by his family as far back as the late fifteenth century and providing a detailed genealogy of his ancestors. Pablo's story was confirmed by the authority of several elderly men. Two of them, Agustín Tecpanecatl and Francisco Çohuailacatz, explained that after the death of Pablo's father, named Xiuhnel, the property passed from brother to brother. Although such a pattern was typical of the preconquest Tenochtitlan area—contrary to Tetzcoco, where, as far as the household structure and inheritance were concerned, the emphasis was put on the parents-children bond rather than on collateral ties—other factors may also have influenced the process (Offner 1983: 205–207). The high mortality rate due to epidemics and recent wars often left landholders without adult heirs. Bernardino's witnesses stressed that only one of his sister's children was alive at the time of her death and suggested that she was the rightful heir. On the other hand, the explanations of the traditional practice given by Bernardino's witnesses could have been an attempt to adjust the native patterns to the Spanish concept *por linea recta*. If such was the case, Pablo's supporters did not choose to employ this strategy. Instead, they stressed that Xiuhnel "kept [the land] in the times before the coming of the Marquis." The chronology they gave suggests that he died around 1538—a date that coincides with that of Magdalena's death, or a few years earlier—and that he had been succeeded by two of his sons over the next ten or fifteen years. Eventually, the disputed land was bequeathed to Pablo by his elder brother, Juan de Santiago.

As I have already suggested, both parties in the lawsuit employed various strategies in an attempt to prove their ownership rights. They do not refer explicitly to any written documents, relying instead on the oral testimonies of the men of authority. These testimonies focus on the long-lasting possession of the land by each family, providing a detailed enumeration of purchases and bequests, meticulously memorized despite wars and epidemics that interfered with the local history. It is also possible that the memory of the elders was in this case reinforced by some kind of written or painted record kept by the community. Nevertheless, even if the record had existed, it would not have been a piece of evidence that outweighed the authority of the *calpolli*'s representatives. Another strategy consciously employed during the lawsuit and associated with memory is the apparent emphasis placed by Pablo Huitznahuatl on his noble ancestry and the continuous chain of inheritance within the family (see Kellogg 1995: 45). As Susan Kellogg notes, the difference between elite and non-elite litigants consisted in the former detailing their connections to precontact nobility, and the latter presenting themselves as humble, poor, and orphaned (1995: 26). The history of Huitznahuatl's family may have been used to create his image as a noble and trustworthy person in contrast to the newcomer, Magdalena, whose siblings had not been able to provide any kind of prestigious details, due to the fact that the land they were fighting over had simply been bought.

Rather than using Spanish-style dating, the witnesses locate events in the past either counting back years or positioning the events in regard to landmarks, such as the arrival of Cortés or the reign of Ahuitzotl. Both sides stressed that traditional procedures involving town elders were observed, pointing to the community's body of representatives as the source of legal rights. A description of these procedures may be, on its own, a strategy of legitimizing the account before the Spanish judges, who might have needed explanations in order to understand that an actual legal act had taken place (Lockhart 1991: 66–67). Spanish authorities are almost absent from the text, although one reference to an *alcalde*'s previous (and unjust) judgment suggests that the piece of land had been argued over for many years before the recorded lawsuit took place. The judges who listened to the testimonies seemed to be interested in one question in particular: who had been working the field for the past few years. Interestingly, this becomes a point of strategy for both parties, who eagerly provide evidence of their involvement in the agricultural activities.

Together with valuable information on preconquest cultural patterns and early colonial legal strategies, the document contains some interesting vocabulary items. Suprisingly, the testimony of Domingo Xochitl, a citizen of Santa María Concepción, includes the word *çohuatzintli*, known as a Tlaxcalan counterpart of *cihuatzintli* 'a revered (or small) woman'. The text has several loanwords associated with legal procedures and documentation: *juez*, *juramento*, *testigo*, and *alcalde*, as well as the term *pesos* and a borrowed pattern of dating. Nevertheless, some of the linguistic changes that are seen throughout the late sixteenth-century Nahuatl sources are not yet present in the document. The term *piya* still retains its original meaning, 'to keep' or 'to guard', instead of copying the meaning of the Spanish verb *tener*. When informing that the document had been "signed," the notary says *quitlali imachiyo* 'he set down his sign,' instead of working from the Spanish loanword *firma*, which only twenty years later is already extensively employed in the *Testaments of Culhuacan*.

DOCUMENT 3

Lawsuit Brought by Juan Jiménez, Ocotelolco, Tlaxcala, Mexico, 1560[1]

AGNIESZKA BRYLAK

[Exp. 26, fol. 1r]

+

En la leal çibdad de tlascalla
cenpoalilhuitl metztli de Abril yn isiho
yn tut° Jhu xpo Extzutli oncastolpoalli
pan Expualli sihuitl yspan yn muy noble
senor pablo de galizia alcalde hordinario
y nican cibdad yvan provincia tlascalla
por su magestad yva nispa nehuatl fabian
rrodrigues escrivano de cabildo nezqui
yn itvca Juan ximenez pillj nican chaneh
çibdad ytech povi yn alhtepetl ocutelolco
quihtv Justj[a] niquihtlani yn itechcopa
ytuca miguel petztetl ça yoaltica
oquitvcac nocue oncan itvcayohca
tvchpan ahu yvan ça no yoaltica yn
otlasq yalhua yoan yehjca yn Justj[a]
niqhtlani tleyca yn ça yoac quitvcac

+

In the loyal city of Tlaxcallan, on the twentieth day of the month of April in the year of Our Lord Jesus Christ, the year 1560, a noble and local citizen belonging to the *altepetl* of Ocotelolco, named Juan Jiménez, appeared before the very noble lord Pablo de Galicia, *alcalde ordinario* for His Majesty here in the city and province of Tlaxcallan, and before me, Fabián Rodríguez, municipal council notary. He said, "I request justice concerning the person named Miguel Petztetl. Right during the night he sowed my field in the place named Tochpan. And likewise, yesterday right during the night he broke ground for planting. And

1 Archivo Histórico del Estado de Tlaxcala (AHET), 1560, caja 1, exp. 26, 22; A transcription of this document and its translation into Spanish were published as two separate texts in *Catálogo de documentos escritos en náhuatl siglo XVI* by the Gobierno del Estado de Tlaxcala (2013). The transcription and translation included here are based entirely on the original manuscript.

DOI: 10.5876/9781607328346.c003

nocue yva çan yuac tlasquj tle quimachotia ynic nellj niquihtva nocue oquipiaya y notahtzin oncan icalhua maniah yvan ocan icuezcohua maniah miec tlacatl quimatjh ynic huel nellj nocue hvel quimocaguitj yn senor alcalde quinahoati yn Joan ximenez quilhui aço ume yey tlacatl sicvalhuica testigus yn aquihque quimati ynic huel nellj mocue quihtv yn Juan ximenez nican ohoallaqueh y quimatih

for this reason I ask for justice. Why, just at night, did he sow my field, and just at night break ground for planting? What confirms that I truthfully say that it is my field, is that my father owned it. There were located his houses and there were located his granaries. Many people know that it is truly my field." The lord *alcalde* listened to it carefully. He issued orders to Juan Jiménez. He said to him, "Bring two or three people as witnesses, those who know that it is really your field." Juan Jiménez said, "Here have arrived those who know it."

pablo de galizia [*signature*]

Pablo de Galicia [*signature*]

nispam mochiho Fabian rr^{o}s
Escrivano

It was done in my presence Fabián Rodríguez, notary

[*signature*]

[*signature*]

[Fol. 1v] y Aho ça no yhcvaqn[2] in ilhujtl metztlj sihuitl tlacpac omíhtv yspan yn senor alcalde pablo de galizia alcalde hordinario yva nispa nehoatl fabian rr^{o}s Esno. nezqueh y testigos yntoca luys pane yvan benitu yyactly yvan pedro tutol yn imizquin Juramento quicuique ypa quimanque yma yn cruz^{+}. niman contenamicque quimilhuj yn senor alcalde ypaltzinco yn Dios[3] yvan ypaltzinco yn santa maria melahoaqu in aquihtozque amotlahtol yn isquich atlahtlanilozque intlacamo melavac aquihtvzque mictla tlacatecvlotl amechvicaz yntla melavac anquihtvzque tvt^{e} dios yc amechtlaoculiz yn imizquin quihtvque melavaqu i tiquihtvzque tutlahtol Amen

On the same day, month, and year mentioned above, the witnesses named Luis Paneh, Benito Yactli, and Pedro Totol appeared before the lord *alcalde* Pablo de Galicia, *alcalde ordinario*, and before me, Fabián Rodríguez, notary. All of them took an oath, putting their hands on the cross. Then they kissed it. The lord *alcalde* said to them, "In the name of God and in the name of Holy Mary, may you speak the truth in everything that you will be asked. If you do not speak the truth, the devil will take you to hell; if you speak the truth, then Our Lord God will have mercy on you." All of them said, "The words that we speak will be true. Amen."

2 What appears to be a crossed-out *n* at the end of *ihcvaqn* is a actually a *u*, which was inserted into the phonological phrase formed when *ihcuac* and the following *in* were combined, for the purpose of preserving the /k/ sound of *c* followed by /i/.

3 The document is damaged and it is impossible to determine whether the notary wrote the word *Dios* with a capital or a lowercase letter.

[left margin: test°]

luys paneh. chaneh san nicolas. yn tlacath quihtv aço ya epoasihuitl ahno ya nepa.

[left margin: witness]

The person Luis Paneh, resident of San Nicolás, said that he was born sixty years ago or perhaps more.

v yvan ic tlahtlaniloc cuis quisimati yn itvca miguel petztetl. quihtv niquisima[ti] noteyccahu ça çe yn itech otiquizque tachto

And therewith he was asked if he perhaps knew the person named Miguel Petztetl. He said, "I know him. He is my younger brother. We came from the same progenitor."[5]

v yvan ic tlahtlaniloc cuis quimatj ỹ cuemitl yn oca mani tvchpa cuis ya nellj ycuen yn Juan ximenez quihtv huel nicmatj huel icuen yn itah ocan mania ycal yvan icuezcohoan yn cetlj onca quitemaya hu[e]l[4] mocuiya acatepec aho yn cuemitl cocuica ytvca tenpilçaca aho nechomacaca aço castvlsihutica yn çano çacaquiztimania çano quichihchjllaquetzaya quehetlacuemaya

And therewith he was asked if he perhaps knew whether the field which is there in Tochpan is indeed the field of Juan Jiménez. He said, "I know well that it was indeed the field of his father. His house was located there, along with the granaries in which he deposited maize. Indeed it extends to Acatepec. The one named Tenpilçaca had taken the field, but he had given it to me. The field was just left fallow for perhaps fifteen years; from time to time he planted chile and beans.

aho y cuemitl onotech pohvtimania aho yn Joan ximenez nehuatl huel onicmacacqu icuen oqujpis yn itah miec tlacatl quimatj yn

The entire field belonged to me, but I indeed gave it to Juan Jiménez. The one who sowed and kept it was his father. Many people know that . . .

[Exp. 22, fol. 1r] ypa ticalaquíz yn ipa cuemitl yn ocâ motocayotia tochpa ypampa huel oniccac yva huel onicmah amo mocue yvan ayc vticpis aho nitlanahuatia nimitznahoatia yntla cui[6] cepa ocan ticalaquiz yn ipa cuemitl yn ocan tochpa notencvpa. [left margin: so pena] macuilpoalli mecatl

(. . .) you will [not] enter into the field located in the place called Tochpan because I have fully heard and learned that it is not your field and that you never owned it. I have issued an order, [in which] I inform you that if you ever again enter the field which is in Tochpan,

4 The document is damaged and the letter between *hu* and *l* is illegible.

5 In the manuscript the word *tach* 'our older brother' is used. The term **achtli* means 'older brother of a woman'. However, when it is incorporated onto the affective noun (*-ton*), it takes on the meaning of 'grandparent' or 'ancestor'. I would like to thank Justyna Olko and John Sullivan for this observation.

6 The final *x* of *cuix* 'perhaps' has elided with the initial *c* of the following *ceppa* 'again' or 'once again'.

mitzteqlizque onca tianquizcv yva cenpoalilhujtl teilpiloya tiez tepoztlj mocxic yezquj yva tiquistlavaz mahtlac ps° De minas. occa moselvz y cequi ytech poviz yn camara yfiscv de su mg^{d} yn oc no isquich yn no occa moseloz cequi ytech poviz tlascalla hospital yn oc no isquich ytech poviz yn aquin juez [. . .]

by my order [left margin: under penalty] they will give you one hundred lashes in the marketplace and you will spend twenty days in prison, and there will be shackles on your feet; and you will pay ten *pesos* of mine gold. [The money] will be divided in two parts: one will belong to His Majesty's fiscal chamber and the other half will further be divided in two parts: one will belong to the hospital in Tlaxcallan; the other half will belong to whoever the judge is [. . .]

[nitlazō]tequiz aho yn tehoatl Juan[7] ximenez sicpia y mocue yn ocan tochpa yn quenin oquipis motahtzin çan iho sicpia yva huel onicmah vel oniccac yn oquipiaya omitzmacac omochiho nican leal çibdad tlascal[la] yc. çepouallj ômome ylhujtl [mez]tli de ~~agosto~~^{blir} yn i[s]iho tvt° xpo ex[tzon]tli ōcastolpoalli [ip]an epoalli sih[uitl] de [illegible]

As for you, Juan Jiménez, may you keep your field located in Tochpan. Just as your father kept it, keep it the same way. And I understood well, I heard well that he had given you [the field] he had been keeping. [The document] was made in the loyal city of Tlaxcallan on the twenty-third day of the month of April in the year of Our Lord Christ, [the year of] 1560.

[Fol. 1v] [. . .] alguaziles agustin ytzcuinnacatzin yvan alexandro tolontzin yva tersco nemitl huel qcac aho. qtv amo ninovelmatih[8] oc niqtvz yspa señor alld mayor onpa noyollo pachiviz yn ilhuitl metztlj xivitl tlacpac vmihtv

[. . .] the constables Agustín Itzcuinnacatzin, Alejandro Tolontzin and Tersco Nemitl.[9] He listened carefully but he said, "Lest I remain displeased, I will say it again before the lord *alcalde mayor*, then I will be satisfied." On the above-mentioned day, month, and year.

Fabian rr^{o}s
Escriuano
Dr^{o}s gratis [*signature*]

Fabián Rodríguez
notary
No fee for service [*signature*]

7 The paper is torn into two parts, with at least one line of the text missing. The fragment [*nitlazō*]*tequiz aho yn tehoatl Juan* is a reconstruction of the line whose upper part is missing and not fully legible. The first word is probably *nitlatzontequiz* 'I [the judge] will issue the sentence'. Given the lack of the context, the translation begins with *aho yn tehoatl Juan* "As for you, Juan . . ."

8 *amo ninohuelmatih* seems to be a vetative or amonestative phrase, although in this mode, the final singular *h* should only be used with Class 1 verbs, and *mati* is normally Class 2.

9 The identity of Tersco Nemitl is not clear. The document itself suggests that it is the name of the third constable. However, according to the records of the municipal council of Tlaxcala on January 1, 1560, the constables elected were Juan Caro, Juan Bautista, Agustín Ytzcuinaca, Alejandro Tolon, Juan Tlacohtzin, Martín Tizamoyotl, Francisco Xochiteuan, and Francisco Motecuzoma (Solís, Valencia and Medina Lima 1984: 377). Also, in no way is the name Tersco Nemitl similar orthographically or phonetically to any other Tlaxcalan official's name from that period.

The documents presented here come from the collection of the Historical Archive of the State of Tlaxcala (Archivo Histórico del Estado de Tlaxcala, AHET) and have been catalogued under two different signatures. However, after a thorough verification they proved to be part of one and the same manuscript concerning the lawsuit brought by Juan Jiménez, in which he accuses another man, Miguel Petztetl, of sowing his field at night. Both fragments were written by the same hand and signed by the notary of the municipal council, Fabián Rodríguez.

The first part (AHET XVI, c. 1 exp. 26) begins on April 20, 1560, when Juan Jiménez, a nobleman who at the time was one of the four *alcaldes ordinarios* of the city of Tlaxcala, representing Ocotelolco, appeared before the municipal council and another of its *alcaldes*, Pablo de Galicia, requesting the execution of his rights. In order to confirm that the cultivated land invaded by Miguel Petztetl indeed belonged to Juan Jiménez and to his father, he was asked by the officers of justice to bring along three witnesses. He did so immediately, and on the very same day Luis Paneh, Benito Yactli, and Pedro Totolin presented themselves before the *alcalde* and the notary. Unfortunately, only a partial record of the testimony of one witness has survived. According to his own statement, Luis Paneh was the one who acquired the field fifteen years earlier from a man called Tenpilzaca and, since it was left fallow, he decided to cede it to Juan Jiménez. Afterwards, the land was taken care of by Juan's father. The witness also attested that he and the accused Miguel Petztetl were relatives. Luis calls him his "younger brother" (*noteiccauh*)—meaning literally a sibling or possibly a cousin—and explains that they came from the same ancestor, identified in the text as *tachton* 'our grandparent', which might also refer to another earlier forebear. With all probability it is due to the blood ties between the two men that Miguel did not recognize the plaintiff's exclusive rights to the cultivated field and felt free to use it secretly as if it belonged to him.

The testimony of the first witness is interrupted when the page ends, and we do not get to see the declarations of Benito Yactli and Pedro Totolin. What we do learn, thanks to the document catalogued in AHET XVI c. 1 exp. 22, which contains the outcome of the complaint, is that the first stage of the legal process ended three days later, on April 23, 1560. The sentence prohibited the accused from entering Juan Jiménez's field again under penalty of public flagellation (one hundred lashes), spending twenty days in prison clapped in shackles, and paying a fine of ten *pesos* of mine gold. A part of the manuscript is deteriorated and thus it is not clear whether, in addition to the warning, Miguel Petztetl was punished in any other way. Most likely the answer to this question is affirmative. Nevertheless, the decision did not seem severe enough to satisfy Juan Jiménez, who announced to the constables his plans to file an appeal with the *alcalde mayor*.

In addition to offering an insight into a private conflict in which one of the most important Tlaxcalan city officials was involved, the document contains some interesting data concerning the course of the legal process itself. It provides us with a detailed description of the oath taken by the witnesses before giving their testimony: they placed their hands on the cross, kissed it, and pronounced a legal formula that included the threat of eternal torments in hell in case of perjury. We can also learn what happened to the money paid as a fine. Half of it was to end up in the fiscal chamber of His Majesty, and the rest was to be equally divided between the judge and the hospital of Tlaxcala, probably as a form of charitable gift.

The notary who wrote this document in Nahuatl, Fabián Rodríguez, consistently marked the glottal stop with the letter *h*, and every time he omitted a nasal consonant, he signaled it with a tilde above the preceding vowel. Interestingly, an *h* is also used once in the spelling of *alhtepetl* to reproduce the devoicing of the syllable-final *l*. The text does not contain many loanwords from Spanish. Those that do appear in the manuscript are names of different Spanish offices introduced during the colonial period (*alcalde ordinario, juez*), expressions related to administration and legal process (*juramento, testigo, ciudad*), and very few terms belonging to the religious domain (*Dios, cruz*); however, the notary prefers to render the concept of "devil" with the Nahuatl word *tlacatecolotl* instead of using the Spanish *diablo*.

DOCUMENT 4

Interrogation of Diego Xiuhnel, Tepeticpac, Tlaxcala, Mexico, 1563[1]

Agnieszka Brylak

[Fol. 1r]

+

En la leal çibdad tlascalla yc çenpoallj omahtlactlj de marçv yn isiho yn itlacatiliz tvtemaquisticaho Jhu xpo Etzuntlj o castvlpuall ipan[2] epoallj omey sihuitl y muy noble senor antvnyo flores alcalde hordjnario y nican çibdad yva probinçia tlascalla por su mag yva nispa nehuatl sabastian rrodrigues escriuano nom[do] del cabildo. tlanahoati ynic tlahtlaniloz yn itvca diego sihonel chane santa clara atzopan ypan yn tlahtvcayotl tepeticpac de santiago. ahu nima Juramentv quicuic ynic nellj quihtv ytlahtol quitēnamic ȳ cruz[+] quinepano yn ima ytepa quima ytechcvpa monehtvlti yn tt[o] dios yvan nochipa huel ichpochtlj çoapillj santa maria. ynic melahvac quihtvz.

+

In the loyal city of Tlaxcallan, on the thirtieth of March in the year of the birth of Our Savior Jesus Christ, in the year of 1563, before me, Sebastián Rodríguez, appointed notary of the municipal council, the very noble lord Antonio Flores, *alcalde ordinario* for His Majesty here in the city and province of Tlaxcallan, issued an order to question a person named Diego Xiuhnel, a citizen of Santa Clara Atzompan in the head town of Tepeticpac de Santiago. Then he took an oath. And so he spoke his words truly, he kissed the cross, and he put his hands together against his lips, in order then to swear by Our Lord God and the Holy Lady Mary, Eternal and True Virgin, to speak the truth.

1 Archivo Histórico del Estado de Tlaxcala (AHET), 1563, caja 2, exp. 13; A transcription of this document and its translation into Spanish was published in *Catálogo de documentos escritos en náhuatl siglo XVI* by the Gobierno del Estado de Tlaxcala (2013). The transcription and translation included here are based entirely on the original manuscript.

2 The final *i* of *caxtolpohualli* has elided with the third personal singular possessor of *-pan*.

DOI: 10.5876/9781607328346.c004

y yn achtv yc tlahtlaniloc cuis quisimati yn ilpitica ytvca diego sasan quihtv amo niquisimatj yvan amo nicmati tl[3] ytvca.

First he was asked if he knew a prisoner named Diego Zazan. He said, "I don't know him and I don't know what his name is."

y yvan ic tlahtlaniloc. cuis quimati tle ypampa yn teilpiloyan oquitlali senor alcalde antº flores. quihtv amo nicmatj.

And then he was asked if he knew why the lord *alcalde* Antonio Flores had put him in prison. He said, "I don't know."

y yvan ic tlahtlaniloc. cuis nelli yn cuemitl quimacac yn ya yehoatl ylpitica ytuca diego sasan quihtv amo nellj amo nicmacac tleyca y nictemacaz cuemitl maço tvtech pohuj cuemitl yn ocan yc tipohuj teccalco ycha quetzalcvatecuitlj ahv cuis amo cate yn teccalli quipiah yehvatl diego panpez cuis amo yehua quitemacazqz ynin cuemitl tlallj

Therewith he was asked if it was true that he had given fields to this prisoner, named Diego Zazan. He said, "It is not true. I did not give them to him. Why would I distribute the fields? Even though the fields belong to us, we belong to the lordly house, to the home of Quetzalcoateuctli. Are there not those who administer the lordly house? Diego Sánchez [is in charge of them]. Aren't they the ones who should distribute the fields, the lands?"

y yvan ic tlahtlaniloc cuis quimati yquin quicuic tlallj yn itvca diego sasan yva quesquich yn oquicuic. quihtv ycquin ipan yn ascā tvquiztlj mochihva aço ya cēpuallj ahno ya nepa ahno nipahual[4] yn otvcac aho yn ya sihujtl amo quitlay ayc quitvca ȳ cuemitl opa manj atzopan ynahoac. metlatl onoc. yn quicuj omecatl ohupoal patlahoac aço ohotzotlj omatlatlactly ahno [*signature*] [Fol. 1v] nepa: ahno nipahoal çequi çacatl aho yn huel cuemitl quicuj castolpoallj yn omecatipa.

And he was asked if he knew when the one named Diego Zazan had taken the land and how much he had taken. He said, "It happened during the current planting season. Perhaps some twenty [units], here and there, is what he sowed. For a year he has not worked the land. He never sows the fields that are there in Atzompan, close to where the grinding stones are.[5] What he has taken are two long plots, each forty [units] wide and perhaps eight hundred ten [units long], [signature] [with] some grass here and there. As for that which is actually planted field, he has taken three hundred [units] on the two long plots.

3 The *tl* probably stands for *tleh* 'what', which has been partially elided with the initial *i* of *itocah* 'his name'.

4 It should be read as *nepahual* 'over there'.

5 It is possible that *metlatl* 'grinding stone' is used here to refer to a Spanish *molino* 'mill'.

v yvan ic tlahtlaniloc yn ya sihuitl ya osihuitl ac quitlay ac quitoca y cuemitl y ya nepa aqu jtech pohuj qhto huel tehoan otictlayya yn ya sihujtl ya ôsihuitl ya vehcaho yvan intahuan ~~ŷculhoan~~[6] yn diego probe çan iho tiquintlaylic yntech tipohuj yvan yc tiquinmacah yn tlen teccalcv yc techialo yvan yn oc cequi yntech monequj tvpilhvan teccallj quipiah

And therewith he was asked, "For a year or two years now, who works and sows the field there? To whom does it belong?" He said, "We ourselves had been tilling the land a year ago, two years ago, for a long time. And we just worked the land for Diego Probe's parents, we are their dependents. With this, we give them what is expected of people in the lordly house, as well as other things that our lords, who are in charge of the lordly house, need."

v yvan yc tlahtlaniloc cuis teishuihvcuemitl yn ya yehoatl tlallj tlacpac vmihtv cuis no tecujtlallj teccuemitl quihto amo teishuihucuemitl tecuitlallj yehuatl huel itech pvhuj yn nopiltzin diego probe ypampa teccallj yn quipia no ypampa yn itech pohuj yn totahua tvcohcvluan çan ihu quimahtihuj tecuitlallj amo teyshuihucuemitl

And he was asked if the land mentioned above was a field for dependents or if it was also lordly land, a lordly field? He said, "It is not a field for dependents, it is lordly land. It indeed belongs to my master Diego Probe, since it is the lordly house that keeps it, also because it belongs to our parents, our grandparents. Thus to their knowledge, it is lordly land. It is not a field for dependents."

v yvan ic tlahtlaniloc yn itoca diego sasan yllipitica cuis ic ahu quipisqueh yn intah~~uan ycvhcvlhūa~~[7] yvan cuis quimati cuis qujpiah cequi y cuemitl yn innemac yntahoā yncohcvlhvan ~~quihto~~[8]. yva cuis no onca pohuj yn teccalcv ycha quetzalcvatecuitly quihtv. ya nellj y no onca pohui ocan chanehque ahv yehatle cuemitl ynemac. ayc cuemitl oquipisque yn iñtah~~ōā yn cvlhcolhūa~~[9] ya ysquich yn itlahtol diego sihunel amo huel quitlalj yfirma ytoca ypampa aº quimatj amatl yn senor alcalde nica [*signature*]

And he was asked about the prisoner named Diego Zazan: if his parents kept [the field]; and if he knows if they hold some fields inherited from their parents, their grandparents; and if they are also dependents there, in the lordly house, the home of Quetzalcoateuctli. He said, "It is true that they are also dependents there, they are residents there. And the field is their inheritance, [but] his parents never worked the field." These are all of Diego Xiuhnel's words. He could not put his signature, his name, because he is not literate. The lord *alcalde* here . . . [*signature*]

6 The term *ŷculhoan* 'their grandparents' was inserted and then crossed out.

7 Parts of the original phrase *yn intahuan ycvhcvlhua* 'their parents, their grandparents' were crossed out.

8 The verb *quihto* 'he said (it)' was crossed out.

9 Parts of the original phrase *yn intahoa yn cvlhcolhua* 'their parents, their grandparents' were crossed out. What remains of the phrase is *intah* 'their father' but the intention, given the plural subject of *quipisque* 'they kept it', was probably *itahuan* 'his [Diego Zazan's] parents'.

The present document, housed in the Historical Archive of the State of Tlaxcala (Archivo Histórico del Estado de Tlaxcala, AHET), contains the interrogation of the witness Diego Xiuhnel, resident of Santa Clara Atzompan (Tepeticpac), concerning a prisoner named Diego Zazan. Reluctant at first to acknowledge his acquaintance with the accused and his knowledge of the case, Diego Xiuhnel eventually produces testimony that sheds much light on the sociopolitical institution of the *teccalli* 'lordly house', a typical institution for the Tlaxcala region and, more widely, for the eastern area of Central Mexico.

Diego Zazan was charged with having appropriated two long, narrow fields, and having sown them. The interrogator attempts to determine the status of the allegedly misappropriated land and to whom it belonged. Judging from his own words, the witness, Diego Xiuhnel, was most likely a dependent, bound to the *teccalli* identified as the Home of Quetzalcoateuctli (*ichan quetzalcoatecuitli*). Its head was Diego Probe, a member of a noble lineage that certainly could have been traced back to the *teccalli*'s founder. Diego Xiuhnel admits to having cultivated the land in question in the past in order to contribute to maintaining his "lordly house," that is, probably as a part of tribute obligations. When asked about it, he explains that the field pertains to the *teccalli* rather than to *teixhuiuhhuan* (lit. 'one's grandchildren,' that is, dependents). This particular group of dependents bound to the *teccalli* were people who had some distant and, possibly, though not necessarily, kin relations with the founder of the lordly house. They were considered to be of noble ancestry but, unlike *pipiltin*, were not able to trace their lineage back to a particular ancient nobleman (Madajczak 2015). They could possess land but were obliged to fulfill tribute duties, a commitment from which the *pipiltin* were probably exempt. For this reason, James Lockhart proposed that they should be viewed as occupying a transitional position between the noble class and the commoners (1992: 98). Diego Xiuhnel's explanation allows us to surmise that lordly lands and the lands of *teixhuihuan* were distinct units with different status. However, it is difficult to infer from his statement whether or not the imprisoned Diego Zazan belonged to the group of *teixhuihuan* linked to Diego Probe's *teccalli*. What we do know is that the land in question was the inherited land (*innemac*) pertaining to his family for generations and during the major portion of this time was cultivated by such commoners as Diego Xiuhnel, most probably with the consent of the *teccalli*.

This short document shows that forty years after the Spanish conquest the institution of the *teccalli* functioned in the Tlaxcalan region in an almost undisturbed manner and did not seem to be in decline. The basis for its existence was the tribute work of the common people (*macehualtin*) and probably also of other social groups, such as dependents (*teixhuihuan*). The text also demonstrates that members of the lordly house could not manage and distribute the fields freely; the only ones authorized to do so were the leaders of the *teccalli*.

Valuable although this document is, there are some major obstacles preventing its complete interpretation. First of all, wider contextual information regarding the case is lacking, and the outcome of the judicial process is unknown. We can assume that Diego Xiuhnel was not the only witness summoned by the authorities, but we have no access to their declarations, and even his testimony is not complete. The page certainly formed part of a larger set: the text is interrupted and the closing formulas and signatures are missing. What is seen at the bottom of the reverse side of the *foja* is a flourish indicating that it will continue on the following page, which is either lost or hidden among other documents of this kind.

Another difficulty concerns the dating of the manuscript. Even though in the text itself we can read that the interrogation took place on March 30, 1563, there is another date on the document, 1562, which was written in a different hand and in different ink after the document itself was prepared. With all probability it was added by someone from the staff of the archive at an undetermined moment, but the criteria for such a procedure remain unknown. The identity of the notary does not provide arguments that would put the original dating into doubt. However, there may be an explanation for the correction in the dating of the document that is related to a confusion surrounding two notaries from the family Rodríguez. The handwriting of the principal text of the interrogation follows quite closely the style of the 1560 documents (in this volume), signed by Fabián Rodríguez. He held the notarial office of the municipal council through 1562, but was not reelected the following year, ceding his position to Diego de Soto and Tadeo de Niza. Nevertheless, his signature appears on many of the Tlaxcalan municipal council minutes from 1563 (as it had on many previous ones beginning in 1547), even when the official title of the notary of the municipal council was assigned to someone else. The notary who wrote down Diego Xiuhnel's testimony presents himself as Sebastián, and not as Fabián, Rodríguez. In their edition of the records of the Tlaxcalan municipal council (1976: 10), James Lockhart, Frances Berdan, and Arthur J. O. Anderson noted that from 1567 on, Fabián Rodríguez was officially accompanied in his work by a younger apprentice, his relative Sebastián Rodríguez. The present document proves that the latter worked in the trade as early as 1563, and the close resemblance between his and his master's penmanship indicates that they followed the same school of handwriting. Thus, there is no evidence for attributing the writing of the present manuscript to Fabián Rodríguez and, consequently, there seems to be no reason for adjusting the date to the period during which he officially held the office of municipal council notary.

The Nahuatl in which the document was written does not contain many loanwords from Spanish; these are limited to its administrative (*alcalde ordinario, juramento*) and religious (*Dios, Santa María, cruz*) vocabulary. Sebastián Rodríguez does not seem to have been as consistent in marking the glottal stop as his more experienced relative, Fabián. However, the text does not lack interesting examples of contact phenomena. One of them is the new use of the word *amatl*. Traditionally meaning 'bark paper', in the manuscript it extends to 'alphabetic writing'. It appears in the expression *amo quimati amatl* 'he is not literate' (lit. 'he does not know writing'), quite often inserted in mundane documents, and in this case explaining why Diego Xiuhnel's signature is missing at the end of his testimony.

DOCUMENT 5

Investigation Regarding a Murder, Aquetzalpan, Tlaxcala, Mexico, 1564[1]

Agnieszka Brylak

[Fol. 1r]

En la leal çibdad Castvlli omome ylhuitl metztlj de abril. de mill y quinyºs y sesenta y quatro anos. y muy noble senor Juan de la tvRe alcalde hvrdinario y nican çibdad yva probinçia tlascalla por su magestad yspan neçico yn itvca maria sihmaticol chane aquetzalpa ypan in tlascalla tlallj qhtv Justª niquihtlani ma tlatemolo aqui quimicti nonamic catca ytvca diego teculomani ya oviptla sabad. oc yoapa y quizqui cvahcvavitv ompa yn icuentla ytvcayohcan temetzûtla ahv y yalva nicchis amo vallaya qui yehoa yvapa oniqz onictemotv ahu oniquihtac omicqui vel mocac yn itlahtol nima tlanahvati yn senor allde yn Campa micvac umpa yaz çe escrivano yva alguaziles tlahtlanitihuj yn quenin micqui quimatizque açv canah tlavan ahno

In the loyal city, on the seventeenth day of the month of April in the year 1564, a person named María Xihmaticol, resident of Aquetzalpan, [situated] on the lands of Tlaxcallan, appeared before the very noble lord Juan de la Torre, *alcalde ordinario* for His Majesty here in the city and province of Tlaxcallan. She said, "I ask for justice. Let there be an investigation into who killed my late husband, named Diego Tecolomani. He left the day before yesterday, Saturday, early in the morning, to go gather firewood in his field at the place called Temetzontlan. Yesterday I waited for him [but] he did not return. Shortly afterwards, early the [next] morning, I left to go looking for him. I saw that he was dead." Her words were heard

1 Archivo Histórico del Estado de Tlaxcala (AHET), 1564, caja 2, exp. 19; A transcription of this document and its translation into Spanish was published in *Catálogo de documentos escritos en náhuatl siglo XVI* by the Gobierno del Estado de Tlaxcala (2013). The transcription and translation included here are based entirely on the original manuscript.

DOI: 10.5876/9781607328346.c005

acameh ycvcvlicnihva quinhuicatinemia yn ihcvac sabado. yn senor alcalde mofirmati testigos. pablo sochmilcatzin alcayde ant° vitlalotl alguazil yn ilhuitl metztli sihuitl omihtv	attentively. Then the lord *alcalde* issued an order, "A notary will go with the constables to the place where the death occurred in order to inquire into how he died. They will find out if perhaps he got drunk somewhere or perhaps there are some angry friends of his whom he was accompanying." It was Saturday when the lord *alcalde* placed his signature. The witnesses were Pablo Xochmilcatzin, jailer, and Antonio Huitlalotl, constable. On the aforementioned day, month, and year.
[*signature*] Juan de la toRe	[*signature*] Juan de la Torre.
Nispa͡mochiho	It was done in my presence
[*signature*] sebastian rr°z	[*signature*] Sebastián Rodríguez
ca niman ihcvaqu in ilhuitl metztlj sihuitl omihtv yn tehoa sebastian rr°z svano yvan alguaziles alonso tlictzin yva ant° teçvn. nican san Juan tvtvlla tevpan tiquihtaque y͡ micquetl ytvca catca Diego tecvlomanj. çan isquatvlcv yn sipehotica yua ehtlj ycamac quiztoc yvan ytla͡cvac sipehotica	Then, on the aforementioned day, month, and year, we, the notary Sebastián Rodríguez and the constables Alonso Tlictzin and Antonio Tezon, saw here, in the church of San Juan Totollan, the deceased person whose name was Diego Tecolomani. His eyelids were flayed and blood was coming out of his mouth and his knees were flayed.
[*signature*]	[*signature*]
[Fol. 1v]	
aho vel tictemolihque yn itla capa yntla canah oc cecca coyo͡tica ahno ezicuiçitica? aca͡ tiquihtaque. ypa͡ titvfirmatique timotocayotihque	We examined [his body] carefully [to see if there was] something somewhere, or [if] in some other place it was perforated or there were bloody wounds. We did not see any [such] place. We put our signatures and our names on [the document].
[*signature*] sebastian rr°z	[*signature*] Sebastián Rodríguez
Evano de la çibdad [*signature*]	Municipal notary [*signature*]
v çа͡ no yhcvac titlachisque y͡ nican motocayotia salatlahvte͡cv yn o͡can ic vetztvya ȳ micquetl aho titlachisque ynic vnoya micquetl eztli chichipicatihcac ahu titlachisque aço onpoallj icsitica yn quivilaque ynic cec°ca quitlaçatv	Also at that time we looked around here [in the place] called Xalatlauhtenco, where the deceased had been lying. We observed how the corpse lay and how the blood was spattered. We noticed that they had dragged him some forty feet

yvan tiquihtaque yn icacva [2] micquetl
onca vetztoque vel ehççvque yva
tictemohque yn cvahuitl quivalmemeya
micquetl acā çe tiquihtaque y cvavitl
miecca titlatemohque ypa titvfirmatique
timvtvcayotihque

in order to throw him in a certain place. And we saw the shoes of the deceased, lying there, completely covered with blood. And we looked for the firewood that the deceased had been carrying on his back; nowhere did we see a single piece of wood. We searched in many places. We put our signatures and our names on [the document].

[*signature*] sebastian rruz

[*signature*] Sebastián Rodríguez

Evano de la çibdad [*signature*]

Municipal notary [*signature*]

[Fol. 2r]

+

Yn nican temetzutla de san frans.co
ypan altepetl tlapitzavaca tehoan alonso
tlictzin yva Juan teçotzin alguaziles
yva nehoatl sebastian rrvz svano de la
çibdad. tictlahtlamihque yn itvca antº
tlasich nican chaneh quihtv yhcvac
sabado açv ya chicuej hvras valla yn
itvca diego tecvlomani chaneh sa nicvlas.
aqtzalpan notes catca vel nican ehuac
çan opa tlacuitv yn aquetzalpan ahu
tepoztli cvCuitiquiçacv y nican ya nelli
ome y nica cvnitiqçacv octlj. ahu yahqui
~~quihuicac nopiltzin ytoca Gregorio aho~~
~~yn valla amo yuintiya quivalmeme yn~~
~~Coavitl quiseselotv. çi~~ ychan ymach.
ytoca poçelotl. aho amo nicnati cuis quic
ompa octlj cuix anomo aho yn oquiçacv
ça çe y quitiquiçacv octlj nima yayahu
quihuicac nupiltzin ytvca gregoryo
quicavazqz yn icha ypapa ymachtzin
ya isqch yn itlahtol ypa nimofirmati
nimotvcayoti. nehoatl svano

+

Here in Temetzontlan de San Francisco, in the town of Tlapitzahuacan, we constables, Alonso Tlictzin and Juan Tezontzin, and I, Sebastián Rodríguez, municipal notary, questioned a person named Antonio Tlaxich, a resident here. He said, "[The person] named Diego Tecolomani, a resident of San Nicolás Aquetzalpan and my late brother-in-law, came on Saturday, it could have been already eight o'clock. He left right from here in order to get something in Aquetzalpan. He came here to pick up an axe and, it is true, to drink two *pulques*. He went[3] to the home of his nephew, named Pocelotl.[4] I do not know if he drank *pulque* there or not. Up until the time he left, he had drunk just one *pulque*. Then it got dark, [so] he took my son, named Gregorio. He was going to take him to his house because he is his nephew." This concludes his testimony. I, the notary, placed my signature and my name on [the document].

2 The Nahuatl term for shoes, *cactli*, is in the possessive form and pluralized.

3 The lines that are crossed out read, *quihuicac nopiltzin ytoca Gregorio aho yn valla amo yuintiya quivalmeme yn Coavitl quiseselotv. çi*, 'My son, named Gregorio, accompanied him. When he came he was not drunk. He carried on his back the wood that he went to cut up.' The letters *çi* belong to the next word that the notary intended to write down right before making the decision to cross out the entire fragment.

4 It seems to be an abbreviation for *Pedro* or *Pablo Ocelotl.*

[*signature*] sebastian R°z

Esvano de la çibdad [*signature*]

[*signature*] Sebastián Rodríguez,

Municipal notary. [*signature*]

ça niman ihcvac quihto yn itoca maria teyacapa yn ihcvac nican oquiztiquiz Di° tecvlomani umpa huia y nochan nechilhuia nicvavicv aho ayacqu ih notlavical yahqui ychcatla ça nehuatl y nopan ehuatv aho nechihtlaniliaya yn octlj aho atle nicmacac ya isquich yn itlahtol

Right after that, [the person] named María Teyacapan said, "When Diego Tecolomani left here, he was going to my home. He told me, 'I've come to gather firewood.' My husband[5] was not present, he went to Ichcatla [Ixcatla]. It was just me whom he went to help. He was asking me for *pulque*. I did not give him any." This concludes her testimony.

gregorio piltútli aço ya matlactli omome omey sihuitl nemi quihtv nichuicaqu ī notlatzin catca Dj° tecolomanj aho nispan yn quixexelo cvahuitl vel miec yn ya quimeme vele tehcihota nechilhuia nopiltzin ca xiloti. ȳtla miec nocvaho tinechpalevizqz aho ynī maca niahtiho ypa visperas y ya yaho aho yn ya quiyahui ya calaquih tonatiho machu oahçic yn ichan ya isquich yn itlahtol

Gregorio is a child, he is perhaps twelve or thirteen years old. He said, "I accompanied my late uncle Diego Tecolomani. In my presence he cut up firewood. He already carried quite a lot on his back, it was hailing heavily. He said to me, 'My little boy is only just sprouting up. If my [load of] wood were great, you would help me. But this will not be so. I'll just go [walking].' It was late Saturday evening when he went. It was already raining and the sun had gone down. It is known that he arrived home." This concludes his testimony.

Maria sihmatiloc quihto nonamic catca yn Diego tecvlomani. aho yn sabadotica valla y nican çan ic valcequiz aho amo nicmati aço ytlah yc quicvcvlia ȳ atanomo nican at anomo yeh nochipa yn vallani ypapa nica mani ycuetzin nican chaneh catcah. aço ya cenpoasihotica yn onechmonamicti aho ayc onechpilhoati. ya isquich yn itlahtol ypa ninofirmatiq timotocay[o]tique ~~tynilhuitl~~ omochiho yc castolli omome ylhuitl metztli de abril de mill y quinj°s y sesenta y quatro anos. testigos bartholome acatl Damia ant° cvahotzo alguazil temetzuntla oc miec tlacatl ixpan

María Xihmaticol said, "My late husband was Diego Tecolomani. On Saturday he came here having won a lot of money gambling. I don't know if for some reason those that are here hate him. Perhaps not. He comes all the time because his fields are here, he was a resident here. He married me about twenty years ago but he never made me pregnant." This concludes her testimony. I put my signature on [the document]. We provided our names. Done on the seventeenth day of the month of April in the year 1564. The witnesses were Bartolomé Acatl, Damián Antonio Cuauhotzon, constable in Temetzontlan, and [it was done] in the presence of many other people.

5 An alternative translation of *notlavical* would be 'my servant'. However, *tlahuicalli* is the eastern Nahuatl (to which Tlaxcalan Nahuatl belongs) equivalent of the central *namictli*. This term is also attested with the meaning of 'spouse' in some documents from Central Mexico, such as *Arte de la lengua mexicana y vocabulario* by fray Andrés de Olmos (1547: 229r). Fray Bernardino de Sahagún in Book 6 of the *Florentine Codex* pairs *motlavical* 'your husband' with *monamic* 'your spouse' (1969: 102).

+ [*signature*] Sebastian Ro[z]	+ [*signature*] Sebastián Rodríguez
scrvano de la çibdad [*signature*] +	municipal notary [*signature*] +
[Fol. 2v]	
procesSo ypampa çe miquiztlj yc micquj ytoca catca Diego tecvlomanj chane aquetzalpa	The lawsuit concerning the death of a deceased person named Diego Tecolomani, a resident of Aquetzalpan.
En tiempo de 1564 a[os]	In the year of 1564.
Juez Juan de la toRe	Juan de la Torre
svano sebastian R[o]z [*signature*]	Notary Sebastián Rodríguez [*signature*]

The genre of the present manuscript written in April of 1564 is defined in the text itself as a *proceso*, that is, a 'trial' or 'lawsuit'. Its contents, however, are highly unusual if we compare it to the known corpus of colonial mundane documents in Nahuatl. In it María Xihmaticol, a resident of San Nicolás Aquetzalpan, asks Juan de la Torre, one of the four *alcaldes ordinarios* of Tlaxcala, to carry out an investigation concerning her husband's death. Immediately after hearing the request, the *alcalde* assigned two constables (*alguaciles*), accompanied by a notary, to examine the case.

Among the testifying witnesses were María Xihmaticol, her brother Antonio Tlaxich, his underage son Gregorio, and a woman named María Teyacapan, whose relation to the dead person is not specified, though she was probably the wife of Pocelotl, Antonio Tlaxich's older son and Gregorio's brother. Their statements allowed the constables to reconstruct the events that took place on that tragic Saturday and thus solve the mystery of Diego Tecolomani's death.

As we can learn from the testimonies of the persons who were interrogated, Diego Tecolomani left for San Francisco Temetzontlan to gather firewood. When he did not return, his wife became worried, went in search of him and found him dead. She reported it to the authorities, suspecting that someone must have killed him. Thus the constables had to decide whether it was an accident or a murder. It was determined that Diego Tecolomani has first gone by his brother-in-law's place in Temetzontlan. He wanted to borrow an axe and the two men drank some *octli* (*pulque*), that is, an indigenous alcoholic beverage made of fermented maguey juice. Afterwards and on the way back home to Aquetzalpan he planned to go to the house of his nephew, Pocelotl. It was already dark and it had started to rain, so young Gregorio accompanied him. The next thing we know is that he visited María Teyacapan, whom he was to help with some chore. Based on this piece of information, it is plausible that the woman was Pocelotl's wife, and that she needed assistance in her husband's absence. There Diego Tecolomani asked to be served some more *pulque* but the hostess refused. The constables examined the body of the deceased, which by the time they got to San Francisco Temetzontlan, had been removed from the crime scene and laid out in the church of San Juan in Totollan. They found it all covered in blood, with some skin peeled off but with no signs of wounds or perforations that could indicate an attack with a weapon. They also examined the scene of the alleged crime, where they encountered Diego's scattered shoes and found indications that his body had been dragged. However, there was no wood, even though the adolescent Gregorio testified that Diego Tecolomani had cut it in his presence.

The document does not contain a clear expression of the final conclusions of the investigation. María Xihmaticol, the deceased person's wife, testified that her late husband had won a lot of money gambling, and for this reason he may have been the victim of a mugging that ended tragically. Another possible scenario that can be inferred from the documents is that Diego Tecolomani's death was not a murder but rather an unfortunate accident, caused perhaps by the bad weather conditions, especially given his state after consuming alcohol. The latter aspect points to one of the major social problems in New Spain faced by Spanish authorities, that is, the inebriation of the indigenous population. One of its causes frequently indicated by scholars is the postconquest relaxation of the rigid restrictions concerning the ritual consumption of *pulque* in the prehispanic period. Some authors also indicate that native alcoholism was fomented by the Spaniards themselves, mainly those involved in the production of this type of beverage (see the summary on this subject in Ruz Barrio 2007). The document also reveals the general procedure put into motion when a possible crime was reported to the authorities of the local municipal council.

The notary who wrote down the text of this investigative document did not use many loanwords from Spanish. Those that do appear are mostly nouns related to time and the calendar (*sábado, vísperas*) and the names for colonial officials (*alcalde ordinario*, *justicia, alcaide*). Some are in the plural form, which in all probability was not analyzed but rather borrowed in the plural as a singular form (*alguaciles, testigos*). In fact, the singular and plural forms, *alguacil* and *alguaciles*, were used interchangeably. The text also contains a quite rare use of the Nahuatl word *icxitl* 'foot/feet' for measurement, apparently not attested before the conquest, and, therefore, an example of a calque of Spanish *pie* (see Lockhart 1992: 144).

DOCUMENT 6

Land Sale Document, Tlaxcala, Mexico, 1607/1608[1]

Agnieszka Brylak

[Fol. 1r]

Solar del Pu^{o} de s^{n} Phelipe

House lot of the village of San Felipe

San Felipe
para pedro de muoñbe
que bendio Alonso. Sanches moreno
Oi le toca A Antt^{o}, Munibe dha tierra que se A labrado Ya en ella

San Felipe
to Pedro de Muoñbe
which Alonso Sánchez Moreno sold
Now the mentioned land will belong to Antonio Munibe[2], who has already been cultivating it.

[Fol. 1v]

yc. 6. ilhuitl. metztl. de agustos. 1607. anos. ypã. yn otimononotzque. ypã. Domigo. oquihualtitlan. yn ihuepol. yn itoca. baltasal. quechol. auh. nimã onechilvi. oquito. onechvaltitla y nohuepoltzín. quihualitova. cuix quimaniliz. y nosulal. auh. nimã. oniquilhui. ma oc nimononotza. auh. nimã. yqu eto[3] comitalhuiz. nimã. hopã.

On the sixth day of the month of August of the year of 1607, Sunday, we made an agreement. She sent her brother-in-law, named Baltasar Quechol, here. Then he spoke to me and said, "My sister-in-law has sent me. She says, 'Will he take my house lot?'" Then I said to him, "For now I agree." Then he ended by saying, "Then we will go there to meet you,

1 Archivo Histórico del Estado de Tlaxcala (AHET), 1607, caja 4, exp. 7.

2 Perhaps *Munive*, a surname attested in Tlaxcala in the twentieth century.

3 The expression *yqueto comitalhuiz* apparently stands for *ic yeto comitalhuiz*. The verb *ye* is the vehicle for the purposive *-to*, with the sense of 'to wind up doing something', 'to end up doing something'. I would like to thank John Sullivan for this explanation.

DOI: 10.5876/9781607328346.c006

toyazque. y monahuactzinco. ca huel itech monequi. y tomitzin. auh. çã nimã. y çãn ipa. domigo. amo ce ora. yn ohualaque. ymeysti. yhuepol. yn itoca. bal^r. quechol. yhuã. yn itoca. Ju^o. ceron. yach. yhuã y tlanamacani. ytoca. ~~namie~~ ãna. cohuacihuatl. auh. yn ixpã. yn iach. y~~p~~huepal. yn oticchiuhque. y tococierto y tonenonetzal. auh. nimã. onicmacac 6 ps^o. yhuã 2 ts^o ca huel imatica. oquicel. y tomines. homohuelma. ca hue~~h~~l yecyotica. omo[4] nictetequihui. nimã. oquito. ca y naxca. huel ninovelmati. camo tinechtequiviya. ca noyolocacopa. y nimitznamaquiltiya. y nosulal. ca notlatqui. y naxca. nimitzmaca. xicmopilli ca y notlatqui. ca ya nimitzmomaquillia[5]. camo tinechtequihuiya. auh. ynic huel yecyotica. timononotza. auh. ynic nicã. yc titlamachiyotiya. cruz +. tomesti. yvã y testicosti. no yc tlamachiyotique. cruz +. amo cepa. timoxicozque. ca huel yecyotica. otimononotzque. y tomesti. y timotlacohuillia. ynic timotocayotiya. yc ticneltillia. y totlatol. y nehuatl. nitlacuilo. nimochiuh. nimofilmati. y nimotocayoti. yc nicneltilli. yn ilhuitl. y xihuitl. tlacpac. homito

+ y ãna. cohuacihuatl

+ y Jhuã ceron

+ y baltolome sanchez

+ y baltasal. quechol

+ Diego minor [*signature*]

because she really needs the money." Immediately afterwards, on that same Sunday, in less than an hour, the three of them came: her brother-in-law named Baltasar Quechol, and the one named Juan Ceron, her elder brother, and the seller named Anna Cohuacihuatl. In the presence of her elder brother and her brother-in-law, we made an agreement, a deal. Then I gave her six *pesos* and two *tomines*, indeed she personally[6] received the money. All were satisfied that [it was done] truly in the right way; I did not force her. Then she said, "It is my property, I am satisfied, you do not force me for I voluntarily sell you my house lot. It is my possession, my property, I give it to you, may you keep it. It is my property, I have now given it to you, you have not forced me [to do it]." Thus truly in the right way we make an agreement. So here in this way we both confirm it with a cross +. And thus the witnesses also confirmed it with a cross +. We will not enter into dispute in the future, for the two of us who make the purchase have truly made our agreement in the right way. For this reason, we put our names in order to certify our words. I did the writing, I did it, I signed it, I put my name. Thus I confirmed it. The day and year as mentioned above.

+ Anna Cohuacihuatl

+ Juan Cerón

+ Bartolomé Sánchez

+ Baltasar Quechol

+ Diego Minor [*signature*]

4 It should be read as *amo*, negative particle.

5 The reflexive pronoun *mo* used in the first person singular instead of *no* is common in eastern variants of Nahuatl, to which Tlaxcalan Nahuatl belongs.

6 Literally, 'with her hand'.

[Fol. 2r]

yn iquac. homomiquili. quimonahuatilitehuac. yn inamic ytoca bal^{e}. sanechez oquilhui. y nosulal. yn onicnamacac. yn onicnamaquilti. yn itoca. thomas. yaotl. aya quiteq͡pachoz. ca naxca. ca notlatqui. ma cemicac. quimopilli. yehuatl. quimati. ca ya yaxca. ca ya ytlatqui. ca ya onicuic ytomines. 6 ps^{o}. 2 ts. ca nomatica. ynic nimitznahuatehua. y tinonamic. aya q̄tequipachoz ca yc onitlamachiyoti. yn icruz +. yn tt^{o}. dios. amo nechmotlatoleviz. yn ixpatzinco. ca onicnotenehuilli.

When she died, she left an order to her spouse named Bartolomé Sánchez, she told him, "As for my house lot, I sold it. The one to whom I sold it is named Tomás Yaotl. No one should bother him about it because it was my property, because it was my possession. May he forever keep it. He knows that it is now his property, it is now his possession. I have already taken the money, six *pesos* and two *tomines*, [I did it] personally.[7] Thus, my husband, I leave you the order that no one should bother him about it. Thus I confirmed it with the cross + of our lord God. He will not accuse me of falsehood as it was before him that I said it."

v̲ + ana. cohuacihuatl

+ Ana Cohuacihuatl

v̲ + bal^{e}. sancchez

+ Bartolomé Sánchez

v̲ Auh. ynic opa. hotlanahuati. quinahuati. yn itoca. mathias. quiyauhtzín. yhuã. feliphe. cohuatl. yhuã. Juliano. quauhtli. ca huel quimati. ynic notlatqui. ynic naxca. ca occepã. namechnahuatitehuã. ayac ytla quitos yn ameyxtin. anotesticoshuã. ca ya onic^{na}macac. y nosulal. ca ya yxquich. y notlatol. y niquitohua. ca huel melavac. hypã. sabato. yc nitlanavatia. yc 4 ilhuitl. metztli. de henero. 1608. ãnos

For the second time she issued an order. She ordered the one named Matías Quiyauhtzin, and Felipe Cohuatl and Juliano Quauhtli, "Because they know well that it was my property, that it was my possession, once again I leave you the order that no one will say anything [against it]. The three of you are my witnesses that I have already sold my house lot. These are all my words. What I say is really true. I order it on Saturday, the fourth day of the month of January of the year 1608."

ymixpã. mochiuh.

It was made in the presence of:

v̲ + lucas. perez

+ Lucas Pérez

v̲ + aña. cohuacihuatl

+ Anna Cohuacihuatl

v̲ felipe. cohuatl

Felipe Cohuatl

+ mathias. quiyauhtzín

+ Matías Quiyauhtzin

+ Diego minor [*signature*]

+ Diego Minor [*signature*]

---

7 Literally, 'with my hand'.

The present manuscript is a bill of sale concerning a house lot located in San Felipe, Tlaxcala, bought by Tomás Yaotl from Ana Coacihuatl. It is composed of two documents, dated in August 1607 and January 1608, respectively.

The first text (folio 1v) describes the transaction, though in an unusual manner: rather than a third-person narration of the events, it is the direct testimony of the buyer, Tomás Yaotl (though his name appears neither in the document itself nor among the signatures that conclude it), which even includes bits of conversations in first person. According to Tomás, on Sunday, Ana Coacihuatl delegated Baltasar Quechol, her brother-in-law, to go to the house of the potential buyer in order to inquire whether he was interested in the purchase. Immediately after having received an affirmative answer, Baltasar Quechol, accompanied by Ana Coacihuatl and her elder brother Juan Cerón, reappeared at Tomás Yaotl's residence to close the deal, since Ana was in urgent need of money. Unlike in other documents of this genre, there is no mention of the location, dimensions, or boundaries of the lot; neither are there any details concerning the buildings constructed on it. The only specific information provided is the price: six *pesos* and two *tomines*.

The second document (folio 2r), dictated by Ana Coacihuatl on her deathbed on January 4, 1608, is addressed to her husband, Bartolomé Sánchez. In an admonitory tone she reminds him that the house lot, which was sold, was her property and that the transaction was carried out with her consent, which is why he should not claim it in the future. Ana also indicates the names of three witnesses who made a declaration confirming that her words were true. It should be noted that the owner of the lot is Ana rather than her husband, though it is not specified whether it was inherited land or a part of her dowry. Such a situation was quite common in the sixteenth century, when prehispanic patterns still prevailed after the conquest. However, things gradually started to change, and it seems that by the mid-seventeenth century women did not frequently possess goods or, when they did, they were represented by their husbands in the legal sphere (Kellogg 1999: 137–139).

Despite the fact that the documents were prepared within the span of five months, they are written by the same hand and apparently with the same ink. From the text itself we learn that Ana Coacihuatl, as well as some of the witnesses, did not know how to write, so they signed with a cross, while their names were supplied by the notary, Diego Minor. In one place, next to the signature of Felipe Coatl, there is no cross, which might suggest that he signed the document himself; however, his signature is in the same handwriting as both other signatures and the main text. These observations, as well as the fact that the 1607 document and the one from the beginning of 1608 appear on two consecutive folios, allow us to assume that they are copies of the original documents. A short note in Spanish, written down on folio 1r, indicates their possible use. It states that the house lot in San Felipe, sold by Alonso Sánchez Moreno, has been turned into cultivated land and that it belongs to Antonio Munibe. Taking this information into account, the copies of the two documents in Nahuatl might have formed part of a much larger set of manuscripts concerning the same parcel, which permitted the new proprietors to trace back its previous ownership and prove their rights to it. In this way the members of the Munibe family could protect their holdings from unjustified claims.

Even though the Nahuatl text belongs to Stage 2 of the chronological outline proposed by James Lockhart, it does not contain many examples of linguistic changes induced by contact with Spanish. The loanwords that appear in the document are relatively few: *solar* 'house lot'; *domingo* 'Sunday'; *pesos* and *tomines,* each of them a monetary unit; *cruz* 'cross'; *hora* 'hour'; and *testigostin* 'witnesses', with both Spanish and Nahuatl plural suffixes. All the legal formulas were expressed in Nahuatl. The notary, Diego Minor, quite consistently substituted the letter *r* for *l*.

DOCUMENT 7

Land Sale Document, Tlaxcala, Mexico, 1612[1]

Agnieszka Brylak

[Fol. 29r]

En la ciudad de tlax.^{a} yc omilhuitl.
metztli. de abril de mill y seys.
sientos y doçe años. ymixpantzinco.
yn yehuatzin. Don. Juã. diaz. don.
mel.^{or} gallego. don. Juã. bau^{ta}. de monde
alegre. don. Juã. ponçe. de leon. y
mendoça. alldes. ordinario. y nicã yn
ciudad. yhuã. probicia. de tlax.^{a} por su
mag^{d}. yhuã. nixpã niesCrj.^{o} de cabildo.
nezque. testigos. yhuã. yehuatin. fran.^{ca}
totoztic. yoa ytelpoch. ytoca. Diego.
de soto. nican chanehque. ciudad.
tlax.^{a} ypan. cabeçera. ocotelolco ./.
quihtoque. tohuelitiliztica. toçeyaliztica.
tonehuelmachiliztica. ticnamaca. tosular.
nican mani. teopancalixpan[2] huel ipan.
yn ohtli. onca. hualquiça. sancta. yglesia.
mayor. yuh ticçenmaca. ticnamaquiltia.
yn yehuatzin. dona. fran.^{ca} maxixcatzin.
yuh ticneltilia. ticmocuitia. yn benta

In the city of Tlaxcallan on the second day of the month of April in the year 1612, the witnesses and Francisca Totoztic, along with her adolescent son named Diego de Soto, all local citizens of the city of Tlaxcallan from the head town of Ocotelolco, appeared before Don Juan Díaz, Don Melchor Gallego, Don Juan Bautista de Montealegre, [and] Don Juan Ponce de León y Mendoza, ordinary *alcaldes* here in the city and province of Tlaxcallan for His Majesty, and before me, notary of the municipal council. They said, "By our authority, by our permission, by our consent we sell our house lot located here, in front of the church, right at the road which departs from the main holy church. Thus we give it entirely, we sell it to Doña Francisca Maxixcatzin. We confirm and

1 Archivo Histórico del Estado de Tlaxcala (AHET), 1612, caja 13, exp. 3.

2 I translate it literally, but it is also possible that the term is a toponym; however, I have not been able to find it in the area of Ocotelolco.

 DOI: 10.5876/9781607328346.c007

rreal. ma yuh quimopiliz. yn axca. yhua. y nochipa çemihcac. auh. yn ticnamaca. tosular. ynic patlahuac. macuilnehuitzantli. yca toma. yhua. yca tocxi. auh. ynic huecapan. yeh tlama. yn atlauhtli. yn çe capal. ytepanco. Diego. lopez. Espanol yn occe capal. ytepanco. gonçalo. gomez catca. auh. yn occe capal. yehuatl. tlahma. yn sular ./. auh. yn ipan mani. tlapancaltin. yetetl. auh. yn ipatiuh. omochiuh. ynic oquipatiyoti. yn yehuatzín. Dona. franca maxixcatzín. mahtlacpohuali. omome pesos. tomines teocuitlatl. oticuique. oticçelique timohuelmati. toyolo pachihuí. ma concuí. ma conana. yn sular. yn oc huel yehuatl. çihuapili. dona. franca maxixcatzin. yhua ypilhua. yxhuihua. ytlacamecayohua. yherederoshua. yn itech quiztazque. ynic temotaz tlacatiliztli. auh. amo quemania. ticuepazque totlahtol. amo ypa tictlalizque. teca necayahualiztli. yhua. amo quemanian. ypan tictlalizque. neteylhuili ./. auh. yntla quenmania yuh ticchihuazque. ca yuh ticmotenehuilia. Timotlatlalilia. mochi tehuatin tuconixtlahuazque. yn danos. yhua. costas. yn dereçes.[3] yni[c] nenemiz. neteylhuili. yhuā. oc opa yexpa. yxquich. tiquixtlahua[z]que. yn teocuitlatl. yn axca ticçelia. huel motlapihuiz. auh yc amo. huel toconcuizque. toconanazque. yn tosular. çan yehuatl concuiz conanaz. yn omoteneuh. cihuapili. dona. franca. maxixcatzin auh. yhu ipa. timotlatenehuilia. yn ixquich totlacayo. yhua. totlatqui. yn axca ticpia. yhua. yn oc ticpiyazque. ynic huecauh. tzonquiça iuh. tiquinmaca. ynin ixquichime. Justincias. yhua Jueçes. de su mag+. yn canpa necitiuh. ynin dotlanamaquiliz.amauh. yn.tla nica. ytec. altepetl. anoço cana. quiyahuacpa. ma

acknowledge the bill of legal sale. May she keep it now and forever. And regarding the house lot we sell, it is five *nehuitzantli* wide, [measured] from hand to foot.[4] And as for its length, it goes along a ravine. On one side it borders with [the property of] Diego López, a Spaniard, and on another side is the border with the [property of] the late Gonzalo Gómez. Along yet another side of the house lot there are three flat-roof houses. And the price which Doña Francisca Maxixcatzin would pay for it was set at 202 *pesos* in gold. We took it, we received it. We are content, we are satisfied. May Doña Francisca Maxixcatzin, she who is indeed a noblewoman, take the house lot, along with her children, her grandchildren, her descendants, her heirs, those who will issue from her as the generations will go along descending. We will never go back on our word, we will never engage in plots against anyone about it, and we will never submit a complaint about it. But if at some point we do so, we promise and declare that we will pay for all the expenses of the reparations, judicial costs, and accrued interest as the complaint proceeds. And if again [it happens], for the second or for the third time, we will pay back all the gold, which we receive today, which [with interest] will greatly increase. In this case, we would not take back our house lot; only she, the aforementioned lady Doña Francisca Maxixcatzin would take it. And we commit to this on our very bodies and all of our current and future possessions. In order that it may be upheld in the future, we give [the document] to all the officers of the law and judges of His Majesty. Wherever this bill of sale of ours appears, whether here in the city or anywhere

3 The Spanish loanword *intereses* is interpreted as the Nahuatl particle *in* and the word *dereces*.

4 The text is redundant since *nehuitzantli* itself is a known unit of measurement consisting of the distance from the foot to the upstretched hand.

quimotzonquixtilizque. yca sentecia. Difinidiba. ynic huel neltiz. yn tlanamaquiliz.amatl ./. yn moteneuhque. alldes. quimocaquitique yhuã quimohuelmachitique. yhuā. niman ipan. quimotlalilique yn imauturidad. y tecreto. Justicial. yxquich. ypan. ynhuelitiliz. justicia. ynic huel neltiz mopiaz. ynin tlanamaquiliz.[Fol. 29v]/amatl.
[*signature*]

outside, may they ratify it with a definitive sentence, so that indeed the bill of sale may be confirmed." The aforementioned *alcaldes* heard it and approved it. And then they exercised their authority with a judicial decree. Everything is with the consent of the judges so that this bill of sale will surely be validated and enforced.
[*signature*]

quimopiliz. yn omoteneuh. cihuapili. Dona. fran^{ca}. maxixatzin yuh quimoneltililique ./. ypan quimotlalilique. ynfirma yntoca yhuã. motocayotique ./. yhuã. yn sular quinamacanĩ . amo huel mofirmatique. motocayotique./. çan cruz+.tica tlamachiyotique. ym[ix] pan testigostin. Juã. de meneçes. yhuã. Juã. regino. yn yehuatin niman nican quimotlalilique. ynfirma. yntoca. y quimo[nel]tililique. auh. y nehuatl. niescrj^{o}. nixpan mochiuh. niquinm[acac?][5] .+. neltiliztli. yn tlanamacani. niquimixmati. nitla[nel]tilia. yca nofirma. notoca.

The aforementioned lady, Doña Francisca Maxixcatzin, will keep it. They confirmed it by placing their signatures, their names on it, and they signed it. And the sellers of the house lot did not know how to sign and put their names on it: they only marked it with a cross in the presence of the witnesses Juan de Meneces and Juan Regino, who here then placed their signatures, their names, and confirmed it. Done before me, the notary; I corroborate the sellers, I know them. I provide verification with my signature, my name.

r ynic neli. nicchipauh. yn izcatqui. traslado. ytech niquit[tac?][6] yn original. yn quenamihtica. çan huel iuhtia. amo ma niqualaqui. amo no ytla nicpolo. çan huel itech niquitac. y[nic] neli. nicchipauh. nehuatl. niescrj^{o}. nima nicã. nictlali [no]firma. notoca. yc nitlaneltili
----

I truly assured the accuracy of the present copy by collating it with the original. It is exactly the same; I did not add anything to it at all, nor did I delete anything. I assured its accuracy by collating it. Then I, the notary, placed here my signature, my name, and in this way I performed the verification.

Luys larios

Luis Larios

escrj^{o}. tlax^{a}

notary in Tlaxcallan

The present document is a copy of a bill of sale concerning a parcel in Tlaxcala. It contains all the elements typical for this genre of mundane documentation: essential data regarding the lot itself (its dimensions, price,

5 Probably for *niquinmacac*.

6 Probably for *niquittac*.

buildings, neighboring possessions, topographic details) and declarations stipulating that the transaction has been carried out voluntarily. It also includes the admonitions that the seller, in this case a woman named Francisca Totoztic, addressed to her offspring, to the effect that they should not question her decision to sell and later claim their rights to the property. The text states that such a claim should have financial consequences for the illicit plaintiffs, who will be forced to pay damages, cover judicial costs, and, should the complaint be repeated, to return to the buyers all the money along with interest.

The purchased lot is an expensive one. Its value of 202 *pesos* is probably due to its central location within the head-town (*cabecera*) of Ocotelolco. It also includes a road that leads to the main church. The buyer is Francisca Maxixcatzin, a noblewoman referred to in the document both by the Spanish title *doña* and by its Nahuatl equivalent *cihuapilli*. The date of the transaction, April 2, 1612, allows us to assume that she was none other than the daughter of Don Francisco Pimentel and Doña María Maxixcatzin, who married the *mestizo* Diego Muñoz Camargo, himself son of the famous Tlaxcalan chronicler, and governor of Tlaxcala in 1612. She was also the only direct heir of the ruling dynasty of Ocotelolco who could be traced back to prehispanic times. Thanks to her social and economic status she could afford such a big expense. The preparation of the document, in the presence of not only the seller, her son, and the witnesses, but also of all four ordinary *alcaldes* of Tlaxcala further indicated that the transaction involved at least one person of high position. What is more, the document contains an unusual amount of legal formulas as compared with other texts of this genre from the same period. Without doubt these are translations of Spanish legal expressions and they serve to protect the rights of the buyer, as well as to confirm her high status. Clearly the usage of so many legal expressions was considered important to safeguard the legal weight of the document.

Along with providing us with information about the acquisition of land by the last remaining descendant of one of the most important ruling lineages from Tlaxcala, the text also contains some details regarding landholding and ethnic relations in this region in general. One of the lots that borders with the purchased parcel belongs to a Spaniard named Diego López. This information suggests that almost a century after the conquest the system of ethnic segregation, the purpose of which was to separate the indigenous population from the Spaniards, did not function in accordance with the policy of the Spanish Crown. As an acknowledgement of its active collaboration with the conquistadors, Tlaxcala had been granted a privilege to remain an indigenous town, whereas in its vicinity a new settlement, Ciudad de los Angeles or Puebla, was founded for the Spanish population. Regardless of whether the aforementioned Diego López or one of his ancestors had come into possession of this lot through the system of land grants (Spanish *mercedes*) bestowed by the king or by way of purchase, a Spaniard owning a piece of land in Tlaxcala violated multiple royal provisions (the first one issued by King Charles V in 1535, and later repeated in 1541, 1563, and 1585; see Gibson 1952: 80) and *cabildo* decisions (the first prohibition of land sale to Spaniards appeared in 1553; Gibson 1952: 86). It should be noted, however, that this was not an isolated case: by the mid-seventeenth century it became quite a common practice (Gibson 1952; Lockhart 1992).

This Nahuatl text, written at the beginning of seventeenth century, contains many examples of contact-induced phenomena. Most of them are borrowings from the Spanish language. Apart from more frequent loans, such as the titles of colonial officials (*alcaldes ordinarios*, *escribano, juez, justicia*), it is rich in legal vocabulary, not recurrent in earlier documents: *venta real* (*benta rreal*)[7] '[bill of] legal sale'; *yherederoshuan* 'her heirs' (written in a double plural form, with both Spanish and Nahuatl plural suffixes); *sentencia definitiva* (*sentecia difinidiba*) 'final sentence'; *decreto justicial* (*tecreto justicial*) 'judicial decree'; *daños* (*danos*) 'damages or reparations'; *costos* (*costas*) 'costs'; and *intereses* (*yn dereçes*) 'interest'. The document also has the attestation of the Nahuatl term *tlapancalli* 'flat-roofed room' in the plural *tlapancaltin*. It is generally acknowledged that the pluralization of inanimate nouns did not occur in prehispanic Nahuatl and that such a change was due to contact with the Spanish language. Its presence in this document suggests that by 1612 the pluralization of inanimate nouns in Nahuatl was already beginning to be used more widely; however, the very same plural noun, *tlapancaltin*, appears in the 1600 copy of a testament dictated in 1576 (Document 13, this volume). No other Nahuatl inanimate noun was pluralized in either of the texts, which may indicate a special function of the noun *calli* 'house' in this process.

7 The term *venta real* refers to a sale that was effectively carried out, as opposed to transactions that were not terminated.

DOCUMENT 8

Land Sale Document, Santa Bárbara Tamazolco, Mexico, 1637[1]

Justyna Olko and John Sullivan

1637 anos

\+

v Ãxcan ypan domigo yc caxtoll ilhuitl
honahui m^{a}ni metztli de ablil de mil y
seyscientos y treinta y siete Ãnos ypã
timononotzque consierto hoticchiuhque
y nehuatl y nitlalnamacani nica
nichane sata balbola tamaçolco ytech
nibohui y cabecera hocotelolco auh
y nictlalnamaquiltia ytoca sabastia
ycnoquauh chane santana acolco
ytech bohui y cabecera hocotelolco y
nitlalnamacani ayac honechcuitlahuilti
noyolocacopa y nicnamaca[no]tlal ayc
cepa nimoxicoz yoã y tlalcohuani ayc
cepa moxicoz ynic neltiliztli ticchihua
tocõçilto ymixpa totesticohuan yn tlali
ypatiuh macuili peso honicceli yspa
nohueltitzin ytoca fra^{ca} castilaxōtl Y[n]
tlali ynic huecapã hobohualomatłactli ^{on}
ma[y]tl ynic pa[tla]huac cebohuali maytl
yn tlacpa^{c} ytepa[co] Juã bauh^{ta} ynic oca

In the year of 1637

\+

Today Sunday, the nineteenth day of the month of April in the year 1637, we convened and made an agreement. I am the land seller, resident here in Santa Bárbara Tamazolco and belonging to the municipality of Ocotelulco. The person I am selling land to is named Sebastian Icnocuauh, resident of Santa Ana Acolco and belonging to the municipality of Ocotelolco. No one forced me, the land seller; I sold my land voluntarily. I will never go back on my word, and the land purchaser will never go back on his word. For the purpose of verification we have made our agreement before our witnesses. I received five *pesos*, the price of the land, in the presence of my older sister, Francisca Caxtillanxochitl. The length of the land is fifty *maitl*; its width is twenty *maitl*. At the top, its border

1 Archivo General de la Nación (AGN), Tierras 145, exp. 7, fol. 13r.

DOI: 10.5876/9781607328346.c008

ytepaco totlaçonatzin - ynic yeca tepatli ça no yehuatl totlaçonatzin satanatzin ynic nauhca ça yehuetl yn tlacoh[ua] ni sebastia ycnoquauh ya ysquich yc tlani toconcielto yn ixpan totesticohuan amo quimati aamatl ça crustica hotlamachiyotique	is (with) Juan Bautista; in the second place, its border is (with the land of) Our Precious Mother; in the third place, the border is (with the land of) our very same Precious Mother, Santa Ana; in the fourth place (its border is with the land of) the purchaser himself, Sebastian Icnocuauh. With this concludes the agreement before our witnesses. They are not literate; they just made a mark with a cross.
hoqui[to]cayoti y escri°	The notary put their names.
y nehuatl $^{+}$andres martino	+ I, Andrés Martino, witness.
testico + fra^{ca} castilaxochitl	+ Francisca Caxtillanxochitl
y nehutl nitlalcohuani + y sebastia ycnoquauh	I the land buyer + Sebastián Icnocuauh.
+ testicoti	+ Witnesses:
+ y bel^{ue} ycoctotl	+ Bernabé Icoctotl
+ y fra^{co}, hernates	+ Francisco Hernández
y Jũa Diego hernates escri° [*signature*]	Juan Diego Hernández, notary [*signature*]

This is a typical land sale document involving seventeenth-century indigenous residents of Tlaxcallan who might have been lower-ranking nobility or middle-class commoners. Those directly involved in the transaction, as well as their witnesses, were illiterate. The seller, not mentioned by name in the main body of the text, can be identified with a considerable degree of certainty as Andrés Martino, a resident of Santa Bárbara Tamazolco in the head town of Ocotelolco. It is he who is mentioned with the first-person pronoun at the beginning of the list of persons who marked the document with the sign of the cross. The principal witness is his elder sister, Francisca Caxtillanxochitl; the text emphasizes that the money was exchanged in her presence. Andrés Martino sold the land for the price of five *pesos* to Sebastián Icnocuauh from Santa Ana Acolco, another locality from the same head town of Ocotelolco. The land, measuring fifty by twenty *maitl*, in fact borders on one side with another property of the purchaser.

The orthographic conventions of the text are typical for local indigenous scribes and differ significantly from those of the more standardized canon of genres supervised by Spanish friars. One feature of this type of indigenous writing is the presence of the glottal fricative before vowels—for example, *honnahui* (for *on nahui*) or *honechcuitlahuilti* (for *onechcuitlahuilti*). Typical phonetic substitutions include *c* [k] for Spanish [g] (e.g., *testico* for *testigo*), *t* for *d* (*Hernates* for *Hernandez*), and *l* for *r* (*ablil* for *abril*). However, *r* has indeed already entered the orthographic repertory because the word *concierto* is once written *consierto* and once *concielto*, but this probably only attests to the transitory character of the Spanish letter, the acquisition of which surely preceded that of the actual phoneme. An uncommon feature is the hypercorrection of a native [p] for [b] at the level of orthography in the word *pohui* 'to belong.' At the lexical level several interesting features stand out. Spanish loanwords are relatively infrequent, limited to the formulaic expression of a date and some basic administrative, legal, and economic terminology (*cabecera*, *concierto*, *peso*, *testigo*, *cruz*). In order to express the lack of literacy, the notary uses the expression *amo quimati amatl,* which also appears with considerable frequency in other colonial texts from Tlaxcala between the sixteenth and the eighteenth centuries. It seems that this expression did not have an exact counterpart in the contemporary Spanish and indeed would have been quite ungrammatical[2]; so rather than a possible lexical calque, it should be viewed as a native creation. The meaning of the word *amatl,* originally denoting a native bark paper, had been extended in early colonial times to refer to European paper and to any kind of written document. Here it is taken a step further, for it means "writing in general" or an "act of writing." Thus, the expression "he does not know paper" became the equivalent for "he does not know writing; he does not know how to write."

Part of the seller's sister's name is Caxtillanxochitl, 'a flower from Castile' (for 'rose'). This neologism, created in the first phase of contact, must have figured quite commonly as a native female name or surname in Tlaxcala because it is also found in other documents from the period. It is interesting that Santa Ana, to whom a field bordering with the property in question belongs (land no doubt cultivated in order to maintain the cult to the patron saint of the town of Santa Ana Acolco) is given the typical name for the Virgin Mary, *totlazohnantzin*, 'Our Precious Mother'. This title became so intimately associated with Mary that indigenous writers often did not bother to provide any further clues to her identity (Anderson, Berdan, Lockhart 1976: 176–177; Madajczak 2015: 152). The unusual application here of this epithet implies a possible ambivalence in the religious hierarchy encompassing the Virgin Mary and female saints as protectors of a community and objects of worship.

2 Eva Bravo García, personal communication, September 2016.

DOCUMENT 9

Land Sale Document, Cholula, Mexico, 1695[1]

Justyna Olko

Ma quimatiCan yn ixquichtin quitasque in noneltililisamatlaCuilol nehuatl notoCa ana maría ahuatl niCan niChane ypan tlatoCaAltepetl siudad San grabiel cholula noCaBesera San Juan Tenaquiyahuac ticpia se tlaltzintli CalnaCastli oquicahuilitehuaque noquichtitzin ytoca diego[. . .] ahuatl oquimomaquilitehuac yn totatzin oCatca ytoCa Diego gimenes ahuatl yn omoteneuh tlali yehuatl yaxca ayac sepa quiquixtiliz auh yn axcan ytech oquimotlalili yn iJustisiatzin yn yn ttºe Dios oquimochihuilitehuac testamento oc sepa nehuatl nechmomaquilitehua noquichtitzin yn omoteneuh Diego paBlo oquimopolhuili Dios amo noconipia[2] tlen yc nicmotoquilis nicnamaCa tlaltzintli yn onechmomaquili yn omoteneuh CalnaCastli [ni]Connamaquiltia Señor Antonio gerero auh [i]namic ytoCa

May all who will see my statement of verification know that I am Ana María Ahuatl, resident of the royal city of San Gabriel Cholula; my head town is San Juan Tenaquiyahuac. We have a parcel of land on the corner of the house that was left to my older brother named Diego [Pablo] Ahuatl: our late father, named Diego Jiménez Ahuatl, gave it to him before he died. The mentioned land is his property, nobody will ever take it from him. Now he has entrusted it to the justice of our Lord God; he made a will before he died. Once again my elder brother, the already mentioned Diego Pablo, bequeaths it to me: God took him. I do not have [any money] with which I am to bury him, so I am selling the piece of land that he gave to me, the aforementioned [land] on the corner of the house. I am selling it to the lord

1 Archivo Municipal, San Juan Ixtenco, Tlaxcala.

2 Probably for *noconpiya*.

 DOI: 10.5876/9781607328346.c009

Señora Jusepa maria BillaloBos no nican chane ypan Altepetl siudad San grabiel cholula yn ipatiuh mochihua tlali maCui peso yhuan nahui tomin onoConseli chipahuac ystac teocuitlatl ynic onicmotenehuili yn itlasoquauhnepanoltzin Dios Santa Cruz ymixpan yn testigos ti[. . .]hua tictamachihua tlali ynic hueya[c qui]pia senpohuali yhuan maCuili Bara yhuan se quarta auh ynic patlahuac quipia senpohuali yhuan yei Bara auh ynic tonali yquisayan quitepanohua otli auh yn icalaquiyan tonali quitepanohua san no ye tlalnamacani ytoCa ana maria auh ynic tlaxcalancopatli auh yn atlixcopa san no tlalnamacani ana maria yni omoteneuh tlali

[v] ymixpan testigos ayac cepa moxicoz tla moxicoz [tla]lnamacani opa yxquich quicuepaz tomin yhuan polihuiz in itlal san no yuhqui tlalcohuani polihuiz yn itomin mixpantililiz justisia Alcalde anoso toteopixCatlatoCahuan Cura Bicario ynic yehuantzitzi quimoyectililizque ymixpan testigos = ynic se ytoca Antonio ahuatl ynic ome ytoca Dŏ sebastian yacanextli ynic yei ytoca santana [es]pinosa yni quineltilia yn itoca no nehuatl niescr[ibano] ynic nicneltilia notoCa yhuan nofirma otitla[cui]loque martes yc 2 de henero ypan xihuitl de 1695 años

Testigo testigo

testigo santana espinosa

Ju[an] de los santos escriu° pasado de cabildo

Antonio Guerrero and his wife, named lady Josepa Maria Villalobos, who is also a resident of this town San Gabriel Cholula. The price of the land is five *pesos* and four *reales*. I received pure silver. I expressed it before witnesses by means of [the sign of] the precious cross of God, the Holy Cross. We measure the land, it is twenty-five and one quarter *varas* in length and twenty-three *varas* in width. To the east it reaches the road[3] and in the same manner, to the west, it borders [with the land of] a land-seller, named Ana María. And [on the sides] that face Tlaxcallan and Atlixco, this mentioned land likewise [borders] with [the property of] the land seller Ana María.

[It was done] in the presence of witnesses. No one is ever to complain. If the land seller complains, then she will give back all the money and her land will be forfeit. Likewise, [if the buyer complains], the buyer will forfeit her money. It will be brought to the *alcalde* or our priestly rulers—the priest, the vicar—so that they will rectify it. [It is done] in the presence of witnesses: the first one named Antonio Ahuatl, the second named Don Sebastián Yacanextli, the third one named Santana Espinosa. I certify it [with] my name and my signature. We wrote [the document] on Tuesday, the second of January in the year 1695.

Witness witness

witness Santana Espinosa

Juan de los Santos, former notary of the municipal council

This land sale document is part of the holdings of the Municipal Archive of the town of San Juan Ixtenco, Tlaxcala. We do not know how a document from Cholula, almost sixty kilometers away, made its way to the predominantly

3 Literally, 'the road is its border'.

Otomi-speaking Ixtenco, but it might have been through family connections between the members of the nobility of the two places. The female seller, Ana María Ahuatl, a commoner living in the town of San Juan Tenaquiyahuac belonging to the jurisdiction of the city of San Gabriel Cholula, tells the story of a parcel of land on the corner of a house, probably her own, given the fact that, according to the description, the land that she was selling bordered on two sides with her other properties. On his deathbed, her father, Diego Jimenez Ahuatl, left this plot to her older brother named Diego Pablo Ahuatl. He, in turn, bequeathed it to his sister Ana María in a formal will. Since she did not have any money for his burial, Ana María Ahuatl decided to sell this piece of land in order to generate the necessary funds. The buyers are presented as Antonio Guerrero and his wife, named Josepa María Villalobos, both residents of San Gabriel Cholula. They are introduced with the title of *señor* 'lord' and *señora* 'lady', which in native documents is rather unusual, even for the highest members of the indigenous nobility, who are usually addressed with *don* and *doña*. These titles are often used in reference to Spaniards, which strongly implies that the couple could have been of non-native origin. Spanish women especially were addressed in Nahuatl documents as *xinola* (a phonetic adaptation of *señora*) and this term survives to this day in many Nahua communities in reference to non-indigenous women. However, considering the relatively late date of the document, it is also possible that the titles, which originally applied to Spaniards, were used here as a prestigious appellation for the high-ranking members of native (or perhaps *mestizo*) members of the local society. According to Lockhart, in the latter part of the colonial period an alternative title for an indigenous ruler or a member of the highest-ranking nobility, usually referred to as *cacique*, was also *señor* (Lockhart 1992: 133). In the case of our document, the buyers had the means and will to invest in land purchases, and the fact that the seller was apparently under pressure to raise funds provided them with a good opportunity. On the day of January 2, 1695, the seller confirmed receipt of five and a half *pesos* in pure silver; the land was measured in the presence of the three witnesses and all necessary legal formulas were invoked. Interestingly, the notary referred to himself as a former notary of the municipal council, which means he no longer held this office, but was nonetheless performing the job for the community members on a permanent basis.

The orthographic conventions are typical for the period and pretty much consistent throughout the document. The letter *s* is used to express a voiceless alveolar sibilant [s]. In one case, with the loanword *henero* (from Spanish *enero*), a hypercorrection *h* precedes the word's initial vowel, a feature often seen in early- and mid-colonial writing by indigenous authors. On the phonotactic level, the consonant cluster composed of [r] and [b] in the word *Gabriel*, each element of which was absent from the Nahuatl phonetic repertoire and, taken as a word-internal cluster, would have been very difficult for a Nahuatl speaker to enunciate, was made more easily pronounceable by moving the [r] before the preceding vowel in order to create a word-initial cluster: *Grabiel*. In fact, this reinterpretation of the name *Gabriel* is widespread in the documents from Ixtenco (where the Cholula document is presently held) from the mid- and late-colonial period, and is used by some native speakers of Mexican Spanish today.

Borrowings from Spanish are not numerous, considering the date of the document. Typical loanwords include legal and administrative terms (*justicia*, *testamento*, *testigo*, *ciudad*), offices (*alcaldes*, *escribano*, *cura*, *vicario*), and monetary and measurement units (*peso*, *real*, *vara*, *quarta*, calendar terms). *Tomin*, originally borrowed with the meaning of a *real*, or one-eighth of a *peso*, and quickly adopting the meaning of "a coin," is already here being used with the extended meaning of money in general, which prevails in Nahuatl to this day. An interesting feature are the doublets that, drawing on traditional native rhetoric, are applied to Spanish terms. Thus, the judiciary office of a municipal *alcalde* is referred to as *justisia alcalde*, while priests are addressed as *toteopixcatlahtohcahuan Cura Bicario* 'our priestly rulers, priest, vicar', where *cura vicario* is a juxtaposition of two Spanish terms referring to a priest, functioning almost as a blend. This blend, or at least a doublet, is paired with and explained by the native neologism—*teopixcatlahtohcahuan*—forming an initial part of the complex doublet or triplet. The document also reveals an example of a lexical-structural calque in the usage of the particle *auh*, in traditional Nahuatl meaning 'and' and 'but' and always used in an utterance-initial position (beginning a new clause). Here it seems to be equated with the Spanish *y* 'and' as a conjunction instead of the word *ihuan* traditionally used in this function: *Antonio gerero* ***auh*** *[i]namic ytoCa Señora Jusepa maria BillaloBos* 'Antonio Guerrero **and** his wife named lady Josepa María Villalobos'. This adaptation implies that a native particle had been reinterpreted on the basis of the Spanish usage of the conjunction, the semantic field, and grammatical functions that partly coincided with that of the native term. Another example of a lexical-structural calque is the use of the verb *piya* throughout the document, the meaning of which had already started to extend in the sixteenth century to copying the Spanish verb *tener* 'to have'. But these new semantic and structural functions overlapped with the traditional meaning 'to keep' and 'to guard', sometimes making it difficult to determine in practice whether an older or more recent meaning was being implied, especially since 'to hold' was also one of the traditional meanings of *tener* at the time of contact. In the Cholula land sale document, however, *piya* is employed not only to refer to the possession of land (where the meaning of the verb could be ambivalent), but also for dimensions and measurements following the Spanish model. This pattern of use leaves no doubt that by the time this document was made, *piya* had already acquired and deeply assimilated typical semantic and grammatical functions of the verb *tener*.

DOCUMENT 10

Dispute over Land Inheritance, Tlaxcala, Mexico, 1706[1]

JOHN SULLIVAN

[Fol. 1r]

En la mui ynsigne y noBle leal
Ciu^{d} tlax,^{an} ynic senpoalli yhuan
chiquasentonalli mani metztli de
febrero de mil cetecientos y seis años
d,^{n} Pasqual Ramires jues go,^{or} ypan
xihuitl de setecientos y sinco an:^{os}
ytlatocaixpantzinco oquihualnextique
se testamento yn ixhuihuan Ju,^{o}
Pasqual catca auh yhuan ce escrip^{a} ic
otlalcouhtehuac intachtoncol ocatca Ju,^{o}
chicuatototl = auh in tlalli quitenehua
mani santa m,^{a} quauhostotitlan auh
in yehuatzin omoteneuh d^{n} pasqual
Ramires san ic oquimotili in escrip,^{a}
motlanahuatilia ma in onpa teniente
ju,^{o} pacheco ixpan yhuan ome noso yei
testigos quimoxelhuisque in motenehua
ixhuihuan ju^{o} pasqual catca auh ye
in tlalli chico quitoa in quesquime
teixhuihuan necoc ayac mochicomatis.
huel qualli xiquintlaxelhuili n titeniente.
= auh in tlen ticchihuas titechmacas
cuenta ca iuhqui timitznahuatia

In the very notable and noble, loyal city of Tlaxcallan on February 26, 1706. In the year 1705, the grandchildren of the deceased Juan Pascual came and exhibited a will in the rulerly presence of judge-governor Don Pascual Ramírez, as well as a document by which their deceased great grandfather, Juan Chicuatototl, bought some land before he died. The land it mentions lies in Santa María Cuauhoztotitlan. As soon as the aforementioned Pascual Ramírez saw the document, he ordered that the aforementioned grandchildren of the deceased Juan Pascual distribute the land among themselves, in the presence of the deputy, Juan Pacheco, and two or three witnesses: "All of the grandchildren argue among themselves about this land. Let no one have any doubts (about this). Distribute things among them very well, deputy, and inform us of whatever you do. Thus we order you, in the name of

1 Archivo Histórico del Estado de Tlaxcala (AHET), 1706, caja 14, exp. 5.

DOI: 10.5876/9781607328346.c010

yhuan no iuh quimoneltililia in motenehua testamento yca yn itocatzi in tohueitlatocatzi Rey su mag,[d] ticaprobaroa yhuan ticconfirmaroa in tlen ye iuhqui quenami catqui yn amo aquin quenmanian quinequis quixitinis, yhuan tictlalia ynin auto decreto judicial ynic semicac neltis mopias ynin escrip,[a] testamento yhuan no titlanahuatia yn aquique quimopialitasque ynin tlatocatequitzin in Rey su Mag,[d] ma [Fol. 1v] = ma iuh semicac quinmopalehuilitasque yhuan quimoneltililisq̃ ynin omoteneuhqueh amame = auh ynic nelli nitlanahuatia yhuan nimofirmatia nican sala de cauildo

our great ruler His Majesty the King, to approve and confirm things just as they are, just as the aforementioned will stipulates. No one will ever attempt to undo it. And we file this judicial order so that this testamentary document will forever be valid and in force. We also enjoin those who hold this rulerly office for His Majesty the King in the future to always continue helping [the grandchildren] and to ratify these aforementioned documents. In order to issue my ruling legitimately, I place my signature, here in the municipal council chambers."

v d[n] pAsQual Ramires [*signature*]

Don Pascual Ramírez [*signature*]

Nixpan

Before me,

d[n] diego de torres ess[te] de cauildo [*signature*]

Don Diego Torres, municipal council notary [*signature*]

[Fol. 3r]

\+ v Yca yn itocatzin yn dios tetatzin yhuan yn dios ypiltzin yhuan yn dios espi~~tzin~~ ritu santo yei teotlacacatzitzinti ca sa se huel neli teotl dios ma quimatican yn ixquichtin quitasque yn nomemoria testamento yn nehuatl notoca Juan pascual nican nichane santa M[ra], Quaostotitlan ypan nipoi in tlatocacabesera quiahuistlan yn axcan ~~ypan~~ Nopan asico yn itetlasotlalitzin yn tt[o] dios huel Mococoa yn notlalo yn nosoquio ahu manel mococoa yn notlalo yn nosoquio huel pactica yn noAnimatzin Ahu intla mostla huiptla nitlanahuis Nicmocahuilitehua yn noalbasea d,[n] Juan de los santos chane san fran[co] Mitepec nopan Motlatoltis ynic nitoctos yn itech yteopancaltzin yn notlasonantzin sihuapili santa maria teopancalitec y nopan motlatoltisque yn nopilhuantzitzihuan Ahu in notlamanaltzin mochihuas nahui tomin ma yhuqui nopan motlatoltisque

\+ "In the name of God the Father, God the Son, and God the Holy Spirit, three holy persons and only one absolutely true God, may all those who see my will, know that my name is Juan Pascual, I am a resident of Santa María Cuauhoztotitlan and I belong to the rulerly head town of Quiyahuiztlan. Now, my time has come,[2] my earthly body is sick. But even though my earthly body is sick, my soul is completely sound. If at some point my state should worsen, I leave my executor, Don Juan de los Santos, resident of San Francisco Mitepec, with the responsibility of seeing that I be buried next to the church of my Precious Mother, the Lady Saint Mary. My children will be responsible for matters inside the church. My offering will be four *tomines*; let them handle this for me."

2 Literally, "Now, our lord God's precious love has befallen me."

v oquito yn cocoxqui juan pascual Niquinpia nopilhuan oc achton oniquipix se itoca Maria salomen yn ocse ytoca melchora maria niquinmacatehua yn innemac ma yehuatzin yonictenehu noalbasea quinmoxexelhuilis yn oniquitenehu nopilhuan oc achto

The sick person, Juan Pascual, said, "I have children: the first one that I had is named María Salomé; another is named Melchora María. I bequeath them their inheritance. May my aforementioned executor distribute it to each of my aforementioned eldest children."

v oquito yn cocoxqui ocse nicpia nopiltzin ytoca sebastian ernandes yonicmacac ynn inemac aocmo tlen quimitlanilis yn ocsequin nopilhuan Amo quinnetequipacholmacas yntla mostla huiptla huamoquepa

The sick person said, "I have another child named Sebastián Hernández. I have already given him his inheritence. He will ask for nothing more from my other children; if he should come back at some point, he is not to importune them."

[Fol. 3v]

+ v oquito yn cocoxqui nicpia nonamic ytoca ysabel M_^{ra} yhuan yn nopilhuan yeyme sihuatzitzintin se itoca micaela maria yn ocse itoca fan^{ca} maria yn ocse itoca mariana niquincahuilitehua . yn noxacaltzitzinhuan maquili yhuan yn tlali ypan ca y. caltzitzintin ye n mecatl ytlacohual yn nococoltzin ocatca quipia yn nopilhuan yn tlalnamaquilisamatl motocayotia escrituradebenta ca oncan ~~yehuatzin~~ quimoyeyecahuilis yn noalbasea ycuac quintlaxexelhuis yn nopilhuan

+ The sick person said, "I have my wife, whose name is Isabel María, and my children, three daughters: one is named Micaela María; another is named Francisca María; and another is named Mariana. I bequeath them my five small huts and the land upon which they stand. The small houses, together in a row,[3] were the purchased property of my deceased grandfather. My children have the land sale document, which is called a bill of sale. My executor will evaluate the property carefully when he distributes it to my children."

v oquito yn cocoxqui ocse nicpia notlalcoal teopancalquitlapan nicmacatehua yn nonamic ysabel Maria yc motequipanos Ahu in yn tlalnamaquilisamatl quipia yn onictenehu nonamic ahu in yc huecapan yn tlali yepoali yhuan matlactli nehuitziantli Ahu in ynic patlahuac senpoali yhuan matlactli nehuitziantli contepanoa yn iquisallan tonali yn d^{n}, Mateo de los santos Ahu in yn icalaquian tonali san no ye in tlalcoqui quitepanoa Ahu

The sick person said, "I have more purchased land in back of the church.[4] I bequeath it to my wife, Isabel María, for whom it will be worked. My aforementioned wife has the land sale document. The length of the land is seventy *nehuitzantli*.[5] Its width is thirty *nehuitzantli*. It borders to the east with [the land of] Don Mateo de los Santos. And to the west it borders with [the land of] the very same land buyer. And toward Ahuizco it borders with the very same

3 Perhaps this sequence is *ye (i)n mecatl* but the meaning is not clear. It could refer to the fact that these rooms are strung together in a row, or that the parcel of land on which they stand is long and narrow.

4 "Teopancalcuitlapan" could also be a place name.

5 Unit of land measurement; see the glossary.

in yc ahuiscohuic contepanoa san no ye in tlalnamacani Joseph lis Ahu in yc coliuhcahuic san no nehuatl yn nechtepanohua ma semica quimopialis yn onictenehu tlacpac nonamic ayac aquin quiquilis ma ipan motlatoltis yn noalbasea

land seller, Joseph Luis. And toward Coliuhcan, it borders with my [own land]. May my wife, mentioned above, always have it. No one is to take it from her. May my executor be responsible for this."

[Fol. 4r]

+ v oquito yn cocoxqui ocsentetl nicpia notlal onechmocahuilitehuac yn notatzin ocatca quipia yn caxtiltecatl Agustin de Rocha niquin~~pi~~cahuilitehua yn nopilhuan ca yehuan quimati yn tlen quichihuilisque ca oncan nicpia yn escrituradeBenta ynic oquimocohuilitehuac yn nococoltzin ocatca ma quinmopalehuilis in onictenehu noalbasea

+ The sick person said, "I have another plot of land that my deceased father bequeathed to me. The Spaniard, Agustín de Rocha has custody of it. I bequeath it to my children. They know what to do about it, for I have the bill of sale with which my deceased grandfather bought it before his death. May my aforementioned executor help them."

v oquito yn cocoxqui nechhuiquilia nahui peso yn caxtiltecatl felipe Juares ma quitlanisque yn nopilhuan yehuan quimati

The sick person said, "The Spaniard, Felipe Juárez, owes me four *pesos*. My children are to request it from him. They know what to do."

v San yxquich yn itlatol yn cocoxqui amo ocsequi quilcahua yhuan yn nehuatl niescribano huel ytenco onitlacac yn cocoxqui amo ocsequi onictlapihui nose amo onictzinquixti san yn tlen onechylhuita ahu in yn neli melahua ynic nitlaneltilia tictlalia yn totoca yn tofirma yhuan yn nehuatl niteniente nixpan yhuan yxpan testigos noschtin omotocayotique ynic titlaneltilia yhuan tilalia in tonali martes ic mopa[6] se tonali marso ipan xihuitl 606 a^{os}

This is all that the sick person declared; there is nothing more that he has forgotten. I, the notary, was right next to the sick person listening to everything. I have not added nor excluded anything. It is only what he was telling me. I truly and correctly performed the validation. We put our names and signatures. Before me, the deputy and in the presence of all of the named witnesses. In this way we performed the validation. And we put the date, Tuesday, on the first day of March, in the year 1606.

+ testigo Joseph lorenso

+ witness Joseph Lorenzo

+ Juan de santiago tiniente [*signature*]

+ Juan de Santiago, deputy [*signature*]

+ Esteban ernandes

+ Esteban Hernández

+ Josep de soto [*signature*]

+ Joseph de Soto [*signature*]

Nixpan + d^{n} diego de los santos esribano Nonbrado [*signature*]

Before me, + Don Diego de los Santos, appointed notary [*signature*]

---

6 This is probably *ompa*.

[Fol. 4v]

+ v oquito yn cocoxqui oniquilhui yn escribano oniquilcau ca yca yn amame nechinpilia yn d^{n}, pascual Belasco nicmonahuatilia yn noalbasea quinmitlanilis yonicmacac matlactomin yc quintemacas ma yhuqui quinmopalehuilis yn nopilhuan yn onictenehu noalbasea	+ The sick person said, "I told the notary I forgot about the documents Don Pascual Velasco is keeping for me; I order my executor to ask for them. I already gave him ten *tomines*; my aforementioned executor will distribute the money for the benefit of my children."

In the city of Tlaxcala, sometime in the year 1705, a group of petitioners involved in a dispute over the distribution of some land, originally purchased by their great, great grandfather, Juan Chicuatototl, presented the will of their deceased grandfather, Juan Pascual, to the judge-governor of the city of Tlaxcala, Don Pascual Ramírez. On February 26 of the following year, the municipal notary, Don Diego Torres, prepared the manuscript, which is the subject of this study, documenting the corresponding mediation process ordered by the judge-governor and including a copy of the aforementioned testament. In all likelihood, the petitioners were members of the lower nobility, who could trace their lineage back at least six generations (neither their grandfather nor their great, great grandfather's name appears in the document with the title of *don*, used only by *teteuctin*). They appealed to Don Pascual Ramírez, one of the *tlahtoani* of the Tlaxcalan confederation of *altepetl*, holding the office of *alcalde* or judge on the municipal council. By all accounts, in 1706 the Tlaxcalan high nobility appears to be exercising the same judicial functions through the indigenous *cabildo* that they did at the time of the institution's inception before the middle of the sixteenth century.

We do not know which of the testator's grandchildren were involved in the conflict, but the will itself provides a number of clues regarding its possible nature. The testator had six children and a wife, but these are divided into two groups. The first consists of three children: two women, María Salomé and Melchora María, and one man, Sebastián Hernández; all are probably children of an earlier marriage of the testator, and their mother is not mentioned. The will states that the three have already received their inheritance, but does not specify what it is. This practice is sometimes reflected in Nahuatl documents, in cases where some family members had already received their inheritance while the testator was still alive (see Document 19). The son, Sebastián, is said to have left Tlaxcala, and is cautioned not to bother his siblings with further claims of inheritance. The second group consists of the testator's wife,

Isabel María, and their three daughters, Micaela María, Francisca María and Mariana. All four receive bequests of land purchased by the testator's grandfather, Juan Chicuatototl, and these are backed up by the original bills of sale. There is a further amount of purchased land, currently being worked by a Spaniard, that is to be divided up between the children, although no further details are given. So for starters, we have possibly two households, each of which has received inheritance under different proceedures, an absent and possibly contentious heir, and a general lack of specificity regarding the distribution of the inheritance.

Whenever land was bequeathed in a Nahua will, its type, location, and measurements were usually specified with precision, and if it contained buildings, these were mentioned. Of all the land mentioned in this document, only one parcel complies completely with this norm. The purchased land that the testator left to his wife was located behind the church; it measured seventy by thirty *nehuitzantli*; the parcels with which it bordered on all four sides were mentioned, along with their owners; and the borders were identified with the traditional formulas: east and west were associated with the rising and setting of the sun; north and south were indicated by mentioning two other *altepetl* that lay in each of these directions. Interestingly, two of the bordering parcels belonged to the testator, but we do not know if these correspond to the other ambiguously mentioned bequests in the will. In short, this is not a typical Nahua will, detailed and explicit, the purpose of which was to preclude conflicts like the one that produced this document.

Linguistically, this document needs to be divided into the introductory section, written in 1706 and dealing with the mediation process, and the copy of the testament from 1606. The former contains many language-contact phenomena typical of Lockhart's Stage 3. The process by which Spanish transitive verbs enter Nahuatl—consisting of converting the Spanish verb into an unattested noun, to which is initially added the Nahuatl *-ihui* or *-ahui* intransitive verbing suffix, and then the *-oa* causative suffix—appears in the phrase *ticaprobaroa ihuan ticconfirmaroa*[7] 'you [will] approve and confirm [things]'. The inanimate *amatl* 'paper' is pluralized as *amameh* 'documents'. There is an interesting mixed calque: *titechmacaz cuentah* '[you will] inform us'. All legal terminology appears in Spanish: *escriptura* 'document'; *testamento* 'will'; *testigos* 'witnesses'; and *auto decreto judicial* 'judicial order'. The numeral *ce* 'one' is now taking on the function of the article: *ce escripturah* 'a

7 I have standardized the spelling of all citations from the Nahuatl text using the ACK orthography (see Karttunen 1992; Olko and Sullivan 2014; Sullivan et al. 2016).

document'. And yet all in all, the language of this portion of the document is very traditional, including some very interesting features. Noun compounding is used spontaneously: *itlahtohcaixpantzinco* 'in his rulerly presence'. The second person singular subject prefix is used with a Spanish noun in direct address: *huel qualli xiquintlaxelhuili [y]n titeniente* 'distribute things among them very well, [you] deputy'. The only Spanish particle appearing in the document is *de* 'of', and it is only used in the opening and closing formulae. The testament copy is a typical Stage 2 document. It contains administrative, religious, and temporal loanwords: *testigos* 'witnesses', *teniente* 'deputy', *escribanō nombrado* 'appointed notary', *peso* 'peso', *años* 'years', *dios* 'god', and *espíritu santo* 'holy spirit'. Some of these nouns take the Nahuatl subject and possessor prefixes: *niescribano* 'I, the notary', *noalbaceah* 'my executor', and *noanimahtzin* 'my soul'. There is one instance of bilingual compounding or blending: *tlahtohcācabecerah* 'rulerly head town', and another of a common bilingual doublet, *in totocah in tofirmah* 'our names and signatures'. There are two cases in which Spanish concepts are stated and then further explained. In the first case, the Spanish phrase, *escritura de venta* 'bill of sale' is reanalyzed as one word and explained in Nahuatl: *in tlalnamaquilizamatl motocayotia escrituradebenta* 'the land sale document, which is called a bill of sale'. The second consists of two words: *nomemoriah testamento* 'my account, the will'. *Testamento* is probably referring to the specific subgenre of wills within the larger genre of accounts, which has the prefixed Nahuatl possessor *no-* 'my'. There are some surprising language phenomena in this document. In *noxahcaltzitzihuan macuilli* 'my five small huts' the inanimate *xahcalli* 'hut' is pluralized, but the number five, *macuilli*, remains in the singular. In the phrase, *amameh nechinpilia* 'the documents [he] is keeping for me', *amatl* 'paper' is pluralized in the same way as in the 1706 document; however, it also serves as the referent for one of the two objects of the applicative verb *nechinpilia* 'he is keeping them for me'. The object prefix that refers here to "documents" is the seldom-seen *-im-/-in-*, which is only used for a third person plural specific object when a verb has two specific objects. There are what appear to be two very early attestations of fusion of the particle *ye* 'already' and the antecessive preclitic *-o* that is so common in Tlaxcalan Nahuatl today: *yonicteneuh* 'I already mentioned [it]', and *yonicmacac* 'I already gave [them to him]'. And finally, *teotlacacatzitzintin* 'holy persons' seems to have a reduplicated form of *tlacatl* 'person'; this is either a scribal error for *tlatlaca-* or a heretofore unattested plural form of the noun.

DOCUMENT 11

Dispute over Land Inheritance, San Juan Ixtenco, Mexico, 1758[1]

JUSTYNA OLKO AND JOHN SULLIVAN

YPan ynin Altepel S.^{n} Jũ^{o} Yxtenco ca yc mactlactlonse de Abril xihuil de m̄il setesientos y sinquenta y ocho Cabd̄o yxpantzinco ne nithe^{e}. notoca Antto Xabier yhuan yxpan no Alhuasil Mayor fran^{co} Pe^{o} yhuan no ixpan niess.^{no} de Cabildo omoyxpantico yn Sebastiana M.ª Ynamic Jp̄h Antto yxpotzin yn Nicolas Antt.^{o} axto ynamic ocacca y^{n} Rosa M^{a} ytexpa se xolal oquicahuili yn inamic axca ynahuac omocahua yn omoteneuh nooxpox Sebastiana ca ma quimomase[2] yn tlen yaxca ytatzin yo omoteneuc sanno yhuan ome calme sacal ytex mocahua yn omoteneuh Sebastiana yhuan quiqui[c] quitepequili chiquasen mayl nahui ynahuac yn Fran^{co} Manuel yhuan ome aca oc sequin mitlanique aca saso quimotehuiquilia yhuan tlaco mecal tlali mantica xolaltenco ye quisa yn

In this *altepetl* of San Juan Ixtenco, on the eleventh of April in the year 1758, Sebastiana María, daughter of Nicolás Antonio and wife of José Antonio, whose first spouse was the late Rosa María, came and appeared before the town council, me, the deputy [governor] named Antonio Xavier, and also before the chief constable Francisco Pérez and also before me, the town council notary, in relation to a house lot that her husband left to her. Now it has been left to my aforementioned daughter, Sebastiana. Let her inherit what was the property of her aforementioned father. Likewise two huts are left with the aforementioned Sebastiana. And she seized, she took for herself [the field that is] six *maitl* [long], four [*maitl* wide] next to [the field of] Francisco Manuel. And then another two

1 Archivo Parroquial, San Juan Ixtenco, Tlaxcala.

2 This is probably a reduced form of the verb *mahcehua* 'to obtain or deserve something', although technically, as a class 2 verb, it should not reduce in the optative mode.

 DOI: 10.5876/9781607328346.c011

tonali yq^{co}[3] fran^{co} mati.[^{s}] yc calaquia yn tonali yq^{co} Pe^{o} lorenso yc quamancohui[c] yquentenco Agustin Benito ic San Pablo yquentenco Jph Antt^{o} yc tlami nauhtepantli

people were asked if she is indebted to anyone at all [for this land]. And a half of a *mecal*[4] of land is located in Xolaltenco. To the east [it borders with] the field of Francisco Matías, to the west [it borders with] the field of Pedro Lorenzo, toward Huamantla with the field of Agustín Benito, toward San Pablo with the field of Joseph Antonio, and thus end its four sides.

yhuan yei s^{to} de Bulto s.^{n} Nicolas s^{n} Antt^{o} yhuan s^{ta} ynes = yhuan yn xolal yc quisa yn tonali yquentenco Mig^{l} mati^{s} yc calaquia ycuen^{co} sa ye yn octlica yc quamancohui[c] yq^{co} Ju^{o} mendes yc san pablo yq^{co} Ju^{o} sebastian yc tlami nauctepantli = sanno yhuan oc tlacomecal tlali amo huel asitica san onicmasce ne sebastiana maria Ca ma quesqui tonali quimopielis noahuitzin yc panos yntla queman quichihuati yn ytestamento yn omotheneuh Jph^{a} Maria ocsepa mocuepas yn tlali ne nonahuac sebastiana M.^{a} ynin tlali oquimese y notatzin ytex nositzin ocacca ynes maria yhuan nitlapalehuis yca yn s^{o} s^{n}. Mig^{l} ome tomi tlapalehuis yca yn s^{n} lasaro moconcahuisque[5] yhuan yhuan yn s^{n} Pedro san no yhuan ytex mocahua yca ne nictlaxtlahuas sebastiana M^{a} ynin tlali onictenuac amo huel asitica yc quisa yn tonali yque^{co} grabiel de la Cruz yc calaquia yn tonali yquentenco

And three saints [carved] in the round: San Nicolás, San Antonio, and Santa Inés. And a house lot [that borders] to the east with the field of Miguel Matías, and to the west [it] just [borders] with the road, and toward Huamantla [it borders with] the field of Juan Mendez; toward San Pablo with the field of Juan Sebastián; thus end its four sides. "Likewise, I, Sebastiana María, just inherited another piece of land not reaching half of a *mecal*.[6] How long will my aunt yet keep it? The way it will happen [is that] when the aforementioned Josepha María winds up making her will, the land will be again returned to me, Sebastiana María. My father inherited this land from my late grandmother Inés María. I will help with [the maintenance of the image of] the saint San Miguel with two *reales*, which will [also] help with San Lázaro: they will share it. And, the same [amount] is to be left for San Pedro. I,

3 Abbreviation for *icuenco* 'on or at his or her field'; from the third person singular possessor *i-*, *cuemitl* 'field', and the relational word *-co* 'in, on, at'.

4 This word *mecal*, or *mecalli*, also appears in Document 11 (San Luis Chalco Tlamanalco) of this anthology, and does not appear defined or discussed in any works that we are aware of. It seems to be a long, narrow piece of land with somewhat standard measurements in length and width.

5 Here, the benefactive verb *cahuia* 'to leave something for someone', along with its third person singular specific object prefix *c-* and its outbound directional prefix *on-*, have been reanalyzed as a new verb root *concahuia*, with the same meaning as the original verb. It is then conjugated in the future with the third person singular subject *Ø-* and with the third person reflexive prefix *mo-*.

6 It is also possible that the expression 'not quite reaching [sth]' does not refer to the size of this field, but was part of spontaneous speech and was meant to specify the location, and the speaker then changed the focus of the utterance.

Ju° SanChes yc huamanco yq^{co}- Fra^{co} martin yc san Pablo yc sa ye yn atlaco yc tlami nauetepantli = san no yhuan noyolocacopa nitemaca notlahtol ne sebastiana M^{a}, yca nictlalpachos yn noNantzi Jp̄ha M^{a}. yca misa bigilia yhuan Responso yca nochi maquili p^{s} yhuan ome tomi sa ye: yn Ma. fran^{ca} tlapalehuis yca se Responso y Manuela sanno tlapalehuis yca se Responso ynin ytlanequilistica: yhuan axca yomoyectlali quayotica yn quenami D^{s}. otlanahuati sano yhuan omoyecxexo[7] yn ocse xolal tlaco oconana yn M^{a}. fran^{ca} yhuan oc tlaco oconana yn Manuela M^{a} ynin omoyecxeloc ypanpa amo ocacca testameto axca oquimoyecmasehuiqui yn topilhuan yca grasia yhuan Donasion axcan yhuan semiuccac niquinmoaxcatia ca niman axca oniquinmomaquili yn posesion yca yahuto Judisial ytexpa ynin mopenatia ca amo mostla huitla aca quiaccomanas quimacas netequipapachol yn omoteneuh chane ytla aca colinis tlahtol quixtlahuas pena caxtoli p^{s} yhuan motlatzaquiltis yhuan ynin tlaquiloli nesis campa saso mocaquis yhuan timofirmatia ytex ynin Cabildo tlacpac omoteneuh etc^{a}

Antt° xabier The^{e} de Gov^{or}
[*signature*]

Jp̄h Martin
[*signature*]

Sebastiana María, will pay for it with the land I mentioned. Toward the east it does not quite reach the field of Gabriel de la Cruz, to the west [it borders with] the field of Juan Sánchez, toward Huamantla [with] the field of Francisco Martín, and [toward] San Pablo it just [borders] with a ravine. Thus end its four sides. Likewise, I, Sebastiana María, sincerely give my word that with [the income from the land] I will bury my mother Josefa María with a vigil mass and responses for the dead. In total, it will be five *pesos* and two *reales*; that's all. In the same way, María Francisca is to help with responses, and Manuela will likewise voluntarily help with responses. And today it was set right, in a good way, just as God ordered. Likewise, another house lot was correctly divided: María Francisca has taken one half; Manuela María has taken the second half. This was correctly divided because there was no will. Today our children inherited it correctly with favor and generosity. Now and forever I endow them with the property because today I have granted them possession with a legal order." Punishment will be levied in regards to this [order], for never will anyone in the future disturb or cause distress for the aforementioned citizen [Sebastiana María]. If someone goes back on their word, they will pay the fine of fifteen *pesos* and will be arrested. And this document is to be disseminated wherever it will be heard. And we put our signatures in the presence of the above-mentioned municipal council, etc.

Antonio Javier, deputy governor
[*signature*]

Joseph Martín
[*signature*]

7 It should read *omoyecxelo*.

fran^{co} Pe^{o} alguasil May^{or} [*signature*]	Francisco Pedro, chief constable [*signature*]
Diego Ber^{no} testigo [*signature*]	Diego Bernardino, witness [*signature*]
Jua^{o} Ber^{o} testigo [*signature*]	Juan Bernardino, witness [*signature*]
Ju^{o} sebastian testigo [*signature*]	Juan Sebastián, witness [*signature*]
yxpan Mig^{l} de los s^{tos} Cortes ess^{no} [*signature*]	In the presence of Miguel de los Santos Cortés, notary [*signature*]

JUSTYNA OLKO

The form and content of this document, made in San Juan Ixtenco, Tlaxcala, in 1758, is not very common. Confronted with the lack of a valid testament, the heir Sebastiana María appears before the municipal council of the town of Ixtenco, represented in the document by the deputy governor and chief constable and accompanied by a notary, who resolve the issue. The purpose of her appearance is to take legal possession of a property bequeathed to her by her father, including wooden images of the saints Nicolás, Antonio, and Inés, carved in the round (*santos de bulto*) and several pieces of land, the most important of which is a house lot that Sebastiana María's father received from his first spouse. Among the other parcels, there is also a field kept by her aunt. Sebastiana María demands to have it back and goes on to clarify that this land was inherited by her father from her grandmother. She adds that when her own mother, Josepha María, makes her will, the land in question will be immediately restored to her, Sebastiana María. This suggests that her father, from whom the whole inheritance was drawn, is no longer living. He is not explicitly referred to as dead in the text, but his first wife is, because she has *ocatca* 'late' next to her name.

The document is characterized by an abundance of direct discourse. After the initial presentation of the case, made in the first person by the deputy governor of Ixtenco, Antonio Javier, the speaker is switched to one of the parents of the claimant, since Sebastiana María is referred to here as *nooxpox* [for *nochpoch*] 'my daughter'. With all probability this voice belongs to her mother, who is likely either on her deathbed or at least very sick, and this condition is probably what motivated the legal procedure by her daughter, whose inheritance was not properly secured. Sebastiana María says that if her mother makes her will, she will have no problem claiming back the field to which she was entitled, and then she commits to paying for the burial of her mother with a vigil mass and responses.

Thus, after the supposed declaration of her sick mother and a detailed description of the properties, Sebastiana María proceeds to speak, voicing her commitment to her mother and to the saints to whom some money will be donated from her property. She also made sure that two other women, probably her sisters, help with the cost of the responses. The next speaker in the document is the deputy governor, who announces that, given the absence of a formal will, another house lot is to be shared by these two women. He concludes by issuing a confirmation, backed by the legal power that he represents, to the effect that the legal situation of the family has been put in order, and that all those entitled to receive property have in fact received it. Interestingly, he refers to these people as *topilhuan* 'our children', drawing on the traditional preconquest conceptual terminology by which a ruler addresses his subjects as his "children," thus transmitting his words and wisdom to them (Madajczak 2015). The entire construction of the document reflects the multivoice dynamics of the process of the production of a legal text, and consists of a constant switching of voices between the protagonists involved in issuing declarations or providing explanations. As such, it sheds light on an inherently native way of expression, typical for literary creations that contain a large amount of orality: it permeates even written legal records where one would expect rigid and standardized formulas and descriptions. The resulting fluidity in a changing order of speakers may sometimes be difficult to follow, but it gives us a good idea how the whole investigation and procedure was carried out. Whereas this characteristic is quite often found in early colonial documents, here it stands out as the essential feature of a local eighteenth-century text, by no means standardized according to the norms of Spanish legal genres.

Another issue worth mentioning is the promise made by the heir to provide offerings to the saints Miguel, Lázaro, and Pedro, that would be taken from the agricultural production of the land she inherits. The fact that these commitments are practically inserted within the descriptions of the pieces of land to be taken over by Sebastiana María implies that these were patron saints ascribed to particular fields and whose cult, feasts, or images were maintained by these same fields, an arrangement widely attested in Nahua communities across the colonial period (e.g., Lockhart 1992: 546–567). What is even more interesting, however, is that San Miguel and San Lázaro are to share the two *reales* promised to them: Sebastiana María employs an expression *concahuisque*, which in testaments often referred to two family members who were to share a joint inheritance. This detail offers a glimpse into the ontology of Nahua culture: saints are considered real protagonists, not only in individual or family life, but also on the legal stage, enjoying the same status as other beneficiaries mentioned in legal documents. They are to share the donation as real, living persons and members of a family.

At the orthographic level, this document reveals roughly consistent local scribal conventions. The letter *s* is often used for the phoneme [s], and a single *l* is employed for a double [ll] cluster. Priority is given to the rendering of phonetic pronunciation, as in writing *ocacca* for *ocatca*, marking the recessive assimilation of [t] toward [k]. Spanish impact on Nahuatl here is not very striking: loanwords are limited to specialized religious and legal vocabulary, and borrowed verbs are missing, but the usage of the pluralized inanimate noun *calli* in *ome calme* 'two houses' speaks to the increasing structural influence of the Spanish pattern. This is the only pluralized inanimate noun in the entire text but there are other examples of early pluralization of this specific noun in Tlaxcalan Nahuatl. There is also evidence of two steps in the process of conversion of the particle *ye* 'already', which traditionally preceded a preterite verb, into a preclitic, which then fused with the antecessive *o,* itself also on the way to becoming a preclitic. In the first step, *ye* and *o* fuse in *yo omoteneuc* 'already mentioned'. In the second step, they attach to the verb as a compound preclitic in *yomoyectlali* 'already corrected'. This structure is typical of modern Tlaxcalan Nahuatl and, as we can see, was appearing already in eighteenth-century regional Nahuatl.

WILLS

DOCUMENT 12

Testament of Catalina Papan, Tehuitzco, Mexico, 1571[1]

JUSTYNA OLKO

v Ascan lunes . x . dias . de deçiembre . de mill . y qui.os y setenta . y vn años . Yn nehuatl . catalinan . papan . nochan . tehuitzco . Ca nicnoneltoquitia in dios . tetatzin . yn dios . tepiltzin . yn dios . Espu. sancto . yn imeistin. personas.me . Ca çan ce huel nelli . dios . ysquich yhuelli . yn oquimochihuilli . yn ilhuicatl . yn tlalticpac . Etc . yn axcan noce.yollocopa . nictlalia . yn carta . testameto . ypanpa . cocoliztli . notech . oquimotlalili.tzino . ỹ notecuiyo . dios . Cenca ninomiquiliznequi . yn iquac . yntla ninomiquiliz . ỹ nanima . Ca ycemactzinco . nicnocahuillia . yn notecuiyo . dios. ypanpa . Ca ipan . ninomiquiliz . in tlaneltoquiliztli . sancta fee catholica . auh ỹ nonacayo . Ca ytic. motocaz. yn tlalli . yn ocan . yn ichanco . noteo . dios .yn iteopanco . Sanc Juan bapa

Today Monday, the tenth day of December of the year 1571, I, Catalina Papan, resident of Tehuitzco, [declare that I] believe in God the Father, God the Son, and God the Holy Spirit, all three persons only one very true God Almighty, who made heaven and earth, etc. Now with all my heart I issue my testament because my Lord God has visited me with an illness. I am about to die. When I pass away, I leave my soul entirely in the hands of my Lord God, for I am to die in the faith, the holy Catholic faith. But my body is to be buried in the earth at the home of God, at the church of Saint John the Baptist.

1 McAfee Collection, 339, UCLA.

DOI: 10.5876/9781607328346.c012

v Ynic centlama[2] . ynic nitlanahuatia . yn iquac . yntla ninomiquiliz. i ps. yc nechmaniliquihui . y huey teopan . cuicanime. y nican nochantzinco . ihua ce tomin . nohuetzin . nicchihua yn itechpatzinco sacta. della velacruz yua . ~~no~~ ii ts°. nohuetzin . nicnomaquilia . nostra . señora . derrosario . yuan . ii ts°. nohuetzin . nicchiua . yn itechcopatzinco . sancto . Comunion . no . yua . ii ts°. nohuetzin . nicchiua yn ichanco . sacto. san franco. no iua ~~iiii~~ ts°. nohuentzin nicchihua yn ichanco . sancto . apostol sanctiago ii[3] ts°. yc motziliniz y campana . yn huey teopan . ii ps . yc ninotocaz yn ocan calitic . yn teopan . yn cani nihuelitiz . auh ynic missa . mayor nopan mitoz . ontetzintli . ocan nichuechiuhtiuh yn ichanco . note°dios . mocahuatiuh ps . xii . inic nicnitlanitiuh . ontetl . missa mayor . yuan . onxihuitl. nocontlalia missa nopan . mitotiaz . cecexihuitl . nicnitlanitiuh . auh in quimocuitlauizque y n.aia . niquimisquetztia[4] . Ju.°pablo . teoyotica tepisqui . yc ome . dı°. de san migl . yniquey . marcos . de san Ju°. ynic nahui tlacatl . domingo . couatl nahuistin . in quimocuitlahuizque yn . aia .

First, I order that when I die one *peso* [will be my offering] so that the singers from the main church will come here to my home to get me; and one *real* will be my offering to [the confraternity of] the Holy True Cross,[5] while two *reales* will be my offering that I give to Our Lady of the Rosary; and I make an offering of two *reales* for the [confraternity of] the Holy Communion; likewise I make my offering of two *reales* for the home of Holy Saint Francis; likewise I make my offering of two *reales* for the home of the Holy Apostle James; two *reales* for the bells to be rung in the main church; two *pesos* so that I will be buried wherever possible inside the main church. And I am making an offering for two high masses to be said for me; twelve *pesos* are to be delivered to the home of my Lord God, for which I request two high masses. And I order masses to be said for me for two years; I request one each year. And as to those who are to look after my soul, I name Juan Pablo, church official; second, Diego de San Miguel; third, Marcos de San Juan; and the fourth person, Domingo Coatl. These are the four who will look after my soul.

auh yn milla mochiuaz çintli yn ocan . yn oniquimmamacac yn nopilhua . yn tlalli . oc ocan quicaz[6] . yn q quicuazque . yn ıtech monequiz . yn nech.tlalilizque . yn missa .

And from the maize that will be produced on the land that I have distributed to my children will additionally come what those who will arrange the masses for me will need to eat.

2 The absolutive ending *-tli* seems to be missing.

3 The numeral is smudged and not very legible; it could very well be *iiii*.

4 The letters *tia* are smudged and not very legible.

5 Literally, *Santa de la Veracruz* would be 'Holy of the True Cross'. This is probably mistaken syntax, given that the name of the confraternity in many other sources is *de la Santa Veracruz* 'of the Holy True Cross'.

6 This should be *quiçaz*, with *ç* instead of *c*, *for* quiza 'to exit [from a place] or to issue [from sth]'.

auh y̑nocuetzin . yhuan . nohuipiltzin . yn oteixtih[7] . monamacaz . auh . yn ipatiuh mochiuaz . yn tsº. yeuatl yc mocohuaz in qualloz [. . .][8] tozino . ynic ninotocaz yuā ontetl . tecomatl . monamacaz . yn ipatiuh yez . tsº. mochi nopan poliviz . yhuā mocohuaz . ~~cayamāço castilla.yeh~~tilmatli . yc niq̃milliuhtiaz . yn iquac . oninomiquilli .

Both my skirt and my shift are to be sold, and with the cash from the transaction, bacon will be bought to be eaten when I am buried. And two jars are to be sold; all of the cash from the transaction will be spent on me: and a cloak[9] will be bought, with which I will be shrouded when I am dead.

v̲ ynic ontlamatli . ynic nitlanahuatia . yn itechcopa . y̑noconetzin yn itoca Juana . franca. nicnomaquilia . x . pˢº . yn tomintzin . yuā nicmaca yn calli [v] yn mexico.pahuic . ytzticac . yuā yn ipan icac yn tlalli . ynic huiyac mactlatlomome quahuitl . yc patlahuac . chicuhcnahui quahuitl . yuā inic occan nicnomaquilia yn tlalli onpa mani . tlacues yquiahuac . chicuhcnauhcuemitl . y̑ tlaltzintli . yniqu escan . in tlalli nicnomaquilia . ynic huiyac . hequahuitl . yc patlauac . cē quahuitl ōcan mani . tlaquilyaualtitlan yescannistin in tlalli . nicnomaquilia yn Juana . fran.ca. yuan cētetl . petlacalli nicmacatiuh . yuā . xicalli . ontetl . yuā tecomatl . hetetl . no nicmaca . yuā . centetl metlatl nicmaca . ytech nicpohua . amo ac quistoquiliz . in Juana . franca

Second, I issue an order concerning my child named Juana Francisca: I give her ten *pesos* in cash, and I give her the house facing toward Mexico and the land on which it is standing, twelve *quahuitl* long and nine *quahuitl* wide. At a second place I give her land outside of Tlacuex, the field is nine furrows. At a third place I give her land three *quahuitl* long and one *quahuitl* wide in Tlaquilyahualtitlan; I give the land at all three places to Juana Francisca. And I am giving her one reed coffer and two gourd vessels; I also give her three jars and I give her one *metate*. I assign it to her; no one is to covet it from Juana Francisca.

v̲ yniquetlamatli . ynic nitlanahuatia. in centetl. tilmatli. yn ōca . yn iq̃c intlacamo neciz . in castilla.ichtilmatli. yeuatl . yc niquimilliuhtiaz. in iquac ninotocaz .

Third, I issue an order: there is a cloak. If at that time a cloak of Spanish cloth cannot be found, I am to go shrouded in it when I am buried.

7 For *onteixtin*. The final *h* probably represents a word-final neutralized *n*.

8 A letter or two here are smudged and illegible.

9 The original phrase, ~~*cayamāço castilla.yeh*~~*tilmatli*, all of which was crossed out except the final morpheme, was a doublet, pairing the Spanish *cañamazo* 'course hemp cloth' (*tela tosca de cáñamo*; DRAE) and the Nahuatl neologism *caxtillanichtilmahtli*, *Ø-caxtillan-ich-tilmah-tli* [SBJ.3SG-Spain-maguey_fiber-blanket-SBS.SG] 'course hemp blanket'.

v̱ ynic nauhtlamatli . ynic nitlanahuatia . ytechcopa . ỹ notelpoch . yn itoca . Joseph . gabriel nicmacatiuh . yn çihuacalli . yn tonatiuh . iquiçayanpa . ytzticac . yuã yn icallalo . mochiuhtica in tlali . ynic patlauac . nahui quahuitl yc huiac matlactli . quauitl . ynic ocã . nicmaca in tlali . hepan temi . ynic patlauac . necoc matlactli . quahuitl . yq̃auac mani antõ quauhtlotlollin yvã imiltitlan . augustin de galinçia omomiquili . chane catca . apçolco . yuã acha . centetl . quaquaohua[10] no nicmacatiuh . yuã tecomatl ontetl no nicmaca . yuan metlatl cẽtetl no nicmaca yuã xicalpechtli . ontetl . nicmaca . yuan casa tepito . cẽtetl . no nicmacatiuh . yxquich in yn itech pouhqui in Joseph gabriel amo ac . quistoquiliz . neltiz . mochiuaz. yuã . v ps̊ . nicmacatiuh yn tomintzin . momacaz . ỹ Joseph . gabriel

Fourth, I issue an order concerning my son named Josef Gabriel. I am giving him a woman-house, facing east, and the land that has become its house-plot, four *quahuitl* wide, ten *quahuitl* long. In a second place I give him the land on which there are three rows of *chinampas*, ten *quahuitl* wide on both sides; it is in front of the house of Antón Quauhtlolin and next to a field(s) of the late Agustín de Galicia whose home was in Apçolco. And I am also giving him an axe with a wooden handle. I also give him two jars and also one *metate* and two gourd bowls. I am also giving him a small chest. All this belongs to Joseph Gabriel, nobody is to covet it from him. This is to be carried out and done. And I am giving him five *pesos* in cash; it will be given to Joseph Gabriel.

v̱ ynic macuillamatli . inic nitlanahuatia . yn itechpa . yn noshuiuhtzin yn itoca fran. co in piltõtli nicmaca . cẽtetl tlaltepoztli . quin iquac quicuiz yn otzõquiz . onxihuitl ỹ nomissa . ỹ notlaocoliloca yez . ysquich in in niquitoua . notlatol . yn ipan notlanahuatil ỹ notestamẽto . amo ac . quixitiniz . amo ac quitlacoz . neltiz mochiuaz . yn imispan onictlalli ỹ namauh . testigusme . diego . de san miguel . miguel pz̃ . barnabe . Juº. pablo . pº. telpochpil —

Fifth, I issue an order concerning my grandchild named Francisco, who is a little child. I give him a hoe; he is to take it later when he has grown. After two years have passed, masses will be celebrated for my benefit. This is all that I have to say in my instructions, my will. No one is to undo it, no one is to vitiate it; it is to be carried out and executed. I have issued my document in the presence of the witnesses, Diego de San Miguel, Miguel Pérez, Barnabé, Juan Pablo, and the youth Pedro.

yṉ ye mochi ts̊ . yn itech ca . testamẽto . ỹ mocenpouah xxxi . ps̊ . v ts̊ . Onicneltilli . amatlacuillo . ambrosion rrapael

I, Ambrosio Rafael, notary, verified it; All the money that is in this will totals thirty-one *pesos* and five *reales*.

. m . d . lxxi años .

The year 1571

10 If we incorporate the noun *quauhyotl* 'an axe or knife handle' [personal communication from Joe Campbell] onto the preterite agentive noun of possession *-huah*, we get *quauhyohuah* '[the axe] has a handle'. The additional *qua-* that appears at the beginning of this word in the text could either be a reduplication, *quahquauhyohuah* '[the axe] has several handles', or the combining form of *quahuitl*, *quauh-* 'wood', indicating that the handle is made of wood.

v ytestamẽto . catalina papã chane . tehuitzco .	The will of Catalina Papan, whose home is in Tehuitzco.
v yn omopouh . yn t°s yn ye tlamachiyotilli ymispanco omopouh . y p.eme clxiii [iiii?] p°s.	The money was counted, it is confirmed. 164 *pesos* was counted in the presence of the priests.
v auh yn omopouh yn çan oc . tlachipauazhualli teocuitlatl . yn omocecetepouh . cxcix .	And when the gold that is still only purified (and not weighed or made into coins) was counted, when each piece was counted, there were 199.

The testator, Catalina Papan, was the victim of *cocoliztli*, which in this case was almost certainly an epidemic. Major waves of epidemics usually referred to as *cocoliztli* are documented for the years 1545 and 1576; however, the second is reported to have begun as early as 1571 (Carral Cuevas 2008), the year of Catalina's death, and reached its peak in 1576. She appears to have been a woman of relative wealth and status: in addition to numerous properties, she owned 164 *pesos* in cash—not mentioned in the will itself except for the more modest quantity of thirty-one *pesos* and five *reales*!—which was counted in the presence of witnesses only after the will was made. Either additionally or in total—this is not entirely clear in the document—she had the equivalent of 199 pesos in unpurified gold. Apparently a widow, since she did not mention her husband, she bequeathed everything to her daughter, the principal heir, and her son and a small grandchild. However, despite her elevated status, Catalina did not bear the prestigious title of *doña*, so we cannot be sure if she belonged to the nobility proper. Even so, the lack of the title is not conclusive, given the fact that in the first decades after the conquest it tended to be reserved for the high nobility, but was sometimes employed as a sign of an attained position, usually prestigious municipal offices. For this reason, *doña* was even less common among female members of the Nahua nobility because they could not become holders of such offices; also many a highborn woman would not be associated with the title if her husband were of lower status (Lockhart 1992: 126). So, although lacking the appellation of *doña,* Catalina Papan may well have belonged to a local noble class.

In fact, her noble status is indirectly confirmed by her request to be buried inside the *huey teopan*, the main church of San Juan Bautista (in whichever place it would be possible). This reference of Catalina, herself a resident of Tehuitzco, to one of the *tlahxillacalli*, or districts of the head town of Coyoacan, points to the main church of this *altepetl*. We know from historical records that, especially in early colonial times, well-off or prominent community members often requested burial inside the church, while burials in the churchyard became more and more frequent in late colonial times (Pizzigoni 2007: 142). Catalina gave relatively precise and detailed information regarding funeral arrangements, as well as instructions concerning care for her soul after she died. She secured an offering so that the singers from the main church would come to her house and take her body into the church. After confirming donations for different confraternities, she made sure that the bells would be rung during her funeral and that she would be buried inside the church, as already mentioned. Catalina also secured a separate offering to ensure that two high masses would be said for her soul, one each year after her death. Four executors, including a church official, were to oversee this process. She ordered that some of the maize that would be harvested from the land that she bequeathed to her offspring would be used to feed the people who wound up arranging the masses for her. In addition, she indicated that her skirt and shift should be sold in order to secure cash for purchasing the bacon that would be consumed during her funeral. Catalina did not forget about her final attire: she ordered a cloak to be purchased in order to shroud her corpse. Interestingly, the original phrase referring to the cloak was crossed out except for the final morpheme: *~~cayamãço castilla.ych~~tilmatli*. The term in question is a doublet, pairing the Spanish *cañamazo* 'course hemp cloth' (*tela tosca de cáñamo*; DRAE) and the Nahuatl neologism *caxtillanichtilmahtli* (lit. 'Spanish maguey-fiber cloak' or 'Spanish course hemp cloak'). Later on she came back to this point in an unclear statement that seemed to indicate that if the Spanish hemp cloth "does not appear," there is another cloak with which she is to be shrouded.

Catalina gave some of her cash and three pieces of her land to her female child, Juana Francisca; this included a house lot and some household equipment. Her son, Josef Gabriel, received a *cihuacalli*, or a 'woman-house', along with the land on which it stood, another field with three rows of *chinampas*, as well as some cash and house equipment, including an axe with a wooden handle. Of those bequests, the most interesting is the reference to *cihuacalli*. As pointed out by Lockhart (1992: 66), this term is rendered by some Spanish sources as *cocina* 'kitchen', contributing to its identification by scholars as a place where women met and worked. He identified the term on a 1593 map from San Hipólito Teocaltitlan in Mexico Tenochtitlan as a single structure that was the property of a female—a *cihuacalli* was normally owned by a woman, and whenever it had a male owner, he was expected to bequeath it to a women upon his death. The building mentioned in Catalina's will seemed also to be a freestanding structure on its own separate house plot. However, she decided to give the *cihuacalli* to her son, and not to her daughter, who would have been the natural heir if the strict inheritance rules regarding this kind of building were in fact obligatory.

The orthographic conventions of the document reflect the unstandardized writing of a local native scribe, with the proliferation of *h* preceding word-initial vowels (*hepan*, *hequahuitl*) and the insertion of a syllable and word-final *n* in Spanish loanwords, attesting to their phonetic adaptation to Nahuatl (*galinçia*, *ambrosion*). Other loanwords, such as *casa* ('chest', from Spanish *caja*) or *acha* ('axe', from Spanish *hacha*), attest to the absorption of European material culture into the daily life of the Nahuas. The word *tomin* is used both as a monetary unit (= *real*, one eighth of a *peso*) and to refer to cash in general, reflecting a semantic extension of this loanword that occurred in early-colonial Nahuatl and gradually replaced its original meaning.

DOCUMENT 13

Testament of María Toztecayatl, Tlaxcala, Mexico, 1576/1600[1]

Agnieszka Brylak

[Fol. 2r]

[left margin: Traslado]

v Izcatqui. nomemoria testam̄eto. nicchiua y͡ nehuatl notoca maria. toztecayatl .//. yte͡copatzinco. yn ttº. Jesu xp̃õ .//. huel noyollocacopa ypaltzinco yn dios .//. ȳ nopilhua͡tzitzihuan ayac ynca mocahcayahuaz ./. y͡mac niqu͡icauhtehua y͡noquichtitzin. yn itoca matheo. miyahuatzin. canel ypilhua͡ ymachtzitzihuā. yehuatl quimati

v Quito yn cocoxqui. ca͡tellas niccauhtehua. çe͡pohuali pesostica o͡mahtlactica yn ipatiuh: niqu͡imacatehua y͡ nopilhua͡ quimonamaquizque yn imeyxtin. mª ./. yoa Jossanā ./. yoā

[left margin: copy]

Here is my memorandum, the testament that I, María Toztecayatl, make by order of Our Lord Jesus Christ, of my own free will, with the help of God. As for my children, nobody will deceive them. I leave them in the hands of my elder brother, named Matheo Miyahuatzin; after all they are his children, his nieces.[2] He knows what to do.

The sick person said, "I leave candles. Their value is thirty *pesos*. I bequeath them to my children, the three of them, María, Susana, and Juana, so that they will sell them. Likewise, I bequeath

1 Archivo Histórico del Estado de Tlaxcala (AHET), 1600, caja 1, exp. 7. This document was originally published by Thelma Sullivan (1987: 342–345), with some fragments of the Nahuatl text omitted in the Spanish translation. The transcription and translation included here are based entirely on the original manuscript.

2 See the first note of the accompanying commentary.

 DOI: 10.5876/9781607328346.c013

Juā .//. yoā onpetlacali copalli. çā no niquīmacatehua ȳ nopilhuā quimonamacaquizq̄ ./. yn ipatiuh castoli p°s .//.

two chests of incense[3] to my children; they will sell them; their value is fifteen *pesos*."

v yoā yetetl. tlahmachcueytl. yn ōtetl cueytl. ypatiuh chichicohome p°s. yoā nanahui tu^es. Auh yn ocçētetl. yey p°s ypatiuh .//. yoā yetetl huipiltin. mamacuili p°s. ypatiuh. niquīmacatehua ȳ nopilhuā .//. yoā ȳ nosolar. niquīmacatehua ȳ nopilhuā nauhtetl ȳ tlapācaltin ypā manih .//. yoā çētetl tlali nicpiya. motocayotiya xiuhtetelco. niquīmacatehua ȳ nopilhuā quitequipanozq̄ ./. nauhpohuali yn ic huehcapā ./. Auh yn ic patlahuac çēpoualmatl ōmahtlactli ./. yz[4] çecapal ytepāco. dō luys ./. yn oc çecapal. ytepāco. Juā. quauhchita .//. ya yxquich ȳ niquicuilohua .//. yoā ȳ tehuatl noquichtitzin. tle ticmomachitiya Amo tiquīmoxicahuiliz. ȳ momachhuā. Ayac ynca mocahcayahuaz .//. nehuatl onitlahcuilo m̄artin. thobias .//. yn imixpā testigos. pipiltin motocayotique quineltilique yca ynfirma .//. + feleçiano. texolo .//. Matheo. miyahuatzin .//. myn thobias

"And [I leave] three embroidered skirts: the value of two of the skirts is eight *pesos* and four *tomines* each; and the value of the other is three *pesos*. And I bequeath three shirts, valued at five *pesos* each, to my children. And I bequeath my house lot to my children. Four flat-roofed buildings stand on it.[5] And I have a field in [a place] named Xiuhtetelco. I bequeath it to my children and they will work it. It is eighty [units] in length and thirty units in width. On one side it borders with [the land of] Don Luis and on the other side it borders with [the land of] Juan Quauhchita. This is everything that I write. And as for you, my elder brother, what you know is that you should not neglect your nieces. No one is to deceive them." I, Martín Tobías, wrote it in the presence of the witnesses, the nobles. They put their names and confirmed it with their signatures. + Feliciano Texolo, Matheo Miyahuatzin, Martín Tobías.

v oc çepa quito yn cocoxqui. nauhpohuali p°s ȳ nicauhtehua tomines. yc quimizcaltizque ȳ nopilhuā. Amo ynca mocahcayahuaz ȳ nonamic ocatca Antonio. oncate testigos .//. yn ipā mochiuh yn itestamēto. mª. toztecayatl ypā miercoles. çēpohualilhuitl mes. de Julio. de mill y quinientos y setenta y seys. anōs

Once again the sick one said, "I leave eighty *pesos* in cash, with which they will raise my children. My former husband Antonio will not deceive them.[6] There are witnesses." The testament of María Toztecayatl was made on Wednesday, the twentieth day of the month of July in the year 1576.

---

3 In this fragment the word *petlacalli*, referring to a container made of straw, similar to a deep basket with a cover, is used as a numeral classifier, and for this reason it appears together with the numeral two (*on-*).

4 The *n* of *yn* has assimilated the initial *c* [s] of the following word, *çecapal*.

5 The Spanish translation of this text refers to one flat-roof house with four rooms. The expression in Nahuatl clearly refers to four houses or buildings, which does not exclude the possibility that they formed one complex and were adjacent to each other.

6 This suggests that her former husband was still alive, but we do not know if she was in some way separated from him since he is referred to as her "late/former spouse."

[left margin: Auto]

En la ynsigne Muy noble y muy leal çiudad. de tlaxª. matlaquilhuitl oçe mes de henero. de mill y ~~quini~~seyscientos anos. ymixpātzinco do Jua. de ribas. Gon[or]. yoa do feleçiano. ceyynos allde. hordinario y nica ciudad. yoa y proujª. de tlaxª. por su magd: nica audiencia tlaxª. mopuh yn itestameto. mª. toztecayatl catca: quicacque yn ichpoch ytoca Jossana. toztecayatl. yoa teoyotica ynamic. lucas. gadena. yoa tehuayolque. huel quicacque yn izqui tlamatli yc tlanahuatita micquetl catca: yn yehuatzin Gon[or]. yoa alld. nimā quimotlatlanilique y Jossana. toztecayatl. yoa ynamic. yoā tehuayolque .//. quimolhuilique. cuix itla yhtlacauhtica yn ipa ytestamēto amonatzin catca .//. yn yehuatl Jossana. toztecayatl. yoa ynamic. quihtoque. yn izqui tlamatli nica quiteneuhtehuac tonatzin catca. y momiquili huel oc tepipiltzitzintin. atle tiquitaq. ȳ cādelas ȳ copali. yoa y cueytl. y huipili. yoa ȳ nauhpohuali pºs. tomines: ac quipohpolo amo ticmatque canel ya opohpoliuh .//. yoa ca ya omomiquilique y nopihtzin. mª. yoa nicuctzin Jua: ça huel noçel yn onimocauh ./. quema oc çe noquichtiuh ytoca Esteua. morate. ce y ynātzin. atle nicuilia: Auh yn ixquich nica quiteneuhtevac nonātzin catca ./. yoā y tlali cuemitl. xiuhtetelco ./. yoa yn solar. huel ixcoya ytlatqui ytlacohual. y tlali. yoa solar ./. yoa yn ixquich nicā quicuilotehuac huel ixcoya ytlatqui ȳ nonātzin catca .//. yn yehuatzin Gon[or]. yoa allde // quimitahuilique ça yeh ticneltiliya yn iuhtica testameto ./. y Jossana. toztecayatl. Ma yuh quimopili. yn tlali solar .//. yoā ȳ cuemitl quicuhtehuac ynatzin catca. yn ōpa mani xiuhtetelco. ayac cepa acah quicuiliz ./. ypapa ça huel içel yn omocauh omomiquilique yn ipih. yoa ycuctzin. ayac çepa huel quicuiliz y Jossana huel neltitica yniqu itlatqui .//. ynic neli yn yehuatzin Gon[or]. yoa allde. ynic neli yc

[left margin: Auto]

In the distinguished, very noble, and very loyal city of Tlaxcallan, on the eleventh day of the month of January of 1600, here in the Audiencia of Tlaxcallan, the testament of the late María Toztecayatl was read in the presence of Don Juan de Rivas, the governor, and Don Feliciano Ceynos, the ordinary *alcalde* here in the city and in the province of Tlaxcallan by His Majesty. Her daughter, named Susana Toztecayatl, and her legitimate husband, Lucas Cadena, and the relatives heard it. They heard very well everything that the deceased person ordered before dying. The governor together with the *alcalde* then questioned Susana Toztecayatl and her husband and the relatives. They said to them, "Is there anything wrong with the testament of your late mother?" And Susana Toztecayatl and her husband said, "We have not seen any of the many things that our mother mentioned—when she died we were still little children—neither candles, nor incense, nor skirts, nor blouses, nor eighty *pesos* in cash. Who spent it? We do not know. Surely it was spent. And since my elder sister María and my younger sister Juana have already died, I am the only one left. Yes, there is one more elder brother of mine named Esteban Morrate, of the same mother, [but] I take nothing from him. Everything here that my late mother mentioned before dying, including the land, the field in Xiuhtetelco, and the house lot, it was indeed her own purchased property. And the land, the house lot, and everything that she wrote down here before dying was truly my late mother's own property." And the governor together with the *alcalde* said to them, "Thus we confirm the testament as it is. May Susana Toztecayatl then keep the land, the house lot, and the field that her late mother had bought before dying and which is there in Xiuhtetelco.

quimoneltilique ypā quimotlalilique ynfirma yntoca .//. yōa nehuatl fran^{co}. de st. mathias. Escrj^{o}. tlax^{a}. ynic neli. ypā nictlali. nōfirma notoca. yc nicneltili // tlilhuahuāqui amo no yehuatl ./. mihtoz. y seysçientos

No one will ever take it from her because she is indeed the only one who is left; her elder sister and her younger sister died. No one will ever take it from Susana: it is completely verified that it is her property, that it is true. The governor together with the *alcalde* verified it and put their signatures and their names on it. And I, Francisco de San Matías, notary from Tlaxcallan, put my signature, my name on it in order to verify its authenticity. I confirmed it with a cancelation mark [so that] no one will contradict it. 1600.

Jhua de Ribas

Juan de Rivas

Dō Feliçiano Çaynos

Don Feliciano Ceynos

Nixpā mochiuh Fran^{co}. de s^{n} mathias escrj^{o}. tlax^{a}.

It was done in the presence of Francisco de San Matías, notary from Tlaxcallan.

The protagonists of the set of texts which is the focus of this brief introduction are María Toztecayatl and her daughter Susana, whose family affairs are recorded between the beginning and ending legal formulas of the official documents. When María dictated her testament to Martín Tobías in 1576, Susana was only a little child, just like her two other siblings, her elder sister María and her younger sister Juana.[7] Apparently, María Toztecayatl had separated from her husband Antonio, whom she mentioned as *nonamic ocatca* 'my late husband'. Having been afraid that after her death he might want to take advantage of the situation and deprive her daughters of the possessions bought with *itlacohual* 'her own assets', she decided to write down the testament in order to ensure her underage children a means of support. According to the will, Susana Toztecayatl and her sisters were to remain in the custody of their uncle, Matheo Miyahuatzin, María's elder brother. This was in accordance with an uncle's social role among the prehispanic Nahuas (Sahagún 1950–1969 X: 3; see also Document 2 commentary).

Among María Toztecayatl's bequests to her offspring were *cātellas* 'candles' and *onpetlacali copalli* 'two chests with incense' with a total value of 45

7 The text of the testament itself, and contrary to its translation in Spanish, renders the child's name as Juā, an abbreviation normally used for Juan. However, the fact that María Toztecayatl left to her three children three skirts and blouses favors the identification of the youngest child as a girl.

pesos, which were to be sold so that the girls could be raised with the income. For the same reason, she also left them eighty *pesos* in cash (in the Nahuatl text a Spanish loanword *tomines* is used with this broader sense). Along with this, Susana and her sisters inherited three embroidered skirts and three shirts worth twenty-six *pesos* and four *tomines* in total. Nevertheless, the most valuable part of the legacy was a house lot and a cultivated field of eighty units in length and thirty units in width, located in Xiuhtetelco, today part of the city of Puebla. The dimensions of the field are measured in units described by the Nahuatl term *matl*, literally 'hand' or 'arm' (see Glossary).

The house lot that María Toztecayatl passed on to her daughters had a building on it: a construction consisting of *nauhtetl ȳ tlapācaltin ypā manih* 'four flat-roofed rooms are on (the lot)', probably four separate structures surrounding a small *patio*. Interestingly, in this particular fragment of the will not only did the testator use the Nahuatl counter *tetl* to indicate the number of rooms, but she also pluralized the inanimate, unpossessed noun *tlapancalli* by adding the suffix *-tin* to it. The latter linguistic phenomenon, apparently nonexistent in preconquest Nahuatl and induced by contact with the Spanish language, is hardly attested at such an early stage, that is, in the year 1576 (Karttunen and Lockhart 1976; Lockhart 1992).

Twenty-four years after the testament was written, Susana Toztecayatl, one of María's daughters, together with her husband, Lucas Cadena, appeared in the Audiencia court of Tlaxcallan in order to execute the terms of the will. According to Susana's testimony, the death of her two sisters, María and Juana, made her the only heir still alive. She did not recall ever having seen candles, incense, clothes, or money and suggested someone must have taken them. It is possible that Matheo Miyahuatzin had indeed fulfilled the request of his sister and sold these goods, later spending the money to bring up the girls. In Susana's statement, she mentioned another sibling of hers (and María Toztecayatl's son), named Esteban Morrate, who was absent from her mother's testament. Probably he was one of the reasons why she presented herself before the local authorities in the first place. As Susana explained, she was not depriving her brother of any of their mother's property, and the testament was the proof which confirmed her being the only heir. The omission of Esteban Morrate in the will fits into an overall pattern, traced back to prehispanic tradition, of indigenous women bequeathing more often to their female than to their male offspring (Kellogg 1986; Wood 1997). However, due to the lack of additional pertinent information in the testament we do not know whether Esteban, Susana, and her two sisters had the same father, or if this father was the above-mentioned Antonio. There is a possibility that Antonio was only Esteban's father and that upon his death he would have provided his son with means of support, whereas María felt obliged to secure the future of her daughters from the previous relationship.

The execution of the testament of the late María Toztecayatl was supervised by the most important representatives of the indigenous authorities: the governor Don Juan de Rivas and the ordinary *alcalde* Don Feliciano Ceynos. This fact raises the question about the social status of the document's female protagonists. The lack of the Spanish title *doña* might suggest that they were commoners or at least that they did not belong to the highest nobility. What we know about María is that she was a wealthy woman, with enough resources to have purchased a field and to have bequested candles worth thirty *pesos* to her offspring, a considerable sum in the second half of the sixteenth century. On the other hand, her son, Esteban Morrate, and her son-in-law, Lucas Cadena, bear names quite unusual for indigenous people, possibly indicating their Spanish or *mestizo* origin. Based on this naming pattern we can assume that María Toztecayatl was in a relationship with or was married to a *mestizo* or a Spaniard, just like her daughter Susana. This, together with her economic situation, hints that she belonged to the indigenous nobility; nevertheless, the possibility that she was a wealthy commoner cannot be excluded.

Both the testament, dated in 1576, and the *auto* or judicial decree from 1600 were written in the same hand and with the same ink. What is more, there are no signatures at the end of the will, which leads to the conclusion that it is a copy of the original, made by Francisco de San Matías, the notary who produced the decree. This observation brings up a series of important questions: Did the writer make a faithful copy of the manuscript dictated by María Toztecayatl to Martín Tobías? Or did he manipulate the data so that Susana Toztecayatl would become the only possessor of the house lot and the lands in Xiuhtetelco? The latter supposition could explain the unusual presence of the above-mentioned linguistic phenomenon of pluralization of an inanimate and unpossessed noun in Nahuatl (*tlapācaltin*) in the will, as it could have been added automatically by the notary in 1600. Nevertheless, Francisco de San Matías seems to have thought that someone might level this kind of accusation at him, and so in order to emphasize his trustworthiness he closed the set of two documents with a formula that is quite unusual, athough not unattested elsewhere: "I confirmed it with a cancelation mark [so that] no one will contradict it. 1600." This would have precluded anyone from later adding to the document's content.

DOCUMENT 14

Testament of Tomás Feliciano, Omaxac Huehuecalco, Coyoacan, Mexico, 1579[1]

Justyna Olko

[Fol. 1r]

+v yn ica ytocatzin tetatzin yoan
tepiltzin yoan es̃pu santo nicpeualtia
notestameto neuatl tomas feliz.º nochan
omaxac ueuecalco macihui ȳ mococoua
nonacayo yece y noyollo y nocializ
y notlalnamiquiliz y notlacaquia çan
pactica yc nicchiua notestamento huel
achto ytech nipeua naniman ymactzinco
nocontlalia note̊ d. ma q̂ualmanili Ca
ytlachihualtzin auh y nonacayo nicmaca
in tlali Ca ytech quiz auh yn onimic
ninotocaz tohueiteopan san joan bapa
macuil ts̊ macoz vic̊ ome tomi yc
tlatziliniz ueiteopan ce tomi yc tlatziliniz
ospital naui ts̊ niquinmaca cuicanime
naui ts̊ yc mocouaz cantella tlatlatiaz
otlica ome ts̊ yc mocouaz cacauatl [ma]
cozq̃ cocosque ospital ome ts̊ nouētzin
cõz ome ts̊ nouētzin ver[a] cruz ome ts̊
nouentzin cofradia de rosario yeuatzin
quineltiliz fiscal å̊l benavides auh
niquitlani ontetl misa mayor nopan

+ In the name of the Father and the Child and the Holy Spirit, I, Tomás Feliciano, whose home is in Omaxac Huehuecalco, begin my will. Although my body is ill, my spirit, my will, my memory, and my understanding are sound. For this reason, I make my testament. First of all, I begin by [saying that] I place my soul in the hands of my Lord God, may he take it unto himself for it is his creature. But I give my body to the earth because from there it emerged. And when I have died I am to be buried in our main church of San Juan Bautista. Five *reales* are to be given to the vicar, two *reales* for the bells to be rung in the main church, one *real* for the bells to be rung in the hospital; I give four *reales* to the singers, four *reales* to buy candles that will be burned [in the procession] along the road, two *reales* to buy cacao that the sick will be given in the hospital, two *reales* will be

1 McAfee Collection, 339, UCLA.

 DOI: 10.5876/9781607328346.c014

m[i]toz mocauaz nouētzin teopan chiquacē p̊s macoz vic̊. oc no chiquacen pesos moxexeloz inic tlacocoualoz cantella yoan in uen[tli] motlaliz auh in macozque cuicanime in quexquich monequiz ni[qui]mixquetza albaceasm̄e franco de s.to domigo inic ome joan m̃in + ye ixquich in itechpa naniman amo ytlacauiz

my offering for [. . .][2], two *reales* will be my offering for the Confraternity of the True Cross, and two *reales* for the Confraternity of the Rosary. The *fiscal* Alonso Benavides will carry it out. And I request that two high masses be celebrated for me. My offering of six *pesos* is to be left at the church, it will be given to the vicar. Another six *pesos* are to be divided so that various things will be bought, including candles, and an offering that will be given; and the singers will be given as much as they need. I name as executors of the will Francisco de Santo Domingo and second, Juan Martín. + That is all that concerns my soul; it is not to be altered.

v̲ ynic ontlamantli nitlanauatia yn onpa mani notlaltzin atliztacan ymilnauac franco monuz nouentzin nicchiua ospital intech pouhq' cocosque

Second, I declare that I am making an offering of my land at Atliztacan, close to a field of Francisco Muñoz. It belongs to the sick in the hospital.

v̲ yniqu etlamantli yc nitlanauatia yexcan notlal niq̲uinnomaquilia teopisque yc misa nopa quimitalhuizque inic cecni mani acxotlan quap[pa]nauazyacac inic ocan mani çimatlan yniqu excan mani texpolco necoc onpoali omatlactli nechcuili franco sayapedra quichiua in tlaxilacaleque moteylhuizque in peme

Third, I declare that I am giving land of mine in three places to the priests so that they will say mass for me. The first place is in Acxotlan Quappanahuazyacac.[3] The second place is in Cimatlan. The third place is in Texpolco. It is fifty units [long] on each side. Francisco Saavedra took it from me and the citizens of the *tlahxillacalli* are working the land. The friars are to make a complaint.

v̲ ynic nauhtlamantli nitlanauatia in nopiltzin ytoca ambrosio omextin nonamictzin mariana nican nicteneua in izquican niquinmacatiuh notlal çan uel concauitiazque in iz moteneua inic cecni ~~ueuecalco mili mani acuecuexco~~ inic ocan notlal mani chiltonyapan yniqu excan notlal mani copilco inic nauhcan tlalxopan yquiyauac yecatetzin ytlal catca yn achto nonamictzin catca ychan ueuecalco çan iuian quimocauiliz nouexiuhtzin po paulino auh yn

Fourth, I declare that I am bequeathing land of mine to both my child named Ambrosio and my spouse Mariana in all of the places that I mention here. They are to share to the fullest extent what is mentioned here. The first place [is in Huehuecalco: it is a field in Acuecuexco].[4] My land in the second place is in Chiltonyapan. My land in the third place is in Copilco. The fourth place is in Tlalxopan at the entrance to Ecatetzin's [property]. It was the

2 It is not clear what *cõz* refers to.

3 *Quappanauazyacac* is either a place name or it refers to the specific location of the parcel of land, in this case, 'at the end of the bridge'.

4 The bracketed passage has been crossed out in the manuscript.

onpa mani notlal omaxac çan tepiton yquiyauac maga ypan mani tzapotl macuilli imiltitlan sosana yoan franca auh yn onpa yquiyauac diº çiltecatl yei tzapoquauitl amo tle ytlallo çan actimani y[z] catqui cueçalco mani nocalcoual yoan uerta yc ocan tepantitlan quimati nonamic auh yniqu excan onpa mani yquiauac nonamic mariana notlalcoual occan quiztica neuan temi in itlal i[n no] monnan yoan cenpantli yquiauac felipe yoan xallali auh yn [om]pa mani notlal cenpantli chinamitl justiçiatica nimacoc nicpia mandamiento yeuatl quitzontec franco pinelo juez onpa tlilac ymiltitlan baltasar benito in yeuatl luis camacho nechpielia notomi cenpoali oncaxtoli psº itetzinco ninocauhtiuh vicº fray franco de la mina quimitlanililiz intech nicpouhtiuh nopiltzin omextin yn[an]tzin[5] auh in tsº. notlal yc quicouh yn espanol miecpa oniquitlanili o yxquich in intech nicpouhtiuh ambrosio yoan mariana nonamictzin ye ixquich inic niquintlaçotlatiuh

land of my first wife, whose home was in Huehuecalco; my fellow father-in-law,[6] Pedro Paulino, is to relinquish it peacefully. And just a small piece of land of mine is in Omaxac at the entrance to Magdalena's [property]. Five *sapote* trees grow on it, next to Susana and Francisca's field. And at the entrance to Diego Çiltecatl's [property] there are three *sapote* trees. The land where they grow is not [my property]; they just grow [on the other property]. Here in Cueçalco is a purchased house of mine with an orchard. The second [purchased] place is in Tepantitlan; my spouse knows about it. The third [purchased] place is at the entrance to my spouse Mariana's [property]. My purchased land is divided into two parts. It is together with the land of my mother-in-law: one row [of *chinampas*] is at the entrance to Felipe's [property], and there is some sandy land. And there is land of mine there, one row of *chinampas* that was given to me by a judicial decision. I hold the order issued by the judge Francisco Pinelo. [It is] in Tlilac, next to the field of Baltasar Benito. Luis Camacho is holding some of my money, thirty-five *pesos*; I leave myself in the hands of the vicar fray Francisco de la Mina, he is to ask for it. I assign it to my both my child and his mother. And as to the money with which the Spaniard [Luis Camacho] bought my land, I asked him for it many times. I am assigning all of this to Ambrosio and Mariana my spouse; it [shows] how much I care for them.

[Fol. 1v]

v ynic macuillamantli nitlanauatia in ueuecalco mani calli ontetl mixnamictimani yoan icallalo in quauhtlacopauic miluiac monamacaz in

Fifth, I declare that two houses in Huehuecalco that face each other and their house plot that is toward the forest/ to the south, a long field, are to be sold.

5 The two letters in brackets fall at the end of a line of text at the edge of the page and are very difficult to read, but *ynantzin* 'his mother' fits the context.

6 In other words, Pedro Paulino is the father-in-law of one of one of Tomás Feliciano's children.

ipatiuh yez misa yc topan mitoz tomextin yn achto nonamictzin catca yn oncan chane amo ytlacahuiz

With its price a mass is to be said for both me and my late first wife, who was from there. It is not to be altered.

v ynic chiquacentlamantli ycnitlanauatia y nochpoch ytoca ceçilia nicmaca in calli tonatiuh yquiçayan ytzticac yoan nicmaca in inemac catca notelpoch ytoca catca juan garª in tlali caltitlan mani inic ocan nicmaca in tlali onpa mani tlaxopan ymiltitlan franco leonardo iniqu excan nicmaca in tlali onpa mani tlapopoxalpan niccouilica i nochpoch oc cepa nicmaca yn axcan auh ome pso quipielia in iicuhcton juº garª misa mayor quichiuiliz ynic quixtlauaz

Sixth, I declare that I give the house facing east to my grown daughter, named Cecilia. And I give her what was the inheritance of my deceased son, named Juan García, the land next to the house. In a second place I give her the land at Tlaxopan, next to the field of Francisco Leonardo. In a third place, I give my daughter the land at Tlapopoxalpan that I had bought from her; now I give it to her again. She owes two *pesos* to her younger sibling Juan García; she is to repay it by having a high mass said for him.

v ynic chicontlamantli nitlanauatia y noxuiuh bernaltino thomas nicmaca noçiuatlal mani chinanpa necoc cenpoali ueuecalco quauhtlali yoan occan notlalcoual inic cecni caltitlan atlacomoli ypan ca ynic ocan nicmaca ymiltitlan metzapaltzin yn ocanixti çan oquimocuilica notelpoch juan sarano yn omextin ynamic auh yn [ni] can[7] nicneltilia nicmaca y noxhuiuh bernaltino thomas auh nitlanauatia y nouexiuh pº paulino intla ytla yc quitlaçotlaz in ixuiuh ca yehuatl quimati

Seventh, I declare that I give to my grandchild Bernardino Tomás my "woman land" that is in [the district of] Chinampan at Huehuecalco. It is fertile land,[8] measuring twenty units on both sides. And [I give him] my purchased land in two places: one next to the house with a well on it; in the second place, I give him [land] next to Metzapaltzin's field. My grown son, Juan Serrano, together with his spouse, had just taken both of them. Here I verify that I give it to my grandchild, Bernardino Tomás. And I declare that my fellow parent-in-law, Pedro Paulino, will decide whether or not he wants to esteem him with something, he will decide.

v ynic chicuetlamantli nitlanauatia in teoyotica nopiltzin catca omic thomas feliçiano in inemac catca in tlalli xochcayapan mani yetetl misa

Eighth, I declare that the land at Xochcayapan was the inheritance of my deceased godchild, Tomás Feliciano.[9] The three low masses I requested [for

7 The two letters that are postulated in brackets fall at the end of a line of text at the edge of the page and are not visible, but *nican* 'here' fits the context.

8 *Quauhtlalli* is literally 'wooden land'.

9 *Teoyotica nopiltzin* usually means 'godchild' but in the very earliest documents it was also used for the legitimate children of a church marriage, which could be true here, because the child was also named after the testator.

tepi~~pit~~zitzin oniquitlan omochiuh yn axcan notech pouhqui ez[10] cecexiuhtica misa yc nopan mitotiaz ca ye ixquich inic nitlanauatia testigosme p̊ leonardo domigo de san juan yoan baltasar [es] teva auh in ciua juana inic ome ana iniqu ei maria auh in imixpan onez memoria testameto alguaçiles pedro nunez tochco inic ome bonauentura tlalxopan intencopatzinco senores alldsme don juan de guzman ål benabides omicuillo xxv de abril 1579 anos joseph jacobo escrivano

him] were already celebrated. Now it will belong to me, and with it each year a mass will be said for me. That is all that I order. The witnesses are Pedro Leonardo, Domingo de San Juan, Baltasar Esteban, and the women Juana, the second one Ana, and the third one María. The memorandum of testament was presented before the *alguaciles* Pedro Núñez of Tochco and the second one, Buenaventura of Tlalxopan, by order of the lord-judges, Don Juan de Guzmán and Alonso Benavides. It was written on the twenty-fifth of April in the year 1579. Joseph Jacobo, notary.

justiçia oq'chipauh ytlacauhq' ocatca testamento occan tlalli inic cecni mani acuecuexco inic occan mani ycaltech yecatetzin auh omacoc y ixhuiuh p̊ paulino yxpantzinco nez don franco plaçito gouernador

The officers of the law cleared up what was mistaken in the will: the land [is] in two places, the first one at Acueuexco, the second one next to the house of Yecatetzin, and it was given to the grandchild of Pedro Paulino in the presence of Don Francisco Plácido, *gobernador*.

Rescebi de franco de sto domingo seis pesos de dos misan catãdas q̃ se dijerõ por este difũto en este testamẽto cõtenido frai lorẽço de la assũption

I received six *pesos* from Francisco de Santo Domingo for two high masses that were celebrated for this deceased person who is mentioned in this will. Fray Lorenzo de la Asunción

ye nelli omacoc ospidal iii ts̊ nevatl fabia de sando tomingo dipodado

It is true that three *reales* were given to the hospital. I, Fabián de Santo Domingo, deputy.

ye neli otimacoq̄ nahui tomines ypãpa misa Req'em oticuicaq̄ timochintin teopantitlaca capitanes luis de tapia gabriel muyse

It is true that we were given four *reales* for the requiem mass that all we church people sang. Captains Luis de Tapia and Gabriel Moisés

Although he does not use the prestigious title of *don*, Tomás Feliciano was a man of considerable wealth and position, no doubt a member of the nobility of the *altepetl* of Coyoacan. In his will he gave considerable attention to detail, not only regarding the precise description and destination of his material properties, but also with respect to spiritual matters. The latter consideration seemed to be of significant importance for him: he wanted to secure his burial

10 *Notech pouhqui* 'it is my property' and *yez* 'it will be' were written together as a phonological phrase, and the *y* of *yez* was elided.

place inside the main church of San Juan Bautista; he made sure the vicar got his payment and that the bells both in the church and in the hospital were rung during his funeral; he arranged for singers to accompany his corpse with music, and specified that they should be provided with everything they might need; and he envisioned that candles would be lit along his last journey to the church for the funeral. Tomás Feliciano made donations to the church, to the vicar himself, to buy cacao for the sick in the hospital, and for two confraternities with which he was perhaps involved during his lifetime. On top of that, he donated one of his pieces of land to the hospital, and another three to the priest to make sure that holy masses would be said for his soul. Interestingly, one of these plots had been taken from him and was being tilled by some community members at the time he composed his testament; he expected the friars, who were the beneficiaries, to take care of this situation and get the land back for themselves. In addition, a little later in the will he ordered the sale of two houses in Huehuecalco, stipulating that the money be invested in a mass or masses for both his soul and that of his first wife who, as he explained, had come from that same place. Finally, the land that belonged to his godchild (or legitimate son, since the phrase *teoyotica nopiltzin* is ambivalent) was to be used to pay for one mass each year for the soul of the testator. All of these detailed instructions and concerns give us some idea about indigenous devotion relatively soon after the Spanish conquest.

The bequests to the family members came only after most of the spiritual matters had been taken care of. A large portion of his numerous land holdings went to his wife Mariana and his son Ambrosio: each of these bequests is described with precision in the will. One of them included purchased land, along with a purchased house and an orchard. We also learn that one plot of land had been sold for thirty-five *pesos* to a Spaniard who never made the payment. Tomás Feliciano entrusted the execution of this debt to the vicar so that the money could eventually be received by his wife and son. It is clear that the testator had great faith in the legal power and ability of the friars to solve the economic and legal issues that he had not been able to successfully straighten out during his life. One of his houses went to Cecilia, a daughter most likely from his first marriage; however, he insisted she settle her debt with his deceased son, her brother, by paying for a mass for his soul. Another beneficiary was the testator's grandchild, Bernardino Tomás, who received land originally assigned to the latter's son. Tomás Feliciano classified some this land as *cihuatlalli* 'woman land', perhaps referring to inheritance from a female forebear. This type of land was most often held by women, but the meaning was broader than "a female's property" and probably implied some form of inheritance (Lockhart 1992: 159–160; see also the discussion of *cihuacalli*, Document 12). Another of his properties was described as *cuauhtlalli*, literally meaning 'wooden land' and referring to fertile land, or land enriched by the humus of decaying trees. This land category appears among the different kinds of soil listed in the *Florentine Codex* (11: 251); it was already correctly identified by Gibson (1964: 300), and is often mentioned in Coyoacan land holdings (Horn 1991: 128–129). However, despite this logical identification, there is a confusion in the literature based on the similarity of the combining forms of *cuahuitl*—that is, *cuauh-* 'wood' and *cuāuhtli, cuāuh-* 'eagle'—which has led some researchers to interpret the term as 'eagle land' rather than 'wood land', and hence to affirm that it refers to land conquered in war (Carrasco 2012: 453; Hassig 1989: 271).

There are additions to the will informing us about actions taken after the death of the testator. First, we learn that a legal procedure was implemented in order to rectify things that were "mistaken in the will," such as assuring the transfer of property that had been intended for the grandchild of the deceased (identified incorrectly in the will as the grandson of Pedro Paulino, the parent-in law of Tomás Feliciano) in the presence of the very governor of the *altepetl* of Coyoacan. From another added note we learn that one of the friars acknowledged the receipt of money for two high masses and that these were indeed celebrated for the deceased; that money was given to the hospital; and that all the singers sang the requiem mass for which they received payment. These details show us the continuing "life" of the will and its execution, of which it was important to leave written evidence. Again, this is the confirmation of the status and power of the deceased, even after his death.

The language of the document is typical for the epoch in which it was made. There are quite a few loanwords from Spanish, mainly used for religious, administrative, and legal issues. The document employs the benefactive form of the verb *piya* 'to guard' in order to render the concept of a debt: *nechpielia notomi* 'he keeps my money for me', and *ome pso quipielia in iicuhcton* 'she keeps two *pesos* for her brother'. It is used here instead of the benefactive form of the verb *huica, huiquilia* 'to owe something to someone', which in this context is much more common. This usage corresponds to an experimental phase in the development of Nahuatl, in which native equivalents for common Spanish concepts were sought and tentatively applied.

DOCUMENT 15

Testament of María Lapan, Ydcar *Ayllu*, Peru, 1596 (?)[1]

Patrycja Prządka-Giersz, Jan Szemiński, and John Sullivan

Tes^{to} de maria lapan, biuda del *ayllo* Ydcar.

e^{n} eL n^{e} de dios, amen. Se Pan quantos esta Carta detestamento vieren como io m^{a} lapan yn^{a} biuda del *ayllo* ydcar estando como estoy enferma y sana de la voluntad y enmi çeso y entendim^{to} natural y temiendo me dela muerte y creyendo como creo elmisterio dela santi̓ssima trinidad, padre y hijo y espiritu santo, tres personas y Vnsolo dios verdadero, y en todo aquello q̃ tiene y confiessa La s^{ta} madre ygl^{a} romana ydeseando po^{r} mi anima encarrera desaluaçion otorgo y Conosco este mi testamento e^{n} lamanera siguiente

Testament of Maria Lapan, a widow, from Ydcar *ayllu*.

In God's name. Amen. May all who see this testament letter know that I, Maria Lapan, Indian widow from Ydcar *ayllu*, sick but sound of will, and in possession of my God-given judgment and understanding, in fear of death, and believing, as I do, in the mystery of the Most Holy Trinity, the Father, the Son, and the Holy Spirit, three Persons and the only true God and in all that the Holy Mother Roman Church adheres to and acknowledges, and wishing to put my soul on the road to salvation, I establish and comprehend this, my testament, in the following manner:

1 Archivo General de la Nación (AGN), Lima, Testamentos de Indios, leg. 3, exp. 313. We would like to thank Marcos Gildemaro Alarcón Olivos, whose help has been instrumental in the transcription of the wills from the AGN and the Archiepiscopal Archives of Lima (Archivo Arzobispal de Lima).

DOI: 10.5876/9781607328346.c015

[Fol. 19r]

∾Primeramente mando y encomiendo mi anima a dios ñ̃ro s^{or} q̃ La crio y rredimio por su preçio ssa sangre y el cuerpo ala tierra de donde fue formado ____

First, I remit and entrust my soul to God, who created it and redeemed it with His precious blood, and my body to the earth, from which it was formed.

∾yten mando quesi dios ñ̃ro s^{or} fuere seruido de me lleuar desta pressente vida que mi cuerpo seasepultado e^{n} laygl^{a} deste pu^{o} desantiago de surco de adonde soy natural y soy cofadre en la cofadria de ñ̃ra s^{a} del rrosario yconçep^{on} questa fundada eneste dho pu^{o}. Por her^{na} menor della y rruego a los hermanos dela dha cofadria acompañen mi cuerpo como ataLher^{na} conla sera nesçesaria y hagan bien Pormi anima conforme a las constituyçiones desta dha cofadria ___

Also, I order that should Our Lord God deign to take me from this life, that my body be buried in the church of this town of Santiago de Surco, of which I am a native. Also I am a member of the brotherhood of Our Lady of the Rosary and the [Immaculate] Conception, which has been founded in the aforementioned town, at the rank of younger sister. And I entreat all the brothers of the aforementioned brotherhood to accompany my body as a sister of the same, with the necessary wax candles, and to do what can be done for my soul according to the statutes of the aforementioned brotherhood.

∾yten mando quesedigan Por mi anima dos misas cantadas y Vnrressada y se paguen La limosna acostumbrada de misbienes ___

Also, I order that two chanted masses and one mass be said for my soul and that the accustomed alms be paid from my property.

deudas queledeuen

Debts owed to her.

∾yten declaro que no debo aninguna persona assi rropa, Plata, como gallinas ni otra cosa ninguna___

Also, I declare that I do not owe any clothing, silver, or poultry or anything to any person.

∾yten declaro que me deue di^{o} mita paca, yn^{o} deste Pu^{o} vna camiseta de tafetan carmessi nueua de dos *varas* y sessenta caxcaueles quelepreste Para dançar y nunca me lo abuelto ni pagado porello cossa ninguna mando que se cobre losusodho del dho di^{o} mita y si estuuiere manchado, ofaltare algunos caxcaueles Lo pague lo que seaveriguare q̃ Valen ãtela Just^{a} y conesto es mi Voluntad se pague la limosna delas misas __

Also, I declare that Diego Mita Paca, an Indian from this town, owes me a shirt of two *varas* of new crimson taffeta and sixty hawk-bells, which I lent to him for dancing, and he has never returned it to me nor paid anything for it. I order the aforementioned shirt to be retrieved from the aforementioned Diego Mita. And, if it is stained, or some hawk-bells are missing, he shall pay the value of the damage, to be determined before a judge, and with this I wish the alms for the masses be paid.

∾yten declo [sic] queme deue p^{o} ñalqui hutuy ocho *rreales* quelepresto mando se cobre dL susodho__

Also, I declare that Pedro Nalqui Hutuy owes me eight *reales*, which I lent to him. I order it to be collected from the aforementioned person.

∾yten declaro queme deue luys hunos doze *rreales* que le preste mando se cobre del susodho___

Also, I declare that Luys Hunos owes me twelve *reales*, which I lent to him. I order it to be collected from the aforementioned person.

∾yten declaro que medeue di^{o} decarauaJal tres *patagones* de tres cantaros chicha quelleuo fiado mando que se ~~pague~~] ^{cobre} de sus bienes___

Also, I declare that Diego Carvajal owes me three *pataqones* for three jugs of corn beer, which I sold to him on credit. I order it to be collected from his property.

[Fol. 19v]

∾yten declaro que medeue diego guama, yn^{o} deste Pueblo, Vna *f^{a}* de *ssora* demaiz quelepreste mando se cobre del susodho___

Also, I declare that Diego Guama, an Indian from this town, owes me one *fanegada* of corn *sura*, which I lent to him. I order it to be collected from the aforementioned person.

∾yten declaro queme deue Luçia chaopin, muger de fran^{co} quilan Vn pollo quele preste mando que se cobre de la susodha quatro *rreales* por eL___

Also, I declare that Luçia Chaopin, Francisco Quillan's wife, owes me one chicken, which I lent to her. I order that four *reales* be collected from the aforementioned person for it.

∾yten declaro que me deue m̄n macoay |ocho *r̄les* de vn cantaro de chicha mia que le fie mando que se cobre del susodho___

Also, I declare that Martín Macoay owes me eight *reales* for a jug of my corn beer, which I sold to him on credit. I order it to be collected from the aforementioned person.

∾yten declaro que me deue fran^{ca} achim yn^{a} ocho *rreales* de un cantaro de chicha q̄ lleuo fiada mando quese cobre delasusodha___

Also, I declare that Francisca Achim, an Indian, owes me eight *reales* for a jug of corn beer, which she bought on credit. I order it to be collected from the aforementioned person.

Bienes que tiene.

Property that she possesses

∾yten declaro q̄ tengo siete gallinas ponederas, y quatro pollitos pequeños___

Also, I declare that I possess seven egg-laying hens and four little chicks.

∾yten declaro q̄ tengo Vnapetaquilla de guardar hussos ya traydo en cassa de m^{a} quipan___

Also, I declare that I possess a small used box (*petaquilla*) for keeping spindles, which is in María Quipan's house.

∾yten declaro q̄ tengo Vna madexa grande de hilo de algodon teñido enleonado en poder de La muger de luis hunos___

Also, I declare that I have a large hank of tawny-dyed cotton thread, which is in the possession of Luis Hunos's wife.

∾yten declaro q̄ tengo Vna cassa enquebiuo quees enla plaça deste pu^{o} que Linda con las casas de p^{o} vayoc yconlas casas de don domingo ychima nayto enque ay apossentos y ay Vn apossento de Palomar.

Also, I declare that I own the house in which I live, which is on this town's public square, bordering with Pedro Vayoc's buildings, and with Don Domingo Ychima Nayto's buildings. In it there are rooms and also a pigeon loft.

∞yten declaro q̄ tengo tres ollas de cozer chicha___[2]

∞

[*Inserted*: Also I declare that I possess three pots for brewing corn beer.]

mandas que haze.

Her bequests

Yten declaro quees mi Voluntad dedar delimosna a la cofadria de Lamadre de dios del rrossario y conçep^{on} y assi mando queseden demisbienes quatro *Patagones* a La cofadria Para quesegaste en lo mas nesçessario y estaes mi Voluntad___

Also, I declare that I wish to give alms to the brotherhood of Our Lady of the Rosary and the [Immaculate] Conception; thus I order four *patagones* from my property be given to the brotherhood for urgent needs, and such is my will.

[*On the left margin*: Heredera] E instituyo Por mi heredera a fran^{ca} ñacan, mi her^{na} menor, muger de luis tauic sumo, porque no tengo, otro, [Fol. 20r] heredero mas propinco y quesuçeda conmas dr^{o} sino Lasusodha La qual nombro y Elixo por tal mi heredera para que despues de pagado y cumplido las mandas y legados contenidos eneste mi testam^{to} aya y herede y suçeda entodo lo rremaniente demis bienes assi muebles ~~y~~ ^{como} rraizes y estaes mi Vltima y final Voluntad___

[*On the left margin:* Heiress.] As my heiress, I appoint Francisca Ñacan, my younger sister, Luis Tavic Sumo's wife, because I do not have any closer kin with more rights to the inheritance than the aforementioned person, whom I name and designate as my heiress, who will possess and inherit and assume from me all of my remaining possessions, including movables and real estate, once the bequests and legacies contained in this, my testament, have been paid and completed, and this is my last and final will.

[*On the left margin*: ∞ *and below*: albaçeas] f para cvmplir y Pagar este mi testamento dexo y nombro Por mis albaçeas a domingo yucuna, alcalde, y a luis tauic sumo a los quales y a cada uno dellos ~~po~~ doy poder cvmplido tal qual ental casso se rrequiere Para que puedan entrar enmis bienes y tomar los que bastare para cvmplir estedho mi testam^{to}.

[*On the left margin:* ∞ *and below: executors*] In order to pay and carry out [what is stipulated in] this, my testament, I appoint and leave Domingo Iucuna, *alcalde*, and Luis Tavic Sumo as my executors, to each one of which I confer the plenary power required in each case for accessing my property and availing themselves of whatever is needed to carry out [what is stipulated in] this, my testament.

y Reboco y doy porninguno qualesq^{er} testamentos, memorias, cobdiçilios q̄ yo aya hecho y otorgado antes deste por palabra, o porescrito para que no Valga - saluo quiero queste valga portal en testim^{jo} delo qual otorgue La presente carta antel pres^{te} scriuano y tes^{os} de yuso

I revoke and nullify any testaments, records, codicils, that I may have made and established before this one, either verbally or in written form, so that they will not be valid; I only wish this one to be valid as such. And in corroboration, I execute this document in the presence of

2 Inserted line.

escripto e yo el dho scriu° doy fee que conosco a la| otorgante La qual no firmo porque no ssauia escriuir

the notary and the witnesses who have signed below. And I, the aforementioned notary, certify that I know the testator, who did not sign because she does not know how to write.

Te^os *don* di° chocas y Juan loro, rregidor, y el dho domingo yucuna alcalde se hallo pres^te a to lo susodho y por no sauer firmar nofirmo eneste registro.

The witnesses, Don Diego Chocas and Juan Loro, alderman. And the aforementioned mayor, Domingo Iucuna, was present for all the proceedings described above, and since he does not know to sign, he did not sign in this register.

Ante mi

Don Lor° Yanchic [*signature*]

Chumbi, scriu° de Cabil

In my presence

Don Lorenzo Yanchic [*signature*]

Chumbi Town Council notary

PATRYCJA PRZĄDKA-GIERSZ

The will of María Lapan from Ydcar *ayllu* was written possibly in 1596[3] in the town of Santiago de Surco,[4] one of the first indigenous reductions founded in the sixteenth century by the viceroy Francisco Toledo. Because the testator could not write, the document was signed only by the council clerk, Don Lorenzo Yanchic Chumbi, representing the indigenous nobility that spoke the Spanish language and knew the notarial formulas. The clerk usually used fixed legal forms as recommended by the Toledo ordinances. This style is characteristic of early documents (Nowack 2006: 51–77; Navarro Gala 2015).

In the clause arranging details of the place of burial, María Lapan stated that she was a sister of the brotherhood of Our Lady of the Rosary and the [Immaculate] Conception,[5] and requested the presence of the sisters of the brotherhood on the day of her funeral. In addition, the testatrix only asked for two chanted and one recited mass, which indicates that she was not very well off. However, the following clause reveals that she had no debts, and the fact that she illustrates this by mentioning clothing, silver, and chickens, a sequence of items potentially valuable in her social sphere, is quite interesting. Fabrics and garments were highly valued by the natives of this period, just as they were in prehispanic times. This part of the document provides interesting data regarding the value of different things like clothing, bells, vessels

3 The will does not mention the year it was written, but the notarial book that contains it is dated 1596.

4 Today one of the Lima Province districts.

5 *Nuestra Señora del Rosario and Concepción.*

for *chicha*,[6] and chickens. As is clear from the text, María Lapan was engaged in the craft production of *chicha* to be sold to the residents of the town. It is important to understand that this was one of the common activities engaged in by women that would allow them to live without financial worries in the urban areas of the colony. It is likely that by exercising this craft María Lapan was able to gain economic independence and social prestige. Her home was located close to the houses of the indigenous elite on the central square of the settlement.

Just as in prehispanic times, both the production of *chicha* itself, as well as the cultivation of maize used for the manufacture of the beverage, formed a significant foundation of political and economic existence. The pots for preparing the drink were also very important and were bequeathed through wills to other family members. In the case of this document, the testatrix claimed to have three such containers in her possession. What is more, people involved in the production and distribution of *chicha* developed important relations with the elite of colonial society. These relationships and social ties also appear in other colonial documents, especially wills of the Andean area (Charney 2012: 342–344; Salomon 1988).

In addition to what is mentioned above, the testatrix did not accumulate many material goods throughout her life; in fact, the inventory of her possessions is quite short. Hens and chickens, which in the early colonial times had special value, were mentioned. Other important objects listed include a small chest used to keep spindles[7] and a skein of cotton thread. The presence of these artifacts in the will reflects the importance at this time, just as before the conquest, of all accessories and tools related to textile production. Carefully fashioned baskets with decorations that were used to store utensils and other personal items, confirmed by archaeological evidence, were also among her personal effects.[8] Having apparently no other option, María Lapan appointed her younger sister, Francisca Ñacan, as her heiress. Her sister's husband, Louis Tavic Sumo, together with the mayor (*alcalde*) Dominic Iucuna, were the executors of her will. María Lapan's high social position is revealed by the fact that among the witnesses participating in the signing of the will were representatives of the local authorities: Don Diego Lisocal, member of the indigenous elite, Juan Loro, alderman (*regidor*), and the aforementioned town mayor, Dominic Iucuna.

6 *Chicha*, a beverage with a long prehispanic tradition, is produced from the fermentation of corn.

7 Chests of indigenous origin of this kind were useful containers, being small in size and easy to transport, and were common in the early colonial period (Campos Carles de Peña 2013).

8 Prządka-Giersz 2014: 100–127.

DOCUMENT 16

Testament of Catalina Carguay Chumbi, Guarochiri, Peru, 1608[1]

Patrycja Prządka-Giersz, Jan Szemiński, and John Sullivan

[Fol. 1r]

+ [*On the left margin: illegible*, En] nombre de Dios amen Sepan quantos estacarta detestamento Yltima e postrimera boLuntad Vieren como Yo Catalina carguay chumbi yndia natural quesoy del rrepartimiento de guarochiri hija legitima que soy de Lorenço ocho anupa y de ca [*On the left margin*: 1608] talina caxa ticlla, naturales del dho rrepartimiento que al presente soy moradora eneste d̄ho puº desantiago del çercado, estando enfermo dela enfermedad que dios n̄ro señor fue seruido de me dar ques cossa natural atoda criatura creyendo como firmemente creo el misterio de La santissima trinidad, padre e hijo y espiritu santo tres personas E Vn solo Dios Verdadero y tomando como tomo por mi abogada E intersessora ala gLoriossa Virgensanta maria madre

+ In Gods name. Amen. May all those who see this testament letter, [my] last and latest will, know that I, Catalina Carguay Chumbi, an Indian and native of the Partition of Guarochiri, legitimate daughter of Lorenço Ochoanupa and Catalina Caxactilla, natives of the aforementioned Partition, now living in this aforementioned town of Santiago del Çercado, sick with the illness that God Our Lord deigned to give me, which is a normal thing for every creature, believing as I do firmly believe in the mystery of the Most Holy Trinity, the Father, the Son, and the Holy Spirit, three persons and only one true God, and taking as I do the glorious Holy Virgin Mary, Mother of God, for my advocate and intercessor, whom I implore to beseech her precious Son to pardon my sins and guide my soul on the road

1 Archivo General de la Nación (AGN), Lima, Testamentos de Indios, legajo 1, exp. 21.

DOI: 10.5876/9781607328346.c016

de Dios a La qual suplico Ruegue a su preçiosso hijo perdone mis pecados y encamine mi anima en carrera de saluaçion, y estando como estoy en my sseso, Juizio y entendimiento naturaL por tanto, otorgo y conozco que hago y ordeno este my testamento vltima e postrimera boluntad a sseruiçio de Dios n̄ro señor en la forma siguiente

of salvation, and being sound of mind, judgment, and my God-given understanding, thus do I make and know that I do and order this, my testament and last and final will, for the service of God, Our Lord, in the following way:

∽ Primeramente enComiendo mi anima a Dios n̄ro señor que La crio y rredimio porsu preçiosso sangre y mi cuerpo alatierra dedo fue formado i criado.

First, I entrust my soul to God, Our Lord, who created it and redeemed it with His precious blood, and my body to the earth, from which it was formed and created.

∽yten digo que sidios n̄ro señor fuere seruido de llebarme deesta enfermedad en que estoy quiero que mi cuer sea sepultado Enla yglesia del señor Santiago eneste diho pu^{o} del cercado___

Also, I state that if God Our Lord deigns to take me from this state of illness in which I find myself, I wish that my body be buried in the church of Lord Saint James in this aforementioned town of Cercado.

∽yten mando quesemedigan Vna missa de rrequien cantada, decuerpo presente si fuere ora competente y sino otro dia siguiente y se paguen lalimosna acostumbrada___

Also, I order a chanted requiem mass to be said for me, with my corpse present if the time is suitable, and if not, on a subsequent day, and the accustomed alms to be paid.

[Fol. 1v]

∽yten asi mesmo mando que se me digan diez missas rrezadas y se paguen La limosna acostumbrada___

Also, in the same manner I order that ten masses be said for me, and that the customary alms be paid.

∽yten quealpress^{te} fran^{co} poma mi marido natural de guamanga esta ẽfermo ẽL hospital de s^{a}. santaanna Digo que sidios n̄ro señor fuere seruido dellebarle desta presente vida mando que seledigan porsu anima vna missa cantada decuerpo pressente y otras diez missas rrezadas La qu^{a}L cumplan Los d̄hos mis alvaçeas | esto se entiende desu mismo bienes que en otro capitulo adelante declarare dello___

Also, since at this time Francisco Poma, my husband, native of Guamanga, is ill in the hospital of Lady Saint Ann, I say that if Our Lord God deigns to take him away from this present life, I order a chanted funeral mass to be said for his soul, and another ten masses, all of which my executors will carry out, (and pay for) obviously from his own property, which I shall explain in another section.

∽yten digo y es mi voLuntad queentro por cofrada ẽLa cofradia del santissimo ssacramento fundada ẽLa yglesia destedho pu^{o}. porhermana veinte quatro mando seden delimosna veinte *pessos de a ocho rreales* y seme asienten. mi

Also, I state and it is my will that I enter as a member into the brotherhood of the Most Holy Sacrament, founded in the church of this aforementioned town, as the twenty-fourth sister. I order that alms of twenty *pesos de a ocho reales*

nombre En el libro donde alosdemas Hermanos se asientan porque asi es mi voLuntad___

be given as charity, and that my name be registered in the book in which all of the other members register, because such is my wish.

∽yten mando quel cura deste dho pu^{o} acompañe mi cuerpo con la cruz † alta y conel sacristan ysemedigan tres possas en tres esquinas y se paguen la Limosna acostumbrada___

Also, I order that the priest of this aforementioned town accompany my body with a high † cross and with the *sacristan*, with bell tolls, and that processional chants be said for me in each of the three corners, and that the customary alms be paid.

∽yten mando que digan porelanima delorenço ocho anupa mi padre difunto Vna missa rrezada_

Also, I order that one mass be said for the soul of Lorenço Ochoanupa, my deceased father.

∽yten mando q̄den demis bienes de Limosna ala cofradia dela madre de dios del pilar de çaragoza vn *rreal de a ocho*___

Also, I order that alms of one *real de a ocho* be taken from my property and given to the brotherhood of the Mother of God, of the Pillar de Zaragoza.

∽yten mando ala cofradia delas animas del purgatorio deste d̄ho pueblo vn *real de a ocho.*

Also, I leave one *real de a ocho* to the brotherhood of the Souls of Purgatory of this aforementioned town.

∽yten mando a la cofradia del señor santiago vn *rreal de a ocho*___

Also, I leave one *real de a ocho* to the brotherhood of the Lord Saint James.

∽yten mando a las *mandas forçossas* a todas ellas [*qu*]atro *reales* conloqual aparto de todos mis bienes.

Also, I leave four *reales* for all of the *mandas forçossas*, and with this I cancel any of their claims to my property.

[Fol. 2r]

∽yten digo que soy cassada segunorden dela santa madre yglesia con fran^{co} poma mi marido legitimo aquenos cassamos tres años aesta parte poco mas o menos y no ~~emos~~ tenido ningun hijo paraser n̄ro heredero sino es La que fuere mi voLuntad___

Also, I state that I am married according to the law of the Holy Mother Church to Francisco Poma, my legitimate husband. It has been more or less three years to date since we were married, and I have not had any child to be our heir, so [the bequests] are up to me.

∽ Para en cumPLimiento de todos Los vienes quetengo declaro sonlos siguientes___

In order to carry out [the preceding bequests] of all of the property that I possess, I declare that it consists of the following:

∽ Primeramente duçientos y çinquenta *pesos de* ~~*Don rreales*~~ *a ocho* *rreales* y digo q̄los çiento y Vte cin^{co} [*canceled illegible*] son mias y los otros ciento y Vte çinco ~~son~~ de fran^{co} poma, mi marido, porque lo emos ganado con n̄ro trabajo

First, two hundred fifty *pesos de a ocho reales*. And I state that one hundred twenty five are mine, and the other one hundred twenty five are Francisco Poma, my husband's, because we have earned them with our toil and sweat. And the

y sudor delosquales d̃hos *pessos* contenidos seade distribuir ẽlas d̃has missas arriba declaradas y ẽlas demas mandas quese a͡ho, enella seentienda conlos *pesos* perteneçientes ami parte yse cumplan Los d̃hos mis albaçeas porque asies mi voLuntad___

aforementioned *pesos* listed here should be distributed for the masses mentioned above, and for the other bequests listed. It is understood [that this will be done] with the *pesos* belonging to me. And my aforementioned executors will carry it out because such is my will.

∾yten digo queal presente esta ẽfermo El͡dho fran^{co} poma mi marido ẽL hospital deseñora santa anna. ysi dios ñro s^{r}. fuere seruido dellebarle desta press^{te} uida mando seledigan ~~vn~~ La misa cantada y diez missas rrezadas comolo tengo ya declarada ẽL capitulo antes deste o como mejor ordenare El͡dho mi marido de los *pesos* perteneçientes asuparte que son los çiento y beinte çinco *pesos de a ocho* y esta es mi uoLuntad___

Also, I state that at this time Francisco Poma, my husband, is ill in the hospital of Lady Saint Ann. If Our Lord God deigns to take him away from this present life, I order one chanted mass and ten masses to be said for him, either according to what I have already declared in the section before this one, or as my aforementioned husband may prefer to order [paying] from the *pesos* that belong to him, which are one hundred twenty-five *pesos de a ocho*. And this is my wish.

∾yten declaro q̃ tengo vna cassa eneste d̃ho pueblo ẽL solar de pisco con dos puertas ~~las dos~~ consus çerraduras $^{y\ llaves}$ ~~y la vna nueba sin cerraduras y llabes~~ mando quesea para fran^{co} poma mi marido, y sie͡ldho mi marido falleçiere y pasare desta presente uida mando se ben^{da} ẽla almoneda y lo procedido della sedistribuya en dezir misas por $^{su\ anima\ de}$ ambos ~~a dos~~__

Also, I state that I possess a house in this aforementioned town on the Pisco plot, with two doors with their locks and keys [*cancelled*: and the new one without locks or keys]. I leave it for Francisco Poma, my husband; and if my aforementioned husband dies and leaves this present life, I order it to be sold at auction, and its proceeds distributed for saying masses for the souls of both.

[Fol. 2v]

∾yten declaro que tengo tres paños de manos de *Ruan* y un obillo de algodon parda

Also, I state that I possess three linen handkerchiefs and a ball of grey cotton thread.

+∾yten vna *lliclla* de gerguilla ^{color} de flor de romero con sus pasamanos de eda morada y leonada consu faxa de tafetan tornasul___

Also, a rosemary flower-colored *lliklla* made of serge, with purple and tawny silk laces and a band of sunflower taffeta.

∾yten dos camissas de *rruan* La vna de pecho y la otra alta y mas vna camisilla de niña gayada conseda negra___

Also, two linen shirts, one for a woman, and the other for a man; and a small girl's shirt, trimmed with black silk.

+∾yten vn faldellin de paño V^{er}de m^{do}. que todo lo suso se den aJoan Masmayauri mi her^{no}. porqueasies mi boLuntad___

Also, a green cloth kilt. I order that everything mentioned above be given to Joan Masmayauri, my brother, because such is my wish.

∽yten Vn par de *mates de madera pintada* pequeña y un tenedor deplata yotro pedaçito deplata qvebrada de un *topo*___

Also, a pair of little *mates de madera pintada*, a silver fork, and another silver piece broken off of a *tupu*.

∽yten declaro qve tengo dos caballos El vno esta ẽL puº de guarochiri q̃ los tiene catalina caxa ticlla mi madre yla otra en mi poder | m^{do}. q̃l caballo queesta en guarochiri sea para Lorenço ocho anupa mi hermano. y el caballo queesta en mi poder se benda para dezir bien de mi anima___

Also, I state that I possess two horses. One is in the town of Guarochiri and is being held by Catalina Caxaticlla, my mother, and the other is in my possession. I order that the horse in Guarochiri be given to Lorenço Ochoanupa, my brother, and that the horse in my possession be sold [for prayers/masses] for the benefit of my soul.

∽yten tengo un faldellin de bayeta ya trayda mando se benda___

Also, I possess a used baize kilt. I order it to be sold.

∽yten declaro qve tengo dos fraçadas mando qve se den La vna dellas blanca a Joan Quispoma mi sobrino y la otra parda sea para fran^{co} poma, mi marido y estaes mi voLuntad___

Also, I possess two blankets. I order one of them, the white one, to be given to Joan Quispoma, my nephew; the other, grey one should be for Francisco Poma, my husband, and this is my wish.

∽yten mando queden a x͡ptovaL sullcauy mi tio vn faldellin de paño azul escuro ya traida___

Also, I order that a used kilt of dark blue cloth be given to Cristoval Sullcauy, my uncle.

[Fol. 3r]

∽yten declaro que tengo doze abes ponederas ysugallo yun pollo mando se venda paradezir bien de mi anima___

Also I state that I possess twelve laying hens, their cock, and a chick. I order them to be sold [for prayers/masses] for the benefit of my soul.

∽yten tres esCofietas de Ruan y un manteles yabieja | ymas dos tijeras y dos cuchillitos pequeños.___

Also, three small linen coifs and an old tablecloth, and two scissors and two small knives.

∽yten declaro qve tengo dose axas medianas mando quea[2] para fran^{co} poma, mi marido___

Also, I state that I possess twelve medium-size adzes. I leave them for Francisco Poma, my husband.

∽yten vn *anaco* morada de caxamarca ya trayda___

Also, a used purple *anaku* from Caxamarca.

∽yten doze platos de barro y una escudilla y mas vn par de medias de paño azul escuro. ___

Also, twelve clay dishes and one bowl, and also a pair of dark blue cloth stockings.

∽yten Vn *anaco* de algodon negro ya traido y otro *anaco* biejo mando quesea para catalina llacxa cargua mi hermana___

Also, a used black cotton *anaku*, and another old *anaku*. I leave them to Catalina Llacxacargua, my sister.

2 Read: *que sea*.

∾yten Vnas Ebillas de ~~ghue~~ hierro y mas Vnos clauos___

Also, some iron buckles and some nails.

∾yten mando a catalina Ysabel mi hermana vna *lliclla* de algodon negro yse les den mis albaçeas.___

Also, I leave a black cotton *lliklla* to Catalina Ysabel, my sister, my executors should give it to her.

∾yten ~~de~~ quatro *Lampas*. Lasdos con sus cabos ylasotras dos sin cabos yuna hacha pequena yun asado, dos baritas de hierro ydos cochillos y quatro llabes de hierro___

Also four *lampas*, two with handles, and the other two without handles, and a small axe, and a spit, two iron tods, and two knives, and four iron keys.

∾yten dos sombreros El vno negro El otro pardo___

Also, two hats, one black and one grey.

∾yten una manta de *rruan*___

Also, a linen blanket.

∾yten una tinaja ___

Also, a large earthenware jar.

∾yten como dos *almudes* de manies___

Also two *almuds* of peanuts.

[Fol. 3v]

∾yten Vna talaguilla de *quingua*___

Also a small sack of *kinwa*.

∾yten vn freno bueno ytres frenos quebradas ydos sogas___

Also, a good bridle and three broken bridles, and two ropes.

∾yten dos banquillos de sentar___

Also two small sitting benches.

∾yten dos botijas y una boteçuela__

Also, two earthen pitchers and a small canister.

∾yten digo qve no deuo aninguna persona___

Also, I declare that I am not in debt to anyone.

∾Y para cumPLir y pagar este mi testamento y las mandas y legatos, obras pias y graciosas enel contenidas ynstituyo por mis albaçeas y testamentamerios [*sic*] y tenedo[re]s de mis bienes a gonçalo benites y a Joan Bautista, fiscales moradores eneste dho puº, y les doy todo mi poder cumplido a ambos. y a cada Vno dellos por si *ynsoLlidum* para que por su auturidad o de la Justiª. o como quissieren tomen de mis bienes Los que bastaren. y los bendan ẽ. almoneda. o fuera della y cumplan y executen este mi testam^{to}. y paguen lo ẽLcontenido Lo qual puedan hazer y hagan no enbargante sea passado El año del. albaceazgo qveyo selo prorrogo por todo El tiempo qve para lo cumplir se a menester___

And in order to carry out and pay [what is stipulated in] this, my testament, and the donations, and bequests, works of charity and grace listed in it, I appoint Gonçalo Benites and Joan Bautista, *fiscales* and residents of this aforementioned town, as my executors and custodians of my property. And I give full power of attorney to both and each of them *in solidum*, so that by their own authority or by the authority of justice, or as they best deem fit, they may take what they need from my goods to sell at auction or without auction, in order to execute this my testament, and pay what is stipulated in it. And they may do this even after concluding the year of executorship, which I extend for as long as is needed in order to carry out [the testament].

∾y CumPLido ypagado este mi testamento. y las mandas y legatos En el contenidas. dexo ynstituyo Enel rremaniente de todos mis bienes. por mi vniuersal heredera a catalina caxa ticlla mi madre $^{\text{que al presste esta en guarochiri}}$ Los quales aya y herede conla bendiçion de Dios ñro señor y La mia porque asi es mi Vltima voLuntad___

And once this, my testament, and the donations and bequests stipulated in it are carried out and paid, I name my mother, Catalina Caxaticlla, who at this time is in Guarochiri, as the universal heiress of all of my remaining property, which she will have and inherit with the blessing of Our Lord God, and my own, because such is my last wish.

[Fol. 4r]

∾Y poresta presente carta rreboco y anuLo y doy por ninguno qualesquier testamentos o codiçilios que ãtes de agora yo aya f͡ho por escrito o de palabra Los quales quiero qve no balgan En Juizio ni fuera del saLuo este que agora hago. que quiero que balga pormi testamento y por mi cobdiçilio o por VLtima boLuntad. o en aquella via y forma quededer^{o} aya mexor lugar En testimonio de lo qual otorgue la presente carta ãteel sCriuano del Cabildo y to^{s} aqui contenidos ques f͡ha en el pu^{o} de santiago del cercado delos Reyes. a diez yocho dias del mes de mayo de mill y seis zyentos y ocho años estando ẽ Las cassas de la morada dela d͡ha otorgante siendo para Ello llamados y Rogados por to^{s} presente don d͡go chumbi manta al[*ca*]lde ordin^{o} eneste d͡ho pu^{o} porel rrey ñro señor y agustin guachapayco y Joan paichu cama y fran^{co} purilla, yndios Ladinos moradores eneste d͡ho pueblo. y La d͡ha otorgante yel d͡ho al[*ca*]lde y to^{s} aquien yo elsCriu^{o} doy ffee que conozco no firmaron por no saber leer ni esCriuir E yo elsCriu^{o} doy ffee Lo firme este dia mes y año ff^{o} ut supra___

And with this letter I revoke, nullify, and declare invalid any testaments or codicils that I may have made before today, either verbally or in written form. They will not be valid either in or out of court; I only want the one I am making now to serve as my testament, my codicil, or my last will or whatever is the most appropriate legal means and form. In confirmation of this, I executed this document in the presence of the town council notary and the witnesses here mentioned. Done in the town of Santiago del Cercado de los Reyes on the eighteenth day of the month of May in the year one thousand six hundred eight, in [my] presence in the residence complex of the aforementioned testator, for the purpose of which were summoned and asked to be witnesses, Don Domingo Chumbimanta, first chairman of the council in this aforementioned town for our Lord the King, and Agustín Guachapayco and Joan Paichucama, and Francisco Purilla, Spanish-speaking Indians and inhabitants of this aforementioned town. And the aforementioned testator and the aforementioned chairman of the council and witnesses, whom I, the notary, certify that I know, did not sign because they do not know to read and write. And I, the notary, certify that I have signed it on this day, month, and year, dated *ut supra*.

Paso ãte my

+

Don fran^{co} defuentes [*signature*]

sCriu^{o} deCab^{do}

Done in my presence

Don Francisco de Fuentes [*signature*]

Town council notary.

PATRYCJA PRZĄDKA-GIERSZ

The will of Catalina Carguay Chumbi was written in 1608 in the town of Santiago del Cercado, located on the eastern outskirts of the city of Lima. This *reducción* had been established at the initiative of the viceroy Francisco Toledo as an autonomous residence for the indigenous people who would serve the city and the governors of Lima. As such, it had peculiar characteristics in terms of the social structure, organization, and occupational status of its inhabitants. They formed a mosaic of ethnic groups from different regions and were generally divided into two categories: those who lived temporarily in the Cercado and the group formed by those residing there permanently. Catalina Carguay Chumbi belonged to the latter, smaller group, although, as mentioned in the part of the will where she identifies herself, was a "natural *yndia*" originally from the Partition of Huarochirí.[3] It is possible that she came to the town of Santiago del Cercado at the initiative of the Jesuits who administered the parishes of Saint James (Santiago del Cercado) and Huarochirí during that period. It is worth noting that the testatrix was not identified in this document by referencing her husband, a practice recommended in the model will of the Toledo ordinances (Nowack 2006: 56). This peculiarity may be explained by the serious condition of her husband, Francisco Poma, "native of Guamanga," who at the time that this testament was issued was interned in the hospital of Lady Saint Ann (Señora Santa Ana) for indigenous people in Lima.[4] Moreover, Catalina requested in her will a chanted mass and ten recited masses in the event of the death of her husband, that should be paid from his share of the inheritance. She also ordered one recited mass for the salvation of Lorenço Ochoanupa, her deceased father. For herself, she requested the same number of masses as for her husband, stipulated the local church of Saint James (Santiago del Cercado) as the place of her burial, asked the priest and the sacristan to accompany her body "with a high cross," and ordered "chants in each of the three corners." In this part of the will we also find a special clause referring to the brotherhood of The Most Holy Sacrament (Santísimo Sacramento), one of four based in the town church. The testatrix bequeathed alms to this brotherhood under the condition that her name would be included in the book of the brotherhood along with names of the other sisters. Catalina also donated money to the other brotherhoods: Mother of God of the Pillar de

3 Huarochirí is currently located in the center of Peru, in the central eastern part of the department of Lima.

4 There was a hospital named San Blas in the town of Santiago de Cercado, but in serious cases indigenous people were treated in the hospital of Lady Saint Ann (Señora Santa Ana) in Lima.

Zaragoza (Madre de Dios del Pilar de Zaragoza), Souls of Purgatory (Ánimas del Purgatorio), and Lord Saint James (Señor Santiago). The names of these last three seldom appear in documents of this era and are apparently unknown to many researchers (Hampe Martínez 2010: 94–96).

In accordance with official standards, immediately following the clauses dealing with topics of a religious nature, information regarding the testatrix's civil status, her heirs, her executors, and her liabilities is provided (Eire 1995: 34–39). Catalina was married for only three years and had no children who could receive bequests after her death. In her will she distributed the entire two hundred fifty *pesos* collected during the marriage between her and her husband. The testatrix left her house "with two doors" to her husband, making sure that in case of his death the property should be sold to pay for the celebration of masses for both of them.

The next section of the will contains an extensive list of Catalina Carguay Chumbi's personal property, including clothing and dresses, both of the traditional (e.g., *lliklla*, *anaku*) and European (e.g., "linen shirts") varieties, as well as other luxury objects. Among the latter, prehispanic items, such as a silver pin *tupu* and a pair of decorated wooden vessels known as *qiru* in Quechua, are particularly striking. It is remarkable that these objects, as markers of prestige, are also documented occurring in pairs in the ancient prehispanic tradition. Some of them are mentioned by their own names in Quechua, and are accompanied by descriptions relating, for example, to color, decoration, state ("old" or "new"), and so on. The inventory also includes a list of a variety of objects, such as various craft tools, pots, benches, and food, which provide valuable information about the material legacy and culture of this period. The heirs to her possessions were her husband; two sisters, Catalina Llacxacargua and Catalina Ysabel; two brothers, Lorenço Ochoanupa and Joan Masmayauri; her uncle, Cristoval Sullcauy; and her nephew, Joan Quispoma. The choice of heirs and the relative proportions of the bequests they receive, can provide important information about the family relationships and the social ties that characterized the life of the testatrix. She gave dresses and traditional clothing, especially that worn by women, such as *lliklla* and *anaku*, to her sisters, while she distributed other garments and textile items, such as kilts or blankets, among the men.

In contrast with other wills from the same period, little space was devoted to the issue of debts. Only a short clause located at the end of the property inventory included information stating that Catalina did not have any debts. It is surprising that none of the testatrix's relatives appear among the executors, testamentaries, and property holders mentioned in the will. The names of two men stand out. Gonzalo Benites and Joan Bautista were "*fiscales* and residents of this aforementioned town," and the testatrix's confidence in them was expressed by a long formulation. Similarly, Catalina named her mother, Catalina Caxaticlla, "as the universal heiress of all of the remaining property," which at the time the will was issued was in the town of Huarochirí.

The will was signed only by the council clerk, Don Francisco de Fuentes, in the presence of four witnesses: "Don Domingo Chumbimanta, first chairman of the council in this aforementioned town for our Lord the King, and Agustín Guachapayco and Joan Paichucama, and Francisco Purilla, Spanish-speaking Indians and inhabitants of this aforementioned town," who did not sign the document because they could neither read nor write.

DOCUMENT 17

Testament of Martín Rimanga, San Gerónimo, Peru, 1612[1]

Patrycja Prządka-Giersz, Jan Szemiński, and John Sullivan

[Fol. 1r]

[*On the left margin*: Testam^{to} de martin rimanca, yn^{o} dft^{o}, 1612]

Yn Dey ynomine[2] , amen. sepan quantos esta carta de testamento vieren como yo m͡yn Rimanga yn^{o} natural del pu^{o} de sanger^{mo}, de Laprouinçia de guayllas y alpresente rrecidente eneste pu^{o} del señor sanctiago del çercado Estando enfermo delcuerpo y sana de la boluntad y en mi libre Juyzio y entendimiento tal qual dios n͡ro s^{r} fue seruido de me dar Creyendo como firme mente Creo enla sanctissima trinidad padre y hijo y espiritu sancto tres personas y Vn solo dios Verdadero que biue y rreyna p͡a siempre Jamas, amen___

∞Primem^{te}: mando mi anima a dios q̃ La Crio y rredemio por su presiosa sangre y el cuerpo ala tierra de q̃ fue form^{do}.

[*Left margin*: Testament of Martín Rimanga, deceased Indian, 1612]

In Dei Nomine. Amen. Know all who see this testament letter that I, Martín Rimanga, Indian, native of the town of San Gerónimo in the Huayllas province, now resident here in the town of Lord Santiago del Cercado, sick as my body is and sound of will, and with my free judgment and understanding such as God Our Lord deigned to give me, believing as I do firmly believe in the Most Holy Trinity, the Father, the Son, and the Holy Spirit, three persons and the only true God who lives and reigns forevermore, Amen.

First, I entrust my soul to God, who created it and redeemed it with His precious blood, and my body to the earth, from which it was formed.

1 Archivo General de la Nación (AGN), Lima, Testamentos de Indios, leg. 1, exp. 20.

2 This is bad Latin for "In God's name" (*In Dei nomine*).

DOI: 10.5876/9781607328346.c017

∾yten mando q̃ mi cuerpo sea sepultado dentro de la yglesia deste dho pu^{o} del cercado y me sea lleuado el dho mi cuerpo desde mi casa con quatro posas en quatro esquinas y paguen alos cantores 4 *patacones*___

Also, I order that my body be buried inside the church of this town of Cercado, and that my aforementioned body be taken from my home with bell tolls and chants in each of the four corners; and the cantors should be paid four *patacones*.

∾yten mando q̃ seme digan diez misas rrezadas pormi anima.

Also, I order ten masses be said for my soul.

∾yten mando a La cofradia de nr̃a senora del pilar de Zaragoza dos *patacones*

Also, I send two *patacones* to the brotherhood of Our Lady of the Pilar of Zaragoza.

∾yten mando se de de limosna ala cofradia del s^{r} santissimo sacramento Vn*patacon*

Also, I order an offering of one *patacon* be given to the brotherhood of the Lord Holy Sacrament.

∾yten declaro q̃ tengo Vn hijo llamado Ju^{o} Quispi q̃ sera hedad de diez o doze años el qual es mi hijo lixitimo

Also, I state that I have a son named Juan Quispi, who should be ten or twelve years old, and is my rightful son.

∾yten declaro q̃ tengo Vncalson de rrazo con sus pasamanos de oro y plata mando q̃ sebenda.

Also, I state that I have a pair of satin breeches with its golden and silver laces. I order it to be sold.

∾yten declaro q̃ tengo dos camisetas listados nueuos m^{do}. q̃ sebenda

Also, I state that I have two new striped shirts. I order them to be sold.

∾yten declaro que tengo otra camiseta pintada nueuo mando que se benda

Also, I state that I have another new painted shirt. I order it to be sold.

∾yten declaro q̃ tengo un calsõ de *rruan* m^{do}. q̃ sebenda

Also, I state that I have a pair of linen breeches. I order it to be sold.

[Fol. 1v]

∾yten declaro q̃ tengo Vnpares de baso deplata mando q̃ sebenda

Also, I state that I have one pair of silver cups. I order them to be sold.

∾yten declaro q̃ tengo Vnpares de sapatos y Vn assuelo y Vn asadon y Vna *Lampa* man q̃ sebenda.

Also, I state that I have one pair of shoes, and one adze, one spade, and one *lampa*. I order them to be sold.

∾yten digo q̃ tengoVuna *guauya* de Vn yn^{o} ya difunto mando q̃ sebenda bendido se den al cura p̃a q̃ diga de misas por los difuntos___

Also, I say that I have a *wawya* belonging to an Indian who is now deceased. I order it to be sold. Once sold, the proceeds are to be given to the priest for masses to be said for the dead.

∾yten declaro q̃ tengo un capote azul trayda m^{do} sebenda

Also, I state that I have a used blue cloak. I order it to be sold.

∾yten tengo Vn espejo y Vna escubilla y Vn compas de hierro y Vna tenasuela de rrancar baruas mando sebenda

Also, I have a mirror and a small brush, and an iron compass and pair of tweezers for beard plucking. I order them to be sold.

∾yten declaro q̃ tengo Vn sõbrero nueuo m^{do} sebenda

Also, I state that I have a new hat. I order it to be sold.

∾yten declaro que tengo Vna rreja con su timon m^{do}. Sebenda

Also, I state that I have a ploughshare with its beam. I order it to be sold.

∾yten tengo Vna manta negra ~~bie~~ trayda y Vna *partiana* mando sebenda.

Also, I have one used black cape and a *partiana*. I order them to be sold.

∾yten declaro q̃ tengo Vna cuxa q̃ me costo 15 *p^{o}s de a nueve* mando q̃ sebenda y seden ami muger maria cancha para su luto___

Also, I state that I have a bedstead that I bought for fifteen *pesos de a nueve*. I order it to be sold and the proceeds given to my wife María Cancha for her mourning attire.

∾yten tengo Vn paño de manos mando q̃ sebenda

Also, I have a hand towel. I order it to be sold.

∾yten declaro q̃ tengo una asta La qual tengo conçertado en quatro *patacones* y me pago doze *rreales* o mas o menos no me acuerdo bien mando q̃ se cobre el rresto y entreguen el asta

Also, I state that I have a pike, [the sale of] which I have agreed to for four *patacones*, and he paid me twelve *reales*, more or less, I do not remember well. I order the rest to be collected and the pike handed over.

∾yten declaro q̃ me deve ana, muger de garçia Colq̃, 1 *patacon* mando se cobre

Also, I state that Ana, García Colque's wife, owes me one *patacon*. I order it to be collected.

∾yten declaro q̃ deuo a Vna yn^{a} llamada beatriz seis *patacones* y quatro *rreales* mando se pague digo es difunta la d͡ha yn^{a} mando q̃ se den al cura para q̃ se digã de misas. por los difuntos ___

Also, I state that I owe an Indian named Beatriz six *patacones* and four *reales*. I order them to be paid; on the other hand, since the aforementioned Indian is deceased, I order them to be given to the priest to say masses for the dead.

∾yten deuo a ynes Xutuy tres *patacones* ~~tre~~ y quatro *reales* tanbien difunta mando seden al cura pa las dhas misas

Also, I owe Inés Xutuy, also deceased, three *patacones* and four *reales*. I order them to be given to the priest for the aforementioned masses.

∾yten deuo a ger^{mo}. esterero Vn *rreal* mando se pague.

Also, I owe Gerónimo, a mat maker, one *real*. I order it to be paid.

∾yten devo a͡xpoual, esterero, do *reales* mando sepague

Also, I owe Cristóbal, a mat maker, two *reales*. I order it to be paid.

[Fol. 2r]

∾yten mando y es mi Vltima boluntad q̃ despues de averse cumplido mi entierro y mi alma to el ~~rremaniente~~ demas rremaniente q̃dare mando a mi muger maria cancha y esta es mi vltima boluntad.

Also, I order, and this is my last wish, that upon completion of my burial, the responsibility for all matters pertaining to my soul and other pending affairs be entrusted to my wife, María Cancha. And this is my last wish,

y para esto nombro por mis albaseas a sanctiago caruayañac y a Ju^{o} Yauri pa q̃ hagan cumplir este mi testamento ques ff^{o} eneste d͡ho pueblo del s^{r} sanctiago

and for this I appoint as my executors Sanctiago Caruayana and Juan Yauri so that they will enforce this testament of mine, which was made in this town of Lord Santiago.

y mando ala d͡ha mi muger esta casa contoda su puerta.[3]

And I leave to my aforementioned wife this house with its entire garden,

a 1θ2 de setienbre de 1607 años siendo testigos her^{do} ger^{mo}. y anton xulca y m^{x}yn caxabillca, rresidentes eneste d͡ho pu^{o} porq̃ los d͡hos no supieron firmar ni el otorgante. rrogaron ager^{mo}. mexia lo firmase de su nombre___

on September 12 of the year 1607, having as witnesses Hernando Gerónimo and Antón Xulca and Martín Caxabillca, who dwell in this aforementioned town. Because neither these nor the testator know how to sign their name, they asked Gerónimo Mejía to sign in their name.

tanbien tengo Vna hacha ~~tanb~~ ya gastada m^{do}. se bẽda

Also I have an axe, already worn down. I order it to be sold.

A Ruego y por te^{o} ger^{mo} mex^{a}

According to the request and as a witness Gerónimo Mejía

[*signature*]

[*signature*]

[Fol. 3r]

\+

∞Quenta quesele toma delos bienes de Martin rimanga, difunto, aJoan Yauri aLuaçea del dho difunto, aPedimiento de Joan Quespi, menor[4] del dho Difunto, son los siguientes___

Inventory of the deceased Martín Rimanga's property, taken by // Juan Yauri, the aforementioned deceased's executor, requested by Juan Quispi, the aforementioned deceased's minor [son], and it is as follows:

∞	Lo Primero vn pares de *cocos* de pla La qu^{a}l dijo que se bendio en U 6 *p^{o}s* r^{ls}___	U 6 p^{o}s r^{ls}	First a pair of silver *cocos*, which he said was sold for six *pesos*.	6 *pesos*
	Yten vn par de çapatos de cordoban La qual dijo que se bendio en U *p^{o}s 4* r^{ls}	U U p^{o}s 4 r^{ls}	Also, a pair of goat-skin shoes, which he said was sold for four *reales*.	4 *reales*

3 The word *puerta* doesn't fit the context; the expected would be *huerta*.

4 *Menor* here refers to a person who is underage.

	Yten una azuela La qual dijo que se bendio en un *Real de a ocho*___	U 1 p^{o}s. r^{ls}	Also, one adze, which he said was sold for one *real de a ocho*.	1 *peso*
∞	Yten un açadon La qual se bendio en dos *Reales*	U U p^{o}s 2 r^{ls}	Also, one hoe, which he said was sold for two *reales*.	2 *reales*
∞	Yten Vna *Lampa* La qual se bendio en catorze *Reales*.	U 1 p^{o}s 6 r^{ls}	Also, one *lampa*, which he said was sold for fourteen *reales*.	1 *peso* 6 *reales*
∞	Yten vn capote de paño azul ya trayda. La qual dijo quese bendio en seis *Reales*	U U p^{o}s 6 r^{ls}	Also, one used blue cloak, which he said was sold for six *reales*.	6 *reales*
∞	Yten vna esCoVilla de çerda La qu^{a}l dijo que se bendio en dos *rreales* ___	U U p^{o}s 2 r^{ls}	Also, a small bristle brush, which he said was sold for two *reales*.	2 *reales*
∞	Yten Vn espejo La qual dijo que se bendio en quatro *Reales*___	U U p^{o}s 4 r^{ls}	Also, a mirror, which he said was sold for four *reales*.	4 *reales*
∞	Yten un sombrero La qual dijo q̃ se vendio en ocho *Reales*	U 1 p^{o}s . r^{ls}	Also, a hat, which he said was sold for eight *reales*.	1 *peso*
∞	Yten vn timon con su cabeza y Reja La qual dixo que se bendio en siete *patacones*	U 7 p^{o}s . r^{ls}	Also, one plowbeam with its head and share, which he said was sold for seven *patacones*.	7 *pesos*
	O____________	U 19 p^{o}s . r^{ls}		

[Fol. 3v]

∞	yten vna manta de algodon negra ya trayda La qual dijo quese vendio en seis *rr^{e}les*_____	U U p^{o}s 6 r^{ls}	Also one used black cloak which he said was sold for six *reales*	6 *reales*
∞	Yten vn cuxa La qual dijo quesebendio en diez *p^{o}s*	1 U p^{o}s . r^{ls}	Also one bedstead which he said was sold for ten *pesos*	10 *pesos*

∾	Yten vn Paño de manos de algodon La qual dijo que se bendio en dos *rr^{e}les*	U U p^{o}s 2 r^{ls}	Also a cotton towel which he said was sold for two *reales*	2 *reales*
∾	Yten vna hasta delança. La qual dijo quese Vendio en dos *p^{o}s*. y quatro Reales_____	U 2 p^{o}s 4 r^{ls}	Also one shaft of a spear which he said was sold for two pesos and four *reales*	2 *pesos* 4 *reales*
∾	Yten Vna camisseta de algodon Pintada nueba La qual dijo que sebendio en ochos *p^{o}s*.	U 8 p^{o}s . r^{ls}	Also one new painted cotton shirt which he said was sold for eight *pesos*	8 *pesos*
∾	Yten vna hasta de hierro La qual dixo quese bendio en ocho *rr^{e}les*	U 1 p^{o}s . r^{ls}	Also one iron lance which he said was sold for eight *reales*	1 *peso*
	Los quales dhos bienes aRiba C^{dos} pareçe ysuma averse venido en 41 *p^{o}s*. 4 rr son estos	41 p^{o}s 4 r^{ls}	All the said goods enumerated above have been sold for the sum of 41 *pesos* and 4 *reales*, that is	41 *pesos* 4 *reales*

[Fol. 4r]

\+

∾ ẽL Pueblo desantiago decercado enCatorze dias del mes de Hebrero demill yseis cientos e doze años ãte d͡go vanegas allde ordinario eneste d͡ho pueblo por el rrey n͡ro s^{r}.- y enpresençia de mi el sCriu^{o} delCabildo. Pareçio press^{te}. Juan Quispe yndio hijo y Heredero de martin rimanCa yndio difunto morador que fue deste dho Pueblo segun Consta por el d͡ho testamento su fh^{a}. endiez y ocho de septiembre de mill y seis çientos y siete años. Elqual estando press^{te}. pidio ãte el d͡ho allde que Joan yauri questa Press^{t}e. fue albaçea Juntam^{te}. consantiago carhua yañac ya difunto del d͡ho m͡rn rimanga difunto su padre y que algunos

\+

In the town of Santiago on February the fourteenth of the year one thousand six hundred and twelve before Diego Vanegas, ordinary mayor in this the said town for the King Our Lord, and in the presence of me, the Town Council Notary, appeared Juan Quispi, Indian, son and heir of Martín Rimanga, Indian, deceased inhabitant who resided in this said town as recorded by the said testament dated September the eighteenth of the year one thousand and six hundred and seven. And being present, he asked the said mayor why Juan Yauri, who is present, and together with the already deceased Santiago Carhua Yañac was the executor of the will

bienes que tenia en su poder y delos pesos proçedidos noseles auia dado quenta como a tal heredero y para su Cumplimiento el d͡ho allde mando que el d͡ho Joan yauri dequenta y Razon delo quesele pide asi. lo mando efirmo____

of the said Martín Rimanga, his deceased father, has not given an account of the goods which he kept in his power or of the *pesos* proceeding (from their sale) to him as heir. To fulfill (the request), the said mayor ordered the said Juan Yauri to give an account of what he was asked to do. Thus he ordered and signed

\+

d͡go venegass

ãte my

Don franc^{o}defuente [*signature*]

\+

Diego Venegas [*signature*]

Before me

Don Francisco de Fuente [*signature*]

\+

∽ ẽL d͡ho dia mes y año susod͡ho pareçio Presente Joan yauri yndio albaçea que fue de m͡in rimanga difunto edio quenta delos bienes que entro en su poder enla forma siguiente___

On the aforementioned day, month, and year, appeared Juan Yauri who was the executor of the deceased Martín Rimanga's will and in the following way gave an account of the goods that had entered in his power.

cargo

∽ Hazele cargo de quarenta y ũ p^{o}s de a ocho Reales y medio que entro en su poder y del d͡ho santiago carhua yañac yà difunto que asie mesmo fue albaçea ___

Obligation:

He is held responsible for forty one *pesos de a ocho reales* and a *medio* which came into his possession and the possesion of the said deceased Santiago Carhua Yañac, who also was the executor.

descargo

Primeramente dio por desCargo çinco patacones que dio aJer^{mo} mexia p^{a} el dia del entierro y mostro carta de pago y notiene f͡ha del mes y año ___

Quittance:

First he gave as evidence of quittance five *patacones* which he had given to Gerónimo Mejía for the day of the funeral, and he displayed a payment letter that has no date of the month and year.

[Fol. 4v]

∽ ytẽ dio por desCargo de treze *patacones* que dio al p^{e} Ju^{o} bazquez. cura deste pu^{o}, y mostro car de pago su f͡ha en 26 de otubre de seis çientos y siete años ___

U 13 p^{o}s . r^{ls}

Also, he gave as evidence of quittance thirteen *patacones* that he had given to father Juan Bazques, curate of this town, and he produced the receipt of payment, dated October 26, in the year six hundred seven.

∽ Yten dio por desCargo de siete *patacones* que dio al padre x͡ptoual de olmedo deLa Comp^{a} de J͡hs, cura que

U U 7 p^{o}s . r^{ls}

Also, he gave as evidence of quittance seven *patacones* that he had given to father Cristóbal de Olmedo of the Jesuit order,

fue deste d͡ho pueblo, para que dijera misas rrezadas su f͡ha en beinte ocho de nobiembre de 1607 ao^{s}___		who had been curate of this aforementioned town, to say masses, dated November 8, in the year 1607.
∾ yten dio Por desCargodiez p^{o}s, 2 *rr* y *medio* que dio en Vestido deluto amaria Cancha muger legitima que fue del dho dif^{to}. su p^{e}___	U 10 p^{o}s 2 r^{ls}	Also, he gave as evidence of quittance ten *pesos* and two *reales* and a *medio* that he had given for the mourning attire of María Cancha, lawful wife of the aforementioned deceased, his father.
∾ yten Por desCargo ~~quatro~~ ^{cinco} *p^{o}s* y ~~quatro~~ ^{vn} *Real* y *medio* que dio bestido deluto aJoan quespi Hijo y heredero del dho difunto y aestos dos capit[ul]os estubo press^{te} el d͡ho Ju^{o} quispe y deClaro que asi Reçibieron conlad͡ha sum^{e} difunta___	U U5 p^{o}s . 1 r^{ls}	Also, as evidence of quittance, five *pesos* and one *real* and a *medio* that provided for the mourning attire of Joan Quespi, son and heir of the aforementioned deceased. And the aforementioned Juan Quispi was present for the execution of these two payments, and he stated that he and his aforementioned, deceased mother so received it.
Por manera Hechas la d͡ha^{s} quentas summa y monta el gasto que se a hecho 40 p^{o}s 4 r^{ls} – y son estos___	U 40 p^{o}s 4 r^{ls}	Thus made, the aforementioned account comes to a sum and total expenditure of forty *pesos* and four *reales*, and it is indeed this amount.

[*on the left margin*: Alcançe] Hechas las dhas quentas quedo por alcançado el dicho Ju^{o} yauri en Vn *Real [on the right margin:* U U 1 p^{o}s . r^{ls}] *de a ocho* y no amas nisehallo que aya entrado en su poder ~~o sus~~ otros bienes del d͡ho difunto. La qual d͡ha quenta se hizo ãte el d͡ho al[*ca*]lde y empresençia de mi el sCriu^{o} y delos to^{s} press^{tes} Joan grabiel y alonso her^{z}. alguazil m^{or} del d͡ho pu^{o} ~~el dho alg~~ con lo qual se feneçio toda la d͡ha qu^{ta}. Eld͡ho allde lofirmo e yo el sCriu^{o} doy ffe e lo firme, entre rreg^{es} .çinco, vn vala. //tes^{do} quatro – quatro no vala

[*In the left margin*: Deficit] After the aforementioned account was settled, the aforementioned Juan Yauri remained with a deficit of one *real de a ocho* and nothing else; and no further property of the aforementioned deceased was found, nor was found to have entered into his custody. The aforementioned account was settled before the aforementioned mayor and in my, the notary's, presence, as well as that of the attending witnesses, Juan Gabriel and Alonso Hernández, high constable of the aforementioned town; and thus the aforementioned account was closed. The aforementioned mayor signed it and I, the notary, validated it and signed it. The insertion above of "five" and "one" is valid; "four" is crossed out — "four" is not valid.

d͡go venegas [*signature*]

Domingo Venegas [*signature*]

ãte my *Don* Fran^{co} defuente [*signature*]

Before me, Don Francisco de Fuente [*signature*]

sCriu^{o} del Cabdo

The council notary

Patrycja Prządka-Giersz

Martín Rimanga's[5] will was written down on September 12, 1607, in the town of Santiago del Cercado[6] in the presence of three witnesses: Hernando Gerónimo, Antón Xulca, and Martín Caxabillca. The document was signed by Gerónimo Mejía, a member of the indigenous society who, based on the presence of certain linguistic errors in the text of the will, probably spoke Quechua as a native language. The composition of the will and its terminology are generally based on the model recommended by the Toledo ordinances of 1575 (Nowack 2006: 51–77).

The testator was one of the permanent residents of Santiago del Cercado, but he came from the town of San Gerónimo in the Huayllas province. Although he did not belong to the indigenous nobility, he was a perfect example of the kind of successful people who strove to improve their living conditions and social position. An analysis of the personal effects registered in this document suggests that the testator belonged to the group of natives who worked in the fields.

As a good Christian, Martín Rimanga requested to be buried in the town church of Santiago del Cercado. He asked that his body be carried for the funeral "with bell tolls and chants in each of the four corners," and paid the cantors four *patacones* (*pesos*) for this service. For the care of his soul, he also requested ten masses, a number that clearly marked his status and position within the indigenous society. He also arranged for the two brotherhoods of Our Lady of the Pilar of Zaragoza (Nuestra Sęñora del Pilar de Zaragoza) and the Lord Holy Sacrament (Señor Santísimo Sacramento) to receive alms in *patacones*.

The sole heirs indicated by the testator were his legitimate son, Juan Quispi, who was ten or twelve years old at the time, and his wife, María Cancha. The list of goods is not extensive but it is written in a style appropriate for wealthy people, and provides interesting data about the material culture and daily life of the inhabitants of the town. Among the things accumulated during testator's lifetime and highlighted in the text are different types of garments, such as clothing, blankets, shirts, hats, and shoes. Some of them were testimonies of prehispanic times; for instance, there is a painted shirt, possibly a short tunic decorated with paint, recognized traditionally as having prestigious and

5 The name *Rimanga* itself provides phonetic evidence that points to the Quechua dialect of the Huaylas region, the testator's place of origin (Jan Szemiński, personal communication).

6 For more on the town of Cercado de Santiago, see the will of Catalina Carguay Chumbi (Document 16, this volume).

symbolic value. In addition, the list contains two silver vessels of prehispanic origin, known in Cusco as *akilla*, normally used for important ceremonies. Listed also are objects, such as field tools (a spade, a hoe, and an axe), that were introduced and distributed within indigenous society after European contact. Martín Rimanga decided to sell all of his property, with the exception of his home,[7] which he gave to his wife. The notarial account included in the will documents the list of movable goods that were sold for a total of forty-one *pesos* and four *reales*. The price noted with each individual item corresponds to its actual value on the colonial market. At the end of the inventory of movable goods, the testator listed four people to whom he owed money. Two were mat makers, Gerónimo and Cristóbal, to whom he was indebted for one and two *reales*, respectively. The other two, interestingly, were women, Inés Xutuy and "an Indian woman named Beatrice." Both were already deceased and therefore the money was to be given to the priest to celebrate masses for their souls. Martín Rimanga had only one debtor, "Ana, García Colque's wife," who owed him one *patacon*.

The executors of the will were Santiago Caruayana, Martín's father, and Juan Yauri, who at the request of Juan Quispi presented to the mayor an account and calculation of the goods, which was attached to the will. Don Francisco de Fuente, the council clerk, and Dominic Venegas, the town mayor, signed the document on February 14, 1612, in the presence of two witnesses, Juan Gabriel and Alonso Hernández, the high constable (*aguasil)* of the aforementioned town.

7 Probably this was a house with a garden; however, in the document the word *puerta* 'gate' appears instead of the word *huerta* 'garden', which in this context does not make much sense.

DOCUMENT 18

Testament of Francisca de los Angeles, San Luis Obispo Chalco Tlalmanalco, Mexico, 1663/1743[1]

John Sullivan

[Fol. 1r]

+ yca in itocatzin tt,° Jes[. . .][2] p̄to, yhua in senquiscaichpochtli dios ytlasonantzin ma quima[t]ican yn aquique quihtasque quipoasque ynin amatl in queni nehuatl fransisca de los angeles nicã nochan in ipa altepetl san luis chalco tlalmanalco ca nipohui ipan barrio tenayacan mazonelihui i ninococotica yese ninoquitia ca melahuac inic nicnoneltoquitia santissima trinidad dios tetatzin dios tepiltzin dios espiritu santo yei personas auh ca sase yn inteoyelistzin ihua in ixquich quimoneltoquitia

+ In the name of our lord Jesus Christ and the perfectly virgin Mother of God, may those who see and read this document know that I, Francisca de los Angeles, am a resident here in the *altepetl* of San Luis Chalco and that I belong to the *barrio* of Tenayohcan. Although I am sick, I acknowledge that I truly believe in the Holy Trinity—God the Father, God the Son, and God the Holy Spirit—three persons, but only one in their divinity; and in everything that our mother, the Holy Roman Church,

1 Manuscripts/Collection 49/(1), Indian Language Series, Manuscripts Collection, Latin American Library, Tulane University. It is mistakenly titled "Will of Francisco de los Ángeles" (the name of the testator is actually *Francisca*). The document is a 1743 copy of the original document, made at the request of the testatrix's descendants.

2 A large amount of the surface area of each of the three pages of this manuscript is gone, probably due to moisture-related deterioration of the paper. Everything between square brackets in the transcription represents an approximate measurement of the length of the missing writing. I have attempted to reconstruct as much of this material as possible; an ellipsis indicates where I have been unable to do so.

DOI: 10.5876/9781607328346.c018

tonantzin santa iglecia Romana ca mochi nicneltoca ihua ninosenetoltia ca mochipa ipa nimemis ihua ipa nimiquis i melahuac tlaneltoquilistli santa fe chatolica et[a]

believes. I believe everything and I unreservedly vow that I will always live and that I will die in the true belief, the Holy Catholic Faith, etc.

/v huel achtopa niquitoa y noyolia nanima ca isemactzinco niccahua in tt,[o] dios yeica ca oquimochihuili oquimoyocolili[3, 4] ma quimohuiquili in canpa quimohuiquilis quimoyeyamaquilis ca oquimomaquixtili yca in itlasoesotzin ihua in ixquich ytlazopassi[y]ontzin auh i nonacayo ca nicmaca in tlali yeica ca itech oquis ca ihuanpo

From the very first, I say that I leave my soul entirely in the hands of our Lord God, because He made it, He created it. May He take it where He will take it to give it a home, for He freed it with His precious blood and the entirety of His precious passion. On the other hand, I give my flesh to the earth; from there it came and is therefore its counterpart.

/v yhua niquitoa yn caltzintli yhuan in calali ca mochi nicnocahuililitiuh y noconetzin x̃ptobal de los Angeles ca ayac quitehuilis ca nicnemactia yaxca ayac quiquixtilis ca catqui quadrado ca nicnotlaltenamiquilia y nohueshuatzin pelaxtitlan in canpa totlaltenamiqui mochiuhtica quaxochtli senuelas

And I say that I am leaving the house and the house plot in their entirety to my son Cristóbal de los Ángeles. No one is to challenge him regarding them: I am bequeathing it to him; it is his property and no one is to take it from him. [The plot] is square. I share a border with my sister-in-law in Pelaxtitlan; where we share the border, boundary markers are set.

//v yhua niquitoa nicnemactia y noxhuiuh Juan fran[co] ca ninemactitehua se caltontli mostla huiptla hualas onca quimacas yn ihermano x̃ptobal de los Angeles ca ixquich noxhuihua auh camo[5] nica nesi

And I say that I am making a bequest to my grandson Juan Francisco. I bequeath him one small house. Sometime in the future he will return, and at that time his brother, Cristóbal de los Ángeles, will give it to him, for both are my grandchildren. But he is not present here.

---

3 *Yocoya* 'to make/fashion/create something' is supposedly a transitive verb, the benefactive form of which is *yocolia* 'to make/fashion/create something for someone'. The addition of a reflexive prefix and a second benefactive suffix would produce the reverential *quimoyocolilih* '[God] made/fashioned/created it for him or her' that we have here in the document. However, it is clear from the context that *quimoyocolilih* is meant to form a doublet phrase with the preceeding *quimochihuilih*, and the sense here is clear: '[God] made/fashioned/created [my soul]'. Either the notary made an error or the speakers who produced this document considered *yocoya* to be an inceptive and therefore intransitive verb, formed from an unattested root and the verbing suffix *-ya* 'to be made/fashioned/created'. This kind of verb is made causative and thus transitive with the addition of the suffix *-lia*, resulting in *quiyocolih* '[God made/fashioned/created [my soul]'. The presence of the additional reflexive suffix and benefactive *-lia* that we find in this case gives us the reverential form *quimoyocolilih*.

4 All citations of the Nahuatl text included in the notes and commentary of this document are written with the stardardized ACK orthography.

5 *Ca* and *ahmo* are written together.

//v hompa mani se pedaso tlali mecalli pelaxtitlan caltitlan ca niquincahuilitiuh yn omentin noxhuihuan x̃potobal de Los Angeles yhuan in ihermano diego de Los angeles quimotlacocotonisque mochiuhtica quaxochtli sentetl peras ycaltenpancopa tlantica y nopilotzin Don Luis de rrojas

There is a long, narrow piece of land in the residential area of Pelaxtitlan. I am leaving it to both of my grandchildren, Cristóbal de los Ángeles and his brother, Diego de los Ángeles. They will divide it in half. A pear tree acts as the boundary: it ends at the edge of the house of my nephew, Don Luis de Rojas.

//v nica nicahuilia y nochpoch Mª. de los Angeles se pedasito tlalpitzactontli ic itechcopa norte ca nicnotlaltenamiquilia dn. sebastian basques hualtlamelauhtica itechcacopa tlateli quaxochtli mochiuhtica ic [to]nalli iquisayan ca niquintlaltenamiqui tlalticahuaque

Here I leave a small, narrow piece of land to my daughter María de los Ángeles. At its north end, I share a border with Don Sebastián Vásquez. It comes along straight to the hill, which is the boundary marker. To the east I share a border with the Tlaltecahuahqueh.

[//v omp]a ma[ni o]c se pedaso tlalli nepantla actica ica om[................]hui [..............................]a i nopiluan nio[6] nohueshuahuan i no[..........................] [..............................] auh intla mos[tla] huiptla quiteh[uilisque......................] [.......quitlaxtlahuili]sque maquil[li pe]sos

There lies another piece of land, inserted in the middle with [. . .][7] my children; likewise, my sister's-in-law, my [. . .] But if at some time in the future they challenge [. . .] they will pay five *pesos*.

[Fol. 1v]

[....................tl]alpitzactontli yquapa[8] mani ca niquinemactitehua yn oc[cequi nox]guihuan ca no quimotlacocotonisque franca de los Angeles nox[h]uiuh yhua yn nicolas ortis ca amo aquin quinquixtilis se pedaso tlaltontli tlateli onicnamacac amo aquin quitenhuis ca oticnamacaque tonehua i n[o]coneuh diego de los Angeles ca totech omonec ynic oticnamacaque ayac quitenguis ca oquimocohuili y[n nop]ilotzin in inantzin Dn luis de rroxas Dª Mª

[. . .] small, long field, which is in [. . .]. I bequeath it to some other grandchildren of mine. Francisca de los Ángeles, my granddaughter, and Nicolás Ortiz will also divide it in half. No one will take it from them. I sold a small piece of hilly land. No one will challenge her, for my son, Diego de los Ángeles, and I sold it together. We needed to sell it. No one will challenge her. Doña María, my nephew Don Luis de Rojas's mother, bought it.

6 I'm not completely sure of the meaning of the sequence, *nio*. Perhaps it is *[i]n iuh* 'likewise'.

7 An ellipsis between brackets in the translation corresponds to missing words in the transcription that I have not been able to reconstruct.

8 I'm not sure what *yquapa* means. It most likely functions as an adverb of place, explaining where *[tla]pitzactontli . . . mani* 'a small, long field which is . . .' is located, obligatory information for identifying plots of land in Nahua wills. It could be *ic cuappan* 'around where the bridge is', *in cuappan* 'at the bridge', or even the name of an unidentified *altepetl*.

//v oc se pedaso tlali mani atlay[. . .] enpan[9] nicnemactitehua y noxguiuh xp̃tobal de los Anjeles camo [a] quin quiquixtilis ompa ometzticatca nohueshuatzin ca san tetlasotlalistica onicnotlaneuhtili ypanpa amo quimopielia canpa metzties auh intla mostla huiptla momiquilis ca conanas yn xp̃tobal ic ytechcopa norte totlaltenamiqui don sebastian basques mochiuhtica quaxochtli se durasno ic tonali iquisayanpa totlaltenamiqui in tlatoani D^{n} Juan Bueno ~~auh ynin tlalli ic huiyac quipia ompoalli huan maquilli yhua~~ tlaco ynic ~~patlahuac quipia ompoalli~~ yhuan ome baras yhuan tlaco

I bequeath another piece of land that is in Atla[. . .]npan, to my grandson, Cristóbal de los Ángeles. No one will take it from him. My sister-in-law lived there. I lent it to her with love because she didn´t have any place to live. And when at some point she dies, Cristóbal will take it. To the north, Don Sebastián Vásquez and I share a border. A peach tree serves as the boundary marker. To the east, the ruler Don Juan Bueno and I share a border. And this land has a length of twenty-five and one-half, and a width of twenty-two and one-half rods.

//v yhua niquitoa ca senca niquinotlatlauhtilia y noalbaseas niquinochiguilia don fran^{co} bueno don luis de rroxas ynic ypa motlatoltisque y noyolia y nanima auh intla yuhqui quimochiguilisque ca yehuatzin tt^{o} dios quimotlaxtlahuilis

And I say that I implore my executors—I name Francisco Bueno and Don Luis de Rojas—to advocate for my soul. If they do this, God will repay them.

//v ymixpan omochiuh testigos Antonio Ramires yhua Bartholome Juan quauhpayecac

Done in the presence of the witnesses, Antonio Ramírez and Bartolomé Juan from Cuauhpanyacac.

//v yhua niquitoa ypan chiquei tonalli nechchiguilisque se missa de cuerpo presente ypatiuh maquili peso niquinomemeltilitegua i noxguiuã auh yn aquin nechchiguilis yno missa ca yehuatl nochi conanas yn tlacpac onicteneuh amo aquin quiquixtilis yn aqui nechquimilos auh yntla sa se ca mochi ic mocahuas yn tlen tlacpac onicteneuh

And I say that on the eighth day they will arrange a funeral mass at a cost of five *pesos*. I leave this task to my grandchildren. Whoever arranges that mass for me will take all [of the money] that I have mentioned above. No one will take it from whomever provides me with the shroud. And if [they do] it together, everything will remain just as I mentioned above.

//v yhua niquitoa y nehuatl escriv^{no} Santa yglecia ca inin oquichiuh yn itestamento ca amo senca huel tlanagui ca huel melaguac ynic oquitecpan yn itlatol auh inic nicneltilia ca nicfirmatlalia ic mani metztli henero maquili tonalli yn ipan xihuitl de mil seissientos sesenta y ~~tres años~~ escrib^{no} don Roque Basques _ D^{n} Juan Bueno fiscal # Digo yo fray fran^{co}

And I, the notary of the Holy Church, say that this person made her will, that she is not moribund, and that she expressed herself in an orderly manner. And I placed my signature in order to verify it. On the fifth day of the month of January in the year 1663. Roque Vásquez, notary; Don Juan Bueno, *fiscal*. I, friar Francisco Ruíz, say that I saw what [the testator]

9 This is probably the name of an unidentified *altepetl.*

Ruis y lo que manda de la missa en este testamento le bide y por berdad lo firme en siete [de diciem]bre de 1663[10] años fray fransisco Ruis

ordered with respect to the mass, and signed in verification on the seventh of December of the year 1663. Friar Francisco Ruíz.

[//v ....]lli ic mani ynic hueyac ic itechcopa sur [yhua ic itechcop]a norte quipia[o]npoalli yhua[............................. ....]

[. . .] how it is laid out: its length toward the south and toward to the north is forty and [. . .]

[Fol. 2r]

tlaco auh ynic patlahuac quipia s[empoali] yhua nahui Baras yhua tlaco ic oriente yhua ic poniente — auh [ic[11] pe]laxtitlan caltitlan ca mecaltontli quipia senpoalli yhua na[hui] yhua tlasesencapa huitz mocahuaquiuh quadrado = auh y[..............]tli ynemac maria de los Angeles - ynic hueyac quipia senpoall[yhua matl]actlomei baras — auh ynic patlahuac quipia matlactlamome [varas au]h yn icotonca petlaxtitlan caltitlan mecalli ca noso oquino[co]tonique yn ome hermanos yn oquimomaquilique in mihcatzintli Diego de los Angeles quipie ynic hueyac senpoalli yhua yei baras yhua tlaco ynic patlahuac quipia matlactlonahui baras yehuatl inic mochi motzaqua ynic cate ynin tlaltotõtin[12] =

one-half. And in width it is twenty-four and one-half *varas* to the east and west. And toward the residential area of Pelaxtitlan, for it is [. . .], it measures twenty-four, extending the same on all sides. It comes out square. And with respect to [. . .] that is the inheritance of María de los Ángeles, its length is thirty-three *varas*, and its width is twelve *varas*. But a portion of it, in the residential area of Pelaxtitlan, is narrow. Perhaps, the two brothers who gave it to the deceased Diego de los Ángeles divided it.[13] It is twenty-three and one-half *varas* in length, and fourteen *varas* in width. This concludes everything, the state of these small pieces of land.

auh y nehuatl escribano ytech in tlatoc~~auh~~Republica y nican ypan altepetl S.t S.n Luis OBp.o chalco tlalmanalco nicihtohua[14] ca ynin testamento

I, the notary here for the rulerly municipal council of San Luis Obispo Chalco Tlalmanalco, declare that I made a copy of this testament because it is

10 *1661* was corrected to *1663*.

11 In brackets: *ic* would imply 'toward', although the *in* subordinator is also possible.

12 Beginning here, the writing is done in a different hand, and the ink is a different color.

13 I have interpreted *oquino[co]tonique* as *oquimocotonihqueh*, which is risky on two accounts: there are missing letters; and the *m* of what I am interpreting as *mo-* is definitely an *n*. The verb *cotona* 'to break or divide something', or its benefactive forms, *cotonia* and *cotonilia*, 'to divide something among two or more people', or 'for people to divide something up among themselves', are commonly seen in land-related documents: e.g., '[the brothers] divided it'. So in the context of this document, *quimocotonihqueh* can either be the reverential of *quicotonqueh* 'they divided it' or the reflexive benefactive construction 'they divided it among themselves'.

14 This writer uses *nic-* before an *i*: *niciohua* and *onicixcopin*.

onicixcopin ypanpa huel ye cocotoca ypanpa on onechtlatlauhti ỹ franc^{ca} maria yn isoatzin ometzticatca = D^{n} xptoual Juares de los Angeles ye omomiquili = yhuan ypan in cahuitl m[o]tlatocatilia yn yehuatzin tlatohuani D^{n} Bernardo Velasques ca [i]n quenin [tla]tecpana yn huehue[tes]tamento sayeno yesqui ynin tlaixcopinali auh ynic neltilistli = melahuac inic nitlaneltilia nican tlacxitlan nictlalis notoca yhua axcan ic caxtolli tonalli tlapohua = metztli Junio yn ipan xihuitl de 1743 ca yehuatl in Melahuac Et^{a}

ChristoBal de S^{n}tiago [*signature*]

essn^{o} de Repu^{ca}

//v

already very much falling apart. For that reason, Francisca María, who was the wife of the already deceased Don Cristóbal Juárez de los Ángeles, requested it of me. And this copy will stipulate things exactly as the original will did in the time when the ruler Don Bernardo Velásquez governed. And regarding the certification, I certify it correctly. Here at the bottom (of the page) I will place my name, and today is the fifteenth day of the month of June of the year 1743. It is true, etc.

Cristóbal de Santiago [*signature*]

Municipal council notary

On June 15, 1743, Cristóbal de Santiago, the municipal council notary for San Luis Chalco Tlalmanalco, certified that he had made a true copy of a will that had been prepared in 1663. It was normal practice for copies of older wills to be made and inserted into the legal proceedings of disputes regarding land ownership. In this case, it was done at the request of Francisca María, wife of the then deceased, high noble, Don Cristóbal Juárez, because the original document was literally falling apart. It would seem that she was also the granddaughter of the original testatrix, Francisca de los Angeles, mentioned in the will as "my granddaughter Francisca de los Ángeles"; however, there is a difference of eighty years between the date of the original document and its copy, in which case we may be dealing with a great-granddaughter. It is possible that the copy was commissioned specifically for use in the contemporary dispute that involved the descendants of Francisca de los Ángeles. It could also have been created earlier as a preventive measure, which would highlight the degree to which noble families relied on testaments to safeguard the intergenerational transmission of their property.

The original testament of 1663 does not mention the husband of Francisca de los Ángeles, but she probably had connections to the high nobility because the name of her nephew, Don Luis de Rojas, begins with the title of *don*, reserved for the *teteuctin*, or high nobles, while his mother, the testatrix's sister-in-law, is referred to as *doña*. She bequeathed a fairly large amount of land and houses to her three children, as well as to five grandchildren.

She also charged the same grandchildren with her funeral arrangements, although the notary who prepared the original will made it clear that she was not close to death.

The introductory portion of a Nahuatl will contains an obligatory profession of the Catholic faith, the length and content of which are somewhat flexible. Understandably, doctrinal confusion is often observable, especially considering the problematic nature of New World Christianization. In spite of the efforts of the friars to translate Catholic dogma into Nahuatl, most of it was incomprehensible within the context of indigneous culture. Furthermore, most indigenous converts continued, to a greater or lesser degree, to live within their traditional worldview and practice some native rituals, and for this reason, they were concerned with the image they projected of themselves. Two phrases from the will illustrate this desire to appear orthodox, even in the absence of specific doctrinal knowledge: *ihua in ixquich quimoneltoquitia tonantzin santa iglecia Romana* 'and [I believe] in everything that our mother, the Holy Roman Church, believes', and *ma quimohuiquili in canpa quimohuiquilis quimoyeyamaquilis* 'may He take [my soul] where He will take it to give it a home'.

Some interesting lexical items in the will deserve commentary. The word *-huampoh* 'someone's counterpart' is composed of the preterite agentive noun *-poh* 'someone's companion or peer' and the incorporated relational root *huan* 'in the company of'. *-Poh* can receive other incorporated nouns, but the sense is always to related individual people who share a certain affinity with regard to their name, their work, their gender, and so on. The key word here is *people*, and that is what makes the use of this expression here unique. The writer of the will uses *-huampoh* to establish an affinity between the human soul and the earth: *auh i nonacayo ca nicmaca in tlali yeica ca itech oquis ca ihuanpo* 'on the other hand, I give my flesh to the earth; from there it came and is therefore its counterpart'. The word *mecalli* is used several times in the document, always in relation to plots of land, but it is not defined in any of the standard colonial reference works. I believe it comes from *mecatl* 'vine or rope', which then becomes the intransive verb *mecaya* 'to become like a vine or rope' through the addition of the verbing suffix *-ya*. *Mecaya* can then be converted into the patientive noun, *mecalli*, which would mean something like 'something long and narrow (like a vine or rope)'. For this reason I have chosen to translate it as a long, narrow plot of land.

Finally, I would like to comment on a new area of study in Nahuatl syntax and give two possible examples of it from the testament. Until now, the study of parallel structures in Nahuatl has been limited to what we call in Spanish a *bifrasismo*. This consists of two or more words or short phrases with similar internal structure that are juxtaposed to form a larger phrase. Traditionally, the juxtaposed elements complement each other to form a new, metaphorical concept, such as *in atl in tepetl*, literally 'water, mountain', which in turn means 'city'.[15] With the advent of Nahuatl alphabetical writing, a new kind of *bifrasismo* was created, which juxtaposed a word in Spanish and a similar word in Nahuatl, for the purpose of facilitating the comprehension and assimilation of the usually religious, Spanish concept, among the indigenous people. *In teotl in dios*, composed of the Nahuatl word for a natural deity and the Spanish word for God, is a good example. However, during the 2015 Yale/IDIEZ Summer Nahuatl course, Jeff Pynes, a graduate student in linguistics at the University of Utah, and Allison Caplan, a graduate student in Art History and Latin American Studies at Tulane University, discovered a new, more complex type of parallelism consisting of a central word or phrase that is simultaneously a part of two larger phrases constructed on either side of it. Here are the two examples from the will. I have translated *nicnemactia iaxca ayac quiquixtiliz* as 'I am bequeathing it to him; it is his property and no one is to take it from him.' But actually, it can be divided into two phrases, each built around, *iaxca* 'his property': *nicnemactia iaxca* 'I am bequeathing him his property' and *iaxca ayac quiquixtiliz* 'no one is to take his property from him'. I have translated *hualtlamelauhticah itechcacopa tlatelli quaxochtli mochiuhticah* as 'it comes along straight to the hill, which is the boundary marker'. But again, this can also be interpreted as two phrases built around *tlatelli* 'hill': *hualtlamelauhticah itechcacopa tlatelli* 'it comes along straight to the hill' and *tlatelli quaxochtli mochiuhticah* 'the hill is the boundary marker'.

Regarding linguistic-contact phenomena, the language of the text is typical for the first half of the seventeeth century, perhaps with the exception of the loanword *hermano* 'brother', which, along with some other kinship terms from Spanish is only attested in the later part of the seventeenth century. Lockhart reported the first attestation of *hermano* in a source from 1672 (Lockhart 1992: 84). This is only nine years after Francisca de los Ángeles's testament was written; however, given the fact that usage of this term was still unusual at the time, it is possible that at least the final part of the document, after the closing formula of the will itself, originated later than in 1663.

15 This is attested in Book Six (1961) of the *Florentine Codex*: in oqujmotlanevi in atl in tepetl, in oqujtemjc, in oqujcochitleuh 'the city borrowed him; [it seemed that] it dreamed of him, it saw him in dreams' (Sahagún 1950–1969, VI: 47).

DOCUMENT 19

Testament of Don Diego de San Pedro, a Bill of Sale, and a Declaration of Wages, Santiago Tzacualco, Mexico, 1644[1]

JULIA MADAJCZAK

[Fol. 1r]

este legajo es de los años de 1644 y de 647 // y 97 //	This volume is from the years of 1644 and of 1647 and 1697.
v Testamento de don diego de S. P.º Alcalde Del Barrio De San Tiago tzacualco	The testament of don Diego de San Pedro, *alcalde* of the neighborhood of Santiago Tzacualco.
Lunes, a 21 de Nouiembre del Anõ. - 1644 -	Monday, the twenty-first of November of the year 1644.
de yndios	of Indians
vi este testamento de don diego de San pedro vesino de tzacualco, y esta ya cumplido y porques asi verdad yo firme de mi nombre en guadalupe, oy veinte y quatro de enero de mil y seisientos y quarenta y ocho años –	I have see this testament of don Diego de San Pedro, a citizen of Tzacualco, and it has already been executed and since this is the truth, I have signed [it] with my name in Guadalupe, today, the twenty-fourth of January of the year of 1648.
El B.r luís Lasso de la vega	The bachiller Luís Lasso de la Vega.
[Fol. 2r]	
YN ica ytocatzin Dios tetatzin Dios tepiltzin Dios Spũ St.º Ey Personas yn ça	In the name of God the Father, God the Son, God the Holy Spirit, three persons,

1 Archivo Histórico del Arzobispado de México (AHAM), Caja 199, exp. 58, ff. 1r–5r.

DOI: 10.5876/9781607328346.c019

çe huel nelli Teotl, Dios Tlahtohuani yn nohuian cm̃c, motlahtocatilia Ma quimatican, yn ixquichtin yn quittazque yn quipohuazq̄ yn namatlacuilol yn noTestamento yn quenin Nehuatl, Don Diego De S. P.º AlcalDe, ninamicque, nican nichane yn ipan Tlaxilacalli San Tiago Tzacualco yn huel nocieliztica, notlanequiliztica yn niquihtohua, yn axcan yn nican nopam quimochihuilitzinohua, yn iteylnamicquiliztzin yn iJustisiatzin yn tt.º Dios, yn çan niman, ayac huel yxpampa Ehua quitlalcahuia yn micquiztli, yn huel achtopa niquihtohua, Ca yn nolia naniman Ca yçenmactzinco, nocontlalia yn notlaçotemaquixticatzin, tt,º Jesu xp̄o, ma quihualmaniliz, ma quihualmoçeliliz yn icuac yn oquitlalcahui yn nonacayo yehica Ca ytlaçoEsçoticatzinco, ynic otechmomaquixtilitzinoco yn nican tlalticpac. auh yn notlallo, noçoquio, Ca ytech nicpohua yn tlalli, yehica, ca ytech oquiz. auh ca ye nican, noconpehualtiz. yn ça tlatzacan notlanequiliz. macayac ceppa quihtlacoz. yn ye nican noconpehualtiz. nıctecpanaz. --- ett.ª

but only one true deity, God the Ruler, who rules in the entire world. May all who see and read my document, my testament, know that I, Don Diego de San Pedro, *alcalde*, married, a citizen here, in the *tlahxillacalli* of San Diego Tzacualco, voluntarily and of my own accord declare that today our lord God exerts here upon me his memory of people, his justice.[2] Likewise, no one truly runs away nor separates himself from death. At the very beginning, I declare that I place my spirit and soul entirely in the hands of my dear Savior, our lord Jesus Christ. Let Him take it, let Him receive it when it abandons my body, because it was through His precious blood that He came to redeem us here on earth. As to my earthly body, I offer it to the earth because this is where it came from. I will now begin what is my last will. Let no one even once violate what I will begin to put in order now, etc.

1.º v Ynic çentlamantli niquihtohua yn nehuatl, Don diego De S. P.º Ca oncatqui Caltzintli, çentetl. Tonatiuh ycalaquianpa ytztihcac, huey calli Ca yn axcan niquihtohua, yntla moztla huiptla nechmopolhuitzinozqui Dios, Ca aconmaniliz. Ca ytetzinco nicpohua yn nonamictzin, mag.ⁿᵃ Pascuala yntla quimochicahuilitzinozqui Dios ----

First of all, I, Don Diego de San Pedro, declare that there is one house that faces west; it is a large house. What I declare now is that when God makes me perish in the future, I will not take it. I will assign it to my spouse, Magdalena Pascuala, if God gives her health.

2.º v Ynic ontlamantli niquihtohua yn nehuatl Don Diego De S. P.º Ca oncatqui, ce huey Calli Tenexcalli yancuic, çanno tonatiuh ycalaquianpa ytztihcac, Ca yn axcan Ca niquihtohua yntla moztla huiptla nechmopolhuitzinozqui Dios, Ca çanno ytezinco nicpohua yn tlacpac omoteneuh yn nonamictzin, mag,ⁿᵃ Pascuala yntla quimochicahuilitzinozqui Dios, Canel tonehuan Toçiahuiliz tonecocol, ynic omochiuh -----

Second, I, Don Diego de San Pedro, declare that there is one large house, a new house where the lime kiln is kept, likewise facing west. What I declare now is that when God makes me perish in the future, I will also assign it to my above-mentioned spouse, Magdalena Pascuala, if God gives her health, for it was built with our effort, our pain.

2 In other words, 'today, my time has come'.

[Fol. 2v]

3. v Ynic Etlamantli niquihtohua, yn nehuatl. Don Diego De S. P° ca oncatqui oc çentetl Calli, xancalli calmelaztli çanno tonatiuh ycalaquianpa ytztihcac. auh yn axcan ca niquihtohua yntla moztla huiptla nechmolnamicquilitzinozqui Dios, ca çanno [y]tetzinco, nicpohua yn notlaçonamictzin yn onıcteneuh. magna Pascuala yntla quimochicahuilitzinozqui Dios -----

Third, I, Don Diego de San Pedro, declare that there is another house, made of adobe bricks, long and narrow, likewise facing west. What I declare now is that when God remembers me in the future,[3] I will also assign it to my dear spouse whom I have mentioned, Magdalena Pascuala, if God gives her health.

4. v Ynic Nauhtlamantli. niquihtohua yn nehuatl Don Diego De S. P.º Ca oncatqui oc çe huey Calli xancalli, Calli tictli, xochmilcopa ytztihcac, auh ca yn axcan Ca niquihtohua yntla nechmolnamicquil[i]tzinozqui Dios. Ca ytech nicpohua yn nochpoch yn itoca Juana ABensia, yntla quimochicahuilitzinozqui Dios, Ca yehuatl quimati aço techilnamictiaz yn icuac yn ipam yn miccaylhuit[l] aço cana çe CanDelatzin quitlatitiaz. yn icuac yn huelitiz -

Fourth, I, Don Diego de San Pedro, declare that there is another large house made of adobe, an entry house, facing the garden. What I declare now is that when God remembers me, I will assign it to my daughter named Juana Avencia, if God gives her health. She knows about it. She is either to remember us on the Day of the Dead, or to light candles someplace when she is able to.

5. v Ynic macuillamantli Niquihtohua, yn nehuatl, Don Diego De San P.º Ca oncatqui, ocçe huey Calli xancalli, çanno tonatiuh ycalaquianpa ytztihcac yn axcan oncan texohua, auh yn axcan Ca niquihtohua, yntla quimochicahuilitzinozqui Dios yn omoteneuh nochpoch Juana Agensia , Ca no ytech nicpohu[a] conanaz yntla quimochicahuilitzinozqui Dios. ==

Fifth, I, Don Diego de San Pedro, declare that there is another large house made of adobe bricks, likewise facing west, where the grinding is done now. What I declare now is that if God gives health to my mentioned daughter, Juana Avencia, I will also assign it to her. She will take it, if God gives her health.

yhuan yn itech çaliuhtica, Corredorton, yhuan oncatqui Corral. yn oncan yhcac horno, yhuan oncatqui tepiton ythualco mochi nicmaca ytech nicpohua yn tlacpac omoteneuh Juana agensia Ca yehuatl quimati -----

And adhering to it, is a little corridor and there is a pen where the oven stands and there is a little patio. All of this I give to the above-mentioned Juana Avencia; I assign it to her. She knows about it.

6. v Ynic chicuaçentlamantli niquihtohua yn nehuatl, Don dieg[o] De S. P.º yn axcan yn ocan Calacohuayan Puerta xoch[i]milcopa ytztihcac, yhuan

Sixth, I, Don Diego de San Pedro, declare that [there is a place] where the entry gate now is, facing the garden and there is a patio that likewise adheres to

3 In other words, 'when I die'.

oncatqui ythualco yn çanno ytech [ça?] liuhticatqui yn omoteneuh tenexCalli, ca çanno yehuatzin q[ui]maniliz yn notlaçonamictzin mag,^{na} Pascuala yntla quimochicahuilitzinozqui dios. -----

the mentioned lime kiln building. My dear spouse Magdalena Pascuala will likewise take it if God gives her health.

[Fol. 3r]

v Yn imixpamtzinco yn omochiuh Testamento Santa ysabel Tollan tlaca tetecuhtin, ynic quinmochihuilia Don Diego De S Pº Alcalde, ynic yehuantin mochihua Testigos, Aluaseas, nican quimotlalilia yn intocatzin yhuan yn infirmas. fecho En Santiago tzacualco ----

The testament was prepared before the *cabildo* members of Santa Isabel Tollan. In order for Don Diego de San Pedro, *alcalde*, to prepare it, those who are witnesses and executors put down their names and their signatures here. Done in Santiago Tzacualco.

v Testigos

Witnesses

v Don Juan + Matheo Alcalde Passado

Don Juan Mateo, former *alcalde*

v Juan Pascual + Alguasil mayor.

Juan Pascual, head constable

v Albaseas

Executors

San Juan yzhuatepec tlaca.

Authorities of San Juan Izhuatepec.

v Don Juan + Diego. Regidor mayor

Don Juan Diego, *regidor mayor*

v Don Juan + Diego fiscal

Don Juan Diego, *fiscal*

v Axcan yn omochiuh ynin testamento, Lunes, a 21 de Nouiembre Del Año 1644.

This testament was prepared today, on Monday, the twenty-first of November of the year 1644.

v Ca nehuatl onitlacuilo Oninotzaloc ynic onictlalli onictecpam yn itestamento yn Don Diego De S. Pº Alcalde nican Santiago tzacualco Ca neltiliztli mellahuac Nican nictlalia notoca Nofirma. Miguel + Aparisio Escreº

I was summoned to put the testament of Don Diego de San Pedro, *alcalde* here, in Santiago Tzacualco, in order; I did the writing. This is true and correct. Here I put down my name, my signature. Miguel Aparicio, notary.

[Fol. 4r]

Carta. De Venta

Bill of sale

v Ma quimatican yn ixquichtin yn quittazque yn quipohuazque ynin Carta De venta yn quenin nehuatl niJuachin miguel nicnoquichtli nican nichane yn ipam tlaxillacalli San Tiago tzacualco Ca huel noçieliztica notlanequiliztica ynic nictemaca ynin Carta De venta, yn

May all who see and read this bill of sale know that I, Joaquín Miguel, widower, citizen here, in the *tlahxillacalli* of Santiago Tzacualco, truly voluntarily and of my own accord, deliver this bill of sale. I make the sale to you, Don Diego de San Pedro, a married man[4]

4 This is probably a way of saying that he is a 'head of household' or resident of the community.

tehuatzin nimitznonamaquiltilia Don diego De S. P.º alcalde tinamîq́ Nican titechmopielia yn ipam tlaxillacalli, San Tiago tzacualco Auh yn axcan Ca niquihtohua Ca huel noçenyollocacopa ynic nimitznonamaquiltilia yn notlal, meyotoc auh ompa mani, yn motenehua Cimatlan, auh ynic omotamachiuh. ynic huiac ynic tlecoticac ytech yn petlacaltepetl. ynic huiac, ompohual qùahuitl. auh ynic patlahuac. ynic omotamachiuh, Cempohualli yhuan macuilli quahuitl auh yn axcan Ca nimitznonamaquiltilia, yxquich tinechmo~~na~~maquiliz. Çe~~m~~xto~~hua~~lli yhuan ~~Na~~Ey pesos,[5] de oro comun, auh yn axcá Ca ye nomatica noconçelia yn motomintzin, auh yntla quenmanian ninotlatolcuepatiuh yn aço tlaçotitiuh yn tlalli, amo niquihtoz çacan onixicoloc, Ca amo ypatiuh yn onechmacaque, yn iuhqui quichihua yn oc çequintin yn motlahtolcuepanime, ~~a~~auh yntla yuhqui nicchihuaz, Ca nopam, mochihuaz, Justisia, Ca quimomachiltiz yn yehuatzin, S.r Juez go.r Nitlatzacuiltiloz, auh yn tehuatzin yn timotlacohuiani, amo quen mopam, Ca nehuatl nitlaxtlahuaz. auh yn axcan Ca ye yççenmayan, nimitznaxcatilia nimitznotlatquitilia yn yolizque yn tlacatizque, yn amopilhuan, çaco tle yn ipam anquichihuazque, Caocmo notlamatian, auh yn axcan ca niquihtohua, ynic neltiliztli mellahuac teyxpam, mochihua yn imixpam Testigos Nican quitlalia yn intoca yn infirmas, Axcan yn omochiuh ynin Carta De venta, Martes. a 22 De Nouiembre, 1644 años

and the *alcalde* who is responsible for us here in the *tlahxillacalli* of Santiago Tzacualco. What I declare now is that I sell you my piece of land, planted with *magueyes,* truly and entirely of my own free will. It is in the place called Cimatlan. Regarding the length, it is forty rods long measured to its high point on [the mountain of] Petlacaltepetl. Its width was measured to be twenty-five rods. Now I sell it all to you, you will give me eighteen *pesos* of common gold. Now I receive your money with my hand. If I ever change my mind or raise the price of the land, I will not say that I was deceived in any way or that they did not give me what it was worth, like others, who change their minds, do. If I do such a thing, justice will be exerted upon me, for the lord judge-governor will know it; I will be punished. As for you, the buyer, it will not be your fault, I will pay for it. Now forever and ever I am making it your possession [and the possession] of your [pl.] children who are yet to live, yet to be born. Whatever you [pl.] do with it is no longer of my concern. Now I declare that in order for this to be publicly [recognized] as true and correct, it is done before witnesses. Here they put down their names and signatures. This bill of sale was prepared today, on Tuesday, the twenty-second of November of the year 1644.

~ Juan + matheo fiscal

Juan Mateo, *fiscal*

Bartholomé + garsia.

Bartolomé García

Juan + franco

Juan Francisco

v Auh yn nehuatl Ca niquihtohua mellahuac, ca oninotzaloc, nixpam yn omochiuh onitlacuilo nican nictlalia notoca, Nofirma

I, who have been summoned, declare it correct. It was done in my presence: I did the writing. Here I put down my name, my signature:

5 On the left margin: 18 P.s The numeral *caxtolli* was written over the word *cempohualli*.

Miguel + Aparisio

Miguel + Aparicio

[Fol. 5r]

v Axcan Miercoles, a 23 De Nouiembre 1644 a͞ño͞s nican mochi nicmachiotia ynic otlatequipanoloc tomilpam yn oniquintlaxtlahui tequitque yn nehuatl Don Diego De S. P^{o} Alcalde yhuā nonamictzin mag.^{na} Pascuala -----

Today, Wednesday, the twenty-third of November of the year 1644, I manifest here everything that I paid to the laborers who worked in my and my spouse, Magdalena Pascuala's, fields.

v Çimatlan otlatequipano, andres diego onictlaxtlahui ce peso yhuan otlatequipano, Juan gr̃auiel onictlaxtlahui ome pesos yn mochi y conaçi Ey pesos --- 3 ps

In Cimatlan Andrés Diego worked [for me]—I paid him one *peso*—and Juan Gabriel worked [for me]—I paid him two *pesos*. Everything adds up to three *pesos*.—3 *pesos*

v Çanno ompa yn Çimatlan tlatequipanoloc yn otlatequipano nicmacac ytlaxtlahuil chicome pesos ------------- 7 ps

Likewise, in Cimatlan work has been done; and to the one who worked [there], I made his payment of seven *pesos*.—7 *pesos*

v Auh yn oc çe tlacatl otlatequipano, onictlaxtlahui ome pesos yhuan Nahui tomin – 2 p^{s} 4 t^{s}

To another man who worked [for me], I paid two *pesos* and four *reales*.—2 *pesos*, 4 *reales*

v Auh yn oc çe tlacatl otlatequipano onictlaxtlahui çe peso ---------- 1 p.^{s}

To another man who worked [for me], I paid one *peso*.—1 *peso*

v Auh yn oc çe tlacatl otlatequipano onictlaxtlahui onicmacac Ey pesos ----- 3 p.^{s}

To another man who worked [for me], I paid and gave three *pesos*.—3 *pesos*

v Auh yn oc çe tlacatl, otlatequipano onictlaxtlahui onicmacac Nahui pesos ---- 4 p.^{s}

To another man who worked [for me], I paid and gave four *pesos*.—4 *pesos*

v Auh yn oc çe tlacatl otlatequipano, onictlaxtlahui onicmacac chicome pesos --- 7 p.^{s}

To another man who worked [for me], I paid and gave seven *pesos*.—7 *pesos*

v Auh yn oc çeppa otequitihuac, oniquinmacac yn intlatequipanoliz --- 10 ts. m^{o}

Everyone worked again, I gave them their wage—10 and a half *reales*

v Auh yn oc çeppa otequitihuałc Nahui tomin yn itlaxtlahuil mochiuh -------- 4 ts

Everyone worked again; their payment was four *reales*.—4 *reales*

[Fol. 5v]

v Jusepe Diego, otlatequipano onictlaxtlahui matlactomin mochica yn itlacual ---- 10 ts

Josef Diego worked [for me]; I paid him ten *reales*, including his food.—10 *reales*

v Diego otlatequipano, onicmacac matlactomin mochica ytlacual ----- 10 ts.

Diego worked [for me]; I gave him ten *reales*, including his food.—10 *reales*

v Juan Pascual otlatequipano, onicmacac macuiltomin mochica ytlacual ------ 5 ts.	Juan Pascual worked [for me]; I gave him five *reales*, including his food.—5 *reales*
v Juan bap^{ta} otlatequipano, onicmacac Nahui tomin ytlaxtlahuil ---------- 4 ts.	Juan Bautista worked [for me]; I gave him his payment of 4 *reales*.—4 *reales*
v P^{o} Lucas, otlatequipano onicmacac Nahui tomin yn itlaxtlahuil ------ 4 ts.	Pedro Lucas worked [for me]; I gave him his payment of 4 *reales*.—4 *reales*
v Jusepe otlatequipano, onicmacac macuiltomin yn itlaxtlahuil ----------- 5 ts.	Josef worked [for me]; I gave him his payment of 5 *reales*.—5 *reales*
v Andres diego, otlatequipano onicmacac macuiltomin, yn itlaxtlahuil -------- 5 ts.	Andrés Diego worked [for me]; I gave him his payment of 5 *reales*.—5 *reales*
v Jusepe diego tlatequipano onicmacac macuiltomin yn itlaxtlahuil ------ 5 ts	Josef Diego worked [for me]; I gave him his payment of 5 *reales*.—5 *reales*
v Lucas huehuentzin tlatequipano onicmacac macuiltomin mochica yn itlacual ----- 5 ts	Lucas Huehuentzin worked [for me]; I gave him 5 *reales*, including his food.—5 *reales*
v Jusepe Diego, otlatequipano, onicmacac macuiltomin mochica ytlacual ------- 5 ts	Josef Diego worked [for me]; I gave him 5 *reales*, including his food.—5 *reales*

The will of Don Diego de San Pedro, accompanied by a bill of sale and a statement concerning wages paid to hired workers, is housed in the Archivo Histórico del Arzobispado de México, known for its great collection of the testaments of the Valley of Toluca.[6] This one, however, comes from the Valley of Mexico, a *tlahxillacalli* of Santiago Tzacualco, subject to Santiago Tlatelolco, where Don Diego served as *alcalde*. The location is confirmed by numerous references to neighboring communities: the witnesses were the officials of Santa Isabel Tollan, the appointed executors came from San Juan Izhuatepec, and the execution of the will was reviewed in Guadalupe. This neighbourhood is best known from the primordial title of Santa Isabel Tollan, dated to 1714,[7] seventy years after the testament of Don Diego was prepared. The notary, Miguel Aparicio, was first summoned to the house of the alcalde on November 21, 1644, to write down his last will. Surprisingly, he returned the next day, this time in order to issue a bill of sale of a piece of land in Cimatlan. Possibly he was there again on November 23, when another document was drawn up with similar though less-careful handwriting, and lacking the signature of the notary.

6 See Pizzigoni 2007, 2012.

7 Housed in the Bibliothèque Nacionale de France, published on http://amoxcalli.org.mx/.

Don Diego de San Pedro named only two heirs: his wife, Magdalena Pascuala and their daughter, Juana Avencia. Each of them received a patio with several buildings. The buildings were probably arranged around each patio, although this cannot be ascertained because the testament is not accompanied by a sketch. The structures or rooms are described with very rich terminology, both in Nahuatl and Spanish.[8] Magdalena Pascuala's inheritance consisted of two *huei calli* 'large houses', one of which was a *tenexcalli* 'lime house'; a *calacohuayan puerta* 'gate'; and a *xancalli calmelactli* 'long room made of adobe'. *Calmelactli* and *tenexcalli* are puzzling and rare terms, not found in other testaments, but are included in Molina's dictionary as "a large and long room or the corridor of the house" and "a lime kiln or the house where it is kept," respectively.[9] While in this case *tenexcalli* definitely describes a house rather than a kiln itself, a question arises: why would a noble *alcalde* who was also a landowner engage in burning lime in his house compound? As far as *calmelactli* is concerned, we cannot be sure whether the term refers to a separate structure or to a corridor linking two other buildings. The interpretation of another term, *callitictli*, associated with the bequests to Juana Avencia, poses a similar problem. The daughter of Don Diego was assigned a *huei calli xancalli* 'large adobe house', a *corredorton* 'small corridor', a *corral* with an oven (*horno*), and a *huei calli xancalli callitictli*. The latter term should probably be analyzed as *calli ihtictli* 'the inside of a house' but the other epithets, a "large house" and an "adobe house," indicate that it was a separate building. Perhaps the word refers to the location of the structure within the compound, but until more attestations are found, this will remain mere speculation.

A striking feature of Don Diego's listing of property is the total lack of landholdings, and yet we know that he owned land. In the last of the documents he declares the wages, including cash and food, of the workers who labored in the cultivated fields (*milli*) belonging to him and his wife. He lists seventeen individuals, some of them by name, plus an unspecified group of workers. Some of the names are repeated, which may indicate that the same person was mentioned several times, although this may not necessarily be the case, since the names are quite common and indistinctive. Don Diego does not specify the period of time for which he hired these people, but he stresses that the group from Cimatlan worked three times, perhaps during three agricultural seasons. This section, although probably incomplete, deserves a more profound study, as the information it contains can prove useful for studies on

8 For house terminology in Nahuatl testaments, see Pizzigoni 2012: 22–29.

9 Fray Alonso de Molina 1977, vol. 2: ff. 11v, 99r.

local economy and wage labor in the seventeenth-century Valley of Mexico.

Since Magdalena Pascuala is mentioned as either having some fields of her own, or being a co-owner of her husband's land, it is possible that Don Diego decided to transfer his landholdings to his wife before issuing a testament. He could have also given them to his daughter. It was not an uncommon practice in colonial Nahua communities to distribute cultivated fields among adult children well before death threatened the head of the family. Both cases would explain the lack of land among the property listed in the will. They would not, however, shed light on the mysterious act of acquiring another property only one day after making the testament. It seems that, along with the calculation of wages, the bill of sale had something to do with the final putting in order of all the earthly matters of the testator. The land, planted with *magueyes*, was sold to Don Diego by a citizen of his *tlahxillacalli*, Joaquín Miguel, for eighteen *pesos* in gold. The vivid nature of the document gives insight into this official procedure, recording each step meticulously. The seller delivers the description of the field, he then asks for the money and receives it from the hand of the buyer. Finally, the usual formula for preventing any future claims and calling for the authority of justice is pronounced. Possibly, the transaction had been accorded informally long ago between the two parties and Don Diego simply decided to include its legalization in his attempt to deal with finances before death. An interesting detail is that the property was located in Cimatlan, where Don Diego already owned fields. Perhaps he was trying to accumulate land in this area by buying it from local owners.

While both the testament and the bill of sale follow the conventions typical of the notarial practice of the time, they draw one's attention with carefully, even sophistically, written formulas. This may be due to the attitude of the notary, Miguel Aparicio, who was not willing to abbreviate the elaborate declarations of the testator and the land-seller. Once, however, we can see that he apparently ran out of patience, cutting the elongated preamble of the testament with "etc." There is no way of establishing whether the richness of the document's vocabulary owes to the education of the notary or whether it directly expressed the speech of the people he was recording: probably all of the parties involved contributed in some degree to the final outcome. One of the most precious examples is the use of the concept of "memory" or "remembering," expressed in Nahuatl both with the verb *ilnamiqui* and the abstract noun *teilnamiquiliztli*. Three different contexts lend three subtly different meanings to the expression. First, it is employed in a doublet with the Spanish loanword *justicia*, rendering 'God's memory of people, God's justice' and referring to the power of God to make decisions regarding the life and death of people according to His eternal plan. Then the concept is simplified in the phrase "when God remembers me," which was a common way to say "when I die." Finally, it is employed in the way most familiar to a modern Western reader: the daughter of Don Diego is to "remember" her parents by lighting candles for them on the Day of the Dead. In each of these three contexts "remembering" is conceptually associated with existence, not on the mundane plane but rather in the esoteric dimension of the world beyond.

The use of the loanword *justicia* with the meaning of 'God's justice' is unusual as well, because this term most often comes up in the sources in legal contexts, meaning 'law', 'justice', or 'officers of justice'. The documents contain more rare loanwords, such as *corredor* 'corridor', *horno* 'oven', or the formula *fecho en Santiago Tzacualco* 'made in Santiago Tzacualco'. They show no signs of the letter substitutions characteristic of the orthography of those Nahuas who did not speak Spanish well and who tended to pronounce foreign words in a more familiar manner, for example, without the phonemes /r/ or /f/. Here the correct orthography would suggest that the notary was bilingual and probably literate in Spanish as well. In this context one wonders why a common Spanish loanword *puerta*, already found in the sixteenth-century *Testaments of Culhuacan* (e.g., Cline and León-Portilla 1984: 22), was employed in a doublet with the Nahua *calacohuayan* 'entryway', following the pattern usually interpreted as explaining the Spanish term by juxtaposing it with a Nahuatl synonym. In this case, since the order of the words is *calacohuayan puerta*, I believe that the loanword was used to specify the more general native term, supporting the hypothesis of the notary's mastery of both languages. Finally, interesting terminology is used in reference to the Nahua officials who witnessed the issuing of the documents. While their ranks are described with Spanish terms, such as *regidor mayor*, *alcalde pasado*, *fiscal*, and so on, as a group they are referred to as *Santa Isabel Tollan tlacah teteuhtin* and *San Juan Izhuatepec tlacah*. In precontact times, the terms *teteuctin* 'lords' and *pipiltin* 'noblemen' were assigned to well-defined classes of the Nahua society; however, under Spanish rule they began to be used with the meaning of "*cabildo* members" and as such are known from many sources. The use of *tlacah* 'people' with the same sense, however, is not that common. Or perhaps it has been overlooked by modern researchers who tend to understand phrases such as *San Juan Izhuatepec tlacah* as simply 'the inhabitants of San Juan Izhuatepec'. Nevertheless, it has a parallel in a popular term *teopantlacah* 'church people', that is, 'church attendants', suggesting that the term *tlacah* could have been interpreted in terms of a person in charge of a place or community.

DOCUMENT 20

Testament of Doña Juana Flores, Ambar, Peru, 1649[1]

Patrycja Prządka-Giersz, Jan Szemiński, and John Sullivan

[Fol. 1r]

\+

∞ En el nombre de dios todopoderoso Amen sepan quantos esta carta de testamento vieren como yo *doña* Juª flores, yndia naturaL deste pueº de ambar, del *ayllo* de guacas biuda de domingo poma guaman. estando como estoy enferma del cuerpo y sana del entendimiento. hago y ordeno este mi testamento y mandas de mis bienes para que siendo dios nuestro señor fuere seruido. de lleuarme deste presente vida se haga y cumpla como en este dicho mi testamento se contiene porque esta es mi vltima y postrimera boluntad, ques enla forma siguiente ___

∞ primeramente mando mi alma a dios nuestro señor que la crio y rredimio con su preciosa sangre y el cuerpo a la tierra de que fue formada ___

\+

In the name of God the Almighty, Amen. May all who see this testament letter know that that I, Doña Juana Flores, Indian, native of this town of Ambar, from Guacas *ayllu*, Domingo Poma Guaman's widow, sick as my body is and sound of will, make and order this, my testament and bequeathal of my properties, if God our lord deigns to take me from this present life, so that it will be done and carried out as is stipulated in this, my final and concluding will, in the following manner:

First, I entrust my soul to God, who created it and redeemed it with His precious blood, and my body to the earth, from which it was formed.

1 Archivo Arzobispal de Lima, Testamentos 42, exp.1.

DOI: 10.5876/9781607328346.c020

∞ yten mando que mi cuerpo sea enterrado en la yglesia deste pue^{o} de ambar enlaparte y lugar donde mi albaçea ordenare [*on the left margin*: a la ig^{a}] y doy limosna Para la dicha yglesia un macho mohino claro manso de carga con el hierro deste dicho pue^{o} porque asi es mi voluntad ___

Also, I order that my body be buried in the church of this town of Ambar in the part [of the church] and at the place where my executor decides [*on the left margin*: To the church], and I give alms to the said church of this aforementioned town: one branded tame male pack mule with a light black face and a muzzle, because such is my wish.

[*on the left margin*: Vna missa cantada] ∞ yten mando que el dia de mi entierro se me diga Vna missa cantada con su vijilia de cuerpo presente, si Vbiere lugar para ello, y se pague la limosna acostumbrada de mis bienes ___

[*on the left margin*: One chanted mass] Also, I order that on the day of my burial a chanted mass will be said for me with the funeral vigil, if there be conditions for it, and that customary alms be paid from my property.

[Fol. 1v]

[*on the left margin*: mas tres misas cantadas con Vigilia] ∞ yten mando que se me digan otras tres missas cantadas con sus viJilias y se paguen la limosna de ellas de mis bienes acostumbradamente

___

[*on the left margin:* Also, three chanted masses with a vigil]. Also, I order that three chanted masses will be said for me with the vigils, and the alms for them should be paid from my property as accustomed.

+∞ yten mando para la sera del ss^{mo}. sacramento dies *pessos.* para cuya limosna le cobre de diego fe[*l*]ipe yndio del *ayllo* de rarco que se me debe otros tantos *pessos*. de un caballo que le uendi agora año y medio y no melos a pa[*gado*] auiendo pasado el plaço porque asi es mi voluntad ___

Also, I leave ten *pesos* for the wax [candles] of the Blessed Sacrament, and this offering should be collected from Diego Felipe, an Indian from Rarco *ayllu,* because he owes me such an amount of *pesos* for a horse that I sold him a year and half ago, and he has not paid me by the payment date, because such is my wish.

[*on the left margin*: Seis missas Ressadas] ∞ yten mando que seme diga seis missas resadas por mi alma pagando la limosna de ellas de dichos mis bienes

___

[*on the left margin:* Six masses] Also, I order that six masses be said for my soul, paying their alms from my aforementioned property.

[*on the left margin*: a N. s. deCopacauana] + ∞ yten mando para nuestra s^{ra}. de copacabana dos *llicllas* delana dela tierra. listadas concolores la vna tiene elcampo negro y la otra leonada y vn paño de manos Labrado con vnas puntas chiflonas. y dos tembladeras de plata que pesara ambas. doçe *onsas* poco mas o menos. porque esta es mi voluntad ___

[*on the left margin:* For Our Lady of Copacabana] Also, I leave for Our Lady of Copacabana two colored, striped alpaca-wool *lliklla*s. One has a black background, and the other is tawny. Also, a handkerchief embroidered with floating laces and two silver tankards with round bottoms, both weighing more or less twelve *onzas*, because such is my wish.

[*on the left margin*: ocho Reponsos] ∞ yten mando el dia que el d͡ho mi cuerpo sea lleuado ala d͡ha yglesia seme digan ocho rresponsos. como se acostumbra pagando la limosna por ellos de mis bienes. acostumbradamente ___

[*on the left margin:* Eight responses] Also, I order that on the day when my aforementioned body is to be taken to the aforementioned church, eight responses will be said according to custom and the alms for them will be paid from my property, as customary.

+ ∞ yten mando. parala cofradia del s^{or}. San Pedro un *patacon*. y otro *patacon* para el señor san antonio, - otro *patacon* para señor san marcos. y pido a mi albaçea que cumpla esta demanda mi albaçea pagando de mis bienes por ser asi mi voluntad ___

Also, I leave to the brotherhood of Lord Saint Peter one *patacon*, and another *patacon* for Lord Saint Anthony, and another *patacon* for Lord Saint Mark, and I ask my executor to fullfill this demand, and to pay it from my property, because such is my wish.

[Fol. 2r]

==

∞ yten declaro que no debo a ninguna persona cossa que valga plata y si lo deuiere que mi albaçea lo pague presediendo primero aberiguaçion para ello ___

Also, I state that I do not owe anything of value to anyone, and if I do have a debt, my executor should pay, first having scrutinized it.

∞ yten declaro que me deben las personas siguientes ___

Also, I declare that the following person is in debt to me:

∞ diego felipe me debe dies *pessos* como esta dicho antes desta clausula ___

Diego Felipe owes me ten *pesos*, as stated before this clause.

[*on the left margin*: pagó 5 *p*, debe otros 5 *p* y no deve nada]

[*on the left margin:* He paid five *pesos*, he owes another five *pesos*, and he owes nothing more.]

∞ Ju^{o} martin, *camachico* del *ayllo Ychocan*, me debe dos *pessos*==

Juan Martín, *kamachikuq* from *Ichuqan ayllu*, owes me two *pesos*.

[*on the left margin*: pago]

[*on the left margin:* He paid.]

∞ Ju^{o} de la Crus, de dicho *ayllo* de *Ychocan*, me debe un *patacon*__

Juan de la Cruz, from the aforementioned *Ichuqan ayllu*, owes me one *patacon*.

[*on the left margin:* dio ynform^{on} ante el ałłde como auia pagado a la d͡ha difunta]

[*on the left margin:* He stated in the presence of the mayor that he had paid the aforementioned deceased.]

∞ Ysabel Caxapayco medebe quatro *reales*__

Isabel Caxapayco owes me four *reales*.

∞ *don* Ju^{o} leon debe un *pesso*.

Don Juan Leon owes me one *peso*.

alos quales dichos deudores secobrará por mi albaçea para cumplir con las dichas mandas. y se de un *patacon* a la cofradia del s^{or} san miguel__

My executor will collect from the aforementioned debtors in order to fulfill the aforementioned offerings. Also, a *patacon* shall be given to the brotherhood of Lord Saint Michael.

∽ yten me debe Juan yauri, de *ychocan*, quatro *patacones*

Also, Juan Yauri from *Ichuqan* owes me four *patacones*.

on the left margin: pago 3 *p*^{os}, deue un *pesso*, pago todo]

[*on the left margin:* He paid 3 *pesos*, he owes one *peso*, he paid it all.]

∽ yten declaro que tengo una *lliclla* de lana de la tierra parda fuera de las que tengo rreferidas antes desta clausula. m^{do} q̄ le uenda mi albaçea para satisfaçer las dichas mandas ___

Also, I state that I possess a grey alpaca-wool *lliklla*, not one of the ones mentioned before this clause. I order my executor to sell it in order to fulfill the aforementioned offerings.

∽ yten mando a mi *ahijado* domingo, hijo de graçia, mi *comadre*, un faldellin acetuni ya seruido__

Also, I leave a used olive-colored kilt to my *ahijado* Domingo, son of Gracia, my *comadre*.

[*on the left margin*: entregose lo contenido]

[*on the left margin:* The thing was handed over.]

∽ yten mando a mi *ahijada* barbola vna *lliclla* negra ya trayda y otra manta blanca de lana de castilla ___

Also I leave a used black *lliklla* and another white sheep-wool blanket to my *ahijada* Barbola.

[*on the left margin*: entregose todo lo contenido Barbola -]

[*on the left margin:* All of the things were handed over. Barbola.]

∽ yten mando para mi *ahijado* domingo antonio y a bartolo domingo es mi *ahijado* asimismo un faldellin asul de paño de quito ya seruido para que ambos a dos rrepartan por mitad ___

Also I leave a used blue kilt made of Quito cloth to my *ahijado* Domingo Antonio and to Bartolo Domingo, also my *ahijado*, in the same way, so that they will divide it in half.

[*on the left margin*: entregose lo contenido]

[*on the left margin:* The thing was handed over.]

∽ yten mando un faldellin que tengo de paño de quito asitoni nuebo a Luis geronimo

Also, I leave a new olive-colored kilt made of Quito cloth, which I possess, to Luis Gerónimo,

[*on the left margin*: entregose]

[*on the left margin:* It was handed over.]

[Fol. 2v]

hijo de mi sobrino el cappt^{an} *don* Gaspar Rodrigues Pilco__

son of my nephew, Captain Don Gaspar Rodríguez Pilco.

∽ yten mando a madalena mallao mi ahijada vna *lliclla* parda delana dela tierra nueba

Also, I leave a new grey alpaca-wool *lliklla* to Madalena Mallao, my *ahijada*.

[*on the left margin*: que Vendió la *lliclla* a la mug^{r} de ju^{o} guaman. tres *p*^{os} y 3 *r*^{ls}. deue todo__]

[*on the left margin:* She sold the *lliklla* to Juan Guaman's wife. Three *pesos* and three *reales*. She owes it all.]

∽ yten mando para mi *ahijada* m^{a}. antonia, muger de agustin capcha, vna *lliclla* asul ya trayda__

Also, I leave a used blue *lliklla* to my *ahijada*, María Antonia, Agustín Capcha's wife.

[*on the left margin*: entregose Agustin, su marido__]

[*on the left margin:* It was turned over to Agustín, her husband.]

∽ yten m^{do}. a maria bernarda vna *lliclla* parda ya trayda ___

Also, I leave a used grey *lliklla* to María Bernarda.

[*on the left margin*: huyose la yndia]

[*on the left margin:* the Indian woman ran away.]

∽ yten mando a Ju^{a} Suman $^{\text{mi } comadre}$ vna *lliclla* delana de castilla burda__

Also, I leave a coarse sheep-wool *lliklla* to Juana Sumani [*inserted*: my *comadre*]

[*on the left margin*: entregose]

[*on the left margin:* It was turned over.]

∽ yten mando a mi *ahijada doña* fran^{ca} Rodrigues vna caxa de madera de Vayaquil sin llave y un paño de manos con puntas chiflonas y vn par de botones de cordovan blanco ___

Also I leave a Guayaquil wooden chest without a key, and a handkerchief with floating laces, and a pair of white goatskin buttons.

[*on the left margin*: entregose todo lo contenido]

[*on the left margin:* All the things were turned over.]

∽ yten mando que se venda vna capa de paño de quito açitoni enla almoneda para pagar la limosna delas missas que tengo rreferidas Juntamente vna misa cantada con su ViJilia para mi marido domingo poma Vaman difunto ___

Also, I order an olive-colored Quito cloth cape to be sold at auction in order to pay the alms of the masses that I have referred to, together with a chanted mass with its vigil for my deceased husband, Domingo Poma Guaman.

[*on the left margin*: Vendió esta capa la difunta estando uiua a Juan Quispi a 4 *ps*^{s}]

[*on the left margin:* She, the deceased, when still alive, sold this cape to Juan Quispi for four *pesos*.]

∽ yten mando que asimesmo se bendan en almoneda Vna barreta de hierro. vna *lampa* y un freno de mulas para pagar las limosnas rreferidas__

Also, I order one iron bar, one *lampa*, and one mule bridle to be sold at auction in order to pay all the alms referred to.

∽ yten mando para mi sobrino el capp^{tan} *don* gaspar Rodrigues pilco vna artesa de madera con dos cedasos ___

Also, I leave a wooden bowl with two sieves to my nephew, Captain Don Gaspar Rodríguez Pilco.

∽ yten dexo a mi ahijado Ju^{o} domingo una manta parda y otra manta blanca de lana de castilla.

Also, I leave one grey cloth and another white sheep-wool cloth to my *ahijado*, Juan Domingo.

[*on the left margin*: entregose lo contenido]

[*on the left margin:* The things were handed over.]

∽ yten mando a mi ahijada Ju^{a} maria una fresada negra ya trayda.

Also, I leave a used black blanket to my *ahijada*, Juana María.

[*on the left margin*: entregose lo contenido]

[*on the left margin:* The thing was handed over.]

∽ yten mando a mi ahijado Ju^{o} flores vna *llama* hembra y vna botija baçia vna olla grande ___

Also, I leave a female *llama*, and an empty earthen jug, and a big pot to my *ahijado*, Juan Flores.

[*on the left margin*: entregose todo lo contenido]

[*on the left margin:* The things were handed over.]

[Fol. 3r]

==

∞ yten mando a ysabel caxa payco un cordero de la tierra que esta en el pasto decasca ___

Also, I leave a male alpaca which is in the pasture of Casca to Isabel Caxapayco.

[*on the left margin*: ẽtrego[*se*]]

[*on the left margin:* It was handed over.]

∞ yten mando a mi sobrino el capp^{an}. *don* gaspar dos costales delana dela tierra con siete obillos de algodon, y un santo cruçifixo que terna casi tres *quartas* de largo. una ymagen pequeña de nuestra s^{ra}. copacabana como vna *quarta* delargo. vna cuchara de plata pequeña que terna vna *onsa* y vna *tompina*[2] de plata que terna *onsa* y *media* con otro *topo* de plata pequeña como media *onsa* ___

Also, I leave two sacks of alpaca-wool, with seven cotton clews, and a holy crucifix, which is about three *quartas* long, a small image of Our Lady of Copacabana, about a *quarta* long, one little silver spoon, that should be about an *onza*, and a silver *tompina* that should be about an *onza* and half, and another small silver *tupu* about half an *onza*, to my nephew, Captain Don Gaspar.

[*on the left margin*: entregose todo lo q̃ ressa]

[*on the left margin:* All the listed things were handed over.]

∞ yten mando que se uenda vna cassa vieja que compre delos herederos. de domingo capcha de *ychocan* en tres *patacones* questa Junto ala quebrada Junto al barrio de ~~y~~ los de *ychocan* que bibe en ella Ju^{a} caxa yauca la qual no a pagado del alquiler della de dies años aesta parte y someto al pareser de mi albaçea para que cobre della lo que fuere Justo ___

Also, I order an old house that I bought for three *patacones* from the heirs of Domingo Capcha from *Ichuqan,* which is located near the ravine near the neighbourhood of the *Ichuqan* people, to be sold. Juana Caxayauca lives in it, and she has not paid the house-rent for ten years now. I leave it to the discretion of my executor to collect from her what is just.

[*on the left margin*: pago]

[*on the left margin:* She paid.]

∞ yten dexo vna *asvana* nueba a Ju^{a} clara mi *comadre* y a su hijo Ju^{o} garçia un coton de bayeta blanca

Also, I leave a new *aswana* to Juana Clara, my *comadre*, and a doublet to her son, Juan García.

[*on the left margin*: entregose todo]

[*on the left margin:* Everything was handed over.]

+ ∞ yten mando para la yglesia deste dicho pue^{o} de ambar vna yegua coxa castaño con su muleto questa en el pasto de guacas. ___

Also, I leave a lame hazel mare with its colt, that stays in the pasture of Guacas, to the church of this aforementioned town of Ambar.

---

2 The meaning here is unknown. If *tompina* has been written in error for *tupina*, it can mean a small *tupu* pin.

∽ yten mando para mi sobrino el capitan *don* gaspar Rodrigues pilco vna yegua castaña con ~~m~~ su muleto macho. ___

Also, I leave a hazel mare with her male colt to my nephew, Captain Don Gaspar Rodríguez Pilco.

∽ yten mando. a mi *ahijado* fran^{co} Rodrigues. vna yegua castaña que esta en el pasto de Vacas con las demas rreferidas__

Also, I leave a hazel mare, that stays in the pasture of Uacas with the other [mares that I have] referred to, to my *ahijado*, Francisco Rodríguez.

\+ ∽ yten declaro que Ju^{o} rica me debe un macho de camino mohino, hijo de mi marido domingo poma guaman porque embiando a la omaya el d͡ho su padre a comprar asucar para su medicamento quando estubo malo boluio dela omaya el dicho Ju^{o} rica diçiendo auersele perdido el dicho macho sin dar mas rraçon ni causa para ello se a quedado con el dicho macho que era mio y no de su padre y a esta causa se me debe pagar y mando que se cobre lo que fuere Justo y para que digan misas por el d͡ho mi marido ____

Also, I declare that Juan Rica, my husband Domingo Guaman Poma's son, owes me a male riding mule with a black face. When his aforementioned father was ill and sent him to Omaya to buy sugar for his cure, the aforementioned Juan Rica returned from Omaya saying that he had lost the aforementioned mule. Without further explanation or justification he kept the aforementioned mule, which was mine, and not his father's. And for this reason he should pay me. And thus I order to be collected from him what is just, so that the masses for my aforementioned husband will be said.

[*on the left margin*: dio ynform^{on} bastante el d͡ho Ju^{o} rica porel macho q̄ se lo hizo cargo]

[*on the left margin:* The aforementioned Juan Rica gave sufficient information regarding the male mule, about which he has been accused.]

[Fol. 3v]

==

∽ yten mando que la cassa de mi morada se Venda enla almoneda con beneplacito de mi sobrino el capitan *don* gaspar Rodrigues pilco porque las tierras en que esta plantada son suyas. y de lo proçedido. se paguen de las lim[*osn*] as delas misas rreferidas con cargo que seme digan mas missas para cuyo efeto rremito al gusto [*de*] dicho mi sobrino

___

Also, I order the house I live in to be sold at auction, with the permission of my nephew, Captain Don Gaspar Rodríguez Pilco, because the land on which it is built is his. And from the proceeds, alms should be paid for the masses referred to, with the obligation that more masses should be said for me, and I leave this wish to the discretion of my aforementioned nephew.

\+ ∽ yten mando sinco abes para nuestra señora de copacabana. y otras sinco para el dicho mi sobrino el capp^{tan}. *don* gaspar ___

Also, I leave five birds for Our Lady of Copacabana and another five for my aforementioned nephew, Captain Don Gaspar.

[*on the left margin*: entregose lo contenido ~~q̄ por~~ con las sinco aves la limosna de n. Sr^{a}]

[*on the left margin:* It was handed over together with the five birds as alms for Our Lady.]

∞ yten tengo una obeJa decastilla con su cordero enpoder de lorenso quispi mi compadre el de tarma mando que se trayga para poner en mi sepultura para la ofrenda ___

[*on the left margin*: pussose la ofrenda]

Also, I have a sheep with her lamb in the custody of Lorenso Quispi, my *compadre*, the one from Tarma. I order it brought and put in my grave as an offering.

[*on the left margin:* The offering was given.]

∞ yten mando que to[*dos*] los bienes que paresieren ser mios asi en dentro de mi cassa como fuere [*sic*] della se uendan mi albaçea para pagar las dichas mandas rreferidas ___

Also, I order my executor to sell all the property that appears to be mine, whether inside the house or outside, in order to pay the aforementioned listed offerings.

∞ y nombro por mi albaçea y testamentario a agustin capcha aquien rruego para que lo açeten y execute segun y como rreferido tengo en las clausulas en este dicho mi testam[to]. y mandas. y rreboco qualquier testamento que aya ff[o] por mi antes deste y no quiero que balga sino este, siendo to[s] *don* xpoual chaupis Guaranga. fran[co] rinri, Ju[o] martin alonso malqui, *don* martin pilco quispi, sebastian condor y Ju[o] garçia. ques ff[o] en ambar en veinte y tres de mayo de mill seis çientos quarenta y nuebe años y por no saber firrmar yo *doña* Ju[a] flores rrogue a los t[os]. que supieron firmar firmasen por mi ___

And I name Agustín Capcha as executor of the will, whom I beg to accept [the responsibility] and carry it out according to what I have stipulated in the clauses of this, my aforementioned will and offerings. Also I nullify any other will that I have made before this one, and I do not want it to be valid, only this one. The witnesses are Don Christóbal Chaupis Guaranga, Francisco Rinri, Juan Martín, Alonso Malqui, Don Martín Pilco Quispi, Sebastián Condor, and Juan García. It is done in Ambar, on the twenty-third of May, in the year one thousand six hundred forty nine. And since I do not know how to sign, I, Doña Juana Flores, have asked the witnesses who know how to sign, to sign for me.

don Xpou chau
pis guaranga
[*signature*]

A[o] Malqui
[*signature*]

D[on] mrn naupari
[*signature*]

Don Cristóbal
Chau
-pis Guaranga
[*signature*]

Alonso Malqui
[*signature*]

Don Martín
Naupari
[*signature*]

Ante mi

don Ju[o] Leon Ticçia [*signature*]
toc scru[o] nombrado

In my presence

Don Juan Leon Ticciatoc [*signature*]
official notary

[Fol. 11r]

Memoria delos Bienes de *Doña* Juana Flores difunta que se haze inventario deello para vender en almoneda publica en presençia de alcalde ordin[o] *Don* Matheo Joseph Pilco, *don* Santiago

An account of the deceased Doña Juana Flores's property which is inventoried in order to be sold at public auction in the presence of the first mayor Don Matheo Joseph Pilco, and Don Santiago

pilco quispi y Juan guaman y ante mi *don* domingo pilco quispi escriuº de cauildo, oy Sauado en once dias del mes de Setiembre de seiscientos y quarenta y nueve años ___

Pilco Quispi, and Juan Guaman, being present I, Don Domingo Pilco Quispi, the Town Council notary, today, Saturday, September 11, in the year 649.

∞ Primeramente dos *llicllas* lestadas con vna toca de *Ruan* que dexo para nuestra sª. de copacauana y dos tembladeras de plata ___

First, two striped *lliklla*s and a linen veil that she left for Our Lady of Copacabana, and two silver drinking cups with round bottoms.

∞ yten una *lliclla* para la qual dexa para que se venda por su alma ___

Also, a *lliklla* to be sold for her soul.

[*on the left margin*: Está en poder de Juº guaman]

[*on the left margin:* It is in Juan Guaman's custody]

∞ yten otra *lliclla* parda ya trayda para que se venda por su alma ___

Also, another used grey *lliklla* to be sold for her soul.

∞ yten vna barreta de hierro y vna *lampa* y vn freno de mula para que se venda ___

Also an iron bar, a *lampa*, and a mule's bridle, to be sold.

[*on the left margin*: la barreta y *lampa* lleuo elgou^{or}.]

[*on the left margin:* The governor took the iron bar and the *lampa*.]

∞ yten una casa vieja donde viui Juana caxa yauca de *ychucan* ___

Also, an old house where Juana Caxayauca of *Ichuqan* lives.

[*on the left margin*: pago 2 *p^{o}s*, 4 de alquiler]

[*on the left margin:* She paid two *pesos* and four *reales*, as rental.]

∞ yten sinco gallinas que dexa para nuestra sª. de copacauana ___

Also, five hens that she assigns to Our Lady of Copacabana.

[*on the left margin*: lleuo elgou^{or}.]

[*on the left margin:* The governor took it.]

Los q̃ Bienes no estavan asentado en el testam^{to} ___

Property that had not been mentioned in the will.

∞ yten vn Jobon de damasillo[3] biejo. otro Jobon de lana de *avasca* bieja ___

An old doublet of woofed damask. Another old doublet made of woolen *awasqa*.

∞ yten vn freno de mula quebrado ___

Also, a broken mule bridle.

[*on the left margin*: lleuo la mug^{r}. de Juº rica hija de dgº poma guaman]

[*on the left margin:* The wife of Juan Rica, Diego Poma Guaman's son, took it]

∞ yten ^{vn} bocal de trompeta de payla ___

Also, the brass mouthpiece of a trumpet.

[Fol. 11v]

∞ yten una navaja de cortar pelo ___

Also, a razor for cutting hair.

3 This is probably *damasquillo*, a "woofed damask, or half threaded and half woofed" (Stevens 1706: 133).

[*on the left margin*: llevo el go^{r}]

[*on the left margin:* The governor took it.]

∾ yten un candelero de payla ___

Also, a brass candlestick.

[*on the left margin*: elt[*ilegible*]]

[*on the left margin: illegible.*]

∾ yten sinco aguJas de hazer media__

Also, five knitting-needles.

[*on the left margin*: Vendio en iii *R*^{l}.]

[*on the left margin:* Sold for three *reales*.]

∾ yten dos agujas de harriero__

Also, two muleteer's needles.

[*on the left margin*: Vendio en iii *R*^{l}.]

[*on the left margin:* Sold for three *reales*.]

∾ yten vna ventosa de vidro ___

Also, one cupping-glass.

[*on the left margin*: llevo el gou^{or}]

[*on the left margin:* The governor took it.]

∾ yten vn poco de añil ___

Also a little bit of indigo.

∾ yten dos hachas de biejas ___ vna hacha de su marido.

Also, two old axes. An ax of her husband's.

[*on the left margin*: lleuo la mug^{r} de Ju^{o} rica. hijo de d͡go poma guaman]

[*on the left margin:* The wife of Juan Rica, Domingo Poma Guaman's son, took it.]

∾ yten vn machete de cortar leña - de su marido –

Also, her husband's machete for cutting firewood.

[*on the left margin*: tambien se la llevo el machete]

[*on the left margin:* She also took the machete.]

∾ yten una asuela de carpinteriar ___

Also an adze for carpentry.

[*on the left margin*: lleuo el gov^{or}.]

[*on the left margin:* The governor took it.]

∾ yten vna hoçe de cortar yerua ___

Also, a sickle for cutting grass.

[*on the left margin*: tambien se la lleuo la hoçe__]

[*on the left margin:* He also took the sickle.]

∾ yten vna tegerita chiquita ___

Also, a small pair of scissors.

∾ yten vna manta de lana castilla ia traydo ___

Also, a used sheep-wool blanket.

∾ yten vna *lliclla* negra ya traida ___

Also, a used black *lliklla*.

∾ yten vn manteles chiquita ya traido ___

Also, a used small table-cloth.

∾ yten vna alforJa bieja de lana castilla__

Also, an old sheep-wool saddle-bag.

∾ yten vn bellon ~~yquartilla~~ de lana blanca dela t^{a}.__

Also, a fleece of white alpaca-wool.

∾ yten vna sobre carga nueba ___

Also, a new rope for fastening packs.

∾ yten vna *suysuna* chiquita de algodon dehaçer chicha ___	Also, a small cotton *suysuna* for corn beer brewing.
∾ yten vn seruiçio chiquillo biejo __	Also, an old small chamber-pot.
∾ yten dos sinchas biejas. ___	Also, two old cinches.
∾ yten vna Jaquima de cuero con su cadena ___	Also, one leather headstall with its chain.
∾ yten vna sobrecarga sin sincha con dos lasos ___	Also, one rope with nooses at each end for fastening packs, without a cinch.
∾ yten tres platillos de barro ___	Also, three small clay dishes.
∾ yten trece *mates* chicos y grandes ___	Also, thirteen small and large *matis*.
∾ yten nueue *mates* de comer pintados ___	Also, nine painted *matis*—plates.
∾ yten tres potes chicos i grandes ___	Also, three small and large pots.
[Fol. 12r]	
∾ yten Veinte y tres *mates* biejos chicos i grandes.	Also, twenty-three old small and large *matis*.
∾ yten vn Jarrito de barro de ueuer agua __	Also, a clay pitcher for drinking water.
∾ yten vna ~~p~~bassi[ni]ca de payla ___	Also, a brass basin or chamber pot.
∾ yten vna espuela de hierro biejo ___	Also, an old iron spur.
∾ yten otro hoçe de cortar yerua ___	Also, another sickle for cutting grass.
∾ yten vn asedon de hierro ___	Also, an iron spade.
∾ yten vna enxalma con su lomillo biejo __ mas otra enxalma bieja ___	Also, a pack saddle with its old saddle pad, and another old pack saddle.
∾ yten veinte sinco ollas chicos y grandes ___	Also, twenty-five small and large pots
mas tres *macmas* ollas grandes de haçer chicha __	and three *maqmas*, big pots for corn beer brewing.
∾ yten vna tinaja de barro de veuer agua __	Also, a clay jar for drinking water.
∾ yten vna escodilla blanca de barro ___	Also, a white clay bowl.
∾ yten doçe botiJas baçias ___	Also, twelve empty earthen jugs.
∾ yten dos çedasos bieJos ___	Also, two old sieves
∾ yten ~~vna~~ [media] *hanega* y tres *quartillo* de mayz du[*l*]çe _	Also, [*inserted*: half] an *hanega* and three *quartillos* of sweet corn.
∾ yten dos Vancos chiquitos de madera de Sause __	Also, two small stools of willow wood.

∞ yten desender[4] micha de hierro con su cadena __	Also, an iron tube for lighting wicks, with its chain.
∞ yten otro Vanco grande de madera ___	Also, another large wooden bench.
∞ yten vna *hanega* y dies *selemines* de mays blanco __	Also, an *hanega* and ten *selemines* of white corn.
∞ yten vna hanega de *taure* ___	Also, an *hanega* of *tawri.*
∞ yten ~~dies~~[ocho] *selemines* de mais blanco ~~de~~ polillado ___	Also, eight *selemines* of worm-eaten white corn.
∞ yten vna asuela chiquita de cubre[5] ___	Also, a small copper hachet.
∞ ~~yten Vna manta chiquita de color parda bieja~~	[*inserted and canceled*: Also an old small grey-colored blanket.]
∞ yten quatro *selemines* de frixoles dela tª. ___	Also, four *selemines* of kidney beans.
∞ todo los dh̃os bienes de la dh̃a *Dª* Juana flores, difunta, se entrego a augustin capcha. su alvaçea, en presençia de los dh̃os tosˢ. como lo Refiere arriba ques ffᵒ. dia, mes y año. Vt supra ___	All of the aforementioned property belonging to the deceased Doña Juana Flores was handed over to Augustín Capcha, her executor, in the presence of the aforementioned witnesses as listed above. It is dated on the day, month, and year *ut supra.*
ante mi	In my presence
D dGo pilco quispi [*signature*]	Don Domingo Pilco Quispi [*signature*]
escriº de cabdo	Town Council notary

Patrycja Prządka-Giersz

The testament of Doña Juana Flores was dictated on May 23, 1649, in the town of Ambar, which is currently located in Huaura Province, department of Lima. It includes an inventory of the deceased's assets, consisting of a total of twelve *folios* (twenty-four pages), an amount that clearly reflects the high economic and social status of the testatrix. Doña Juana Flores belonged to the local elite *ayllu* of *Guacas* of the town of Ambar; she was the widow of Domingo Guaman Poma.

It is important to note that no Spanish authorities were involved in drafting the document, although they should have been. Doña Juana did not know how to write, and for this reason the will was signed by three witnesses, among them two representatives of the local elite: Don Cristóbal Chaupis

4 This is probably *de encender*.

5 This is probably equivalent to *llaqllana* in Quechua, since it is made of copper.

and Don Martín Naupari. This was done before the notary, Don Juan León Ticciatoc. The will, with each of its formal sections, was composed according to the laws and practices of sixteenth-century European notaries (Eire 1995: 34–39). Both scribes, the one who wrote the will and Don Domingo Pilco Quispi, who created the inventory of the deceased's assets, belonged to the indigenous nobility. They spoke Spanish very well, and were able to use notarial formulas; however, the scribe who wrote the will did not copy the legal phrases exactly as recommended by the Toledo ordinances, as can be seen in earlier testaments, but instead used his own style for expressing them (Nowack 2006: 51–77).

Doña Juana ordered that her burial should take place in the church of the town of Ambar, as required by Catholic practices of this time (Eire 1995: 24–34). The testatrix also set aside a special bequest of "one branded tame male pack mule with a light black face and a muzzle" for this church. To express her high social status Juana ordered ten chanted masses: one mass on the day of burial, three chanted masses with vigils, and six additional masses for her soul. Also among the *mandas pias*, the testatrix ordered six masses celebrated for her soul and eight responses on the day of her funeral.

The next section of the document, which deals with personal property endowment, contains interesting facts regarding clothing and objects traditionally linked to the indigenous elite. Among Doña Juana Flores's first bequests are two shawls, or *lliklla*s, garments traditionally associated with women of the indigenous nobility, that she leaves to the brotherhood of Our Lady of Copacabana (Nuestra Señora de Copacabana). It is not known whether the shawls were to be given to the common people, as was the practice during this period, or if they were intended as an adornment for a holy picture or sculpture,[6] in which case it would be interesting to see if they were dressed according to the native custom with all of the elements of prestige. Indeed, the testatrix bequeathed other luxury items, such as "a handkerchief with floating laces and two silver tankards with round bottoms,"[7] precisely for this purpose. Doña Juana donated only money *en patacones* to the other brotherhoods, Lord Saint Peter (Señor San Pedro), Lord Saint Anthony (Señor San Antonio), and Lord Saint Mark (Señor San Marcos).

---

6 It is not known exactly whether the document refers to the local image or to the one from Copacabana today in Bolivia. The same names of brotherhoods can be found in other churches, as in Lima or Cajatambo (the latter located in the province to which the town of Ambar also belonged).

7 Vessels called *tembladeras* were used in water rituals related to fertility.

The next part of the will, dealing with the debts and debtors of the testatrix, sheds light on the social relations that characterized the daily life of Doña Juana. After declaring that she does not have any debts, she lists seven people who owe her money in *pesos*, *patacones*, and *reales*. Among them were men such as Juan Martín, a *kamachikuq* 'leader of workers', who owed her two *pesos*. Some of the debtors were from another local *ayllu* called *Ychucan*,[8] with which the testatrix had close relations.

One of the largest parts of the document refers to goods and heirs. This section provides interesting facts about the persistence and transformation of ancient traditions that manifests itself in material culture after European contact. In prehispanic times, the most successful people had numerous luxurious fabrics and articles of clothing in their possession, and this was also true in early colonial society (Ramírez 1998: 225–226; Castro Vásquez 2005). Both the quality and the quantity of property had symbolic value and reflected the wealth of the owner. Doña Juana Flores had multiple items of clothing and other things fashioned from textiles, some of traditional and others of European origin. It should be noted that the prestigious items of traditional origin were recorded in the will in pairs, according to an ancient Andean tradition. These articles were distributed among the godchildren of Doña Juana Flores, demonstrating their social relationships and family ties. Among the objects of prestige mentioned were two pins, or *tupus*, made of metal. These indispensable feminine dress accessories were used for the *llikllas* and other types of robes in prehispanic times, and symbolized the social status of women. Doña Juana's list included other items that had special value in the ancient society. There were small objects, such as utensils, pots, and dyes, which provide interesting facts about different cultural activities and work but that are often ignored in studies dealing with this topic. During this period it is apparent that items of European origin quickly enter into property records, especially those of the indigenous nobility, and begin to function parallel to traditional objects. Doña Juana's list contains various articles of Western-type clothing, including blankets, kilts, and shirts, as well as a tablecloth and bedcovers.

Doña Juana's will includes animals and agricultural products. A llama, a sheep (and a lamb), a horse, and a mule are mentioned, as well as "birds." The relevant clauses also give the Quechua names of pastures where animals were fed. This information tells us more about activities related to animal husbandry and adds to our knowledge regarding the custom of naming fields,

---

8 In Quechua *ichuqan* means 'one from the left' (personal communication from Jan Szemiński).

known from other regions of Peru (Charney 2012: 329–331). Some types of food listed in the will had special value, among them "white corn," "sweet corn," and beans. Other types of grain cultivated at this time are also listed in the will.

One of the clauses in this section of the document is very special because it provides information on burial practices rooted in prehispanic times. Doña Juana asks that an offering of a sheep be performed on her grave on the day of her funeral, just as it was practiced in the past when some animals, especially llamas, were sacrificed.

The list of the testatrix's assets is complemented by an interesting inventory of additional items of her property that was created on September 11, four months after the issuance of the will. It consists of goods that were found in her house and that, according to the testatrix, were given to Augustín Capcha from Ychocan *ayllu*. This part of the will contains interesting data about different aspects of Doña Juana's life, related to craft, agricultural, pastoral, and medical activities, among others.

Both lists of goods provide information about terminology in the Quechua language. Some objects of traditional use were mentioned using their original names: for example, *lliklla*, *azwana*, *mati*, *suysuna*, and *awasqa*. The items are often accompanied by short descriptions regarding decoration, the type of material they were made with, and their state at the time the will was prepared.

At the end of the operative part of the will, and in accordance with official standards, the testatrix revoked any previous testaments she might have ordered, and appointed her executor, Agustín Capcha. The fact that he was the husband of Doña Juana's goddaughter, María Antonia, once again demonstrates the nature of the bonds uniting the members of the family.

DOCUMENT 21

Testament of María Juana, San Juan Ixtenco, Mexico, 1739[1]

Justyna Olko

Yca (i)n itocazin Dios tetazin Dios yPilzin Dios hesPiritu Sn.tos yeiyn[tin] Personas onicteneuc ca huel ycelzin yn tto. dios Nicmoneltiquitia yhuan yn tto. CenquisCananzin Sn. Maria mochipan huel neli ychponzintli auc ca yeuazin nicmotlatlautilia yCa quimotlatlauhtilis yn itlasomahuisconezin yn tto. temaquixtiCazin yCa nechmotlapopolhuilis yn ixquich notlatlacol onitlapilchihua nican tlalticpac ma yehuazin quimohuiquilis y Noyolia y Noanima yN onPa ytlatocachanzinco yn ilhuiCac ahu in axca ma quimatica yN ixquichme y Nohualyolque yn quitasque y nomemoria y Notestamento y Nehuatl Nican onicchihua onictecpana Nehuatl NiCocoxqui Notoca Maria Juana Nican nichane Sn. JuaN Nichtenco NotlaxilaCal Sn. Antto. axCa yc Caxtolomei mani tonali de octubre de 1739 aos. __________

In the name of God the Father, God the Son, God the Holy Spirit, the three persons that I have mentioned, but indeed [only] one our Lord God, in whom I believe, and the eternal mother of our Lord, Santa María, always truly virgin, and this is her whom I implore so that she would supplicate her precious and venerable son, our Lord Savior so that He would forgive me all my sins that I have committed here on earth, may He take my spirit, my soul to His royal house in heaven. Now may all my kinsmen who will see my statement, my will, know that here I have made and composed it, I, the sick person named María Juana, citizen of San Juan Ixtenco, [from] the *barrio* of San Antonio. Today is the eighteenth day of October, of the year 1739.

1 Archivo Parroquial, San Juan Ixtenco, Tlaxcala.

 DOI: 10.5876/9781607328346.c021

Oquittº. yn cocozcatzintli yntla nimomiquilis yCa nimotoca ce misas yhuan ce Vijilia yhuan ce Responsos yca ypalehuiloCa y noanima yn onpa S.[n]to Purgatorio yn tlachipahualoya ________

The sick person said: when I die, I am to be buried with a mass, a vigil, and responses for the aid of my soul there in holy purgatory, the place of purification.

Oquittº. yn CoCoxqui Niquitohua NixPanzinCo yn ttº. Dios Ca melahua chiquance peso onechcahuilitehua Notazin oCatCa ytoca anttº. hernandes yCa quimochihuilisque matlactli misa Resada yn totlasomahuisNanzin del Carme yhua ome misa Resada quimochihuilisque yn tohueitazin senor S.[n] anttº.________________________

The sick person said: I declare in the presence of Our Lord God that indeed my late father named Antonio Hernández left me six *pesos* before dying; with that they will perform ten recited masses of our precious revered Mother of Carmel and they will perform two recited masses of our great father Lord Saint Anthony.

Oquito yn CoCoxqui Niquitohua NixPanzinco yn to Dios ome metePantli solar NicmoPialia ytech mantiCa S.[n] antt.º Ca nicahuilia y nocnizin ytoCa Rita Nicolasa yhuan oc tlaComecatlalCohua NicPia sano niCahuilia y nocnizin ytoCa Rita nicolasa yhuan Ce Caxa NicPia monamaca yCa quimochihuilisque ResPonsos y nonanzin Ocatca ytoca Cesilia Ma. Yhuan nahui ichCame nicPia Ce niCahuilia y nocnizin ytoca Rita Nicolasa yhua oc Ce Nicahuili y noquixtizin antt.º Baes yhua Ce niCauili y notlazin Ju.ª B.[no] yhuan oc ma monamaca yca mortaja yua chicome tomi quihuiquilia y notazin oCatCa Diego B.[no] quimochihuilisque ce misa resada y notazin ocatca ant.º hernandes yhuan ce respondos yhuan andres ichan Alonso dias ce peso quihuiquilitica y noquixtizin ocatca migel hernandes yhua Ce Cemana yCa onitlaneti notijeras yn diego antt.º ca nechtlaxhuilis yhuan ce peso yhua nahui tomi techhuiquilia ce tlaca ycha s.[n] antt.º yntla onesi yca mochihua ResPonsos. ____________

The sick person said: I declare in the presence of Our Lord God that I have two fields planted with rows of *maguey* located next to the *barrio* of San Antonio. I leave them to my sister named Rita Nicolasa. And I also have half a *mecatl* of purchased land that I leave as well to my sister named Rita Nicolasa. And a chest that I have is to be sold; with it, responses for my late mother named Cecilia María will be performed. As for the four sheep I have, I leave one to my sister named Rita Nicolasa and I have left another to my older brother Antonio Báez. And I have left one to my uncle Juan Bernardino and another one is to be sold in order to [buy] a shroud. And [with] seven *reales* that Diego Bernardino owes to my late father, one recited mass and responses are to be performed for my late father Antonio Hernández. And in the house of Andrés, Alonso Díaz still owes one *peso* to my late older brother Miguel Hernández. One week ago I lent my scissors to Diego Antonio, he should pay me [for them]. And a person in the house of San Antonio[2] owes us one *peso* and four *reales*. When [the money] has appeared, responses are to be performed with it.

2 Probably the *barrio* of San Antonio mentioned in the beginning of the document as a *tlahxillacalli*.

Oquitto yn Cocoxqui Niquitohua [i] n ixpanzinco yn tt.º Dios acmo NicPia yn tlen niquitos Ca san ixquich yn tlen yonictenquixtin Ca ixpan noalbaCea yhuan notestigo yhuan toixpa titehuanti titequihuaque fiscal yhuan nehuatl NihesCriVano ictilia tictlalia yn totoca yn tofirma

The sick person said, I state before Our Lord God that I have nothing more to say, this is all that I have already declared before my executor and my witness. And before us, the officials, the *fiscal* and me, the notary, we verify [the document] and we put our names and our signatures.

antt.º Baes albacea — Antonio Báez, executor

Ju.n S.nches testigo — Juan Sánchez, witness

tereza maria albacea — Teresa María, executor

Fran.co martin fiscal — Francisco Martín, *fiscal*

Fran.co Contreras hescrivano — Francisco Contreras, notary

The will of María Juana, the resident of the *barrio* of San Antonio in the town of San Juan Ixtenco (Tlaxcala), was made on October 18, 1739. It is preceded by an elaborate formula of the declaration of Christian faith, beginning with a descriptive rendering of the nature of the Holy Trinity, whose understandable and unambiguous translation into Nahuatl had posed problems ever since the introduction of the testament genre in the sixteenth century. Then the Virgin Mary is evoked as an intermediary and supplicant of her Son for forgiveness of the testator's sins. María Juana also orders that she is to be buried with the mass with a vigil and responses; in addition, she wishes for twelve recited masses to be performed to help her soul in purgatory. She also wants a chest of hers to be sold in order to pay for a mass with responses for her deceased mother, and, with the money that a certain person owes to her late father, one recited mass and responses are to be performed for his soul. Two pieces of land go to her sister, while three of the four sheep she has are to be divided among the same sister, the older brother of the testator, and her uncle, and the fourth sheep is to be sold in order to secure money for a shroud. María Juana does not forget that she lent her scissors to another local citizen who should pay for them, and that another debtor owes her one *peso* and four *reales* which should also be spent for responses. Thus, the expenditures linked to spiritual matters are of primary concern to the sick person, who makes sure that her soul and those of her deceased parents are taken care of by means of adequate ceremonies. The surname of Antonio Báez, who is mentioned as an elder brother of the testatrix, provides a link to a noble family that was very influential locally in the eighteenth century. This implies that María

Juana might have belonged to the local nobility. Several testaments of the members of the Báez family have been preserved in the corpus of Nahuatl documents from Ixtenco, including for example a 1744 will of Don Joseph Antonio; however, given the lack of the title *don* in the reference and in the signature of Antonio Báez we cannot be conclusive about his status, though it seems rather plausible that both he and his sister belonged to the Báez family. Although in at least some cases the Nahuatl testaments from San Juan Ixtenco represent voices of commoners, in addition to members of the noble class, it seems that the use of this language must have been of considerable prestige in this Otomí-speaking (and perhaps, at least to certain degree, bilingual) native community. It no doubt served as the language of communication with the main *cabecera* of Tlaxcala and its elites, to which, according to the eighteenth-century local documents in Nahuatl, the *altepetl* of Ixtenco was linked at political and administrative levels.

In terms of the language of the document, several phenomena are worth mentioning. While the abundance of Spanish loanwords is not surprising, considering the date of the document, the usage of a doublet composed of a loanword and a native neologism at such a late date is an interesting example of the continuity of contact-related expressions typical for the early colonial period. This is the case of *S.^{n}to Purgatorio yn tlachipahualoya* 'holy purgatory, the place of purification', attested in almost an identical form in the early seventeenth century. The numeral *ce* (*ce tlaca[tl]* 'un hombre'/'a man'), used as a calque of the Spanish indefinite article, represents a typical feature of this stage of language change. Another typical calque is the expression *acmo NicPia yn tlen niquitos* 'I do not have anything [else] to say', modeled on Spanish *no tengo nada [mas] que decir*. On the other hand, the preterite *yonictenquixtin* 'I have already declared' is a bridge between the traditional older form *ye onictenquixtih* and the typical modern usage in Tlaxcalan Nahuatl in which the particle *ye* has become fused with the antecessive *o*. As regards the terminology of rank, the expression employed to identify the municipal officials, *titehuanti titequihuaque,* is based on the preconquest military title *tequihuah* that has been adapted to the new municipal hierarchy (though probably not immediately after the Spanish conquest). It provides a late colonial example of the durability of traditional vocabulary related to power and political/military functions, now extended to designate new roles in the local community.

PETITIONS AND LETTERS

DOCUMENT 22

Petition of Don Pedro de San Juan, Yauhtepec, Mexico, 1545–1559 (?)[1]

JULIA MADAJCZAK, JAN SZEMIŃSKI, AND JOHN SULLIVAN

[Fol. 1r]

+

.s.c.m.R.

v don pedro de san Juan caçique y goũ̊r
del pueblo de avtepeque y sus subjetos
y estancias ques en el marquesado del
valle de la nueva spaña beso los piês de v.
alª. y por persona de mi procurador digo
que v.m̃. por hazernos bien y m̃d a los
caçiques prinçipales y demas naturales
destas yndias vr̃os` vasallos. /ordeno
y mando ansi por sus leyes como por /
otras provisiones y çedûs que nos fuesen
guardadas nr̃as buenas costumbres y
se nos hiziese todo buen tratamĩ̊ como
se haze a los demas vrôs vasallos de
los Reynos despaña y ansi mismo que
a los caçiq̃s y prin͡çipales lo tuvieron
antiguam̃ͤ. señorio siendo naturles fuesen
conservados en ellos y no se los quitasen
pues conforme a la ley de naturaleza
confirmada por vrâs leyes les pertenesçe
y no deven de ser molestados ni

+

Holy Imperial Royal Majesty

Yours, Don Pedro de San Juan, *cacique* and governor of the town of Autepeque and of its subject [towns] and farms, which is in the Marquisate of the Valley in New Spain, kisses Your Highness's feet, and through the person of my attorney declare that Your Majesty, in order to benefit and favor the *caciques,* rulers, and other natives of these Indies, your vassals, ordered and commanded as much through your laws as through other writs and decrees that our good traditions should be preserved, and that we be treated well, as are your other vassals in the realms of Spain. And likewise, that the *caciques* and rulers, who formerly exercised dominion, as they are natives, should not be deprived of them, because according to natural law and upheld by your laws, it belongs to them. And they should not

1 Archivo General de Indias (AGI), Mexico 96.

DOI: 10.5876/9781607328346.c022

desposados dellos por ningũ vıã mayorm̃te no hazıendo cosa alguna tan fuera de termınos por que se deva de hazer y yo siendo como soy caçique natural del dḣo pů y subjetos de mi y padreś y abuelos y de tanto tıenpo que memorıã de honbres no es en contrario constando ser ansi por Recados ẏ provanças muy bastantes fuy avıdo por tal y ansi por v. avdĩa. Real de mex̃co. de la nueva españa me fue adjudıcado el dḣo señorio y caçicato. y gouernaçion. y como yo este debaxo de la jurĩon. del marques del valle. y la pretension de los que gouíernan el dḣo marquesado. es que no aya caçíques nı otros gouernadores para tener mayor líbertad y mano en las cosas que quieren hazer de hecho yo y los demas prinçipales somos molestados y vexados por manera que los caçiques y caçicatos se pıerden lo qủal [Fol. 1v] Redundá en daño vniversal de todos. los naturales vasallos vṙos del dḣo marquesado y por cavsas muy lıvıanas y muy flacas nos prıvan de los caçicatȯs y ansi. hızıeron a mi lo qual se Remedio por vṙa avdĩa Real viendo ser mas genero de vexaçion que de Justiçia

be bothered nor stripped of them by any means, especially since they are not overstepping the limits of accepted conduct. And given that I am a native *cacique* of the aforementioned town and of the subjects who have pertained to me, my parents and my grandparents for such a long time that human memory will not contradict it, and that this is stated in many testimonies and inquiries and was confirmed as such by your Royal Court of Justice in Mexico in New Spain, the aforementioned dominion, *cacicazgo*, and rulership were granted to me. And since I am under the jurisdiction of the Marquis of the Valley, and the intention of those who rule the aforementioned Marquisate is that there no longer be *caciques* or other governors, in order to have more discretion and power in the things they wish to do, in fact, I and the other rulers are offended and mistreated. Because of this, the *caciques* and *cacicazgos* are disappearing, which results in general harm to all the natives, Your vassals, from the aforementioned Marquisate. And based on very frivolous and feeble arguments, they deprive us of *cacicazgos*. And this is what they did to me, but it was corrected by your Royal Court of Justice, which considered it more in the realm of mistreatment than justice.

v supco. a v.m̃. que atento quel dḣo caçicato conforme a drco me esta adjudıcado por vıã de naturaleza y subçesioñ vṙa mag.+ sea serbıdo de me lo confirmar y quel dhȯ marques del valle nı sus subçesores ni gouernadores a mi ni a mis desçendıentes ni subçesores a quieñ pertenesçiere el dhȯ caçicato no nos hagan molestia vexaçion nı perturbaçion alguna y quė ansi confirmado por cavsas lıvıanas no traten de nos hazer las dhȧs molestıas en Razon

I implore Your Majesty, given that the aforementioned *cacicazgo* is legally granted to me, based on natural law and succession, to agree to confirm this; and may neither the aforementioned Marquis of the Valley nor his successors and governors bother, mistreat, or annoy in any way neither me nor my descendants and successors to whom the aforementioned *cacicazgo* may belong; and may they not attempt to subject us to the aforementioned annoyances, based

de suspensiō̄ perpetua nı tenporal del dħo cacicato y demas desto en las estançias tıerras y otros heredami^{o}s anexos al dħo caçicato como a m̄ı propıo patroni^{o} no me perturben en la posesiō̄ dello. En lo qual aliende de ser nr̄o s$^{o}_{r}$. y. v.m̄. enello servıdo yo Preçebıre mucha m̄d /.

don p^{o} de sanct jů

on frivolous arguments, concerning the temporary or permanent suspension of the aforementioned *cacicazgo*, as well as the farms, lands, and other landed properties attached to the aforementioned *cacicazgo*; the same goes for my own patrimony, may they not disturb me with regard to its possession. With this, in addition to Our Lord and Your Majesty being honored, I will be greatly favored.

Don Pedro de San Juan

[Fol. 2r]

q̄ fe[2] Ju^{o} de cordoua por̄ el gou^{or} de yahutepec

Juan de Córdova signs for the governor of Yauhtepec.

Julia Madajczak

The petition of Don Pedro de San Juan, the ruler and governor of Autepeque, is not dated but it most likely comes from the same period as the documents issued by Don Antonio Cortés and Don Francisco de Verdugo, that is, from the 1550s. "Autepeque" can be identified with Yauhtepec, one of the pre-conquest city-states included in the hereditary grant for the Cortés family, the Marquesado del Valle de Oaxaca. The dramatic struggle described in the text is not for privileges or income but for the very existence of the *cacicazgo* and its dynastic rule. The aim of the letter is to prevent any attempts of the Cortés family to deprive Don Pedro and the noblemen of Yauhtepec of their patrimonial lands. The native ruler's mistrust seems to be well justified: he mentions the case he won at the Royal Audiencia, dealing with the Marquis's effort to take away his property. At the same time he emphasizes that many other *caciques* and noblemen were not that lucky and that the threat is ongoing. A set of sixteenth-century documents written in Nahuatl and known as the "Marquesado del Valle Codex" confirms that, due to the project of creating extensive sugar plantations, the possessions of local nobility were constantly endangered and gradually lost to the Cortés family.

One can find among the arguments Don Pedro de San Juan produces with the help of a lawyer a reference to the antiquity of the ruling lineages of the Marquesado, but it is clearly subordinated to the Spanish notion of

2 We are not sure what the abbreviation "q̄ fe" means, although the context suggests something like "que firma" or "que firmó".

"natural law." However, the biggest emphasis is put on the legal procedures and documents that have guaranteed the integrity of local *cacicazgos* ever since the conquest. Don Pedro reminds the king that he and his compatriots are royal vassals and implies that mistreating them undermines the authority of the Crown as the source of justice. He additionally mentions numerous documents issued by royal authorities favoring the indigenous rulers of the Marquesado city-states and stresses that the Royal Audiencia of Mexico has also confirmed his position. Such a line of argumentation, obviously prepared by the Spanish lawyer, suggests that Don Pedro has decided to make the most of the Crown's bureaucracy, viewing it perhaps as the last chance to defend the social and economic position of his class.

DOCUMENT 23

Petition of Don Antonio Cortés, Governor and Lord of the Town Called Tlacopan, Mexico, 1552[1]

Julia Madajczak, Jan Szemiński and John Sullivan

[Fol. 1r]

+

s. c. c. m.

Don Antonio Cortes Gouernador y Señor del pueblo llamado Tlacopan que es en la nueua españa beso los pies y manos De .v. mag.t y le hago saber que quando el marques del valle vino a esta tierra luego de grado y voluntad Recebimos la palabra y fe de ñro señor Jesu x̃po y ansi mesmo Recebimos a .v. mag.t por ñro Rey /y señor/ y fuimos en ayudar a los españoles quando çercaron y conquistaron a mexico ansi mesmo hago saber a .v.c.c.m. como mi padre que era señor quando vino el marques del valle y mis aguelos señores de tlacopan etc. ñunca tributaron a mexico ni a otro señor ninguno con vn tomin ni vn grano

+

Holy Imperial Catholic Majesty

I, Don Antonio Cortés, governor and lord of the town called Tlacopan, which is in New Spain, kiss Your Majesty's feet and hands, and inform you that when the Marquis of the Valley came to this land, with pleasure and willingness we then received the word and faith of Our Lord Jesus Christ, and also we received Your Majesty as our King and Lord, and we went to help the Spaniards when they besieged and conquered Mexico. Also I inform Your Imperial Royal Majesty that neither my father, who was lord when the Marquis of the Valley arrived, nor my grandparents, lords of Tlacopan, etc., ever paid taxes to Mexico or to any

1 Archivo General de Indias (AGI), Mexico 96. This document was previously published in Pérez-Rocha and Tena 2000. It has also been included in the Corpus Electrónico del Español Colonial Mexicano (COREECOM), developed by the Grupo de Estudio del Español Colonial Mexicano (GEECOM) of the Instituto de Investigaciones Filológicas, UNAM.

DOI: 10.5876/9781607328346.c023

de cacao antes el señorio De tlacopan demas de muchos pueblos que aqui tenia subjetos y tributarios tenia juntamente con mexico y tezcuco parte en los tributos De .cxxiii. prouinçias y pueblos Como pareçera por vna memoria que con esta va / y quando los españoles salieron de mexico heridos y desbaratados que avian muerto mas de la metad dellos si como aqui los Reçebimos de paz / y dimos comida les dieramos guerra no q̃ dara hombre dellos y por este hecho los mexicanos fueron muy enojados contra nos despues que mexico se tomo ansi Repartieron el señorio de tlacopan que ningũ pueblo le dexaron antes de los subjetos a esta cabeçera estan algunos Repartidos y dados a españoles y esto por auentura no lo sabe .v. mag.t agora suplico A .v. m. lo mire y mande descargar su Real conçiençia lo que agora yo suplico a .v. mag.t es mande boluer a este pueblo su subjeto que son /ocho/ o nueue estançias que nos quitaron y como tributamos a vn español que se llama Juan cano siruamos daqui adelante y tributemos a .v.m. y para mi me haga v. mag.t merçed del pueblo q̃ se llama xiquipilco que esto es pedir que de vn gran pan que me quitaron me mande .v. mag.t dar vna Reuanada y ansi mesmo suplico que por quanto yo soy señor natural y lo fue mi padre llamado Totoquivaçi. y mis aguelos y a mi me llaman gouernador que daqui a tres /o quatro años quitandome [Fol. 1v] la gouernaçion me quedare sin nada me mandes Confirmar mi señorio para mejor seruir a .v.m. y demando en pago de lo que yo y mi padre sirvio en la conquista de mexico y despues aca que siempre emos seruido lealmente vn escudo de armas y que dentro entren estas que nosotros antiguamente teniamos / y a este pueblo de tlacopan lo mande .v.m. hazer çiudad y dar / otro escudo darmas y para el Reparo y bienes desta Republica nos haga .v. mag.t merçed del pueblo llamado Tlallachco Guarde

other lord, not even a *tomin*, or a grain of cocoa. Furthermore, the Seigniory of Tlacopan, aside from many towns it had here as subjects and taxpayers, partook together with Mexico and Tetzcoco of the taxes from one hundred twenty-four provinces and towns, as it appears in the record presented together with this [document]. And when the Spaniards left Mexico, wounded and defeated, because more than half of them had been killed, if instead of receiving them in peace and giving them food, we had waged war on them, not a man among them would have remained. And for this reason the Mexicans were very angry at us. After Mexico was taken, they divided up the Seigniory of Tlacopan and left this capital with none of the towns formerly subject to it. Some have been distributed and given to Spaniards. And this, by the way, is not known to Your Majesty. Now I beg Your Majesty to consider this and order what your Royal conscience considers just. What I am begging now of Your Majesty is to order its dependencies restored to this town, which are eight or nine farms that were taken from us. And since we pay taxes to a Spaniard named Juan Cano, may we from now on serve and pay taxes to Your Majesty. And as for me, may Your Majesty make me the grant of a town called Xiquipilco; this amounts to my asking Your Majesty to order that I be given a slice of a great loaf that was taken from me. Also, since I am a lord by descent, as were my father, named Totoquihuatzin, and my grandparents, and though I am titled governor, if in three or four years they take the governorship from me, I will be left with nothing, I beg you to order that my Seigniory be confirmed so that I may better serve Your Majesty. And in payment for my father's and my service during the conquest of Mexico and later here, given that we have always served loyally, I demand a coat of arms, which

avmente ñro señor el felicissimo estado De .v. mag.t por muchos años en su sancto seruiçio. Amen.	should contain the arms we formerly had. And may Your Majesty order that this town of Tlacopan attain the rank of city, and give it another coat of arms. And may your Majesty grant us the town called Tlallachco for the restoration and good of this commonwealth. May Our Lord preserve and increase Your Majesty's most happy condition for many years in his holy service. Amen.
Hecha en tlacopan Dia de los Reyes Año. De. 1552.	Done in Tlacopan, on the Day of the Kings,[2] year 1552.
/ D.V.C.C. M.[3] minimo sieruo y vasallo. Don antonio cortes	/ From the least of Your Catholic, Imperial Majesty's servants and vassals, Don Antonio Cortés
[Fol. 2r]	
A la Sacra .C.C.M.[4] Del Inuictissi.º Emperador Don carlos Rey ñro señor.	To the Sacred, Catholic, Imperial Majesty of the Supremely Undefeated Emperor Don Carlos King, Our Lord.
nueua esp^{a} +	New Spain +
1552	1552
A Su m^{tj}	To His Majesty
en tlacopan	In Tlacopan
d don Antonio cortes /yndio/	from Don Antonio Cortés/Indian/

Julia Madajczak

The letter of Don Antonio Cortés Totoquihuaztli, *tlahtoani* and governor of Tlacopan, to Charles I, king of Spain, is only one example of the vigorous petition writing of this indigenous ruler. It was issued on August 6, 1552, and soon the Spanish emperors received at least three other documents signed by Don Antonio (dated 1552, 1556, and 1561; Castañeda de la Paz 2009:

2 January 6.

3 De Vuestra Católica Cesárea Majestad.

4 Católica Cesárea Majestad.

135), all presenting a rather critical attitude towards the economic aspect of the colonial system. The present text, which is the earliest, is structured around two major goals: improving the economic situation of Tlacopan and achieving a grant of personal privileges for Don Antonio, allowing him to get closer to the status of Spanish nobility. The former point includes petitions to assign eight or nine subject settlements to the town—these had been distributed among the Spaniards after the conquest—and to take the *encomienda* of Tlacopan away from its current owner, Juan Cano, so that the *tlahtoani* would be able to pay tribute directly to the Crown. Along with these demands, Tlacopan was to receive the status of a city and a coat of arms, privileges requested by many indigenous towns, Tlaxcala being one of the most famous examples. Additionally, Don Antonio asks the king to grant him the town of Xiquipilco, to confirm his status of indigenous ruler, which implies a stable income even when he is no longer governor and thus part of the Spanish administration, and to bestow on him a coat of arms. These issues are not treated in the 1556 petition, of a much more general character and dramatic tone, signed by all of the most important indigenous rulers of the Valley of Mexico (Paso y Troncoso 1942: 64–65). Yet from the 1561 document it is obvious that the privileges requested for Tlacopan had not been received. So in the final petition, everything heard by Charles I is repeated to Philip II, from the plea for a grant of settlements to the appeal for a coat of arms for the city (Paso y Troncoso 1942: 71–74). This latter wish was finally fulfilled in 1564 (Castañeda de la Paz 2009: 135).

Arguing in favor of his stance, Don Antonio emphasizes the legitimity of his position as a dynastic ruler: "I am a lord by descent, as were my father, named Totoquihuatzin, and my grandparents." He also claims to be son of the most famous *tlahtoani* of Tlacopan, Tetlepanquetzaltzin, who was executed along with the rulers of Tenochtitlan and Tetzcoco during the fatal expedition of Cortés to Honduras in 1526. The strategy of Cortés, after cutting off the heads of the Triple Alliance, was to replace the reportedly rebellious *tlahtohqueh* with others loyal to him. The name of Don Antonio, Cortés, is the same as the name of another successor to the executed rulers, Ixtlilxochitl of Tetzcoco. It may indicate that Hernando Córtés was their godfather, but that he was their protector is more than certain. Don Antonio must have been very young in 1526, which made him vulnerable to the influence of both the conquistador and the training in Spanish culture that all of his protégés received. In spite of his loyalty to Cortés, Totoquihuaztli named one of his sons Pedro Cortés Tetlepanquetzaltzin (Chimalpahin 1997, 1: 171), thus establishing a link with the preconquest dynasty. Another son, Juan Cortés, secured the continuity of the Totoquihuaztli dynasty by succeeding to the throne in Tlacopan (Chimalpahin 2006: 46).

Two strategies of argumentation are particularly salient in the 1552 petition: putting emphasis on the role of Tlacopan as an important ally of Cortés, and pointing to the important position of the *altepetl* before the conquest. The latter is in line with the common strategy of justifying the right to sovereignty by tracing family rule back a few generations. And both arguments respond to the respect Spaniards paid to the antiquity of institutions and natural law. The authors of the petition also seem to be aware of the value, for the Spanish legal system, of written (or painted) documents, given that the document was accompanied by a record of tributary provinces that belonged to Tlacopan (now lost). The list of merits during the conquest is quite common for this type of documentation—see, for example, the petition in Nahuatl of the council of Huexotzinco to the king of Spain (Anderson, Berdan, and Lockhart 1976: 177–191) or the letter from the Nahua nobles of Xochimilco to the king of Spain (Restall, Sousa, and Terraciano 2005: 66–71; see also: Castañeda de la Paz 2009: 126)—typically recalling to the king's attention the warm welcome given to the Spaniards by the natives, their immediate conversion to Christianity, and the nutritional aid they gave to the wounded and terrified Spanish soldiers after their escape from Tenochtitlan. There is even a suggestion of Mexica hostility towards Tlacopan, a tactic undoubtedly intended to dissociate the latter from the biggest loser of the conquest. The entire line of reasoning, though designed to impress the royal officials, is also characteristic of the emerging postconquest identities of the Central Mexican *altepetl*. The fall of Tenochtitlan becomes the frontier between the highly valued noble past and the era of Christianity, which brought ultimate legitimization of local dynasties. Double heritage mirrors—in a way—the precontact Toltec-Chichimec tradition and along with the quest for prestigious privileges, plays a crucial role in creating space for the indigenous ruling class within colonial society.

DOCUMENT 24

Letter of the Municipal Council of Tollan Xicocotitlan, Mexico, 1557[1]

Anastasia Kalyuta

[Fol. 63r]

\+

Axcan martes . yc . 23 . ylhuitl metztli de març̧o . año de mil E quinientos . y ç̧incuenta y siete años . otitocentlalique yn tehuantin titollantlaca yn tixquichtin tictocuitlavia yn taltepeuh tullan ỹ nican cabildo ticate yn tehuãntin talcaldesme nitoribio feliciano . yoã nimiguel gar.ª yhuan tehuantin tiRegidoresme niJoachin tlacatecuhtli . niJuan damian . nimiguel de luna . nibar.[me] martinez . nipablo marcos . yvã nehuatl nialonso mentez . yoã yn tizq̃ntin tictocuitlavia altepetl yn tullã . nipº esteban . yn timuchintin nicã tichaneq̃ yn tullã. tlaahuililpan . nifelipe de los angeles . / Auh in titlacpactlaca . niJoachin . yoã nitoribio feliciano . / Auh in tiquetzalhuacãtlaca nimiguel de

\+

Today Tuesday, on the twenty-third day of the month of March in the year 1557, we people of Tollan gathered together: all of us who take care of our *altepetl* Tollan, who are here in the municipal council, we *alcaldes,* I, Toribio Feliciano, and I, Miguel García, and we *regidores,* I, Joaquín Tlacatecuhtli, I, Juan Damián, I, Miguel de Luna, I, Bartolomé Martínez, I, Pablo Marcos, and I, Alonso Méndez; and all of us who take care of the *altepetl* of Tollan, I, Pedro Esteban, all we residents here of Tollan Tlahuililpan, I, Felipe de los Ángeles; and we people of Tlacpac, I, Joaquín and I, Toribio Feliciano; and we people of Quetzalhuahcan, I, Miguel de Luna,

1 Archivo General de la Nación (AGN), Vínculos y mayorazgos, vol. 256, cuaderno 12, exp. 1, fol. 63r–63v. Also in the file is a corresponding, contemporary translation of the manuscript into Spanish. John Sullivan participated in the transcription and translation of the manuscript.

 DOI: 10.5876/9781607328346.c024

luna nidi.º lopez . niJuan ytzcotecatl . / Auh yn titlalcovalcotlaca . nibartolome martinez . niJuan quetzalhua . / auh yoã tehuantin vztutenpan titlaca nipablo marcos . nidi.º cuauhpotonqui . / yoan tipanoayantlaca . niJuan tlacuchcalcatl nidi.º atenpanecatl . niJuan chalchiuhtlaol . nifran.co tlacatecpanecatl . / no tehuantin yn ticalpuleque yn timexica . yn tizquitlaxilacaltin ticuañalteca . nipº mĩn . nipº gar.ª niJuan chochõ . nidi.º moysen . / yoan vapalcalco . alonso mentez . Juan de san miguel . mĩn mexicatl . / titepexiccalque niJuan atzaqualcatl . nipablo culhua tlapixq̃. matheo tequiva . / titepetlapancalque . nimiguel gar.ª nip.º tlaylutlac . / titzaputlatlaca . nimiguel de santa m.ª nimartin tecpanecatl . / vel timuchintin y[2] . ỹ nican otiticuiloque yn titullantlaca ça centetl yn totlatol yc titocẽnunutza ynic temechpepena[3] temechixquetza yn amotech ticcava yn toveli yn topoder temechmaca amotech ticcencava . ynic amehuantin anq̃nanquilizque yn don pº motecuhçoma yn quixnamiquico taltepeuh yn çan tlapic motlaltitivitz[4] yn tullan . amehuantin anq̃namiquizque anquinanq̃lizque yn tleyn quitoz . auh no vel anq̃xnamiq̃zque yoã anquipanavizque . yehica ca no vel amomachiz yn altepetl . yn tamechtocayotia yn ipan tamauh y tehuatzĩ tiJuan damiã yoan tigabriel de soto . yoan tipº mĩn . vel anquichicavazq̃ vel anquivapavazq̃ yn toten yn totlatol ca vel antixiptlavan antopatillovã temechchiva . auh ca vel tonellatoltica . toneltiliztica yn otemechpepẽque. yn

I, Diego López, I, Juan Itzcotecatl; and we people of Tlalcohualco, I, Bartolomé Martínez, I, Juan Quetzalhuah; and we people of Oztotempan, I, Pablo Marcos, I, Diego Cuauhpotonqui; and we, people of Panoyan, I, Juan Tlacochcalcatl, I, Diego Atempanecatl, I, Juan Chalchiuhtlaol, I, Francisco Tlacatecpanecatl; also we *calpolli* elders, we Mexihcah, we people of all the *tlahxillacalli*, we people of Cuanallan, I, Pedro Martín, I, Pedro García, I, Juan Chocho, I, Diego Moisén; and [the people] of Huapalco, Alonso Mendez, Juan de San Miguel, Martín Mexihcatl; and we people of Tepexic: I, Juan Atzacualcatl, I, Pablo Colhuah, the *tlapixqui*, Mateo, the *tequihuah*; we people of Tepetlapan, I, Miguel García, I, Pedro Tlailotlac; we people of Tzapotlan, I, Miguel de Santa María, I, Martín Tecpanecatl. Indeed all of us who have registered ourselves here as people of Tollan here, agree with one voice to choose you, to appoint you. We delegate our authority to you, we give and relinquish our power to you, so you will respond to Don Pedro Motecuhçoma who has come to confront our *altepetl*, who comes under false pretenses to take land for himself in Tollan. You will counter and respond to what he says. And you will also be able to contend with him and overcome him. It is because of your great knowledge of the *altepetl* that we name you Juan Damián, and you Gabriel de Soto, and you Pedro Martín, in our document. You will aggressively argue and support our case, for we make

2 This is probably the demonstrative *īn* 'this/these'. A literal translation of the entire phrase would be 'all these of us'.

3 The first person plural subject prefix *t(i)-*, and the second person plural specific object prefix *-amech-*, appear together ten times in the manuscript. With the normal vowel ellision that is characteristic of Central Mexican variants of Nahuatl, we would expect to see the sequence *tamech-*; however, in nine out of ten instances, we see *temech-*. This is a case of vowel harmony that I have never seen before.

4 The verb is *tlaltia* 'to provide someone or oneself with land'.

otemechixquetzque . yn otemech-tocayotique . ca vel am̃achizeq̃ . [Fol. 63v] Ca vel nican amaltepeuh yn tullan vel anquimati yn quenin mani altepetl yn huel amomac catqui . yehica vel anquichicavazq̃ yn totlatol vel anquichicavacatlaçazq̃ yn ixpan Justicia

you truly our representatives, our deputies. With our endorsement and authorization, we have chosen you, we have appointed you, we have named you. For you are very knowledgeable; for Tollan here is truly your *altepetl*; you know how the *altepetl* is laid out. It is completely in your hands. For this reason, you will aggressively argue our case, you will forcefully present it before the judge.

Yvan yn amehuantzitztĩ yn temechtixiptlatia yn tizquintin yn techteixpanhuitivitz yn don pº tlacavepẽ yn õpa otechicuilo yn audiençia rreal . yn iuh quitoa yn oticcuilique yn itlal . yn iuh techteixpahuia . yn nicã titocayeticate yn nehuatl niJoachin yoã nigabriel de soto . nitoribio feliciano . / nipº estevã . niJº damian . nigabriel de san fran.^{co} nifelipe de los angeles . nipº bassilio . nifran.^{co} chalchiuhtepeva niJuan tuchtli . / nimiguel de luna . niJuan tlacuchcalcatl . nidº cuauhpotonqui . nidonJuº clemente . nigonçalo fabian . nibar^{me} martinez . niJuan quetzalhua . / yn tixquichtin techteneva yn don pº . yn itlal oticcuilique ca ça yztlacati . ca çã nimã ticcauhquẽ. auh ca amo çan io yn tlalli topan yahyaca ca yoã yn macevaltin yeq̃ne amo çan tizquintiny . ca miec tlacatl yn õpa macoca tlalli yn calpixcapã . auh no vel amotechtzĩco titocẽcava yn anpipiltĩ tiJuan damian . tigabriel de soto . tipº mĩn vel anq̃momelavilizq̃ ymixpan Justicia . yn totlatol yn iuh timamacoca yn tlalli . no yoã yn iuh ticcauhq̃ vel ãquimaxitilizque yn totlatol . ye ixquich yn tocentlatol yn ic temechtonavatilia . auh nican ypan titofirmatia yn totlatol .

We make you representatives of all of us who Don Pedro Tlacahuepan comes to accuse in the Real Audiencia, where he has filed against us. He says that we took his land. He accuses us who are named here: I, Joaquín and I, Gabriel de Soto, I, Toribio Feliciano, I, Pedro Estéban, I, Juan Damián, I, Gabriel de San Francisco, I, Felipe de los Ángeles, I, Pedro Basilio, I, Francisco Chalchiuhtepehuah, I, Juan Tochtli, I, Miguel de Luna, I, Juan Tlacochcalcatl, I, Diego Cuauhpotonqui, I, Don Juan Clemente, I, Gonzalo Fabián, I, Bartolomé Martínez, and I, Juan Quetzalhuah. We are all named by Don Pedro as having taken his land from him. He is just lying, for we have just now abandoned it. We are not the only ones to whom the benefit of these lands had fallen: there are also the *macehualtin*. Furthermore, it is not just us: there are many people who had been given land in the tribute area. We entrust ourselves entirely to you nobles: to you, Juan Damián, to you, Gabriel de Soto, to you, Pedro Martín. Before the judges, you will present our case in relation to how each of us had been given land, and also [why] we abandoned it. You will indeed make sure our case is heard. This concludes our joint statement by which we entrust you [with this task]. Here we sign our statement.

Toribio Feliciano allde [*signature*]

Toribio Feliciano, *alcalde* [*signature*]

[*signature*] miguel garcia allde

[*signature*] Miguel García, *alcalde*

Joachin

Joaquín

Miguel de Luna Regidor [*signature*]	Miguel de Luna, *regidor* [*signature*]
Bar[me] martiniz Regitor [*signature*]	Bartolomé Martínez, *regidor* [*signature*]
pablo marcos Regidor [*signature*]	Pablo Marcos, *regidor* [*signature*]
a[o]l mendez Regitor [*signature*]	Alonso Méndez *regidor* [*signature*]

This is an interesting and in many respects unique manuscript. Within the entire corpus of documentation that deals with the prolonged litigation from 1540 to 1569 between Don Pedro de Moctezuma Tlacahuepantli, the youngest son of the last Mexica ruler, Moteuczoma Xocoyotzin, and the ruling elite of the *altepetl* of Tula Xicocotitlan, this letter is apparently the only document written in Nahuatl on behalf of all the Tula residents. It is addressed to the *procuradores* Juan Damián, Gabriel de Soto, and Pedro Martín, members of the local nobility whom they appoint as their legal representatives before the Spanish courts, including the Real Audiencia of Mexico, the highest judicial and administrative body of the viceroyalty of New Spain.

As was often the case in the early colonial period, the apple of discord was real estate, more precisely twenty-one *estancias*—dependent communities within the *altepetl* and around it occupied by tenants and commoners, *ciertas tierras con sus indios labradores e maceguales* ('certain lands with their Indian workers and commoners') as it was indicated in one of Don Pedro's petitions (Pérez Rocha and Tena 2002: 139). Don Pedro and his mother, doña María Mihuaxochtil, claimed these lands as their private property, inherited from their ancestors on both the paternal and the maternal lines and illegally seized by a group of nobles headed by Tula's colonial governor Francisco Aztatl in 1540 when Don Pedro was in Spain (AGN, Vínculos y mayorazgos 256, cuad. 12, exp. 1, fol. 78r/v). However, the municipal council of Tula rejected these claims, stating that these *estancias* had always belonged to the *altepetl* and therefore had been legally distributed among Tula's nobles and commoners in order to help them to pay tribute to the Spanish authorities. The conflict between Don Pedro and the Tula residents had its origins in prehispanic times. Between the late fourteenth and early sixteenth centuries, when the Mexica state was rapidly growing, the lords of Tenochtitlan took pains to secure political and economical control over Tula Xicocotitlan and its surrounding areas. They sent their sons, grandsons, nephews, and half-brothers to govern the *altepetl*, married women from the Tula ruling house, and purchased community lands there. By the eve of the Spanish conquest they had managed to concentrate in their hands a large portion of the *altepetl*'s real estate. The documents mention vast land holdings owned by the sixth *tlahtoani* of Tenochtitlan, Axayacatl, and his sons, Moteuczoma Xocoyotzin and Ixtlilcuechahuacatzin; the latter was the last preconquest ruler of Tula Xicocotitlan and the maternal grandfather of Don Pedro. In his letters and petitions addressed to the Real Audiencia and to Emperor Charles V,[5] Don Pedro put particular emphasis on the endogamous marriages between his ancestors, which made him the only legitimate heir of the disputed properties on both the paternal and the maternal sides (AGN, Vínculos y mayorazgos 256, cuad. 12, exp. 1, fol. 15–16v). He also stressed that all the *estancias* formed part of the private estate of his grandfathers and parents. Nobody challenged his rights before his voyage to Spain.

The defendants, local dignitaries and hereditary nobility, all *pipiltin* of Tula Xicocotitlan, presented a quite different version of events as their main strategy. First of all they stated that the twenty-one *estancias* were community holdings and that they had never been the private property of Don Pedro, his parents, or even their distant ancestors. They also reported that all the income from this land had traditionally been used to pay tributes, as well as a sort of salary in labor and commodities to the local officials when they served their term. Therefore, according to their argument, even the prehispanic rulers of Tula could enjoy these properties just because they fulfilled their duties as the highest dignitaries of the *altepetl*; however, they never owned them (AGN, Vínculos y mayorazgos 256, cuad. 12, exp. 1, fol. 319–320). After the conquest and the premature deaths of Ixtliltcuechahuacatzin's successors, a new administrative unit, the *corregimiento* of Tula, was established by the Spanish authorities with an elected governor and city council. Around 1532, the Franciscan friars who were in charge of the Tula parish insisted that their candidate, Don Pedro de MoctezumaTlacahuepantli, be chosen as governor; they prevailed, against the will of the *altepetl* residents (AGN, Vínculos y mayorazgos 256, cuad. 12, exp. 1, fol. 319). Thus, Don Pedro received the temporary right to use the income from Tula's *estancias*. However, in 1539 he was removed from office for numerous abuses and was exiled forever from Tula. From that point on, he no longer had any rights to its lands. Juan Damián, one of the legal representatives (*procuradores)* of the Tula *cabildo* even raised credible doubts as to whether Don Pedro's mother, doña María Mihuaxochtzin, was really the daughter of Ixtlilcuechahuacatzin, or at least his legitimate offspring (AGN, Vínculos y mayorazgos 256, cuad. 12, exp. 1,

5 King Carlos I, as he was known in Spain, was also the fifth emperor of the Holy Roman Empire with that name.

fol. 319–320). Given these circumstances, Don Pedro's claims to the *altepetl* lands became totally unfounded, from both the indigenous and the Spanish points of view. Finally, Juan Damián and the other *procuradores* affirmed that the loss of the twenty-one *estancias* would have seriously affected the normal functioning of Tula and its capacity to fulfill tribute obligations (Kalyuta 2011: 493). Indeed, all of the *estancias* claimed by Don Pedro were situated in the limited zone of the Tula Valley where irrigation was possible. Given the semiarid climate of the area, this was of critical importance for obtaining good harvests. In fact, the twenty-one *estancias* in question might have yielded the lion's portion of the *altepetl* crops, used both to pay tribute and to support indigenous and Spanish authorities.

The value of the disputed properties might explain why the litigation with Don Pedro lasted almost three decades, from 1540 to 1569, and was accompanied by numerous incidents. Potential supporters of Don Pedro in Tula were imprisoned and his house there was robbed and destroyed. Enraged residents made it a practice to insult the Mexica prince and his mother, and at least once they attempted to assassinate him (Ramírez Calva 2005: 171).The situation escalated in 1557, when Don Pedro presented to the Spanish *corregidor* of Tula, Diego de Almódovar, declarations of sixty witnesses, mainly residents of the twenty-one *estancias* including their *tequitlahtohqueh*—administrators and tribute collectors—who unanimously testified in his favor. It was evident that Don Pedro had a good chance to win the case. Given the circumstances, the residents of Tula, headed by the municipal council, decided to act and elected their own representatives before the local court of Tula's *corregidor* and the Real Audiencia of Mexico in order to refute all of their adversary's claims. This procedure is recorded in the letter, dated March 23, 1557, and is contained in this anthology. The letter of Tula's *cabildo* contains interesting and valuable testimony that gives us new insights into the situation of the indigenous nobility in the *altepetl* that once played such an important role in Central Mexico. First of all, we have an example of a document composed at an assembly of the entire local elite: the members of the municipal council; the *calpolehqueh*, elders of the *altepetl* subdivision; and the *pipiltin,* hereditary nobles who obviously at that moment did not occupy any administrative office but nevertheless attended the meeting. The tradition of gathering all the *altepetl* noblemen in order to make collective decisions in critical situations has prehispanic antecedents and it is well documented by both native and Spanish historians. In this respect, the document resembles the collective letter of the Huexotzinco *cabildo* to the Spanish king, Philip II, dated in the year 1560 (Anderson, Berdan, and Lockhart 1976: 112).

The second point of interest is the self-identification of the Tula elite who attended the assembly as Mexica, which confirms ethnohistorical and archeological evidence referring to the Mexica presence in Tula in the Late Postclassic period. It is likewise noteworthy to mention that several nobles who attended the assembly, Joaquín Tlacatecuhtli, Juan Tlacochcalcatl, Diego Atempanecatl, and Mateo Tequihua, still have as part of their personal names traditional prehispanic titles. *Tlacochcalcatl* literally means 'he of the house of darts', *atempanecatl* 'he of the water shore place', *tlacateuctli* 'the lord of men', and *tequihuah* 'he who has a duty'. The sources associated with the tradition of the Chronicle X[6] link their appearance in Tenochtitlan with the victory over the Tepanecs, the main enemies of the Mexica in the early to mid-fifteenth century (Alvarado Tezozomoc 1944: 57–58). Later these titles are frequently mentioned in the context of preconquest Tenochtitlan governmental organization as the titles of high-ranking offices. *Tlacateuctli* was the honorific title of the supreme Mexica ruler and of noble warriors who took at least ten prisoners. *Tlacochcalcatl* referred to his closest adviser and military commander, responsible for providing the Mexica army with arms; for this reason Spanish authors often translated it as *capitan general* 'commander-in-chief' (Sahagún 1954, 8: 55, 61). *Atempanecatl* is generally described as an executor of the supreme ruler's orders, including the death penalty (Sahagún 1954, 8: 55). *Tequihuah* is a general title for warriors who took four captives and served as army offices and messengers of the Mexica rulers. However, according to other sources, including the earlier letter of Don Pedro and his mother doña María Mihuaxochitl to the Real Audiencia, dated February 7, 1543, the majority of Tula's population were Otomí-speaking groups (AGN, Vínculos y mayorazgos 256, cuad. 12, exp. 1, fol. 15r). We can assume that after the conquest the *altepetl* was still governed by a Nahua-speaking elite of Mexica origin.

The third point of importance is the presentation of the motives for the lawsuit, from the defendants' point of view and in their own language, thus reflecting indigenous concepts of justice and responsibility. If the plaintiff Don Pedro de Moctezuma always stressed his individual rights to the properties in question and acted as an individual with the support of specially trained Spanish lawyers, his adversaries, on the other hand, choose a

6 The Chronicle X is a now lost early colonial Nahuatl prototype of several historical works (*The History of the Indians of New Spain* by fray Diego Durán, *Crónica Mexicana* by Hernando Alvarado Tezozomoc, the *Codex Ramírez* by fray Juan de Tovar and the *Codex Cozcatzin*).

collective strategy of defense. They emphasized their unity and cohesion in the face of a common enemy by providing a detailed listing of all the *cabildo* members, prominent residents from all the *altepetl* subdivisions, in order to demonstrate the unanimity and validity of their decision and, therefore, the unquestioned legitimacy of their elected representatives. Such emphasis on collective action seems to have been typical for Nahua prehispanic legal practices. Moreover, the authors of the letter deny Don Pedro's accusation that the disputed *estancias* were illegally taken by a small group of nobles. On the contrary, they state that these lands were divided between many people, including commoners who would have been seriously affected in the event of their loss. In Nahua traditional ethical discourse, protection of the lower social strata as the most vulnerable part of society was one of the main obligations of the authorities, from community elders to supreme rulers. The *cabildo* members and assembled nobles also directly stated that the real estate claimed by Don Pedro was situated in the area of lands assigned for paying tribute, alluding to the critical importance of these lands for the fulfillment of Tula's tribute obligations to the Spanish Crown. Thus, in their defense strategy, the members of Tula's *cabildo* seem to reveal a mixture of preconquest patterns with legal concepts and procedures taken from the Spanish conquerors. It is noteworthy that the document itself is categorized with the Spanish loanword *poder* ('trust, power'). The entire text has a significant number of loanwords. Most of them are directly associated with administrative bodies, court, legal procedures, and documentation: *cabildo*; a*lcaldes* and *regidores* (both with the typical Nahuatl plural ending *-meh*); *poder* (letter of trust with the possessive prefix *to-*); *justicia; audiencia real;* and *firma*. Finally, all of the assembled nobles have Christian names, and some of these are double, like Toribio Feliciano, Juan Damián, Pedro Esteban, and Pablo Marcos, which indicates their relatively high status. Local *alcaldes* (councilmen) even have Spanish-style surnames, such as García, de Luna, Martínez, Méndez, and de los Ángeles, which also denotes high social status in Nahua postconquest society. One of the assembled nobles, Juan Clemente, has the honorific *don*, obviously indicating his noble origin.

At the same time, the language of the document shares common features with the elaborate, elegant style of speech typical of the Nahua elite. First of all, the text contains honorific constructions widely used in polite discourses. The text also has several doublet constructions—paired nouns, verbs, or even adverbs—which together acquire a new metaphorical sense or make speech more expressive and colorful. Two doublet constructions—*toten totlahtol* 'our lips, our words', in a sense "our breath, our speech," and *antixiptlahuan, antopatillohuan* 'you [are] our images, you [are] our substitutes', that is "our deputies, messengers"—are also among the metaphorical constructions documented in the *Florentine Codex* (Sullivan 2014: 349). Other doublet constructions involve verbal compounds: *anquinamiquizque anquinanquilizque* 'you will go to meet him, you will respond to him', *huel anchicahuazque huel anquihuapahuazque* 'truly you will strengthen, truly you will give force to [our speech]', and *yn otamechixquetzque yn otamechtocayotique* 'we have appointed you, we have named you [as our representatives]'. Equally traditional is the adverbial construction *tonellatolticatoneltiliztica* 'truly, certainly', literally 'with our true word, with our verification'. Generally, the language of the document shows features typical of Stage 2 language contact according to the scheme proposed by Lockhart, when Spanish loanwords were being frequently borrowed and assimilated according to Nahuatl phonological and morphological rules (Karttunen and Lockhart 1976; Lockhart 1992).

DOCUMENT 25

Petition for Coat of Arms for Don Francisco Verdugo, Teotihuacan, Mexico, 1558[1]

Julia Madajczak, Jan Szemiński, and John Sullivan

[Fol. 1r]

\+

.c.c.R.m+

Don fran.^{co} verdugo. yndio caçique. y señor. del pueblo. de huey tiguacan. que por/ otro nonbre. se llama. san Juan. besa los rreales. pies y manus. de .v. mg.+ y dize. quė de memorıál tiem̃po a esta parte. el y sus padres. y abuelos. deçienden. del señor. y señores. que son. y fueron de la çiudad. de tezcuco. cabeça. de la gran. trrá. de la nueua españa que tubo. nonbre. el senór. y prinçipal della. neçahualcoyuçi. la qual cabdad de tezcúco. y mandaúa. aquellas trrás. antes y prim̃ero. que los naguales. y açendencia. de motençuma. que despũes vinieron. a señorear y poblar la çiudád. de mex^{co}/. y por̃que agora. el es gouernador del dh. pueblo de San Juan.

\+

Catholic Imperial Royal Majesty+

Don Francisco Verdugo, Indian, *cacique*, and Lord of the town of Huei Teotihuacan, otherwise known as San Juan, kisses Your Majesty's royal feet and hands + and declares that from time immemorial until now, he and his parents and grandparents descend from those who are and were the lord and lords of the city of Tetzcoco, capital of the great land of New Spain, the name of the lord and head of which was Nezahualcoyotzin. The said city of Tetzcoco also ruled those lands before and earlier than the *naguales* and Moteuczoma's ancestors, who later came to rule and populate the city of Mexico. And since now he is the governor of the aforementioned town of

1 Archivo General de Indias (AGI), Mexico 96. The transcription of this document was previously published in Pérez-Rocha and Tena 2000.

DOI: 10.5876/9781607328346.c025

por .v. alª. y el y el dh. su padre. dieron fabor. a tro capitan general. el marqùes del valle. don hernańdo cortes. que en nonbre. de .v. mg+. gano nueùa españa. en las guerras qu[e] tubo. con los naturalès della. hasta que la gano y paçificò y por ser como es xpiáno. ques el mayor bien que puede tener. y deçiende de los dhś señores. suplica a .v. alª. le haga mrd. de dalle por armas una aguila rrapante negra. como esta. que va figùrada en un qrto deste escudo. que presento. y en el otro. un sol. como en el va figurado. ēn memoria. de la luz. que con la fe de isux. cobro èsta nueua españa y porque no se pierda. la memoria de las diuisas. con que sus antepasados peleauan en su antiguedad. se le de . por armas en los otros dos quartos del escudo. segùn quė va figurado en el. juntamente con las demas diuisas. que los dhs. sus anteçesores trayan. como van. figurados. en el y por orlas las. esrpadas. y piernas. como estan figuradas. en el dh escudo. y porque en las dhas guerràs quel dh marques hiżo en la paçificacion y conquista. desta nueua espàna. y ciudad de mexco. perdieron. y cònsumieron. sus vidas muchòs de sus pasados tios y deudos. y ên rrenùmeracion de quel don franco. verdugo. siruio a .v. mg+. eṅ la conquista. que nuño de guzman. su presidente. que fue. hiżo. en su rreal nònbre en la prouincia que agora. llaman. nueua galizia. y aṅsimismo siruio en el alçamº que los naturalės. de aquel rreyno de ġalizia hizieron contra .v. alª quando. su visorrey. don antoño. de mendoça. lo fue apaziguàr se le [Fol. 1v] haga mrd. de le dar. enciṁa deste escudo. Su tinble. Hufa. y apiquines con duisa. encima del tinble. de un leon. de oro. rràpante ~~ansimismo~~ en lo qual. .v. mg+. le hara senialada. mrd. y acreçentara. la memoria de sus pasados. y porque sus hijos y deçendientes. como xp̄īanos gozen. de la dhà mrd. como sus leales. vasallòs/.

San Juan in Your Highness's name, and [since] he and his aforementioned father aided your commander-in-chief, the Marquis of the Valley, Don Hernando Cortés, who in Your Majesty's name conquered New Spain during the wars he waged against its natives until he conquered and pacified it; and since he [Francisco Verdugo] is a Christian, which is the greatest good he can possess, and descends from the aforementioned lords, he implores Your Highness to favor him by granting him as an insignia a rampant black eagle, like this one which appears in the [dexter chief] quarter of this coat of arms that he presented; and in the other [sinister chief quarter], a sun, just as it appears on it, in memory of the light that this New Spain received with the Christian Faith. Also, and in order not to lose the memory of the emblems with which his ancestors fought in their ancient times, may they be be given to him in the other two [base] quarters of the coat of arms, as they appear on it together with the other emblems that his aforementioned ancestors had, as they appear on it; and as orles, the swords and legs, as they appear in the aforementioned coat of arms. And because of the fact that during the aforementioned wars that the aforementioned Marquis waged during the pacification and conquest of this New Spain and the city of Mexico, many of his past relatives and kin lost and forfeited their lives. And in recompense for the fact that Don Francisco Verdugo served Your Majesty in the conquest that Nuño de Guzmán, your deceased captain, waged in your royal name in the province now called New Galicia, and likewise served in [the campaign against] the rebellion that the natives of that Kingdom of Galicia carried out against Your Highness, when your viceroy Don Antonio de Mendoza went to pacify it, may you favor him by granting him a crest atop this coat of arms; a helmet and

	mantling with an emblem, [and] above it, the crest of a gold, rampant lion, with which Your Majesty will favor him immensely and enhace the memory of his ancestors, so that his children and descendants as Christians will enjoy the aforementioned reward as his loyal vassals.
don francisco verdugo 1558	Don Francisco Verdugo 1558
[*signature*]	[*signature*]
Al s^{or} dotor vazquez	To the Lord Doctor Vasquez
[*signature*]	[*signature*]
q̄ de ynformaciô de los serui^{o}s q̄ dize q̄ han hecho el y sus pasados	Referring to the information regarding the services he says that he and his ancestors rendered.
Presentala	He presents it
que se buelba al Sr Doctor	Let it be returned to the Lord Doctor.
q̂ se le den las armas	May he be given the arms.

In contrast with Don Antonio Cortés (Document 23), Don Francisco de Verdugo Quetzalmamalitzin, *tlahtoani* of Teotihuacan, asks Philip II only for a coat of arms for himself. The dynasty of Teotihuacan had a tradition of intermarriages with the ruling lineage of the second most important *altepetl* in Central Mexico, Tetzcoco. Don Francisco does not fail to mention this in his 1558 petition, claiming descent from Nezahualcoyotl. The famous poet-ruler was indeed his great-great-grandfather: Quetzalmamalitzin was son of Teuhtzihuatzin, granddaughter of Nezahualpilli, son of Nezahualcoyotl (Fernández de Recas 1961: 114, 123–124). He continued the tradition, marrying a daughter of the *tlahtoani* of Tetzcoco named Ixtlilxochitl, doña Ana Cortés Ixtlilxochitl (Fernández de Recas 1961: 114, 121).

Although a later relative of Don Francisco, the chronicler Don Fernando de Alva Ixtlilxochitl, insists that Quetzalmamalitzin's father, Xiuhtototzin, was an ally of Cortés and died fighting by his side during the Noche Triste (Alva Ixtlilxochitl 2000: 289), this argument is not used in the petition. Instead, the *tlahtoani* choses to stress his own participation in the conquest of Nueva Galicia conducted by the infamous first president of the Royal Audiencia in Mexico, Nuño de Guzmán, and the subsequent pacification of this land under the command of Don Antonio de Mendoza. It may indicate that the version given by Don Fernando de Alva was false and biased by his general eagerness to present his ancestors as good Christians and friends of the Spaniards. If Don Francisco's father did fight against the Spaniards, it would not be the only important historical fact that the *tlahtoani* of Teotihuacan ignores. He claims that Tetzcoco had actually been more important, in preconquest times, than Tenochtitlan, since its foundation preceded the arrival of the "naguales" (the term apparently comes from *nahualli*, in the colonial period pejorative, and is understood as "sorcerer," the connotation of which was here used in a wordplay, suggesting "people who speak Nahuatl") and "the ancestors of Moteuczoma."

From other documents concerning Don Francisco de Verdugo, we know that the struggle for maintaining the prestige of his position as dynastic ruler was long and painful. The request for the coat of arms was preceded by three judicial trials (1543, 1552, and 1553), in which he fought against one of his tributary towns, Yacapitzahuac, over the amount of the annual tribute payment (Pérez-Rocha and Tena 2000: 389–392). Don Francisco won every one of them, but at the time of his death in 1563, he was engaged in yet another lawsuit, concerning tributary payments from the lands of Tzacatla and Tlacaxoloc. In his testament, he not only ordered his wife to continue the lawsuit, but also forbade her to sell any patrimonial lands he had bequeathed her, thus securing the transmission of property within the family (Pérez-Rocha and Tena 2000: 266–267, 270).

Don Francisco's judicial experience must have made him a skilled diplomat and, indeed, the way he plays with arguments in his 1558 petition is impressive. In preconquest times, the customary marriages of the *tlahtohqueh* of Teotihuacan to Tetzcocan princesses were a sign of subordination of the former *altepetl* to the second-most important member of the Triple Alliance. In Verdugo's narrative this aspect of the practice disappears: the only thing that matters is his relationship with the prestigious dynasty of Tetzcoco. Once this connection is emphasized, Tetzcoco is cleansed of any possible relation to the biggest enemy of the Spaniards: not only was it more ancient than Tenochtitlan, but the latter was only populated by some "naguales," certainly not the same people who had founded the city of Nezahualcoyotl. Interestingly, while the ruler that Don Francisco associated with Tetzcoco is precisely the outstanding fifteenth-century *tlahtoani* Nezahualcoyotzin, the identification of Tenochtitlan is made through the character of the weak and pitiful Moteuczoma.

The text of the petition suggests that it was accompanied by a drawing of the requested coat of arms. It is no longer attached to the document, but the description is detailed enough to make clear that its symbolism referred to both the Spanish (Christian) and the Nahua tradition, which was a very common feature of the indigenous blazons of the time (Castañeda de la Paz 2009: 152). One of the elements, the sun, is so ambiguous that Don Francisco felt compelled to explain its association with the light of the true faith and Jesus Christ. A more subtle piece of evidence of cultural encounter is found in the language of the petition. On the one hand, it uses hispanicized versions of Nahuatl words: *huey tiguacan* ('Huei Teotihuacan') and *naguales*. On the other hand, *huei*, or 'great', was not always added to the name *Teotihuacan* and yet it appears here, as if the Spanish readers were able to understand its meaning. Another possible explanation is that Nahuatl somehow interfered in the process of production of the document: either Don Francisco was speaking Nahuatl or Nahuatlized Spanish to the notary (he might have used the word *huei* as an epithet and the notary understood it to be part of the toponym) or the first draft was written in Nahuatl. In support of these hypotheses, the text includes the Nahuatl metaphor for ancestors, "parents and grandparents," translated literally into Spanish.

DOCUMENT 26

Petition of the Rulers of Amacatlan Mamepan, Soconusco, Mexico, to the King of Spain, 1562[1]

Justyna Olko

[Fol. 29r]

tlatlacohtlatocatin tehuantin

y timomacehualhuan .toconmahuiztenamiqui . ỹ momatzin . ỹ mocxitzin ỹ nican tochantzinco . ytucayocan . Amacatlan . mamepan axca . otitocentlalique / titononoza . t(i)tocalpolcotlatoque pipiltin . ỹ in ipampa . nican . moquixtitiquiza . ce xpiãñõ . ytuca . hernando de s[ta] ella. ypampa . yuhqui totatzin . ticchihua. techtlaçotla. techpalehuia. axca . yuhqui chuloa . yahui yca . ytlatol . presidente . yhuan . oydores. ahu . ytechpa/ ticahua .totlatol . y(n)ic mixpantzinco . netziz. tonetequipacholiz . ypanpa . quemania . techtolinia . ỹ justicias . ca amo huel quipia . ỹ motecoctlatoltzin . amo huel techpalehuia . amo huel techcaqui . çan yuhqui . amo timopilhuan . yuhqui . titlacotin . ỹ tlacamo . nican . onca . ce totlatzin . ytuca fray luis de gueuara .

Our precious ruler,

We, your subjects, reverently kiss your hands and feet here in our home named Amacatlan Mamepan. Today we, the rulers of our *calpolli*, the nobles, have assembled and conferred because the Spaniard Hernando de Santa Iglesia is about to leave. We look on him as our father because he loves us and helps us. Now he seems to be fleeing, leaving, at the command of the president and the *oidores*. But we make a statement about this, so that our dissatisfaction may appear before you, because the officials of justice sometimes mistreat us. They do not really obey your lordly commands, they do not really help us, they do not really listen to us. It is as if we were not your subjects. We would be as slaves if the priest named fray Luis de Guevara weren't here. He helps us, he advises us,

1 Archivo General de Indias (AGI), Guatemala 52, fol. 29r. This document was first published in Olko 2015: 174.

 DOI: 10.5876/9781607328346.c026

techpalehuia . technonotza . techmachtia
. mochipa . huel quimati totlatol
popoloquiztli . timochintin . tipaqui .
ticaqui . paqui toyolo . Axca tictlatlania
. ỹ momahuiz ỹ motlatocayotlatoltzin .
ma can ypanpa . ỹ motlacoh . ycpaltzin
. ma xichualtlali . ỹ ^{mo}tlatoltzin .
ynahuac . ỹ nican probiçial . yhuan .
ynahuac . quipia . justiçias . ynic nican .
motlaliz . totlalpan . yhuan . ca motlal .
titotlatocahu . paquiz toyolo . mochipa .
titotlatocahu . mopaltzinco . tictlatlania
. ỹ moteochtlatol [v] ma çan nican .
mocahuaz . motlaliz ypanpa . quicaqui
totlatol . technonoça techyolcuitia
. yhuan . tictlatlania . motlatoltzin .
hualaz ynahuac . totatzin ỹnic amo
quiçaz ma çan nican motlaliz mamepan
manel quinequiz yn iyolo . macamo
quiçaz ma cenca choçaz toyolo . ỹtla
quiçaz totlatocahue ma ypanpa . dios
. yhuan . ypanpa . ỹ mocpaltzin ỹnic
motlatocayohu . ahu . ynic timopilhuan
. mocxitltlan . tinemi . ỹ nican . yndias
. tlalpan . ca çan yxquichi . totlatol
otitlaquiloq̄ axca . yc castoli meztli enero
. yc yeçontli . ypan . castolpohuali. ypan
yepohuali . ypan omixihuitl . omotlacatili
. totecujyo.s.xpo.

motlaçohpilhuan motlacahuan

Don Alonso

Don Bardasa

Don ju^{o}

he teaches us. He completely knows our
foreign language. All of us are happy;
we listen to him; we rejoice. Today we
request your revered, rulerly command.
For the sake of your precious authority,
please issue your command to the local
provincial and to the officers of justice
here, so that it will be put into effect in our
land, the land of you, our ruler. And we
will always be happy. Through your grace,
our ruler, we request that your lordly
statement just remain and be put into
effect here because he [Luis de Guevara]
understands our language, advises us and
confesses us. And we request that your
command come to our father so that he
won't leave, so that he will just remain
in Mamepan, even if he wants [to leave].
May he not leave, we will weep greatly if
he leaves. Oh, our ruler, [grant us this] for
the sake of God and for the sake of your
throne from which derives your rulership,
since we are your children who live at
your feet here in the land of the Indies.
This is the entirety of the statement that
we have written today, the fifteenth day
of the month of January, 1562 years since
our lord Jesus Christ was born.

Your precious children, your subjects

Don Alonso

Don Baltazar

Don Juan

This petition forms part of a larger group of documents in Nahuatl signed by representatives of native communities in Soconusco, Chiapas, Mexico, directed to the king of Spain, Philip II, and now preserved in the Archivo General de Indias in Seville (AGI, Guatemala 52). The document was signed by the rulers of Amacatlan Mamepan, who present themselves as *tocalpolcotlahtohqueh pipiltin* 'the rulers of our *calpolli*, the nobles', and royal subjects. In general, the set of petitions from the area of Huehuetlan in Soconusco, to which the present document belongs, asks the sovereign to withdraw them from the authority of the Audiencia of Guatemala, return them to the jurisdiction of Mexico, and secure the local presence of mendicant friars, some of whom are already in the communities. After the Spanish conquest this territory was incorporated into the jurisdiction of the Audiencia de Mexico, but in 1556 Soconosco was reassigned to the newly established Audiencia de Guatemala (created in 1543). For example, the indigenous authorities of the community of Tozantlan implore the king not only to be returned to the jurisdiction of Mexico, but also to be placed under the spiritual control of fray Pedro de Betanzos (Hernandez de León-Portilla 2010: 269–270). These letters name an intermediary, the Spaniard and "good Christian" Hernando de Santaella, as the trustworthy person who will deliver the petition. He is portrayed as the ally and benefactor of the community, who has been forced to flee because of persecution suffered at the hands of the president and judges of the Audiencia de Guatemala. The petition from Amacatlan does not directly request a change of jurisdiction; however, its authors accuse the officers of justice of mistreatment and of ignoring royal provisions. In their own words, they would have been enslaved if it had not been for the help and protection of friar Luis de Guevara, who takes care of the community. This friar also appears in the petition from Huehuetenanco Mamepan (AGI, Guatemala 52, fol. 20r). Huehuetenanco and Amacatlan were either neighboring communities or, more probably, subdivisions (*calpolli* is the term used in the Amacatlan Mamepan, Soconusco, petition) of a larger town, since both are identified as Mamepan. Fray Luis de Guevara is referred to here as *padre comendador*, who had been in charge of the community for seven years and understands the local language. It is his superior, the *provincial*, who wishes him to leave despite the will of the native town. In the letter from Amacatlan, the petitioners ask the king to issue a decree to the provincial and the local judges obliging them to keep fray Luis de Guevara in the service of the local community.

One of the arguments employed in the petition is that the friar knows the local language; however, even though the document is written in very good Central Nahuatl, we cannot be sure this is the principal language spoken by the community in question. According to an ecclesiastic document from 1656, this region was highly multilingual, with some predominantly Nahuatl-speaking communities and others that used different Mayan languages (Hernandez de León-Portilla 2010: 271–273). The expression *quimati totlahtol popoloquiztli* means 'he knows our foreign language'. *Popoloquiztli* is an active action noun derived from the verb *popolca* 'to speak a foreign or barbarous tongue, to speak unintelligibly'. In sixteenth-century Nahual, *popoloca* commonly designated foreign ethnic groups and languages, but never Nahuatl itself (Olko 2014b). Thus, it is highly probable that *popoloquiztli* refers here to a language other than Nahuatl that was spoken in the community. A Mayan language such as Mam, which was widely used in the area, is a likely candidate, as the place name Mamepan itself would suggest. The misspelling of *chocaz* '[our hearts] will cry' as *choçaz* cannot be explained by the orthographic idiosyncracies of the manuscript. The scribe could have mistakenly written *ç* for *c*, but this example of orthographic substitution is hardly ever seen in Nahuatl texts. The possibility of interference linked to the use of another language should not be dismissed. The fact that the year 1562 was written out alphabetically in Nahuatl at the end of the document is interesting, precisely because this practice is very rare. Even in documents from Central Mexico large numerals such as years were almost always written in Spanish or in Arabic numerals. At the very least, the alphabetic rendering of the year in the petition proves that the scribe had very good knowledge of the traditional vigesimal system. In general, the document is an example of an elegant, traditional style of expression typical of petitions, and it testifies to the high level of linguistic proficiency of those who employed Nahuatl as the common second language of communication in this region before the conquest. With the appearance of alphabetic script, Nahuatl's usage was expanded as it became the prestigious language of writing and communication with Spanish authorities, of which the present document is a salient example. The petition is both an instrument and an expression of indigenous agency in the colonial reality, an attempt to influence the power relations and administrative/ecclesiastical decisions affecting the life of the local community. But at the same time, it is important to consider the role played in these dynamics by Spanish actors, such as the friars themselves and the mysterious Hernando de Santaella. The latter figure appears in the entire set of documents as the protector and friend of the indigenous communities and the intermediary designated by them to deliver their petitions. We may only speculate about his role in organizing the intercommunity protest. After all, one of the specific goals of this action, which materialized in the set of letters to the king, was the protection of de Santaella's local position, as well as that of the mendicant friars, who were no doubt his allies. All considered, the local elites clearly regarded this alliance and the local presence of its parties as beneficial both to them and to their communities, and decided to play an active role in the political process.

The petition has relatively few Spanish loanwords when compared with other documents from the region contained in the AGI Guatemala 52 collection.[2] They include *xpiãñõ* (here meaning 'Spaniard'), *presidente, oydores*

2 For an example of a document that contains more loanwords, see the petition from Huey Petlahuacan, fol. 17r of the AGI Guatemala 52 collection.

(the president and judges of the *audiencia*), *fray, probiçial, justiçias* (meaning 'judges' or 'officers of justice'), *dios, enero*, and *yndias*. An important orthographic feature is the use of word-final *hu* instead of *uh*, which however is typical for the whole group of Nahuatl documents from this region and, more generally, tends to be included in the conventions of unstandardized local orthographies.

DOCUMENT 27

Petition Concerning Cultivated Land Presented by María Quetzalcocoztli, Ocotelolco, Tlaxcala, Mexico, 1563[1]

Agnieszka Brylak

[Fol. 1r]

\+

muy mag.cos señores

yc cenpualli ôchicuinahuilhujtl metztlj de abril in isiho tut° rx° de mill y quiny°s y sesenta y tres anos. yspantililoque yn senores alldes ynin petiçion nican audiençia. teispan

María qtzalcocoztlí níchane chímalpa sat ypolíto ytech típouí cabeçera / ocotelulco amíxpatzico tímopechteca ceca namechnotlatlauhtiliya in just.a aq̃mopiliya. ma xícmocaq̇tica nĩtlatoleuĩya no[pih] ytoca maría tochomítzi. ypíltzi notla q̄uhtlíztactzi catca / ypapa tvcue ompa manj apíyatzico./ notahtzi. q̇mopiliaya ytoca qtzalpoyotzi ma xocomocaq̇tica atlatoq. y notatzi catca motitlaca. uítzilapa. yq̃c momíq̇li ypanpa atltepeteq̇tl/ auh

\+

Very Magnificent Lords

This petition was presented to the lords *alcaldes* before the *audiencia* court here on the twenty-ninth day of the month of April in the year of Our Lord Christ [=Anno Domini] 1563.

I am María Quetzalcocoztli, a resident of Chimalpan San Hipólito. We belong to the *cabecera* of Ocotelolco and we kneel down before you [pl.]. I greatly implore you [pl.], who are responsible for justice, to listen to how I bring an accusation against my older cousin named María Tochomitzin, daughter of my late uncle Quauhtliztactzin, concerning our field located in Apiyaztzinco. My father owned it, his name was Quetzalpoyotzin. May you rulers hear that my late father had

1 Archivo Histórico del Estado de Tlaxcala (AHET), 1563, caja 2, exp. 17. A transcription of this document and its translation into Spanish was published in *Catálogo de documentos escritos en náhuatl siglo XVI* by the Gobierno del Estado de Tlaxcala (2013). The transcription and translation included here are based entirely on the original manuscript.

DOI: 10.5876/9781607328346.c027

y nehuatl oc uel nítzotzocotzin y nechcauhta. auh in ixq̇ch cuemitl q̇mopiliya. nima yq̃c xixin q̇cuícuíq notlava/ auh ín íq̃c gouernadortíya dō luys xícotecatl alldetíya ín texeda y texeda. q̇navati y notlatzi catca tecpanecatl q̃uhchocholouatzi. yníc nechpílíz nocue. y ayac nechcuilíz. auh y tecpanecatl catca/ ça yuh conavilcauh. ín amo conechíco. notahtzi ycuē yníc q̇mocuicuilique notlava/

been sent to Huitzilapan and then he died because of tribute work for the town. And when I was still a small child, he left me orphaned. All the fields he kept were then immediately divided and taken by my uncles. When Don Luis Xicotencatl was governor, and Tejeda was *alcalde*, Tejeda ordered my late uncle Tecpanecatl Quauhchocholohuatzin to take care of my fields for me, so that no one would take them from me. The late Tecpanecatl merely neglected them, he did not harvest my father's fields, which is why my uncles took them.

auh y nehuatl míyecpa oníctlatlauhtí y nopíh. maría tochomitzin. yníc yuíyā nechmomaq̇líz notahtzín ycue. ça uel tetlacamachiztíca niq̇lhuítíne / auh [i] níc oceyaco. otícmótlahcoteq̇q. neneuhq̇. otíccuíq y cuetzíntly y ompa mani apiyaztzico/ níma nictocac. no yehuatl nopíh q̇tocac. tíccuíq̇z cecepoualmatl ochíchiq̃ce Ahu ȳ tíctomacaq çacatl catca/ otícçacamoq yníc tíctocaq / auh in icue nopíh. y q̇tucac çacatepa [2] / auh yn íq̃c ya píxco. y q̇toua. oníccepixcac. yva ya q̇toua nicxocoua/ auh tlatoq ye amo y ticçepixcaq. cavallome q̇q̃que. yn icē./ auh yníc q̇toua tícxocoua. amo nelli. oq̇tatu ȳ topile/ çaya yuhtíca yn iuh tícmoteq̇q. yva yn q̇tvua nouehpol. pelayo. tíctvcnepanoua. camo nelli. oq̇tato ȳ topile/

Many times did I implore my older cousin María Tochomitzin to give me back my father's fields peacefully and out of sheer obedience. I constantly said it to her. Since she finally consented, we divided them in two equal parts. We took a field located in Apiyaztzinco. Then I sowed it; my elder cousin also sowed it. We took twenty six units [*maitl*] each. On what we assigned to ourselves, there was dry grass; we cleared the land in order to sow it. As for my elder cousin's field, she sowed on the grass. And when the harvest had already begun, she said that I had harvested it all and that I am trespassing on the land. Oh rulers, it is not that we harvested it all; the horses ate her maize. And as for her saying, "You trespass on the land," it is not true. The officer of justice went to see it and it was just the way we had divided it. And my brother-in-law, Pelayo, said that we had joined the fields in regards to planting. It is not true, the officer of justice went to verify it.

yva ma xocomocaq̇tíca atlatoq. uel yehuatl otechchalani ȳ pelayo. yníc axca ya timixnamíq. miyec yn ílivíztlatolly ya tíctolhuiya. ceq̇ pinavíztlatolly ya tíq̇toua.

And may you, who are rulers, hear, that Pelayo really made us argue, so now we fight with each other. We are saying many thoughtless things to each other,

2 This term is probably composed of the Spanish loanword *zacate*, originally derived from the Nahuatl *zacatl*, and the locative *-pan*. It could also be *zacatempan* 'at the edge of the grass', but the expected overbar on the *e* is missing.

auh mach yuh tícchivazneq̇.q̇[3] ça ye otechonetecheuh y pelayo. otechochalani. auh ȳ q̇toua çano nechtlaocolí cuemitl/ qni[4] onechtlaocoly. cuix canapa nívaleva. cuíx cecca nitlacati. yn íuh q̇mati noyolo. ça uel cetlaca ȳ totahua. ce y.na. ce yta. y otechiuhq / ypampa y axca avelítiz ȳ tícmoteq̇zque cuetzintli. nochi y níq̇tlaní.q̇ notahtzi. oq̇piyaya. cuix amo. q̇momachitiya amoyolotzi. y menores. caq̇lilozq yníc just.ª q̇tlani. /auh ȳtla q̇neq̇z noyolo uel Just.ª yc niq̇tlaniz ȳ pelayo. qça yehuatl otechochalani. y moneqz. ça nepātla moqtzazqz / ynic techyecchivazq / auh ȳ q̇toua nopíh y cuemítl q̇moteq̇q. y quauhtlíztactzi. yva qtzalpuyotzi. yc Just.ª [Fol. 1v] níq̇tlaní aq̇q yn íxpā ȳ q̇moteq̇q. cuemítl ma qnnexti. ynopih. /yc Just.ª nictzatziliya ma xínechmupalevilicā ātlatoq. uel ānechmomaq̇lizq. y nochi. notahtzi. ycue / yc xínechycnelícā yca ytlatvcayo Rey. yva yca amoJustª/.	we say some shameful words. Do we really want to do it this way? Pelayo just provoked us; he made us argue. He also just said that he mercifully favored me with a field, that he recently took pity on me. Where am I from? Was I born in a different place? I know very well that our fathers were indeed of one family, their common ancestors engendered us. For this reason, it will not be possible now for us to divide the field. I come to request all that my father had owned. Don't you [pl.] know that appeals for justice from the less influential should be heeded? If it is indeed justice that I desire, then for this reason I will request that Pelayo should leave: he caused discord between us. It is necessary that they [officers of justice] intervene in order to bring us to a settlement. My older cousin says that those who divided the field were Quauhtliztactzin and Quetzalpoyotzin. For this reason I seek justice, may my older cousin reveal those in whose presence they divided the field. I cry out to justice so that you rulers may help me and really give all my father's fields back to me; so that you may show me favor by the king's authority and through your justice.
[2nd handwriting]	
Maria. qtzal	María Quetzalcocoztli
cocotli	
[3rd handwriting]	
r Quimihtahuilique yn senores alcaldes don domingo marmoleJu blas osorio ma quinaquilj yn petiçion yn isnamic nimā Justª mochihoaz yn señores mofirmatique motocayotique yn ispa testigos	The lords *alcaldes* Don Domingo Marmolejo and Blas Osorio said to her/them: "May the person that she has accused answer the petition, then justice will be carried out." The lords signed and wrote their names in the presence of witnesses.

3 It is not clear what the function of the second *q̇* is in this verb.

4 Probably *quin*, *quiniuh*, or *quiniz* 'recently, a short time ago'.

blas osorio	Blas Osorio
don domingo marmolejo	Don Domingo Marmolejo
Nispa͞	In my presence
Sebastian R°	Sebastián Rodríguez
Escrivano	notary

The document is a 1563 petition presented by María Quetzalcocoztli, a resident of Chimalpan San Hipólito (Ocotelolco, Tlaxcala), concerning cultivated land in Apiyaztzinco. It is directed to the *alcaldes* of Tlaxcala who acted, among others, as the judges of the *audiencia* court. In the document the woman reports a conflict between herself and her older cousin María Tochomitzin.

María Quetzalcocoztli's account, in which she argues her rights to the field in question, begins right after the introductory formulae. According to her testimony, the field belonged to her father, Quetzalpoyotzin, who died in Huitzilapan, where he had been sent to perform tribute duties. María Quetzalcocoztli was still underage when she became an orphan, and for this reason her father's property was divided and transferred to the custody of her father's brothers, her uncles. She dates these events to the time when Don Luis Xicotencatl was governor in Tlaxcala, with a person named Tejeda (Texeda) acting as *alcalde*. From other written sources we know that Don Luis Xicotencatl probably died in 1544 (Gibson 1967: 94). The Tejeda mentioned in the text is in all likelihood Don Juan de Tejeda, elected in 1545 as one of the first Tlaxcalan municipal council judges (Baber 2010: 31). According to the document, Tejeda ordered that the fields in Apiyaztzinco be entrusted to one of Maria Quetzalcocoztli's uncles named Tecpañecatl Quauhchocholoatzin. However, due to his neglect of the lands, they were subsequently taken away from him by his brothers, among them Quauhtliztactzin, María Tochomitzin's father.

At the moment the document was written, the plaintiff's father and her uncles had already died. After discussing the problem concerning the inheritance, the two women, María Quetzalcocoztli and María Tochomitzin, reached an agreement and decided to divide the field in Apiyaztzinco into two equal parts (though according to María Tochomitzin, Quetzalpoyotzin and Quauhtliztactzin, the fathers of the quarreling women, were responsible for dividing the lands). The conflict broke out again during the harvest season when María Tochomitzin, incited by her husband, Pelayo, accused her younger cousin of having harvested the crops on both parcels. Through the petition, the officers of justice are asked to inquire into who actually divided the land, in order to establish which fields belonged to María Quetzalcocoztli. The case is not resolved: the authorities demand a response from the accused party before they issue the sentence.

The Nahuatl of this rather early text (the beginning of Stage 2 of Lockhart's contact phenomena classification) does not show much Spanish language influence. It contains some loanwords, mainly legal terms for the type of document (*peticion*), the institutions of colonial administration (*audiencia*), and the titles of colonial officials (*señores alcaldes, justicia, rey*). However, in the latter group there seems to be a clear preference for using, whenever possible, a Nahuatl equivalent of the term, rather than a loanword. Thus, the Spanish term *alguacil* 'constable' is absent; in its place is the indigenous word *topile(h)*. We also find early examples of the coining of native verbs, based on Spanish nouns that receive the traditional Nahuatl inceptive verbing suffixes *-ti* or *–ti(y)a*. Thus, the terms *gobernador* 'governor' and *alcalde* were employed to create the verbs *gobernadorti* and *alcaldeti* 'to become governor/to rule as governor' and 'to become *alcalde*/to rule as *alcalde*', respectively. The Spanish term *firma* 'signature' here takes another Nahuatl verbing suffix, *-ti* 'to have', receives the causative suffix *-a*, and then adds a reflexive prefix, producing *mofirmatia* 'to sign', literally, 'to provide oneself with a signature'.

DOCUMENT 28

Complaint of the Indigenous People from Huamuxtitlan against the Abuses of Local Authorities, Guerrero, 1580[1]

Agnieszka Brylak

[Fol. 1r]

+

muy p^{v} s^{or}

y Piden q̄ atento q̄ los prinzipales y gou^{or} Prosiguen ē hazerles m^{a}los tratamy^{os} y no an cumplido la provy^{on} q̄ se les dio p^{a} q̄ fuesen sueltos / q̄ vn R^{or} [ ][2] a aueriguar los capitulos q̄ p[re]sentan[3] y P^{a} ello se trasunt[an]

+

Highly Esteemed Lord

Considering that the dignitaries and the governor keep mistreating [the commoners] and that they have not obeyed the provision given to them to release [the imprisoned indigenous people], they ask that a *juez receptor* [be sent] to verify the points that they present and that for this reason are translated.

Los yndios calpules y maceguales del pueblo de gumostitlan y sus estancias y sujetos dezimos que por dermas malos tratamy^{os} y otros delictos que los ~~dhos~~ principales del dho pueblo an hecho y cometido ocuriamos a esta rreal aud^{a} para que se proveyese y mandase se les tomase Presidencia y fuesen castigados de sus esesos y nosotros satisfechos de

We, members of the *calpulli* and indigenous commoners of the town of Huamuxtitlan and its outlying settlements and subjects, declare that, because of many abuses and other crimes that the dignitaries of the said town have perpetrated and committed, we have come to this Royal Audiencia court [asking that] a ruling and an order be

1 Bibliothèque National de France (BNF), Mexican manuscript No. 116.

2 Here there is a rip in the manuscript.

3 Here there is a rip in the manuscript, but the meaning is clear.

 DOI: 10.5876/9781607328346.c028

lo mucho que nos son a cargo por lo qual los dhos principales y governador prendieron a ciertos yndios y los tienen en la prision seis meses a siendo favoresidos de la Justª y beneficiado de la dha juridicion porque asimismo acuden a costa y mucho daño nro a darles gusto y aunque se despacho esta rreal provision que haremos demostracion para que los pressos se soltasen no lo an querido ni quieren haser e porque no es justo que semejantes estorciones sin causa se hagan.

issued to take the *presidencia* from them and punish them for their excesses; this will relieve us greatly of the burden that said dignitaries and the governor placed on us when they arrested some natives, whom they have been keeping in prison for six months now. [These authorities] have been favored by the judges and are taking advantage of the said judicial authority, because at our expense and to our great detriment they go and appear before the judges in order to make a good impression. And even though this royal provision ordering the release of the prisoners was issued—and we will show this—they have not consented nor do they consent [to release the prisoners]. It is not fair that this type of unjustified extortion be perpetrated.

a v alª suplicamos mande que un rrecetor des[ta][4] rreal audiª vaya a la aueriguacion de lo contenido en estos capitulos que pressentamos y de los demas que ante el pondremos en el dho pueblo para que vista v alª prouea lo que sea Justª y asimismo se suelten los presos pues asi es [ ][5] que pedimos.

We beg Your Highness to order a *juez receptor* of this Royal Audiencia to go and look into the [allegations] contained in these points that we present, and into others that we will submit to him in the said town, so that once they have been seen, Your Highness may issue a ruling according to the dictates of justice, and the prisoners may be released, since this is what we request.

Otrosi a v alª suplicamos mande que un ynterprete desta rreal audiª trasunte en lengua castellana los dhos capitulos y pedimos Justª

We also beg Your Highness to order an interpreter from this Royal Audiencia to translate the said points into the Castilian language; and we ask for justice.

. . . . de 17 de junyo de 1580

[. . . .] on June 17, 1580

se trasunten y a escrivano [*signature*]

May they be translated and to the notary [*signature*]

[Fol. 2r]

v̲ nica tiguitenehua yn isguichti yspantzīco nezinguihui y tonhueytlatoncatzi tijurey

Here we mention everyone who will come to appear before our great ruler, you the judge-king.

4 Here there is a rip in the manuscript, but the meaning is clear.

5 Illegible.

v Do Jua ponaventolan	Don Juan Buenaventura
v don aloxo te anguilan	Don Alonso de Aguilar
v Do me^{or} te xilpan	Don Melchior de Silva
v p^{o} cohuazancan	Pedro Coazancan
v paltasar te huelascon	Baltasar de Velasco
v Don tienco te satiancon	Don Diego de Santiago
v martin aton	Martín Antón
v xtoval ticocnahuacatl	Cristóbal Ticocnahuacatl
v clapiel sanchez	Gabriel Sánchez
v jusep tlacochcalcatl	José Tlacochcalcatl
v mer^{or} yacanxiuhcatl	Melchor Yacaxiuhcatl
[Fol. 2v]	
v axca ypa metztli de anbil vnconeuhgue tones y ce macehuali onvme tomi ya mochin chicuepohuali p^{ō}s ypan[6] x p^{ō}s	Today in the month of April they collected money, two *tomines* from each *macehualli*, it added up to 170 *pesos*.
v ynic õpan ypa metztli mayos vnconeuhgue onvme tomi y ce macehualin zano ysguich chicueponhuali p^{ō}s yhua x p^{ō}s	In the month of May for the second time they collected [money], two *tomines* from each commoner; likewise in total it was 170 *pesos*.
v nima chili onguehuiligue macehuali yc onguitonlinigue ~~vp~~ vnpohuali guahuacali	Then they collected chili pepper from the commoners: they afflicted them [with the amount of] twenty *quahuacalli*.[7]

6 The use of the word *ypan* in this context is highly unusual. Its traditional function with numbers is to separate multiples of *–tzontli* (four hundred) from multiples of *–pohualli* (twenty), but here it appears between *–pohualli* and the basic unit set (one through nineteen). Possibly the notary made an error and wrote *ypan* instead of *yhuan*, as in other entries.

7 The term *quahuacalli* (from *cuahuitl* 'wood' and *huacalli* 'carrying frame') means "a basket made of sticks or wood holding half a *fanega*" (Townsend 2010: 123, n. 2). The relation of this volume-measurement unit to the Spanish *fanega*, a measure of grain, has also been pointed out by James Lockhart, who used the example from the writings of Chimalpahin, in which *oncuahuacalli tlaolli* 'two *quahuacalli* of maize' is equated with *ce anega* 'one *fanega*' (see UOREGON QUAHUACALLI, http://whp.uoregon.edu/dictionaries/nahuatl/, accessed 01.12.2016).

v̲ auh y tepentlan yn omonechicon 3 põ p[ ][8] ypan ix p^{o}s

As for Tepetlan, sixty-nine *pesos* were collected there.

[Fol. 3r]
nica

here

v̲ yzcatgui ymac poliuhtica do vr^{no} vazquez tlacalaquilin yguac go^{or} mochiuh

Here is the tribute that has disappeared under the charge of Don Bernardino Vázquez ever since he became governor.[9]

[*right margin*] vi põ p^{o}s

120 *pesos*

v̲ auh y ton arosu te anguila yn iguac gon^{or} mochiuh yn imac onpoliuh tlacalaguili 4 põ p^{o}s x p^{o}s

When Don Alonso de Águila became governor, tribute worth ninety *pesos* disappeared under his charge.

[*right margin*] 4 põ p^{o}s x p^{o}s

ninety *pesos*

v̲ auh y mardonato yguac alhuazil maor mochiuh yn oguiponpolo vnfispo ytech moneguizguia

When Maldonado became chief constable, he spent [money] which was supposed to be for the needs of the bishop.

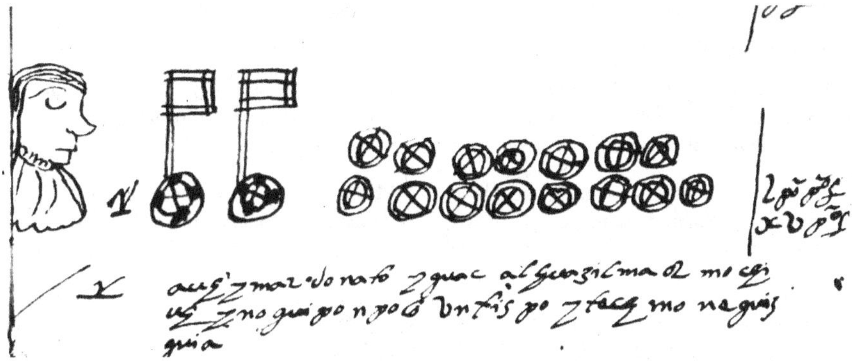

FIGURE 28.1. Representation of the amount of money spent by chief constable Maldonado (redrawn by Joanna Maryniak).

[*right margin*] 2 põ p^{o}s xv p^{o}s

thirty-five *pesos*

[Fol. 3v]

v̲ ayh y do me^{or} de silvan yn iguac alldes mochiuh yn oguipopolo diezmo vi põ p^{o}s

When Don Melchior de Silva became *alcalde*, he spent the tithe, 120 *pesos*.

[*right margin*] vi põ p^{o}s

120 *pesos*

v̲ auh y do Juã ponapetola yn iguac fiscar mochiuh vnguitlãtla[10] domines

When Don Juan Bonaventura became *fiscal*, he used up the money.

8 Illegible.

9 Literally, 'in the hands of Don Bernardino Vázquez it has been destroyed'.

10 Even though the dash is above the first letter *a*, it should be read as *onquitlatlan* and not *oquitlantla*.

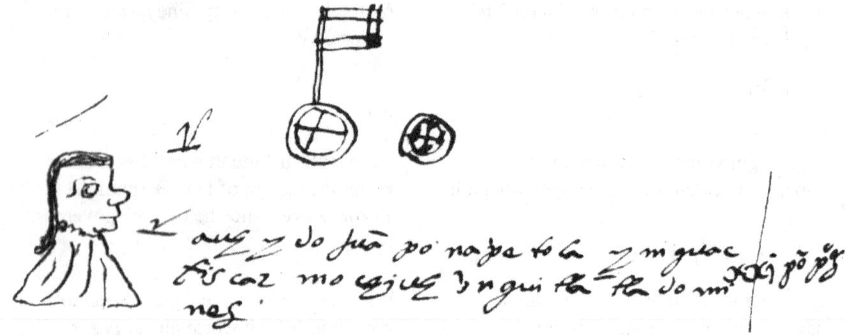

FIGURE 28.2. Representation of the amount of money spent by chief constable Gabriel Sánchez (redrawn by Joanna Maryniak).

[*right margin*] xxi põ[11] p°s	420 *pesos*
[Fol. 4r]	
[right margin] v põ p°s	100 pesos
v ~~auh y crapiner s~~	
v auh y parntasal te huelasco yn iguac escrivano mochiuh yn imac onguiponpolo tlacalaguili v põ p°s	When Baltasar de Velazco became notary, he was responsible for spending 100 pesos from the tribute.
v auh y crapier sanchez yguac allhuazil mayor mochiuh onguiponpolo tzahualtomi	When Gabriel Sánchez became chief constable, he spent money belonging to the prison.

FIGURE 28.3. Representation of the amount of money spent by fiscal Don Juan Bonaventura (redrawn by Joanna Maryniak).

11 In this section the amount of money stated in the alphabetic text, twenty-one counts of twenty, which adds up to 420 *pesos*, does not concur with the amount displayed in the accompanying image, where the number drawn is twenty-one *pesos*. Apparently, the notary made an error and the word *põ* (abbreviation of *pohualli*) is a scribal error.

~~4 x põ~~ 4 põ x p^{o}s

ninety *pesos*.

[Fol. 4v]

ypa metztli apil yhua maosn

In the months of April and May

v yzcatgui y telanma hoguichihuigue yc otlatolinigue y pipiltin ynic otlatolinigue yc otlaxixicoquen

Here is the head tax that they established; because of it the nobles [members of the municipal council] caused much suffering. With [the head tax] they caused great suffering and committed fraud.

[Fol. 5r]

Aqui nonbramos a todos aquellos q̄ an de pareçer ante el Ylle s^{or} Juez

Here we name all those who are to appear before the distinguished lord judge.

v don Ju^{o} buenauentura

Don Juan Buenaventura

v don a^{o}l de aguilar

Don Alonso de Aguilar

v don melchior de silua

Don Melchior de Silva

v p^{o} cohuazanco

Pedro Cohuazanco

v baltasar de uelasco

Baltasar de Velasco

v don diego de santiago

Don Diego de Santiago

v martin naton

Martín Antón

v xpotobal ticocnahuacatl

Cristóbal Ticocnahuacatl

v grauiel sanchez

Gabriel Sánchez

v Jusepe tlacohcalcatl

Jusepe Tlacochcalcatl

v melchior yacanxiuhcatl

Melchior Yacanxiuhcatl

v Agora en este mes de abril echaron de derrama a cada yndio a dos tomines q̄ se monta çiento y sesenta pesos

Now in this month of April they imposed a head tax of two *tomines* on every indigenous person, it adds up to 160 *pesos*.

v La segunda uez por el mes de mayo coJeron de derrama de cada maçegual dos tomines monta lo mismo q̄ son çiento y setenta pesos

For the second time, in the month of May they collected a head tax of two *tomines* from every commoner, it also adds up to 160 *pesos*.

[right margin: ojo] luego de chile tomaron a los maçeguales y los molestaron por quarenta medias hanegas

[right margin: *take note!*[12]] Then they took chili peppers from the commoners, they afflicted them [by taking] twenty *fanegas*.[13]

12 This Spanish term, literally "eye," is a scribal way of drawing the reader's attention to certain passage. It could be translated as "careful!," "look!," "watch out!," "take note!"

13 Literally "forty half-*fanegas*."

v de tepentlan se RecoJo de deRama sesenta y nueue p^{o}s

The head tax of sixty-nine *pesos* was collected in Tepetlan.

[Fol. 5v]

i v Primero Capitulo en q̄ se le haze cargo a don br^{no} bazquez del tienpo que fue gouernador de çiento y ueynte p^{o}s que gasto de los tributos como pareçe

i The first chapter, in which Don Bernardino Vázquez is charged with having spent 120 *pesos* from the tribute [money] during the period when he held the office of governor, just as it is shown.

ii v Segundo capitulo a don a^{o}l de aguilar cuando fue gouernador gasto nouenta p^{o}s como parece.

ii The second chapter [presents] Don Alonso de Aguilar who, when he was a governor, spent ninety *pesos*, just as it is shown.

iii v terçero capitulo a maldonado cuando fue alguazil mayor gasto çincuenta y çinco p^{o}s q̄ eran para el obispo

iii The third chapter [presents] Maldonado; when he was chief constable, he spent fifty-five *pesos* which were for the bishop.

iiij v cuarto capitulo a don melchior de silua cuando fue alcalde gasto del diezmo sesenta p^{o}s

iiij The fourth chapter [presents] Don Melchior de Silva; when he was *alcalde*, he spent sixty *pesos* from the tithe.

v v al quinto capitulo a don Ju^{o} de buenauentura cuando fue fiscal gasto ueynte y un p^{o}s

v The fifth chapter [presents] Don Juan de Buenaventura; when he was *fiscal*, he spent twenty-one *pesos*.

vj v al sesto capitulo a baltasar de uelasco quando fue eriuano gasto de los tributos çien p^{o}s

vj The sixth chapter [presents] Baltasar de Velasco; when he was the notary, he spent 100 *pesos* from the tribute [money].

vjj v setimo capitulo a grauiel sanchez cuando fue alguazil mayor gasto nouenta p^{o}s

vjj The seventh chapter [presents] Gabriel Sánchez; when he was chief constable he spent ninety *pesos*.

Estas son todas las deRamas que echaron los gouernadores y prinçipales molestando a los naturales maçeguales en el mes de abril y mayo

These are all of the head taxes that the governors and chief officers imposed, thus afflicting the indigenous commoners in the months of April and May.

todo lo susodho y escrito es trasuntado por unas memorias y de siete capitulos contra los gouernadores y prinçipales a todo

Everything said and written above is copied in the form of a statement in seven chapters against the governors and chief officers to the best of

[Fol. 6r]

mi saber y entender sin quitar ni poner ni añadir cosa alguna lo cual es çierto y uerdadero sin dolo [. . .] fraude ɏ ni engaño y en testimonio de uerdad fize aqui mi firma acostunbrada que es fecha

my knowledge and understanding, without eliminating or augmenting or adding anything, which is certain and true, without malice nor fraudulent intentions, nor deception, and to confirm

en al cuidad de mexi^{co} a diez i nueue de Junio de mil y quinientos y ochenta y cinco años	[its] authenticity, I place here my usual signature, which is signed here in the city of Mexico on the nineteenth of June of the year of 1585.
Ju^{o} mendez de sotomayor [*signature*]	Juan Méndez de Sotomayor [*signature*]
[Fol. 6v]	
+	
en iij de Jullio de 1585 a^{o}s vistos esos capitu^{os} por el s^{or} d^{or} paredes como se	On the third of July of the year of 1585, having seen how these chapters explain
manexa que fue proueyo y mando que los dhos yndios $\overline{\text{vsen}}$ de la proui^{on} q̄esta librada a su pedimy^{o} sobre l caso	what happened, the lord doctor Paredes ruled and ordered that the said indigenous people may use the *provisión* issued at their request concerning the case.
q̄ vsen dela prouision	May they use the *provisión*.

The following complaint from 1580, concerning the abuses of local rulers against the indigenous inhabitants of Huamuxtitlan (in the present state of Guerrero), is housed in the National Library of France as Mexican Manuscript No. 116.[14] The document is composed of three parts. The first is a letter dated June 17, 1580, written in Spanish on behalf of the indigenous commoners (*yndios calpules y maceguales*) from Huamuxtitlan and directed to the *audiencia* in Mexico. In it the natives complain about the mistreatments and abuses committed against them by local authorities. Among these they mention the apparently illicit imprisonment of some of the indigenous inhabitants of Huamuxtitlan who were not released despite a royal provision. Additionally, they ask the *audiencia* to send a *juez receptor*, a judge in charge of conducting inquiries and taking depositions, in order to investigate the case and sentence the accused.

The second part of the document contains the report on the violations perpetrated by the authorities of Huamuxtitlan and consists of the Nahuatl text and the corresponding pictorial representation. It begins with the list of indigenous governors and officials against whom the accusation is brought,

14 This document was previously published within the project Amoxcalli (http://amoxcalli.org.mx/) directed by Luz María Mohar Betancourt. However, the online edition, authored by Elia Rocío Hernández Andón, contains only a paleography of the document and a comparison of the Nahuatl text with its Spanish translation (*trasunto*) made in the sixteenth century, along with the editor's commentaries. Here I include a revised paleography and a verified translation of the text into English directly from Nahuatl as well as the translation of the Spanish text of the document.

followed by the description of different cases of fraud. The first of those mentioned in the text refers to the events that occurred in April and May of 1580, when the tribute was increased by two *tomines* for every commoner (which added up to 170 *pesos*). The image reflecting this information appears at the end of the complaint, right before the translation into Spanish. According to the document, the tribute obligations of the indigenous people were also raised by twenty *fanegas* (Spanish dry measures equivalent to one and a half bushels) of chili; and sixty-nine *pesos* were gathered in Tepetlan.

After this general information is presented, the complaint centers on the accused officials (some of whom are mentioned in the list included at the beginning of the Nahuatl text) and on their wrongdoings. Among the local authorities accused in the document are the governor, two chief constables, the *alcalde*, the *fiscal*, and the notary, who, it is claimed, pilfered part of the tribute and tithe money. The pictorial data comes first: an image of a male figure dressed in a Spanish shirt with a high collar (and, in the case of Gabriel Sánchez, also wearing a hat) together with the sum of money withheld. In this register a circle with a cross inside it stands for one peso, while a banner above it multiplies the number by twenty. Below each image appears the alphabetic data in Nahuatl, apparently intended as a commentary to it. However, in some of the sections, the Nahuatl text does not correspond to the information conveyed by the graphic representation. In the accusation levied against the chief constable named Maldonado, the alphabetic text states that he removed thirty-five *pesos* from the money that was for the bishop (probably the tithe), but according to the pictorial data it was fifty-five *pesos* (two counts of twenty *pesos* plus fifteen *pesos*). In a similar manner, when the examples of fraud committed by the *fiscal* Juan Buenaventura are mentioned, twenty-one *pesos* are depicted in the image, whereas in the Nahuatl commentary we read that he appropriated for himself twenty-one *pesos* multiplied by a count of twenty, which adds up to 420 *pesos*.

The third part of Mexican Manuscript No. 116 is the translation of the Nahuatl text into Spanish prepared for the judges of the *audiencia*. It is noteworthy that in the fragments that contain discrepancies between the pictorial and the alphabetic data, the author of the *trasunto* follows the information from the image, giving it preference over the Nahuatl script. However, in one passage he made a mistake: according to his version, in April of 1580 the total sum of money taken from the commoners amounted to 160 *pesos*, while both the pictorial and the alphabetic text agree on a sum of 170 *pesos*.

The notary who wrote down the Nahuatl text consistently writes the letter *q* as *g*. He also inserts the letter *n*, usually in place of glottal stop, but sometimes in other contexts, and he is not consistent. He also makes various orthographic substitutions in Spanish loanwords, such as *p* for *b*, *c* for *g*, *t* for *d*, and *r* for *l*. Furthermore, he reduces Spanish diphthongs to a single vowel, which he considers phonetically similar, for example: *ue* to *o*. The text contains many loans from Spanish. These are economic terms, referring to monetary units (*tomines*, *pesos*) or to taxes (*derrama* 'head tax'), names for colonial offices (*alcalde* 'judge', *alguacil mayor* 'chief constable', *gobernador* 'governor'), and expressions related to ecclesiastical administration (*obispo* 'bishop', *diezmo* 'tithe'). In one case the writer creates a new form, *jurey*, which apparently is a fusion of Spanish *juez* 'judge' and *virrey* or *visorrey* 'viceroy'.

DOCUMENT 29

Petition of the Residents of Santa Isabel Xiloxochtlan and San Luis Teolocholco, Mexico, 1624[1]

John Sullivan

[Fol. 3r]

en 26 . de febr . 1624

February 26, 1624

v tehuantin . sancta . ysabel . xilochochtlan . yuã s^{t} lyus teolocholco . tichaneque . yz catqui . ynic techtoliniya yn yehuantin . chaneque. s^{t} fran^{co} . topoyanco . yn fiscal yuã . alguaçil mayor . yuã pipiltin .

Here is manifested how the residents—the *fiscal*, the chief constable and the nobles—of San Francisco Topoyanco mistreat us, the residents of Santa Isabel Xiloxochtlan and San Luis Teolocholco.

v ynic çẽtlamãtlĩ . ynic techcocoliya . õpa . otimohuicaque . mexico . otimotlayhtlanito . yxpantzinco . tohueytlatocatzin . bisorrey . otiquixpatilique . yn tonetoliniliz . oquimocaquiti . yuã oquimocahuili . centetl mãtamie͠ndo y mixpantzinco . oticnextique . yu͠a otimotlanahuatili . ynic oquicauh . fiscal . yn itequiuh

In the first place, they hate us because we went to Mexico in order to make a request before our great ruler the viceroy. We informed him of our suffering. He listened to it and issued an order. We presented it before you and you ordered that the *fiscal* vacate his appointment.

1 Archivo Histórico del Estado de Tlaxcala (AHET), 1624, Caja 23, Exp. 2. This manuscript was collectively transcribed, translated, and discussed in a session of the University of Warsaw's Advanced Nahuatl Online Seminar by Agnieszka Brylak, Eduardo de la Cruz Cruz, Abelardo de la Cruz de la Cruz, Lidia Gómez García, Katarzyna Granicka, Szymon Gruda, Anastasia Kalyuta, Julia Madajczak, Kelly McDonough, Justyna Olko, John F. Schwaller, John Sullivan, Martín Vega, and Stephanie Wood.

 DOI: 10.5876/9781607328346.c029

v yuã . nimã . occe . omixquetz . fiscal . scri° . ocatca yscribano . ocatca . fiscal. / auh yn ax̄ . oc hualca ynic techtolinia ỹ fiscal . yuã . alquaçil mayor yehuatl . ỹ yalhua . oquimilpito . çẽpohuali omatlactli . amo . motencopatzinco . çequi teylpiloyã . yuan teopan .. auh ynin . yc pehua . ynic mixpantzinco . otineçico . ypan sabado . ynic techtoliniya . yn ica . neyxcuitili .

And then another *fiscal* was instated: it is the former notary, the notary of the former *fiscal*. And now, the *fiscal* mistreats us much more. And yesterday the chief constable confined thirty [people] without an order on your part, some in the jail [and some] in the church. And this began because we went to appear before you on Saturday. For this reason they mistreat us with the public spectacle.

[left margin: *signature*]

[left margin: *signature*]

v ye çẽca . timitzmotlactlauhtiliya . ma xitechmopalehuili . ynic quiçazque . yn ilpiticate . yuã . ma mixpãtzinco . neçi . ỹ alguaçil mayor . ma quito . yn queni . yn oquimilpi . no yuã . ma xicmoneltilili yoã . ma xicmoçelili . yc mopiyaz . yn mandamendo yuã . ma xicmoceli . ynformaçion . ynic ticcelizque motetlaçotlalitzin .

We greatly implore you to help us so that those who are imprisoned may be freed and so that the chief constable may appear before you and explain why he confined them. Also please verify and confirm how the order will be carried out. And please receive the testimony, that we may receive your favor.

In this short petition, dated February 26, 1624, residents of two *altepetl*, Santa Isabel Xiloxochtlan and San Luis Teolocholco, file a complaint to an unnamed local authority regarding mistreatment they have suffered at the hands of the *fiscal*, the chief constable, and the nobles of San Francisco Topoyanco. All three of these towns, today named Santa Isabel Xiloxoxtla, Teolocholco, and Tepeyanco, respectively, are located between five and ten kilometers to the southeast of the center of the city of Tlaxcala. The trouble began when the same residents went to Mexico City to report the mistreatment to the viceroy; he, in turn, ordered the local official to depose the *fiscal* who, upon stepping down, simply appointed the town notary to fill his post. The new *fiscal*, according to the residents, increased the mistreatment. The Saturday before writing the petition, the residents appeared before the local official. In retaliation, the chief constable of San Francisco Topoyanco incarcerated thirty residents of the two towns. The arrests were carried out in public manner, described in the petition with the word *neixcuitilli* 'a public spectacle'. This is a patientive noun derived from the passive form of the verb *ixcuitia* 'to provide someone with an example (in the sense of a lesson to be learned)'. The residents of Santa Isabel Xiloxochtlan and San Luis Teolocholco wrote their petition to the local authority to report the public shaming that they had been subjected to, to ask for the release of the prisoners, and to request that the officials and nobles from San Francisco Topoyanco be held accountable for their actions.

Why did the officials of Topoyanco subject Santa Isabel Xiloxochtlan and San Luis Teolocholco to this public spectacle and incarcerate their residents? All of these towns were within the jurisdiction of Ocotelulco, one of the four major *altepetl* that made up the Tlaxcalan province. From the time of its inception, the Tlaxcalan *cabildo* dedicated itself to maintaining the political integrity of the complex *altepetl*. And as Lockhart, Berdan, and Anderson discuss in *The Tlaxcalan Actas* (1986: 75), one of the most important rules was the need to resolve all internal Tlaxcalan conflicts in-house; fines and imprisonment, and punishment in the form of shaming, are prescribed for *cabildo* members who violated this principle. Sometime in the early seventeenth century, a second set of provisional *alcaldes* was named for the Tlaxcalan *cabildo*, one new *alcalde* for each of the four main *altepetl*. Ocotelulco's provisional *alcalde* was located in Topoyanco (Lockhart, Berdan, and Anderson 1986: 125). So when the residents of Santa Isabel Xiloxochtlan and San Luis Teolocholco went to the viceroy and to the unnamed local official, perhaps the Spanish *corregidor* of Tlaxcala, they were in effect inviting Spanish interference into Tlaxcalan affairs, and they received the same punishments that had been prescribed by the *cabildo* for its own members.

The language of the petition is very traditional and it very definitely pertains to Lockhart's Stage 2. The only loanwords used are those dealing with dates, *en 26. de febr. 1624* 'February 26, 1624' and *sábado* 'Saturday'; offices, such as *fiscal* 'church steward', *alguacil mayor* 'head constable', *visorrey* 'viceroy', and *escribano* 'notary', and with the document genres of *mandamiento* 'an order' and *información* 'an investigation or declaration'. There is one possible structural calque from Spanish. The Nahuatl purposive consists of a set of verbal suffixes that indicate whether a subject goes or comes in order to carry out an action. The going or coming is expressed by the suffix and these expressions do not require the presence the actual verbs "to come" or "to go," as they do in Spanish. The petition contains the following sentence, *ompa otimohuicaqueh mexihco otimotlaihtlanitoh* 'we went to Mexico in order to make a request'. Literally it reads, "There we went to Mexico, we went in order to make a request." If we took out *otimohuicaqueh* 'we went (reverential form)', the remaining phrase, *ompa mexihco otimotlaihtlanitoh*, would still mean 'we went to Mexico in order to make a request'. Even with the possible presence of the calque, the sentence provides us with a beautiful example of the newly discovered syntactic structure described in the study of the 1663/1743 Testament of Francisca de los Ángeles (Document

18), in which a central word or phrase is simultaneously a part of two larger phrases constructed on either side of it. In this case, the central element of the "larger structure" is the word *mexihco* 'Mexico', and the two articulated phrases that it forms are *ompa otimohuicaqueh mexihco* 'We went to Mexico' and *mexico otimotlaihtlanitoh* 'We went to Mexico to make a request'. In traditional Nahuatl syntax city names precede verbs; only the presence of an adverbial anticipator allows them to follow verbs. It is precisely the use of *ompa*, 'there'[2] that allows *mexihco* to simultaneously finalize the first phrase and initiate the second, thus articulating them.

2 The word *ompa* 'there' should not appear in the translation. In this sentence it functions simply as an adverbial anticipator of *Mexihco* (Lockhart 2001: 83–85).

DOCUMENT 30

Complaint Concerning a Bad Priest, Coatlan de Puertos Abajo, Jalisco, Mexico, 1637[1]

Justyna Olko

v yn çenca timahuiztililoni
yn tehuatzin yn tixiptlatzin
tto Jso Tehuantin timopilhuan
titlatoque nican altepetl cohuatlã
timitztotlatlauhtilia mixpantzinco
tontopechteca tictotlaçotenamiquilia
yn momahuizmatzin yhuan in
moycxitzin timitztotlatlauhtilia ma
huel xitechmopalehuili tehuantin
timaçehualhuan Dios yn itechcopa
çe toteopixcauh nican onca ypan
toaltepeuh quipachoticatca ypilhuan
Dios auh amo pachihui toyolo yn
yehuatl otinechmomaquilic prohuision
amo quitlacamati oc tlapanauhti çenca
techtolini maca çan yoquin tiyahouã
ypan techmati yoqui tichichimeco ypan
techmati yoquin amo tichristianos yhuan
amo yquin quichiua misa çan yoquin
mocauhtica tosanta ygleçi yhua ca
tictlaqualtia ca ticmomaquilia tlen ytech
monequi yhuã amo yca techtlaçotl çan
huel oc quinequi quixitinis altepetl

Very honorable representative of our Lord Jesus Christ, we your children, we rulers[2] here in the town of Coatlan, address you, we bow humbly before you, we politely kiss your honorable hands and feet. We implore you to help us, the subjects of God, concerning a priest of ours who was governing the children of God here in our town. But we are not satisfied [with him]. He does not obey the provision that you issued to me; it is excessive how very much he mistreats us, as though we were his enemies, he considers us like Chichimecs, he treats us as if we weren't Christians and he does not celebrate the mass on time. It is as if he abandoned our holy church. And we feed him, we give him whatever he needs, and he does not esteem us, he only wants to destroy the *altepetl*. And we gave him a woman, whom they took to the salt works, where she prepared meals for the salt workers. And he does

1 McAfee Collection, 339, UCLA.

2 Probably a broader meaning of the term *tlahtohqueh*, meaning 'notables', 'town officials'.

 DOI: 10.5876/9781607328346.c030

yhuan cihuatl ticmomaquilique salinas oquihuicaque ompa quinchiuiliaya tlaquali salineros yhuan home maçehuali amo quintlaxtlahuiznequi aço quitlatlanilia ca niman qualani qimictiznequi ymanel cihuame huel quintolinia quinhuihuitequi quintilanilia yntzon yhuan oc ce cihuatl huel oquitolini mochican oquitetelicçac oquiyspuliado mochican yhuan amo ticmati capa yca oyac ynõ cihuatl çan yoquin hoticpoloque yhuan quitohua hamo nias oc ce xivitl nicchihuaz nican yoquin nechtlacuilhui tlatohuani hobispo amo huel niaz auh ma motencopatzinco macayocmo onca ya ypan toaltepeuh ma quiça auh xitechmopalehuili ma ytencopatzinco tto Dios in maca çan yoqui egiptotlaca in Rey faraon ynic ymacpa maquixtiloque yn isRael ypilhuan ytencopatzinco Dios ya yxquich oticmocaquiti yn tonetoliniliz yn tochoquiliz yn imacehualhuan Dios nican timofirmatia timopilhua axcã otitlacuiloque virnez mani metztli de junio 19 tonali xivitl 1637 años nican timofirmatia allde juo agostin franco mateho juo chistopal miguel taniyel miguel geronimo juo agoztin miguel franco martin xemenez locaz lopez juo cruz escrihuano

not want to pay two Indians. If they request [their pay], he then gets angry and wants to beat them. Even if they are women, he really mistreats them, he whips them repeatedly, he pulls them by their hair. And he really mistreated another woman: he kicked her repeatedly all over [her body], he used spurs on her all over [her body]. And we do not know where that woman went, it is as though we have lost her. And he says, "I will not go, I will serve another year here, that is what the lord bishop wrote to me; I cannot go." By your orders, let him no longer be in our *altepetl,* let him leave. Help us. [Let it happen] by order of our Lord God, as with the Egyptians, that the children of Israel were freed from the hands of the king pharaoh by order of God. This concludes the affliction and weeping that we subjects of God have informed you of. We put here our signatures. We who are your children wrote it today, on Friday, the nineteenth day of June of the year 1637. Here we sign, *alcalde* Juan Agustín, Francisco Mateo, Juan Cristóbal, Miguel Daniel, Miguel Gerónimo, Juan Agustín, Miguel Francisco, Martín Jiménez, Lucas López, Juan Cruz notary.

v yn cenca timahuiztililoni yn tixiptlatzin tto jso Mixpantzinco timopechteca tehuantin timopilhuan nican altepetl cohuatlan cenca tictotenamiquilia momahuizmatzin yhuan moycxitzin ma xicmocaquiti totlatol tehuantin tiquitohua timopilhuan tipilhuan Dios mochintin pipiltin ayohmo ticnequi ompa motlaliz clerico ticnequi çe teopixqui merçenario ma yehuatl ompa quipachoz toaltepeuh yehuatl quinyolcuitiz ypilhuan Dios yhuan quimochihuiliz misa yhuan estrema uncion quitemaca mochi yehuatl quitequipanoz auh ypanpa timitztomachiltia ypanpa ticmacaz centetl nauatili ypanpa ynic yehuatl tictlatlani timopilhuan yhuan moch maçehuali quitlatlani yuan amo

Very honorable representative of our Lord Jesus Christ, we your children here in the town of Coatlan humbly bow before you, we greatly kiss your honorable hands and feet. Please hear our statement. We your children, the children of God, all the noblemen, say that we do not want a secular priest to be assigned here any more. We want a Mercedarian friar, let him govern our *altepetl.* He will confess the children of God and he will celebrate mass and he will provide extreme unction, he will perform all of that. For this reason, we trust that you will give an order concerning what we your children request, and all the commoners request. And there are not so many people, and it is not a big town;

mic tlacatl amo vey altepetl ca vel çenca motolinia altepetl ma yoquin xicmomachilti yn tiohuispo ya yxquich totlatol oticmocaquiti yn tonetlatlahtiliz yn timopilhuan axcan otitlacuiloque viernez mani meztli de junio 19 tonali nicã timofirmatia juo agustin franco mateho agustin taniel juo chiristopal juo agustin miguel gemenez miguel geronimo juo cruz escriuano

v quimotiliz amatzintli tlatohuani ohuizpo ompa moyetztica ymahuizchantzinco mahuiztic altepetl

but it is one that is greatly afflicted. May you the bishop know it to be so. That is all of our statement; you have heard the petition of us, your children. We wrote it today, on Friday the nineteenth day of June; here we put our signatures, Juan Agustín, Francisco Mateo, Juan Cristóbal, Miguel Daniel, Miguel Gerónimo, Juan Agustín, Miguel Francisco, Martín Jiménez, Lucas López, Juan Cruz notary.

The lord bishop who resides in his honorable place of residence, the revered town, will see this letter.

The manuscript, combining a complaint and a petition concerning a bad priest, was submitted by the representatives of the town of Coatlan de Puertos Abajo in Jalisco in 1637. Despite its relatively modest size, it contains elements of polite, elegant speech, a colorful narrative enriched with many details, and clearly stated demands directed to the bishop, most probably the bishop in Guadalajara under whose jurisdiction the area fell under. The authors of the letter present themselves as local rulers and nobles, all true Christians, and position themselves in relation to the bishop as "we your children, the children of God." Speaking for the entire community, they register a strong complaint against the priest residing there, accusing him of not fulfilling basic Christian duties and services, and thus putting the spiritual order of the town at risk, although the community feeds him and provides him with services. What's more, he physically mistreats members of the community, including a woman assigned to serve him and another one whom he kicked repeatedly and on whom he even used spurs. They also accuse the bad priest of treating the local population as "Chichimecs," as if they were his "enemies" and not Christians. This is a direct reference to the prolonged conflict with pagan Chichimecs, inhabitants of the northern zone who managed to elude Spanish control and thus, in Spanish political and ecclesiastical discourse, became the embodiment of paganism and barbarity (Olko 2014b). The Spanish images of these groups filtered into the sedentary populations that had accepted Christianity, including the inhabitants of Jalisco who defend themselves against the abuses of the vicar assigned to their town. As we can see in this document, they insistently position themselves in opposition to the Chichimecs by assuming the identity, at least in the political context of the petition, of true Christians, "the subjects of God." This argumentation is masterfully enhanced by the use of a metaphorical parallel to the Old Testament, no doubt intended to prove the local nobility's deep familiarity with the Christian tradition. Thus, they compare the bad priest to the evil Egyptians, while equating the local community with the "children of Israel," who, by the grace of God, were freed from slavery: "[Let it happen] by order of our Lord God, as with the Egyptians, that the children of Israel were freed from the hands of the king pharaoh by order of God."

In constructing this elegant petition, the authors prove to be not only proficient users of traditional Nahuatl rhetoric, but also educated enough in the biblical tradition to be able to enrich and adapt it to a new context through their skillful and dramatizing reference to the Old Testament. They adeptly construct arguments against the vicar, a significant portion of which is based on knowledge of Christian doctrine and religious practices. In doing so, they request not only his removal, but also the assignment of a Franciscan friar who would take adequate care of the spiritual life of their town: "We want a Mercedarian friar, let him govern our *altepetl*. He will confess the children of God and he will celebrate mass and he will provide extreme unction." At the level of ecclesiastical politics, this corresponds to the prolonged tension and struggle for control over indigenous communities between the secular clergy and the Franciscans (as well as other orders). The latter's position, no doubt dominant in the sixteenth century, gradually began to be eroded by an increasing presence of secular clergy in the mid- and late colonial period. Local communities often allied themselves with specific mendicant orders against another order, or more commonly, against secular clergy (see also the petition from Soconusco, Document 26 in this volume, and the petitions from Jaloxtitlan in Sullivan 2003). In fact, one may wonder whether a friar or friars were involved in the creation of the document, perhaps providing a biblical parallel in order to strengthen the rhetorical power of the petition. Whereas this remains purely conjectural, taken as a whole, the Jalisco petition stands out as a masterful example of indigenous writing that attempts to influence the power relationships and ecclesiastical politics affecting the life of the community.

The orthography of the document is typical of the conventions pursued by local scribes: the prevocalic *h* stands out, as well as the fact that several words in the manuscript, especially Spanish loanwords, have multiple spellings. Cases of the latter are not very numerous and are limited to specialized terminology of the colonial reality. *Salinas* and *salinero* refer to salt works developed by the Spaniards in the area. Words pertaining to the religious sphere are employed to express arguments related to spiritual matters that are the focus of the complaint. Thus, the bishop is addressed as "the ruler bishop" by using a traditional doublet composed of a native term and a loanword. This doublet is written once as *tlatohuani hobispo*, with a glottal fricative preceding *o*. It also appears as *tlatohuani ohuizpo*, in which case the Spanish word *obispo* became profoundly assimilated to Nahuatl on the phonological level, with the substitution [w] for [b]. The authors also refer to the addressee of their petition in the second person, using a very traditional form of Nahua oratory: *yn tiohuispo* 'you, the bishop'. Other specialized loanwords include *clerico* (for Spanish *clérigo*, [k] for [g] substitution); a further Nahuatl-Spanish doublet, *teopixqui merçenario* 'mercenary priest'; *misa* 'mass'; and *estrema uncion* (from Spanish *extrema unción* 'extreme unction'). References to the Old Testament included the usage of a blend, *egiptotlaca* 'people of Egypt'; *Rey faraon;* and *isRael*. The authors use a common reflexive verb, *firmatia*, meaning 'to sign', which is derived from the Spanish noun *firma* 'signature', as well as the transitive verb *espoliaroa* 'to apply spurs to a person or an animal', which comes from the borrowed Spanish verb, *espolear*. The latter appears here in the preterite, with the third person singular specific object: *oquiyspuliado* '[he] used spurs on [her]'. This form, which differs from the more standardized, phonetically unassimilated spelling of *oquiezpolearoh*, reveals a number of phonetic substitutions: Spanish [r] to [d], [e] to [i], and [o] to [u]. In short, we are dealing with a case of highly proficient usage of Christian terminology, adapted to Nahuatl, and partly expressed by the lexical resources available in this language. In the context of the petition, this no doubt constitutes a strong rhetorical asset of the indigenous authors, who are able to demonstrate their ability to construct complex arguments in their petition to the bishop.

ACCOUNTS AND ECCLESIASTICAL WRITING

DOCUMENT 31

Doctrina Christiana en Lengua Española y Mexicana, 1548

Nahuatl Rulership Terminology in the Christian Text of Sermon 5[1]

Katarzyna Granicka

La p̄mera cosa q̄ os digo al p̄sente es que pa que crios et hizo nuestro gran señor Dios al linage de los hombres y mugeres conuiene que sepays/ que aquellos Angeles malos que cayeron aca a baxo e aquella casa real de nuestro dios antes q̄ pecassen: auia les dios nr̄o señor dado a cada uno una silla real muy excelente en la q̄ se sentauā et alli mismo les auia dado a cada uno un grāpalacio real muy precioso y admirable a dōde estuuiessē. Y como cayerō y como fueron alançados de alla d'l cielo dexarō all alas sillas y palacios

Ynic cētlamātli yn namechnolhuilia in axca tleypampa oquimochiuili yn toueytlatocauh yn Dios yieuhantin tlatcipactlaca: monequi anq̄matizque. Ca yieuhantin amo q̄ltin angelesme yn oualuezque yn ompa yn itlatocachantcinco yn dios yn ilhuicac: yn iquac ayamo tlatlacoa/ ca ceceyacan quīmomaquilica yn dios yn ytlatocaycpaltcin oncan motlaliaya: yuā quimomaquilica cecētetl tlatocacalli cenca uey cēca tlaçotli yuan cenca chipauac yn onca yezquia. Auh yn oualuezque yn

The first thing that I explain to you now is why God, our great ruler, created them, the people on the earth. You need to know that before the bad angels who fell from God's royal house in heaven sinned, he gave each of them royal thrones, where they would be seated. And he had given them each a very grand, very precious, and very beautiful royal palace where they would stay. And when they fell, they were expelled from heaven. There they left behind the royal thrones and the royal palaces, they were just empty. And so, a

1 *Doctrina Christiana en Lengua Española y Mexicana* was prepared by Dominican friars for the purpose of Christianizing the Nahua people and it was printed in 1548 (reprinted in 1550). It is a bilingual Spanish-Nahuatl edition, with text arranged in two columns. It is one of the earliest and broadest doctrinal sources published in Nahuatl.

DOI: 10.5876/9781607328346.c031

reales que estauā vazias y desocupadas: de manera que gran parte d'l cielo q̄do d'l poblada dōde estauan los angeles malos. Por tanto ppuso y determino y tuuo por bien nuestro grā rey y señor Dios de hazer et criar otro genero d' criaturas: cōùiene a saber/ las humanas: pa las lleuar alla a su casa real al cielo: y para les dar aquellos palacios y sillas reales que eran de los malos Angeles que estauan vazias. Y para esto hizo nuestro dios un hombre y una mugger: para que aquestos dos engendrassen otros muchos: y que quando fuessen los hombres en este mundo multiplicados auian d' ser entresacados por los angeles de nuestro dios/ y lleuados alla al cielo/ en cuerpo y en anima: hasta tanto que aquelas casas et sillas reales fuessen llenas/ las quelaes estauan vazias.

oualquixtiloque in ompa yn ilhuicac: ca ompa quiualcauhtiaq̄ yehuatl intlatocaycpalli: yuan yeuatl yntlatocacalli: y çā cactimania: auh ca cēca uey yuhquin otlalpolyhui yn ylhuicac yn ompan catca yn aq̄ltin angelesme. Yehica omotlaçōtequili yuan oquimonequiltitcino yn toueytlatocauh in dios: ynic quīmochiuiliz yuan ynic quiyocuyaz occē tlamātin yn itlachiualhuan: ynic ompā quīmouiquiliz yn itlatocachantzinco yn ilhuicac yhuan ynic quīmomaquiliz ī yntlatocachan: yuan in intlatocaycpal catca: yn amoq̄ltin angelesme y çan cactimania. Yehica oquīmochiuili yn Dios ce oquichtli: iuan ce ciuatl: ynic ym omextin quintlacatilizque in occequintin: auh yn icuac cenca tlapiuiazque[2] cemanauac tlaca çanno yntzatzalan quiualmanilitiazquia yn iangelouā yn totecuyo dios ompā quimouiq̄lizq̄a yn ilhuicac yuā yn inyolia yuan yn innacayo: yxquich cauitl uel temiz yehuatl yn tlatocacalli yn cactimania.

very huge [part of] heaven, where the bad angels were, was left desolate. For this reason God, our great ruler, made a decision: he wished to make and create yet another class of his creatures to take to his Royal House in heaven and give them the royal houses and royal thrones that had belonged to the bad angels and were [now] just empty. Therefore God created one man and one woman so that the two of them would engender others. And when people had multiplied on earth, likewise the angels of our Lord God would select some from among them and take them, along with their souls and their bodies, to heaven. During this time, the royal houses that remained empty will indeed be filled.

The fragment studied here is a part of a much more extensive source. The *Doctrina Christiana en Lengua Espanola y Mexicana por los Religiosos de la Orden de Santo Domingo*, written by anonymous Dominican friars and published in Mexico in 1548, is one of the earliest religious texts printed in Mexico.

2 A possible typographical error: the correct form is *tlapihuizque*, from *tlapihuia*.

The *Doctrina Christiana* is a bilingual composition consisting of parallel texts in Spanish and Nahuatl, arranged in two columns, printed in blackletter type; the book consists of 154 folios in *quarto*. The edition must have been popular because the book was reprinted with no modifications in 1550. The text of the book derives from an older one, a monolingual Spanish *Doctrina Christiana*, printed in Mexico in 1544 under the patronage of fray Juan de Zumárraga, the first archbishop of Mexico. The Spanish text of this edition was in turn based on the older, bilingual materials composed in Spanish and "Antillean" (presumably the Taino language) by Pedro de Córdoba (e.g. the so-called *Manuscrito Antillano* dated 1511), which were used by Spanish missionaries for over twenty years and brought to Mexico by Dominican friars. Currently three copies of the text are known to exist.

Since the Nahuatl version of the text was created as a translation of the Spanish version, the *Doctrina Christiana* is a particularly valuable source for studying the strategies the author/s employed in order to reflect most faithfully the original and express Christian cultural concepts, previously foreign to the indigenous readers and lacking terminological equivalents in the target language. Also, a preliminary analysis of the source suggests the possibility that native speakers of Nahuatl were involved in the process of its creation. This study explores the usage of the Nahuatl terms *tlahtoani* and *tecuhtli/teuctli* in the text, in reference to the Christian God.

The passage in question describes the Kingdom of Heaven, where God created houses and thrones for his angels, which the "bad angels" lost when they rebelled against Him and were expelled from heaven. When their houses and thrones became empty, God decided to create people, with the idea that someday they would repopulate Heaven, taking the bad angels' places. The creation of the indigenous version of this passage required from its authors the usage of vocabulary that would describe Heaven and what had been built there. The terms *Dios* and *angel* (the latter is frequently used in the *Doctrina* in the plural—*angeles* with the Nahuatl plural suffix *-meh*) were borrowed straight from the Spanish language early in the process of Christianization. The authors of the *Doctrina Christiana* also attempted to broadly explain the meaning of the Spanish loanwords to the native readers of the text.

However, more interesting for the purposes of linguistic research and analysis is the use of Nahuatl vocabulary to reflect Christian (or simply European) phenomena, titles, and so on. In the analyzed fragment, this focuses mainly on God, His appellations and ways of referring to Him, and His Heavenly Kingdom. Terms such as *rey* 'king' and *señor* 'lord' and their combinations were translated with the precolonial terms *tlahtoani* and *teuctli* and through neologisms, combining the noun *tlahtoani* with other nouns. The analysis of the contexts in which those terms appear and how they are used shows how the precolonial terminology of power was adapted into the European and Christian context in this source. The choice of the word *tlahtoani,* which in preconquest times referred to the highest ruler of the native state *(altepetl),* to translate the Spanish *rey*, itself used in the Christian context and in reference to God, indicates that the semantic field of this noun had to have gone through a number of changes in the early stages of language contact. First and most obvious is the fact that the precolonial term, reserved for the head of a precolonial political unit, expanded or slightly changed its meaning in order to designate a European king and become an equivalent of the Spanish term. The second change situates the usage of this word in Christian contexts. No longer referencing an actual king, it now metaphorically describes the Christian God as a monarch, ruling from his kingdom over his people. This vision of the king, originating from both the Old and the New Testaments, seems natural from the European perspective, but it could have been foreign to the natives. The preconquest system of beliefs also assumed a connection between a ruler and a deity (Miller and Taube 1993: 168), and therefore the metaphors used to refer to them could have been similar. However, while Nahuatl-speaking rulers were considered to be representatives of deities, the deities were not conceptualized as ruler-like. The implantation of Christian theology in the New World, therefore, must have involved adapting its terminology and corresponding metaphors to the new conceptual system.

The metaphor describing God (or Jesus) as a king ruling over his people derives from both the Old and New Testaments and is deeply rooted in Christian-European culture. At this point it must be said that the attempt to overcome the discrepancies between the meanings of the Spanish *rey* and the Nahuatl *tlahtoani* and unify their semantic fields fits quite well within the general process of translating Christian doctrine that began ages before the conquest of Mexico. For example, the authors of the *Septuaginta* chose the Greek word *basileus* 'king' in order to translate the Hebrew word *melek* 'king, ruler'. However, in *Deuteronomy* the word *melek* was translated with the broader term *archon* 'ruler, lord', probably in order to avoid using a word specifically associated with Hellenistic monarchy (Pearce 2007: 173).

The author of the *Doctrina Christiana* employs two terms to refer to God. In the vast majority of cases in the text, *tohueitlahtohcauh* (literally 'our great ruler') is used as a lexical calque for "nuestro gran rey y señor," and *totecuiyo* (literally 'our great lord') is the equivalent of "nuestro gran señor." A few times, *tohueitlahtohcauh* is also employed for "nuestro gran señor," but the term *totecuiyo* is never used to mean "nuestro gran rey y señor." Analysis of the usage of these Nahuatl terms may reveal that the translators' utilization of *tlahtoani* and *teuctli* was not at all random. First of all, the authors of the text consistently relate *tlahtoani* with *rey* and *teuctli* with *señor*. Moreover, in their eyes *tlahtoani* seems to be a broader concept: they use only this word to translate the doublet "rey y señor" and do not resort to *tlahtoani* and *teuctli*—even though the analysis of the whole text indicates that the authors were very precise and careful in their translation. This in fact is natural and understandable from the point of view of the Nahuatl preconquest pyramid of power. As mentioned by Lockhart, the *tlahtoani* was not merely a large-scale *teuctli* at the *altepetl* level: the term *tlahtoani* included within itself the semantic field of the term *teuctli*, since *tlahtoani* "was at the same time *teuctli* and *pilli*" (Lockhart 1992: 109). So the fact that the authors of the *Doctrina Christiana* closely linked the terms *tlahtoani* and *rey*, and *teuctli* and *señor*, made it possible to translate "rey y señor" through the broader term of *tlahtoani*. And while it was possible to use *tlahtoani* to render "señor," *teuctli* could not be used to render "rey." Therefore, the way that the authors of the Nahuatl version of the *Doctrina Christiana* worked with the semantic fields of these two nouns was very deeply rooted in the preconquest tradition, and was derived from the Nahua world's sociopolitical organization. However, it is hard to be sure whether this careful distinction between the semantic fields of *tlahtoani* and *teuctli*, in relation to their preconquest meanings, was a general tendency in linguistic contact early on, or a category utilized only by those responsible for the translation of the *Doctrina Christiana*. It is worth noting that in other sixteenth-century sources the term *tlahtoani* definitely broadened in meaning, and in mundane sources it began to function in non-royal contexts as an equivalent of the concept of nobility in general.

> *auh yn nehoatl niEscri{o} yuā nialguacil ca ytechhoalmioalique yn señores tlatoque a̅lldes ynic otiquicuiloco ytestam{to} cocoṣq́ auh ynic no ticneltilia ypanpa nicna tictlalia yn tofirmas yca yn totoca*
>
> And I the notary and I the constable whom the lords alcaldes sent to come and write the testament of the sick person, in order to verify it also, therefore we place here our signatures with our names.
>
> (Will of Constantino Felipe from Xochimilco, 1572; Karttunen and Lockhart 1976: 95)

> *auh nima[n] ymoztlayoc lunes nece[n]tlaliloc in Sant Joan onca[n] hualmohuicac in tlatoani p[ro]uisor llicenciado do[n] Esteva[n] de Portillo*

Then on the next day, Monday, the people of San Juan gathered; the lord provisor licenciado Don Esteban de Portillo arrived there.

(Nahuatl account belonging to the annals genre and composed by anonymous native authors from the district of San Juan Moyotlan of Mexico-Tenochtitlan ca. 1564–1582; Reyes García 2001: 28)

The framework for the use of the terms *tlahtoani* and *teuctli* in the *Doctrina Christiana* implies a possible separation of their new semantic fields from the original terms "king" and "lord." However, there are only several usages of both those terms as an additional title accompanying the term *Dios* when there is no mention of either "king" or "lord" in the Spanish version of the text:

Spanish	*Nahuatl*	*English*	*Sermon*
porq̃ el nr̃o **dios** es incorporeo q̃ no tiene cuerpo	ca amo tley in inacayo in **totecuyo dios**	because our lord God has no flesh	Sermon 3 folio 19v
y el poder d'l nr̃o **gran dios** es muy grande	auh in **toueytlatocauh in dios** in iuelitiz ca cenca uey	Because our great ruler God's power is very great	Sermon 4 folio 21v

Thus, it seems that the terms *tohueitlahtohcauh* and *totecuiyo* in a way became an immanent part of the term for the Christian God. As a result they were loosened from their original meanings, which allowed users of the language to employ them in any context denoting the noble or supreme power. This suggests that the loosening of the relationship between the words *rey* and *tlahtoani*, which occurred as part of the latter's process of semantic broadening, may have begun in everyday spoken language, and not just during the careful, word-by-word translation of the text.

DOCUMENT 32

Account of the Commissioning of an Image of the Virgin Mary, Tlaxcala, Mexico, 1600[1]

AGNIESZKA BRYLAK

[Fol. 1r]

xihualhuian notiachcauhtzitzihuan in axca tiquitohua ypan ytonatiuhtzin yn Dios lones yc matlactlonçe tonali mani metztli de mayo ypa xihuitli 1600 años yn nehuatli niquitohua cabriel sachis nica amixpatzinco nica ticate matla^{c}tlonmome tlacatli xihualmohuica yn tehuatzin no^{te}yccauhtzin Jo^{u} pabtista yhua tehu^{a}tzin Jo^{u} marcuztzin yhuan tehuatzin paboltzin mayhuitlatohuane[2] ma yc nechicuiloca pablo te samora yhuan nehuatli antonio de pato yhuan nehuantli caspal quauhtlemani yhuan nehuatli nixpa antonio yaomitzin yhua nehuatli frans^{co} tzacatzintli yhua nehuatli miguel quauhtli nican osequi ymixpan toteyccauhtzitzinhua yn axca nica ticate ychantzinco yn dios nica otinonechicoque[3] tlasomahuizpipiltin ma ticmochihuilica ce totlasunatzin

Come, my honored elder brothers. Today, on God's day, Monday, the eleventh day of the month of May in the year 1600, we and I, Gabriel Sánchez, say that we, twelve people, are here before you. Come, my younger brother, Juan Bautista, and you, Juan Marcos, and you, Pablotzin. O honored ruler, let them thus register me, Pablo de Zamora, and me, Antonio de Pato, and me, Gaspar Quahtlemani, and before me, Antonio Yaomitzin, and me, Francisco Tzacatzintli, and me, Miguel Quauhtli. In the presence of other younger brothers of ours, we are here today in the house of God. We, the precious and honored nobles, have gathered here. Let us make an [image of] our beloved mother; may her beloved son, our beloved savior, Lord Jesus Christ, be fashioned. O ruler,

1 Archive Histórico del Estado de Tlaxcala (AHET), 1600, Caja 1, Exp. 2.

2 The intention here is probably *mahuiztlahtoanie* 'O revered ruler'.

3 For *otimonechicoque*.

DOI: 10.5876/9781607328346.c032

ma ytlasoconetzin mochihuas yn totlasotemaquixticatzin tecuiyo[4] Jesus christo tlatohuane ma quimonequiltitzino yn dius ma tel iuhqui mochua[5] ma cana eetomitzitzin tamemopalehuilisque tlasupipilti seca ticaqui yn amotlatoltzin macamo antechmonencahuilisque amo san ahuilica ma nali[6] ma huel ica yn amochicahualistzin yn aquimochihuilisque

may it be God's will that it be so done. May they take three *tomines* [from] each [of us]. We will help you, beloved noblemen, we greatly value your words. Do not deceive us, [may it] not be just a frivolous matter. Truly put your best effort into it.

Cueta nica tictlalia yc ticnotza maeso ytoca Jo^{o} cabriel ynic quimochihuilis y totlasonatzin asobsiontzin nìman ticma^{ca} castoli peso nima oquito maeso notlasomahuistiachcauhtzitzinhua ma yuhqui noconchihuas yn amonetequipachol ytepatzinco sihuapili santa maria nica no^{co}selia caxtoli peso axca ome metztli nimotlatlalilia ma quimotilisque[7] yn tlatocaychpuchtli sancta maria

Here we present the account of how we called a maestro named Juan Gabriel so that he would make [an image of] our beloved Mother Asunción. Then we gave him fifteen *pesos*. Then the maestro said: "My beloved and honored elder brothers, let me deal with your concern regarding the Lady Santa María in the following way. Here I receive fifteen *pesos*, and now I promise that in two months they will see the [finished image of the] Queen Virgin Santa María."

nehuatli cabriel sachis nica nopehua onoconmacac caxtoli peso maeso

I am Gabriel Sánchez. Here I begin [my statement]: I gave fifteen *pesos* to the maestro.

[Fol. 1v]

nican ipa tictlalia cueta oc sepa quiquixtia noteyccauhtzin ytoca Jo^{o}n paptista patetemnon oc nicquixtia matlactli peso

Here we present the account of how once again my younger brother, named Juan Bautista Patenon, makes a withdrawal.

oc cepa nica nictlilia cuenta quihualitlani maeso tomin n^{i}ca nocunquixtia caxtoli peso nehuatli cabriel saches y noconquixtia ytechpatzinco cihuapili santa maria cenpohuali yhua matlactli peso

Again I take out ten *pesos*. Once again here I present the account of how the maestro requested money. Here I, Gabriel Sánchez, take out fifteen pesos. I take it out for the sake of the Lady Santa María. Thirty *pesos*.

oc se cueta tictlalia

We present yet another account.

4 For *totecuiyo* 'our lord'.

5 For *mochihua*.

6 Probably *nelli*.

7 The sequence is written *maquimotilisque*, and there appears to be a curved bar over the *a*. Given the lack of overbars in the text, this is probably just one of its many wormholes. However, if it is indeed an overbar, the intention would be *ma anquimoittilizqueh* 'you (pl.) should see it'.

yn imixpan oti[~~. . .~~]~~omo~~mononotzque quichihua eeytomin	In their presence we made an agreement that it will be three *tomines* each.
yhuan yn icnocihuantzintzin omotlamatlanilique ce tomin nochi ytetzinco opouhqui cihuapili santa maria	And as for the widows, they were asked for one tomin each; it was all for the Lady Santa María.
noteyccauhtzine tlen ticchihuasque yn axca ye omochiuhtzino sihuapili san^{ta} m^{a} nehuatli niquito^{a} cabriel sachis yntla ce Dios quimochicahuilis nopiltzin quimotequipanilhuiz notlasonatzin auh tlacamo se quimocahuilis nopiltzin nuchi conmanilis notlaltzin	O my younger brother, what will we do, now that the [image of the] Lady Santa María has been made? I, Gabriel Sánchez, say that if God gives strength to one of my children, he or she will serve my Precious Mother. But if he doesn't spare [even] one of my children, [Santa María] will take all my land.
v notiachcauhtzin sano yuhqui niquitohua nehuatli yntla ce Dios quimochicahuilis nopiltzin ma quimotequipamilhuis totlasonatzin cihuapili sancta m^{a} yntlacamo mochi comanilis notlaltzin yuhqui tictlalia yn cuenda yxpantzinco yn Dios	My elder brother, I say the same. If God gives strength to one of my children, may he or she serve our Precious Mother the Lady Santa María. If not, she will take all my land. In this way, we present our account before God.
v Ju^{o} miguel elotzintli onotlacuili	I, Juan Miguel Elotzintli, did the writing.

The present document, dated 1600, is an account (*cuenta*) concerning the commissioning of an image of the Virgin Mary by a group of nobles (*pipiltin*). It can be divided into three parts, of which only the second is the account *per se*. The one-folio manuscript begins with the record of the gathering of twelve noblemen, although we get to know the names of only some of them. Unfortunately, neither their place of origin, the location of the meeting, nor the offices that they held are indicated. From the text we can ascertain that they met in the church where they declared that they would each make a contribution in order to pay for the creation of a holy image (a painting or sculpted figure, the text does not specify which) of the Virgin Mary and/or her son Jesus Christ. From the final part of the document we learn that the image in question was a representation of the Assumption of the Virgin Mary. The text is written in an unusual form: rather than a description of events, it resembles a transcription of the conversations held in the church, quoting the speech of the people involved. This pattern continues throughout the entire document.

The second section contains the list of contributors and the amount of money delivered by them to the *maestro* Juan Gabriel, the artist who was hired to make the holy image. Apparently, the Tlaxcalan nobles were not the only ones who participated in this enterprise; there is also a mention of a group of widows who donated one *tomin* each.

The document concludes with vows made by two of the twelve noblemen before the completed image of the Virgin, though only one of them, Gabriel Sánchez, is mentioned by name. They ask the Holy Lady to protect their children, but state at the same time that if they die without leaving any heirs, their land will be bequeathed to Saint Mary, that is, most probably to the church or the monastery where the declaration of the commissioning of her image took place.

Even though the document was produced at the end of the sixteenth century, it does not contain many lexical or structural influences from Spanish. Loans are limited to some religious terms such as *Dios* 'God', *Jesucristo* 'Jesus Christ', *Asunción* 'Assumption' (written *asobsiontzin*, with some orthographic substitutions and the Nahuatl reverential suffix *–tzin*), names for monetary units (*tomín*, *peso*), and the words *cuenta* 'account' (also spelled *cueta* and *cuenda*) and *maestro* 'master'. A change in Nahuatl words introduced by the writer is the substitution of the Nahuatl absolutive suffix *–tl* for *–tli* (*nehuatli* instead of *nehuatl, tlacatli* instead of *tlacatl*, and *xihuitli* instead of *xihuitl*). It is possible, however, that the intention was *nehuatl i[n], tlacatl i[n]*, and *xihuitl i[n]*.

DOCUMENT 33

T'unapa's Coming

A Fragment of the Chronicle by Don Joan de Santa Cruz Pacha Cuti Yamqui Salca Maygua, Peru, First Half of the Seventeenth Century[1]

Jan Szemiński

[Fol. 3r]

[[2]] dizen que en t̃po de *purun pacha*[3] todas las naciones /de *tauan tin suyo*[4] benieron de hazia aRiba de *poto / ssi,*[5] tres o quatro exercitos en forma de guerra y a/ssi: los Venieron poblando. tomando los lugares. / quedandosse cada Vno delas compañias, en los luga/ res, baldios. à este t̃po se llaman *ccallac pacha*[6]/[7] o *tutayac pacha*[8] y como cada

It is said that at the time of *purun pacha* all the peoples of *Tawantin Suyu* came here from above *Potosi*, three or four armies in battle array. And in this way they came to populate, to occupy places so that each set of troops settled in a wasteland. That time is called *qallaq pacha* or *tutayaq pacha*. Since everyone chose wastelands for their lodgings

1 Don Joan de Santa Cruz Pacha Cuti Yamqui Salca Maygua: *ReLacion. de antiguedadeſ deſte Reyno del Piru*, National Library, Madrid, volume number 3169, folios 131r–174v.

2 On the left margin: "OJO" ('attention').

3 In Quechua, *purun pacha* is 'barbarian times'.

4 In Quechua, *Tawantin Suyu* is 'Four United Parts', the name of the civilized world under the Sun, or Peru, equivalent to the Inca Empire.

5 Potosí. Today this is a Bolivian city; in the sixteenth and seventeenth centuries it was the center of silver production and the largest city in South America.

6 In Quechua, *qallaq pacha* is 'epoch that begins'.

7 On the left margin in Dr. Avila's hand is "tuta" ('night' in Quechua).

8 In Quechua, *tutayaq pacha* is 'epoch of incomplete darkness', before the creation of the Sun.

DOI: 10.5876/9781607328346.c033

Vno. cogieron luga/res. baldios, para sus beuiendas y moradas, es/to se llaman *purun pacha rac Captin*[9] este tp̃o.

and dwellings, this time is called *purun pacharaq kaptin*.

/passaron muchissimos a^{o}s. y al cabo. despues / de aber estado ya poblados. abia gran falta / de tierras y lugares. y como no abian tierras[10] cadal dia / abian guerras y descordias, que todos ~~se~~ en general / Se ocupauan en hazer fortalesas, y assi cadal dia [Fol. 3v] /an abido, en cuentros, y batallas, sin aber La paz. /

Many years had passed, and after they had already been completely settled, there was a great lack of land and spaces. And since there were no lands, each day they waged wars and had disagreements, so that everyone in general was occupied in constructing fortresses. And thus each day there were struggles and battles, with no peace.

en este tp̃o, de tantas. combates. yguerras, in/Justos, que los Vnos y los otros eſtauan Jamas / Seguros, Sin al canssar quietud, ~~llegaron a esta~~ / y por entonces a media anoche oyieron, que los / *happi ñuños*,[11] se despareçieron dando teme/rarios quejas, deziendo. Vençidos Somos, Vençidos somos. / ay que pierdo, mis tierras, a esto se entiendẽ q; / Los demonios, fueron Vençidos. por xesũxpo n. s^{or}. q^{do}. / en la cruz enel monte calbario,

At this time there were so many unjust conflicts and wars that neither one side nor the other was ever safe; there were no prospects for tranquility. Then at midnight they heard the *hap'i ñuñus* going away, moaning dreadfully and saying: "We are defeated, we are defeated. Alas! I lose my lands." This means that the demons were defeated by Jesus Christ our Lord on the cross on Mount Calvary.

porque anti/guam^{te}, en tp̃o de *purumpacha* dizen que los *ha/ppi ñuños* andauan bissiblem^{te} en toda esta tie/rra que no abian seguridad, de andar en anoche / Siendo, porque a los hombres y mugeres y muchachos./ y criaturas. los lleuaban aRebatandoles, co/mo tiranos infernales. y enemigos capitales del / genero humano, &^{a}. y passados algu^{os}. años. des/pues de aber los **ydo y** echado, alos demonios *happi / ñuños* y *achacallas*.[12] desta tierra anllegado./

Because in ancient times, in the time of *purun pacha*, they say that the *hap'i ñuñus* walked in plain sight all over this land, so people were not safe while out walking at night because men, women, children, and newborns were snatched and taken by the *hap'i ñuñus*, the infernal tyrants and mortal enemies of the human species, etc. And some years later, after expelling and driving away the *hap'i ñuñus* and *acha qallas* demons from this land, a bearded man of

9 In Quechua, *purun pacharaq kaptin* is 'when it was still the barbarian epoch.'

10 Bold letters mark Salca Maygua's corrections added to the manuscript.

11 In Quechua, *hap'i ñuñu* is a kind of demon or god, whose name can mean 'the one that catches and sucks', or 'a pregnant, breastfeeding woman'.

12 In Quechua, *acha qalla* is 'the fertile beginners', a class of demons, or gods.

entonçes aestas provyas Y Reyos de *taban tin / Suyo*, Vn home barbudo mediano de cuerpo ycon / cabellos, largos, y con camissas algo largas, y di/zen que era ya home passado, mas que de ~~Vie~~ / moço que trayeya Las canas y era flaco el qual an/daba consu bordon y era que enseñaba alos / naturales, con gran amor llamandoles a to/dos, hijos y hijas. el qual no fueron oydos ni he/cho, casso. de los naturales, y qdo andaba por / todas las prouyas. an hecho. muchos milagros./ &ª. bisibles. solamte con tocar alos emfermos./ los sanabã el qual no trayeya enteres nin/guno. ni trayeya hatos, el qual dizen que / todas las lenguas ha blaua mejor que los natu/rales, y le nombrauã *tonapa*[13] o[14] *tara paca*[15] / *Vira cocham pachayachip Cachan* º *pachaccan*[16,17] [Fol. 4r] [18]*ybicchhay camayoc. cuna cuy camayoc*[19] los ynºs de/ aquel tp̃o dizen que suelen burlar deziendo / tan parlero home aVnque los predicaua Siempre no / fueron oydos, porque los naturales

average build, with long hair and a rather long gown, then came to these provinces and kingdoms of *Tawantin Suyu.* It is said that he was a man, already old rather than young, who had grey hair. He was a lean person, who walked with his staff. And he used to teach the natives with great love, calling all of them sons and daughters. He was not heard nor paid attention to by the natives. And as he walked through all the provinces, he performed many visible miracles, etc. Just by touching the ill, he cured them. He did not carry anything of value nor clothing. It is said that he spoke all the languages better than the natives. They gave him the name of *T'unapa*, or the name of *Tara Paka Wira Quchan Pacha Yachachip kachan* or *pachak'an, iwich'ay kamayuq kunakuy kamayuq*. They say that the Indians of that time used to mock him, saying, "Such a chattering man." Although he always preached to them, he was never heard, because the natives of

---

13 In Quechua, *T'unapa* is 'the Destroyer', an image of the Creator God as the one who punishes and destroys sinners and teaches a new way of life.

14 Left margin note: "a este baron ojo les llamauan" ('take note: they called this man').

15 Left margin note in Dr. Avila's hand: "tarapaca quiere dezir aguila" ('*Tara Paka* means an eagle').

16 In Quechua, *Tara Paka Wira Quchan Pacha Yachachip kachan* o *pachak'an* is the 'envoy' or 'servant' of 'the one who conceals ancestor pairs', 'Nursery of Identities', and 'The one who causes the cosmos to become'. "The one who conceals ancestor pairs" is an image of God as the one in whom the ancestors of all beings are hidden, and according to the Andean religion, the ancestors must be a pair composed of a male and a female. "Nursery of Identities" is an image of God as the one who contains the potential existence of all beings. "The one who causes the cosmos to become" may be an error of the writer, who wrote *pachayachi* instead of *pacha yachachi*, meaning 'the one who gives the world vital force' or 'the one who peoples or teaches the cosmos'. *Pacha Yachachi* as God's name is very frequent in sixteenth-century Cuzco sources, while *Pachayachi* does not occur.

17 Below the line is a note in Dr. Avila's hand: "quiere dezir serujr o criado" ('meaning a servant or retainer').

18 Above the line, there is a note in Dr. Avila's hand: "*yvicchai camajoc*—quiere dezir predor" ('*iwich'ay kamayuq* means a preacher').

19 In Quechua, *iwich'ay kamayuq, kunakuy kamayuq* is 'adviser and preacher'.

de aquel t̄po no hezieron[20] / caudal ni casso. del hom^{e}. pues se llamo aeste / baron *tonapa. Vira cochampa cachan,*[21] pues no sera[22] / ~~fue~~ estehom^{e} el gloriosso. apostol sancto / thomas?

este baron dezen que llegó. al puº, de / Vn caçique llamado *apo tampo,*[23,24] cuyo sujeto fue / el puº. y dizen que llego, muy canssado, en Vna / fiesta q^{do} estaban en las bodas, y assi por el *apo / tampo*, fueron oydos sus razonam^{tos}, con amor / y los ynºs del sujetos. los oyieron mala ganas. / al fin, poraquel dia fue huesped elperigrino./ el qual dizen que dio, Vn palo. desu bordon al dho[25] / *tampo*, Reprehendiendoles con amor afable. / y porel dho *apo tampo*. los oyieron con aten/cion Reçebiendole el dho palo. desu mano. / de modo. que en Vn palo. los Reçebieron lo / que les predicaua seña landoles. y Rayandoles./ cada capitulo de los rrazones, Los Viejos modernos./ del t̄po. de mi p^{e}. don diº. f^{e}. suelen dezir que caçi / caçi era **10** mandam^{tos}, de Dios, prinçipalm^{te} los / siete preçeptos no les faltaua. solam^{te} / nombre de Dios. ns^{or} y desu hijo, Jesu͡xpo ns^{or} / les faltaua que es pp^{co}. notº. entre los Vie/jos. y las penas, eran graues. p^{a}. los que quebran/tauan este baron, llamado *thonapa* dizen / que ~~lle~~ andubo, por todas áquellas prouy^{as} de / los *colla Suyos*.[26] predicando les. sin descanssar

that time did not pay attention to him nor derive any benefit from the man. Well, this man was called *T'unapa Wira Quchanpa kachan*. Could this man be the glorious apostle Saint Thomas?

It is said that the man came to the settlements of a lord called *Apu Tampu*, whose subjects were the people. It is said also that he arrived very weary during a feast when they were celebrating a wedding. So *Apu Tampu* listened to his teachings with love, but the Indians, his subjects, listened to them unwillingly. All and all, on this day the traveler was a guest. It is said that he gave his staff to the above-mentioned *Apu Tampu*, while admonishing him with good-natured love. And the arguments were heard by *Apu Tampu* with attention, while he received the staff from [*T'unapa's*] hand. Thus with a staff they received what he preached to them, marking and drawing lines for each point of the teachings. Old men today, from the time of my father Don Diego Felipe, used to say that those were most surely God's Ten Commandments. Most important, seven commandments were not lacking. Only the name of God our Lord and of His son, Jesus Christ our Lord, were lacking among them. This is commonly known among the old men. And punishments were heavy for transgressors. It is said

20 "*no hezieron*" added at the end of the line.

21 In Quechua, *Wira Quchanpa kachan* is 'envoy of the Nursery of Identities'.

22 In Dr. Avila's hand is added "*no sera*" at the end of the line.

23 In Quechua, *Apu Tampu* is the 'Store of Lords', identified as a forefather of the Inca dynasty in Cuzco.

24 Right margin note in Dr. Avila's hand: "este *aputâpo* es *paccarec tâpu*" ('this *Apu Tampu* is *Paqariq Tampu*'). The name means 'Giving-birth Store'.

25 At the end of the line is added "*apo*."

26 In Quechua, *Qulla Suyu* is one of the four quarters of the civilized word. In the sixteenth century it included lands in the southern portion of modern Peru, Bolivia, northern Chile, and part of the northwestern area of Argentina.

> that this man called *T'unapa* walked through all those provinces of the *Qulla Suyus*, preaching without rest.

This document is a fragment of the *Relación de antigüedades deste Reyno del Pirú* contained in folios 131–174v of manuscript number 3169, which is preserved in the Biblioteca Nacional de Madrid. Don Joan de Santa Cruz Pacha Cuti Yamqui Salca Maygua, probably a local nobleman from the Waywa Qanchi group in the colonial province of Canchis, wrote the *Relación* sometime before 1647. Dr. Francisco de Ávila, owner of the manuscript, died in 1647. The document contains the observations and corrections that he had written in the margins.

In his own words, Don Joan de Santa Cruz Pacha Cuti Yamqui Salca Maygua belonged to the fifth generation since 1532, when Francisco Pizarro and his men imprisoned Ataw Wallpa Inqa and murdered all of his courtiers. The fact that Don Joan de Santa Cruz Pacha Cuti Yamqui Salca Maygua's ancestors visited the Spaniards in Cajamarca suggests that they were old enough to rule their Waywa Qanchi ethnic group. Calculating twenty or twenty-five years for each succesive generation, Don Joan de Santa Cruz Pacha Cuti Yamqui Salca Maygua could have written his text sometime around the beginning of the seventeenth century. I do not know how the text came into Dr. Francisco de Ávila's possession nor how it, together with other manuscripts contained in the same codex, reached the Spanish National Library.

I chose this excerpt to illustrate certain properties of the language used by the author, as well as some of the ways he imagined and understood his own culture. Don Joan de Santa Cruz Pacha Cuti Yamqui Salca Maygua was an educated local nobleman, but at the same time a good Catholic governed by His Catholic Majesty. It seems that he used Catholic teachings to understand the Andean image of the past, and Andean teachings to understand the Catholic image of the past. In both the Spanish text and in the English translation, I have marked all of Dr. Ávila's observations, because as a Spaniard he had the same problems in understanding the native nobleman's words as we do today. I copied the original text, which is accessible through the Biblioteca Cervantina.

The fragment contains a series of Andean myths:

1. The myth of the beginning of humanity in this world, indicated by the Quechua expressions *qallaq pacha* 'epoch of the beginning' and *tutayaq pacha* 'world that is partially night'. Both expressions refer

to the first epoch of the world, before the creation of the Sun, the Moon, and the stars;

2. The myth of the populating of the present world by Andean peoples, which took place in *purun pacha* 'the times of the barbarians'.
3. The myth of *hap'i ñuñu* and *acha qalla*, demons or gods who ruled humanity, simultaneously multiplying and consuming it.
4. The myth of *T'unapa*, vanquisher of former gods and teacher of a civilized way of life, associated with the Second Apparition of the Creator as a teacher.
5. The myth of the ancestor of the Incas who received God's commandments.

It also included at least four attempts to join Andean and Catholic mythology:

6. The identification of *T'unapa* with Saint Thomas, who in traditional European medieval mythology was an apostle sent to the Indies, and therefore to the Indians.
7. The identification of *Wira Quchan*, the Andean creator god, with God the Father.
8. The identification of the change of epochs, when *hap'i ñuñus* lost the power to rule humanity with the death of Jesus Christ on Mount Calvary.
9. The identification of God's Ten Commandments with the Inca's commandments.

We have no information about the author except that which is in the *Relación*. Since he presents himself as a nobleman from a local group, portrays Inca history as the history of all *Tawantin Suyu*, and claims the *Qulla Suyu* people and region as his own, he obviously identifies both with the old elites from the time of the Inca and with colonial indigenous elites. Direct confirmation of this is apparent from the way he uses Spanish and Quechua. He wrote his text is in Spanish, so it was addressed to Spanish speakers and readers. But at the same time it contains prayers in Quechua without translation to Spanish, and many Quechua expressions, also without translation, as in the quote, *iwich'ay kamayuq kunakuy kamayuq*. Even Dr. Francisco de Ávila, a Catholic priest and a Quechua speaker from Cuzco, did not understand some of the Quechua expressions. During the first half of the seventeenth century there were two groups who could read and write Spanish and who spoke both Spanish and Quechua: (1) part of the clergy and the wealthy provincial strata of Creole society, for whom the Inca past and the efforts to demonstrate the presence of the apostles in preconquest Peru was unimportant, and (2) members of the Andean nobility who participated in colonial administration, and who thus, on the one hand, needed an image of their own past in order to become legitimate rulers and administrators in their own ethnic groups, and on the other hand, needed to show the Spaniards that they could not be accused of being pagans, since they had been Christianized (perhaps imperfectly) by Jesus Christ's apostles, such as Saint Thomas. In short, the *Relación* was produced for local native noblemen by a local indigenous nobleman. We should ask why he did not write the entire text in Quechua, as his Mexican contemporaries did in Nahuatl.

The fragment contains words from the author's native or heritage language. We suppose that he spoke Cuzco Quechua fluently, as well as Aymara, since he was familiar with Cuzco and quoted texts in Quechua, and his province was considered among those where Aymara was spoken. The languages of this region together form a *Sprachbund*, and have many common phonetic, grammatical, and lexical traits. Cuzco Quechua shares approximately fifty percent of its word roots with Aymara.

Andean influence is visible in:

Phonetics

1. The mutual exchange of the vowels e/i: "b**e**uienda" [*v**i**vienda*], "d**e**ciendo" [*d**i**ciendo*], "d**e**zen" [*d**i**cen*], and "per**i**grino" [*per**e**grino*].
2. The elision of one of two contiguous vowels: "cadal" [*cada el*].

Grammar

3. The lack of number concordance: "Vencidos somos. Ay que pierdo mis tierras."; "Quando andaba por todas las prouyncias an hecho. Muchos milagros."
4. The lack of gender concordance between adjectives and nouns: "temerarios quejas."
5. The presence of Spanish equivalents of Quechua or Aymara validator suffixes: "dicen que."
6. The direct reporting of speech: "deziendo Vençidos Somos."
7. The use of Spanish past tenses without strict consistence in meaning, which is difficult to demonstrate: "Quando andaba por todas las prouyncias an hecho. Muchos milagros."

Vocabulary

8. Spanish words with an Andean meaning: *camisa* with the meaning of *unku* 'man's tunic', *palo de su bordón*, with the meaning of *k'azpi* 'governor's staff' as a symbol of power.
9. Andean words with a translation—for example, *hap'i ñuñu* 'demons'—without entering into particularities of meaning.
10. Andean words without a translation to Spanish, probably used with the understanding that all readers were familiar with them: for example, *purum pacha* 'epoch of the barbarians', and *Tawantin Suyu* 'Four Sections United', which in the sixteenth or seventeenth century meant the Inca empire, the Viceroyalty of Peru, the whole world under the Sun (South America), or a village divided into four neighborhoods.

DOCUMENT 34

Ritual formulario e institución de curas of Juan Pérez Bocanegra, 1631[1]

The Terminology of Andean Social Hierarchy in the Confession of Kurakas

GREGORY HAIMOVICH

ENGLISH TRANSLATION OF THE SPANISH TEXT

[p. 268]

PREGVNTAS QVE ſe an de hazer a los Curacas acerca deſte Mandamiento, en general: y a los mandones quitando algunas, que solo pertenecen a los Curacas

Questions that should be asked to *kurakas*, about this commandment in general, and to the leaders, omitting some that refer to the *kurakas* only.

[p. 269]

1. As cobrado la taſſa de los Indios, a tí sujetos, conforme a como cada vno está taſſado?

1. Have you exacted the tax from the Indians, your subjects, according to what each of them is assessed?

2. Despues de auerla cobrado, as les pedido mas de lo que suelen dar, cada tercio ò cada año?

2. Having exacted this tax, do you ask them for more than they are used to paying each quarter or each year?

3. Que tanto as cobrado mas?

3. How much have you exacted in excess?

1 RITVAL FORMVLARIO, E INSTITVCION DE CVRAS, PARA ADMINISTRAR A LOS NATVRALES DE este Reyno, los ſantos Sacramentos del Baptiſmo, Confirmacion, Eucaristia, y Viatico, Penitencia, Extrema vncion, y Matrimonio, Con aduertencias muy neceſſarias. POR EL BACHILLER IVAN PEREZ BOcanegra, Presbitero, en la lengua Quechua general: examinador en ella, y en la Aymara, en eſte Obispado. Beneficiado propi-etaario del pueblo de ſan Pedro de Antahuaylla la chica. CON LICENCIA IMPRESSO EN LIMA: POR GERONYMO de Contreras, Iunto al Conuento de ſanto Domingo Año de 1631.

DOI: 10.5876/9781607328346.c034

4. Quãto tiempo à, que cobras mas de lo que estã obligados a dar?

4. How long have you been exacting more than they are obliged to give?

5. As cobrado eſſa demanda en oro, plata, ropa, en semillas ò en otras cosas?

5. Have you exacted this demand in gold, silver, cloths, grain, or in other things?

6. As cobrado taſſa de las mujeres, ó de las biudas, ó de las moças que aun estã en la Dotrina?

6. Have you exacted the tax from women, or widows, or girls who are still learning the Christian Teachings?

7. As cobrado taſſa de los Indios viejos? ó de los que han paſſado ya de los cinquenta años? ò has cobrado taſſa de los moços, que no llegan a los diez y ocho años, ó de los reseruados de taſſa?

7. Have you exacted the tax from old Indians? Or from those over fifty years of age? Have you taken the tax from juveniles under the age of eighteen or from those exempt from tax?

8. As les quitado el maiz, gallinas, pollos, ò hueuos, ò otras cosas, diziendo que es para la taſſa, ó para los gaſtos della?

8. Have you taken maize, hens, chickens, or eggs or other things from them, saying that it is for the tax or for other costs of the tax?

9. As les quitado los carneros, bueyes, ò vacas, ò rejas, diziendo que es para la taſſa? ò as les quitado alguna ropa, auiendo dado de todo lo que son obligados?

9. Have you taken llamas, oxen, or cows, or iron ploughs from them, saying that it is for the tax? Or, have you taken some clothing from them, after they had given everything they were obliged to give?

10. As quitado a tus Indios plata, ò otras cosas, que ayan ganado con ſu trabajo, ò alquiladoſe para los Andes, ò llanos, ó para trabajar en las chacras, ó lleuando cargas, o ſiruiendo en la plaça de alguna ciudad, diciendo que es para la tasa, y quedándote con ello? o has mandado que te den parte de lo que así han ganado?

10. Have you taken silver from your Indians or other things that they have earned by hard work or by hiring themselves out in the Andes or in the coastal lowlands or by working the fields or carrying loads, or serving in a city market, telling them that it is for the tax, and you have kept it? Or have you ordered them to give you a share of what they have earned by working this way?

11. As tomado por fuer[p. 270]ça a tus Indios oro, plata, carneros, ó otras cosas?

11. Have you taken gold, silver, llamas, or anything else by force from your Indians?

12. Haciendo los Indios tu casa, ó tu chacra, ò guardandote tus ganados, ó embiandoles camino, ò haciendoles trabajar en qualquier cosa, as les pagado su trabajo?

12. If you had Indians build your home or your farm, or graze your cattle, or go out on an errand, or perform any kind of labor, did you pay them for their work?

13. Iuntando la taſſa de tus Indios, as les pedido mas de lo que deuen? ó as acrecentado la taſſa, tomando para tí las sobras?

13. Collecting tax from your Indians, have you asked them to pay more than they are obliged? Or have you increased the tax and taken the surplus for yourself?

14. As mandado a tus Indios que te traìgan oro, plata, ò otras cosas para tí?	14. Have you ordered your Indians to bring you gold, silver, or anything else?
15. As gastado la plata de los Indios, para quedarte con el Curacazgo que tienes, trayẽdo pleito injuſto con quien le pertenecía, ò heredaste eſſe Curacazgo, que tienes de tus padres, desde el tiempo del Inca?	15. Have you spent the Indians' money to get the position of *kuraka* which you have, involving the person to whom it belonged in an unfair legal dispute, or did you inherit the position of *kuraka* from your ancestors, since the time of the Inca?
16. Los Indios, que labrã tus chacras, ò guardan tus ganados, ſon por orden de los Gouernadores, ò Visitadores, ó son desde el tiempo del Inca? ò hazesles fuerça para que te ſiruan?	16. Do the Indians who work your fields and graze your beasts do it by order of the Governors or tax inspectors, or do they do it from the time of the Inca? Or do you force them to serve you?
17. Eſſas chacras que tienes, heredastelas de tus padres, ò as las quitado a los Indios, è Indias viejas? ò eran de Indios, que murieron sin herederos? ò siembras las chacras de la comunidad para tí?	17. Did you inherit those fields that you have from your ancestors or have you taken them from old Indian men and women? Or did they belong to Indians who died without heirs? Or do you sow the fields which are communal property for yourself?
18. Embias indios a tus minas, que te traìgã oro, ò plata sin pagarles nada?	18. Do you send the Indians to your mines to bring you gold or silver without paying them?
19. La plata, que los Españoles, ò otras personas te an dado para los Indios, que lleuã cargas, ó traginã, ò guardan ganado, ò trabajan en ſus haziendas, as te quedado con ella, ò con parte della? Y la plata que an de auer los indios de tampu, por el recaudo que dan a los paſſajeros, as te [p. 271] quedado con ella, ò repartiendola, as te quedado cõ parte della para ti?	19. Have you kept the money given to you by Spaniards or somebody else for the Indians who carry loads, or transport them on beasts, or graze livestock, or work in their estates, or a part of it for yourself? Or have you kept the money that the Indians serving in road inns should receive for their services to the travelers, or when you divided it among them, have you kept a part for yourself?
20. As echado derramas entre tus Indios para pleitos injustos, ó para pleitear a los Padres, y Corregidores? Que tantas vezes? que cantidad?	20. Have you imposed levies on your Indians for false legal disputes? Or in order to go to court against the priests or the *corregidores*? How many times [have you done that]? How much [have you collected]?
21. A ſe muerto algun Indio, por auerle tu embiado a los Yuncas, ò minas, adõde entendias que tenia mucho peligro ſu vida?	21. Has any Indian died whom you sent to the lowlands or to the mines, knowing it would put his life in danger?

22. As procurado que no deʃcubran los hechizeros, idolatras, y amancebados? as recebido cohecho por eʃto?

22. Have you attempted to conceal sorcerers, idolaters, and adulterers? Have you received a bribe for this?

23. Tienes algunas huacas en tu tierra, y hechizeros a quien vas a conʃultar y tratar tus neceʃʃidades?

23. Do you keep any *wak'as* and sorcerers on your land, whom you come to consult with and inquire about your problems?

24. As hecho taquies, ò borracheras, ʃecretas, ò públicas, donde se hagan pecados publicos, ò secretos, ritos antiguos?

24. Have you arranged secret or public *takis*,[2] public gatherings for drinking, during which public or secret sins are committed, as well as ancient rites?

25. As leuantado, ó hecho leuantar algun testimonio, a algun Padre, para echarle de la Doctrina? que daño recibio por tu causa?

25. Have you given testimony, or arranged for testimony to be given against a priest in order to expel him from the parish? What damage has he suffered because of you?

26. As eʃtoruado a tus Indios, de la Dotrina, ò Miʃʃa, ocupandolos en cosas de tu prouecho? ò del Padre, ò del Corregidor, ò de otras personas, por darles gusto, ò porque te an dado algo?

26. Have you kept your Indians from attending doctrinal instruction or mass by occupying them in tasks for your own benefit or the benefit of the priest or the *corregidor*, or anyone else, in order to please this person or because they have given you something?

27. As te seruido de las hijas de tus Indios? o as te amancebado con ellas? quantas tienes de eʃta ʃuerte?

27. Have you taken advantage of the daughters of your Indians? Or have you made them your concubines? How many do you have in this situation?

28. As hecho caʃar por fuerça a Indios, ò Indias? ò as eʃtoruado, que se casen, por tus malos fines? que tãtas vezes as hecho esto?

28. Have you forced any Indian man or woman to marry? Or have you impeded them from marrying because of your bad intentions? How many times have you done this?

29. Con achaque de cobrar la taʃʃa, as te aprouechado del dinero de los In[p. 272] dios? ò as tomado para ti el dinero, que pertenece a la comunidad?

29. Using tax collection as a pretense, have you taken advantage of the Indians' money? Or have you taken money belonging to the community for yourself?

30. As hecho que paguẽ taʃʃa los enfermos, ó contrechos, diziendo, que tienen caʃa, y chacras? o as les hecho pagar dos, ò mas vezes la taʃʃa?

30. Have you obliged the sick and the disabled to pay the tax, saying that they have homes and fields? Or have you obliged them to pay the tax two or more times?

2 *Taki* was a song, with the meaning of "to sing the truth," the performance of which was always accompanied by the drinking of corn beer. Hence, the Spaniards saw it only as a *borrachera*, a gathering for the purpose of excessive drinking.

31. As eſcondido Indios de la Viſita, para que te dẽ a ti el tributo, y para que te ſiruan?	31. Have you concealed Indians from tax inspection so that they will pay tax to you and serve you?
32. As hecho que te hagan los indios mita, de yerua, leña, y de otras cosas en mas cantidad de lo que te està permitido?	32. Have you made the Indians perform *mit'a* service by [bringing you] fodder, firewood, and other things in larger quantities than permitted?
33. As te aprouechado, ò tomado el dinero de las Cofradias, ò Fabricas de las Igleſias, ò de las chacras, que se hacen para las Igleſias o para las Cofradias?	33. Have you taken advantage of or taken the money from the confraternities, or from funds for maintaining the church buildings, or from the fields worked for the churches or confraternities?

The *Ritual formulario e institución de curas* was written in both Spanish and Quechua. The original Spanish text and its English translation above can be compared with the original Quechua text and its translation below. Certainly, Pérez Bocanegra tried to adapt his Quechua translation to the necessities of his Quechua-speaking brethren, but the Spanish original was itself adapted to specific local conditions, so it conceivably corresponded better to what the sins of a *kuraka*, an Andean administrator, might well have been, including his opportunities to steal and to force his subjects to serve him in ways not permitted by law or by Christian morals.

TWO ORTHOGRAPHIC VERSIONS OF THE QUECHUA TEXT: THE ORIGINAL AND ITS PHONEMICIZED REINTERPRETATION

We have chosen to provide two orthographic versions of the Quechua text because we wish to call attention to the problems faced by researchers who must reconstruct the phonemes in Quechua texts in order to understand the original meanings correctly. The early colonial Quechua writing, based on the acoustic perception of the indigenous speech by Spanish speakers, did not render the Quechua phonology adequately due to a number of distinct features, for which the Latin alphabet could not have proper solutions in that period (e.g., uvular stop, ejective and aspirated consonants, lack of *i*/*e* and *a*/*o* vowel distinction). The phonemicized transcription used here is based on the conventions proposed by Cerrón-Palomino (1994: 13–26), with inclusion of the opposition between voiceless dorsal *z* (colonial *ç*) and voiceless apical *s*, which existed until the end of the seventeenth century (Mannheim 1991: 153–160).

[p. 304]

PREGUNTAS QVE / se an de hazer a los Cu-/racas, &c.

1. Camachiscayqui runa/manta, chayaquen *tassa*n-/ta,[3] yallintahuan churaicu-/ checchucanqui? chaz-/ quecchucanqui? /	1. Kamachisqayki runamanta, chayaqin tasanta yallintawan churaykuchiqchu kanki? chazkiqchu kanki?
2. Cai *tassa*cta ña chaz/quizcaiquimanta, çapa *ter-/cio*p, cairi, huatap chaya-/ quenmanta, astahuan ma-/ñacchu canqui? /	2. Kay tasakta ña chazkisqaykimanta, zapa terciop kayri watap chayaqinmanta, astawan mañaqchu kanki?
3. Haicactam yallichis-/pa chazquircanqui? /	3. Hayk'aktam yallichispa chazkirqanki?
4. Haica vnaiñatac ça-/pap, chayaquenmanta ya-/llequenta chaçquircan/qui?	4. Hayk'a unayñataq zapap chayaqinmanta yalliqinta chazkirqanki?
5. Chay yallichispa chaz/quiscaiquicta, corepichu/ collquepichu? pachapi-/chu? imana cac muupichu/ imahaicapipas chazquir-/canquichu? /	5. Chay yallichispa chazkisqaykikta, quripichu qullqipichu? p'achapichu? imana kaq muhupichu, ima-hayk'apipas chazkirqankichu?
6. Huarmicunamanta,/ icma huarmicanamanta,/ tazque ama *maria*man ha-/moc, miçcac sipascuna-/ manta,[4] *tassa*cta chazquec-/chucanqui? /	6. Warmikunamanta, ikma warmikunamanta, thazki ama Mariaman hamuq, mizkaq sipaskunamanta tasakta chazkiqchu kanki?
7. Machu runacunaman-/ta, pichca chunca huata-/manta yallec, runamanta-/ pas, *tassa*cta chazquecchu/ canqui? cairi, macta, mana-/racchuncapuçaqueyoc,/ huatamâ chayaccunaman/ta, vnai socsoc, oncoccuna/mantahuampas, *tassa*cta/ chazquecchucanqui? cairi/ *tassa*manta ña llocsecman/ta, chazquectacchu can-/ qui? /	7. Machu runakunamanta, pichqa chunka watamanta yalliq runakunamantapas, tasakta chazkiqchu kanki, kayri maqt'a, manaraq chunka puzaqiyuq wataman chayaqkunamanta, unay zukzuq, unquqkunamantawanpas tasakta chazkiqchu kanki? kayri tasamanta ña lluqsiqmanta, chazkiqtaqchu kanki?

3 Beginning here and throughout the document, the author uses the Spanish loanword *tasa* 'tax'.

4 *Ama Mariaman hamoc* should be translated literally as 'those who do not [yet] reach [the age] of St. Mary.' It is not known, according to the views of the Catholic Church in that period, how old St. Mary was when she received the annunciation nor when she gave birth to Jesus; however, we do know that *tazque* (*thazki*) was a traditional age category, which included prepubescent girls up until thirteen or fourteen years of age. *Miçcac* (in early colonial dictionaries also *michcac*) *sipascuna* literally means 'blossoming girls', while *sipas* generally designates an older age category, namely pubescent and marriageable girls.

8. Cai hinacunamanta,/ [p. 305] çaranta, china atahuall-/panta, *pulli*tunta,[5] ima/ cacllantapas, runtunta,/ cachunta, quechocchu/ canqui, *tassa*pacmi ñispa?/ cairi, *tassa*cta huntachin/campac, ima cacpacpas/ ñispa? /

9. *Tassa*pacmi ñispa, *va*/*ca*nta, yapoc *vaca*nta,[6]/ quellai tacllanta,[7] iman/ tapas, quechupocchu can/qui? cairi, ña chayaquen-/ta coptin, pachacta quæ/ chocchu canqui? /

10. Runap ñacaimana/ tariscanta, collquenta,/ imantapas, quechupoc-/ chu canqui? cairi, yunca/man[8] mincai[9] tucuspa, cha-/cracunamampas[10] rispa, ta/riscâta, quechupoctacchu/ canqui? cairi, quepi apas-/canmanta, pampa tiaicoc/ riscanmanta,[11] *tassa*pacmi/ ñispa, campacchacuspaña,/ hillupocchu canqui? cai-/ri, cai hina llamcaicunapi/ tariscanmanta, as inca coai/ ñispa camachecchu can-/qui mañacchucanqui?/

8. Kay hinakunamanta zaranta, china atawallpanta, pullitunta, ima kaqllantapas, runtunta, q'achunta qichuqchu kanki, "tasapaqmi" ñispa? kayri, "tasakta hunt'achinqanpaq, ima kaqpaqpas" ñispa?

9. "Tasapaqmi" ñispa, vacanta, yapuq vacanta, qillay takllanta, imantapas qichupuqchu kanki? kayri, ña chayaqinta quptin, p'achakta qichuqchu kanki?

10. Runap ñak'aymana tarisqanta, qullqinta, imantapas qichupuqchu kanki? kayri, yunkaman mink'ay tukuspa, chakrakunamanpas rispa, tarisqanta qichupuqtaqchu kanki? kayri, q'ipi apasqanmanta, pampa tiyaykuq risqanmanta, "tasapaqmi" ñispa, qampaqchakuspaña, hillupuqchu kanki? kayri, kayhina llamk'aykunapi tarisqanmanta, "as inka quway" ñispa, kamachiqchu kanki, mañaqchu kanki?

5 The assimilated Spanish loanword *pollito* is the diminutive of *pollo* 'chicken'.

6 From the Spanish loanword *vaca*, 'cow.' *Yapoc* (*yapuq*) *vaca* is literally 'a cow who ploughs,' a hybrid term for 'bullock.'

7 In other parts of the *Ritual formulario, quellai taclla* (*qillay taklla*, literally 'iron plough') is identified with *barreta* 'crowbar'.

8 *Yuncaman* (*yunkaman*) 'to the *yunka*'. Among Quechua speakers, *Yunka* was a general denomination for 'the lowlands', both in the coastal region and on the eastern slopes of the Andes. Acute climatic differences between *puna* (highlands) and *yunka* (lowlands) made work there especially harsh for dwellers of the highlands.

9 *Mincai* or *mink'a(y)* in the native Andean tradition is a type of labor, organized from above, but based on the principle of reciprocity. In other words, an initiator of *mink'a* was obliged to later do work in favor of the recruited laborers (Mannheim 1991: 91). As is the case for many other traditional economic practices, *mink'a* lost its genuine meaning in colonial times, and here only bears the sense of 'wage labor'.

10 *Chacracunamampas* (*chakrakunamanpas*) means 'and to the fields'. Although translated here mostly as 'field', *chakra* in fact originally had a broader meaning, as it could denote any plot of land that could be of benefit to its owner. For example, *chakra* could also mean 'mine', as can be seen in Document 21.

11 *Pampa tiaicoc riscanmanta* (*pampa tiyaykuq risqanmanta*) literally means 'from [what they earned] by going to sit in the square'. However, it is clear that the meaning of *pampa tiyayku-* 'sit in the square' was to sell goods at the market, which usually was situated on a town's central square.

11. Runaiquicunaman-/ta, coricta, collquecta, pa-/chacta, llamacta, imai/mana haicaimanactapas,/ callpamanta quechocchu/ canqui? /	11. Runaykikunamanta qurikta, qullqikta, p'achakta, llamakta, imaymana-hayk'aymanaktapas kallpamanta qichuqchu kanki?
12. huacijquicta huaçi-/chacuptin, chacraiquicta/ llamcaptin, huihuaiquicta michiptin, imapipas runai/quicta llamcachispapas,/ chayaquenta, humpin,/ toquenta, paillapocchu/ canqui? cairi manachu?/	12. Waziykikta wazichakuptin, chakraykikta llamk'aptin, huywaykikta michiptin, imapipas runaykikta llamk'achispapas, chayaqinta, hump'in t'uqinta payllapuqchu kanki? kayri manachu?
13. Runaiquip *tassa*nta/ huñuspa, chayaquenman-/ta, astahuan mañapoc-/chu canqui? cairi, *tassa*-/cta mirachecchu canqui?/ chay miraininta, puchun-/ta, campac ña apacussac/ ñispa? /	13. Runaykip tasanta huñuspa, chayaqinmanta astawan mañapuqchu kanki? kayri, tasakta mirachiqchu kanki? chay mirayninta, puchunta qampaq, "ña apakusaq" ñispa?
[p. 306]	
14. Cammâ chapachisca/ runacta, camachecchu can/qui, cori, collquecta, imac/tapas, camaripuai ñispa? /	14. Qamman chapachisqa runakta kamachiqchu kanki, "quri, qullqikta, imaktapas kamaripuway" ñispa?
15. Hucpa checampi cu/raca cancanta, llulla ñina/cuihuan, quechupurcan/quichu, cai huchapac, ru-/nap collquenta tantachis-/patac? cairi, yayayqui, ma/chuiqui, Inca pachamanta/ curacachucarcan? hinaspa/ rantimpi camchu curaca/ sayanqui? /	15. Hukpa chiqanpi kuraka kanqanta llulla ñinakuywan qichupurqankichu, kay huchapaq runap qullqinta tantachispataq? kayri yayayki, machuyki, Inqa pachamanta kurakachu karqan? hinaspa rantinpi qamchu kuraka sayanki?
16. Chacraiquicta llam/cac chacrachacoc runa, lla/maiquicta michecpas, In-/ca pachamanta, mitaco-/queiquipac, camachisca-/chu? cairi, *visitador*pa,[12] ma-/nañispa? maican apuppas,/ camachiscanchu? cairi, call/pamanta, llamcachiscaiqui/chu? /	16. Chakraykikta llamk'aq chakrachakuq runa, llamaykikta michiqpas, Inqa pachamanta, mit'akuqiykipaq kamachisqachu? kayri visitadorpa, "mana" ñispa, mayqan apuppas kamachisqanchu? kayri kallpamanta llamk'achisqaykichu?
17. Chacraiquiri, machui/quimanta, yayayquimâta/ cacchu? cairi, runacunamâ/ta, payacunamanta, hillus-/caiquichu? cairi mà, ma-/na runamaciyocña, ña/ huañoccunap	17. Chakraykiri machuykimanta, yayaykimanta kaqchu? kayri runakunamanta, payakunamanta hillusqaykichu? kayri má, mana runa maziyuqña, ña wañuqkunap

12 *Visitadorpa* 'of a *visitador*'. A *visitador* in colonial times was a provincial inspector authorized by the Crown.

haquescan cacchu? cairi, pampa,/ sipsi[13] ñisca, chacractachu/ quiquijquipac ña, tarpu-/cunqui?/

haqisqan kanchu? kayri pampa, sapsi ñisqa, chakraktachu kikiykipaqña tarpukunkichu?

18. Collq́, cori coyaman/runacunacta, cachacchu/ canqui, cori, collquecta, a-/pamuai ñispa, mana ima-/llactapas, llamcachiscaiqui/raicu copuspa? /

18. Qullqi, quri q'uyaman runakunakta kachaqchu kanki, "quri, qullqikta apamuway" ñispa, mana imallaktapas llamk'achisqaykirayku qupuspa?

19. Viracochacunap,[14]/ cairi, maicampa collque/ (quepi apac runap, cai-/man, chaiman, chacnaccu/napac, llamacta michec-/pac, cacnimpi llamcac-/cunapachuampas) cos-/canta, huanllacchu canqui?/ llapallâta, cairi, huaquinin-/ta quechupuspa? cairi, tam-/pupipas, runacunap cama-/ricuscanmâta, collq́ vrma/cta, campac ñachu apacoc/ [p. 307] canqui? cairi, cai coll-/quecta aichaspa raquispa,/ asincanhuan, campaccha-/cocchu canqui? /

19. Wiraquchakunap kayri mayqanpa qullqi (q'ipi apaq runap, kayman chayman chaqnaqkunapaq, llamakta michiqpaq, kaqninpi llamk'aqkunapaqwanpas) qusqanta wanllaqchu kanki? llapallanta kayri wakinninta qichupuspa? kayri tampupipas runakunap kamarisqanmanta qullqi urmaqta qampaqñachu apakuq kanki? kayri kay qullqikta aychaspa, rakispa, as inkanwan qampaqchakuqchu kanki?

20. Runaiquicunaman-/ta, collquecta huñuchec/chu canqui, mana caman-/ta cama, llullã ñinacuipac?/ cairi, padre; corregidor/huampas, ñinacuncai-/quipac? haica cutim? hai-/ca chicatac? /

20. Runaykikunamanta qullqikta huñuchiqchu kanki, mana kamanta kama, llulla ñinakuypaq? kayri padre corregidorwanpas ñinakunqaykipaq? hayk'a kutim? hayk'a chikataq?

21. Collque, cori, chacra/man, yuncamampas ca-/chascaiqui runa, huañoc-/chu? cairi, ancha huañoc/ pacha quitiman, runacta/ cachacchu canqui? /

21. Qullqi, quri, chakraman yunkamanpas kachasqayki runa wañuqchu? kayri ancha wañuq pacha k'itiman runakta kachaqchu kanki?

22. Huaca[15] muchaccuna/ sallayoccuna, ama ricuri-/chunchu ñispa, pacachec-/

22. Wak'a much'aqkuna sallayuqkuna, "ama rikhurichunchu" ñispa, pakachiqchu

13 Typesetting error for *sapsi,* a collective name used in the traditional Andean economy for communal property.

14 *Viracochacunap* (*wiraquchakunap* 'of *wiraquchas*'). In Quechua, *Wiraqucha* was a common denomination for Spaniards and, later, creoles. Originally *Wiraqucha* was the name of one of the main Inca deities who, according to early chroniclers, was venerated as a creator of humankind. Apparently, native Andeans started calling Spaniards *wiraqucha* after first contact, taking them for divine creatures, but it is uncertain how this term then became well established in Quechua.

15 *Huaca* (*wak'a*) was a central term in Quechua religious vocabulary that could refer to any deity or to its dwelling place, since in the traditional Andean world-view one was virtually inseparable from the other.

chu canqui? caicunap hu-/chanta yachachcaspa,/ mana yachac tucocchucâ/qui? ima lluqui paillaita-/pas chaçquecchu canqui,/ lluquicocchu canqui, ma-/na anyasca huanachisca/ cancampac? /

kanki? kaykunap huchanta yachachkaspa, mana yachaq tukuqchu kanki? ima lluk'i payllaytapas chazkiqchu kanki, lluk'ikuqchu kanki, mana anyasqa wanachisqa kanqanpaq?

23. Llactaiquipi, chacrai/quipi, mai quitipipas, hua-/cacunacta huacaichacchu/ canqui? laica, vmucunacta/huâpas?[16] imamâta muchus/pa, chai huacacta mucha/occhu rinqui? ima muchus/caiquimanta, haica hucha-/mantahuampas, yanapa-/huaichic ñispa? /

23. Llaqtaykipi, chakraykipi, ima k'itipipas, wak'akunakta waqaychaqchu kanki? layqa umukunaktawanpas? imamanta muchuspa, chay wak'akta much'aqchu rinki? ima muchusqaykimanta, hayk'a huchamantawanpas, "yanapawaychik" ñispa?

24. Suti, pacallapipas, ru-/nacunahuan tantalla vpias/pa, machaspa, ñaupac/ machuiquicunap pacaris-/can taquijta, taquicchu/ canqui?[17] cachuacchu can-/qui?[18] cairi, ima hucha-/ctapas rurachecchu can-/qui? /

24. Sut'i pakallapipas runakunawan tantalla upyaspa, machaspa, ñawpaq machuykikunap paqarisqan takiyta takiqchu kanki? qhachwaqchu kanki? kayri ima huchaktapas rurachiqchu kanki?

25. *Padre*cta llactaiqui-/manta carcuchissac, ñispa/ chussacmanta, chatachec-/chu câqui? cairi caçillamâta/ tumpacchucanqui? ima/ manallimanmi, chaya-/chircanqui, campa tum-/pascaiquimanta, tumpa-/chiscaiquimâtahuampas? /

25. Padrekta llaqtaykimanta, "qarquchisaq" ñispa, ch'usaqmanta ch'atachiqchu kanki? kayri qazillamanta tumpaqchu kanki? ima mana allimanmi chayachirqanki, qampa tumpasqaykimanta, tumpachisqaykimantawanpas?

[p. 308]

---

16 Although Pérez Bocanegra refers to both *layca* (*layqa*) and *umu* as *hechiceros* 'sorcerers', their functions in the preconquest religious hierarchy were more complex; *layqa* corresponded more to 'shaman', while *umu* was probably a more conventional type of priest in the times of the Incas.

17 *Taqui(j)* or *taki* was a ritual practice that combined singing and dancing in preconquest Andean culture. After the rise and subsequent suppression in the 1570s of the spiritual movement known as *taki unquy* 'dancing sickness', the leaders of which opposed Christianization, *takis* were banned by the Church.

18 *Cachua* (*qhachwa*) was the traditional Andean circle dance, which probably had sexual connotations and therefore was not approved of by the Catholic Church.

26. Runaiquicta, llam-/cachispa, imaman cha-/pachispapas, *padre*p, *Co-/regidor*pa, allijninpac pi-/ctapas cussichissacmi ñis-/patac, imallactapas coan-/man, yuyaspapas, *Domin-/go*, *fiesta*cunapi, *Missa*cta,/ *Doctrina*cta,[19] paçuchec-/chu canqui?. /

26. Runaykikta llamk'achispa, imaman chapachispapas, padrep, corregidorpa alliyninpaq, "piktapas kusichisaqmi" ñispapas, "imallaktapas quwanman" yuyaspapas, Domingo fiestakunapi misakta Doctrinakta pazuchiqchu kanki?

27. Runaiquip vssusinta/ yanachacuspa, allcochas-/sac ñecchu câqui? cairi, cai-/cunahuan sallayacocchu/ canqui hai cactam cai hi-/nacta, hatallinqui? /

27. Runaykip ususinta yanachakuspa, "allquchasaq" ñiqchu kanki? kayri kaykunawan sallayakuqchu kanki, hayk'aktam kay hinakta hat'allinki?

28. Pi cari, huarmictapas/ callpamâta, huarmiyachec/ cairi, coçayachecchu can-/qui? coçayacuita munacta-/ri, ama ñecchu câqui, sipa-/ssijquipac, caicunacta mu-/naspa? haica mittam, *casara/*cuncanta[20] collochircâqui. /

28. Pi qhari warmiktapas kallpamanta warmiyachiq kayri quzayachiq kanki? quzayakuyta munaqtari "ama" ñiqchu kanki, sipasiykipaq kaykunakta munaspa? hayk'a mit'am casarakunqanta qulluchirqanki?

29. *Tassa*mâ tumpa runap/ collquenta, tâtachecchucâ/qui? caicollq́ huanri, qui-/quijquipac, mirachicoc-/chu canqui? pampa coll-/quecta, campac apacchu-/ canqui? /

29. Tasaman tumpa runap qullqinta tantachiqchu kanki? kay qullqiwanri kikiykipaq mirachikuqchu kanki? pampa qullqikta qampaq apaqchu kanki?

30. Oncoccunacta, vssu/ricunacta, *tassa* mana côcâ-/ta cocchechu canqui hua/ ciyoc chacrayocmi canqui/ ñispa? mainimpiri, *tassa*cta/ iscai mittapas, chazq́cchu-/palltachu canqui, ma-/ naracmi conquichu ñis-/pa? /

30. Unquqkunakta, usurikunakta, tasa mana qunqanta, quchiqchu kanki, "waziyuq chakrayuqmi kanki" ñispa? mayninpiri, tasakta iskay mit'apas chazkiqchu palltaqchu kanki, "manaraqmi qunkichu" ñispa?

31. Yupasca, yupturasca/ runacta,[21] maicanñin runa-/ctapas pacacchu canqui,/ *tassa* coqueiquipac, yanai-/qui cancampacpas? /

31. Yupasqa, yupturasqa runakta, mayqannin runaktapas pakaqchu kanki, tasa quqiykipaq, yanayki kanqanpaqpas?

19 *Missa* is the Spanish loanword for 'mass'. *Doctrina* here implies doctrinal teachings for the indigenous neophytes, which must have been imparted on a regular basis.

20 *Casaracunca* (*casarakunqa*) 'future marriage' comes from the hybrid verb *casarakuy*, based on the Spanish *casarse* 'marry' and the Quechua reflexive suffix *ku*.

21 *Yupasca* (*yupasqa*) and *yupturasca* (*yupturasqa*) apparently denoted methods by which people were counted before the conquest, while *yupasqa* referred to counting in general, and *yupturasqa* reputedly meant counting by review, in the presence of an inspector (Gonzalez Holguín 1952[1608]: 372, 398).

32. Runaiquicunacta/ mittacuchecchu canqui?/ llamanhuan, cachunhuâ,/ yamtanhuan, imallâhuam/pas, mana mitanan captin. /

32. Runaykimanta mit'akuchiqchu kanki? llamanwan, q'achunwan, yamt'anwan, imallanwanpas mana mit'anan kaptin?

[p. 309]

33. *Iglesia*p, *cofradia*p/ collquenta, imantapas, quechocchu canqui, ca-/ maiquiman yachacuchis-/pa? cairi, *Iglesia*pac, *cofra-/dia*pacpas, chacrachacuscâ/pa collquenta, çuacchu câ/qui? cairi ma? chai collque/huan mirachicocchu can/qui campac. /

33. Iglesiap, cofradiap qullqinta imantapas qichuqchu kanki, kamaykiman yachakuchispa? kayri Iglesiapaq cofradiapaqpas chakrachakusqanpa qullqinta zuwaqchu kanki? kayri má? chay qullqiwan mirachikuqchu kanki, qampaq?

ENGLISH TRANSLATION OF THE PHONEMICIZED QUECHUA TEXT

PREGUNTAS QVE / se an de hazer a los Cu-/racas, &c.

Questions to be directed to kurakas, etc.

1. Kamachisqayki runamanta, chayaqin tasanta yallintawan churaykuchiqchu kanki? chazkiqchu kanki?

1. Do you make the Indians whom you rule, pay the tax owed by them in excess? Do you receive it [in such an amount]?

2. Kay tasakta ña chazkisqaykimanta, zapa terciop kayri watap chayaqinmanta, astawan mañaqchu kanki?

2. Having received this tax, do you ask them for more than they have to pay each quarter or each year?

3. Hayk'aktam yallichispa chazkirqanki?

3. How much have you received in excess?

4. Hayk'a unayñataq zapap chayaqinmanta yalliqinta chazkirqanki?

4. How long then have you now been receiving in excess of the amount that must be paid each period?

5. Chay yallichispa chazkisqaykikta, quripichu qullqipichu? p'achapichu? imana kaq muhupichu, ima-hayk'apipas chazkirqankichu?

5. [Was] this excess that you received in gold or in silver? In clothing? Do you receive it in some kind of seed or anything else?

6. Warmikunamanta, ikma warmikunamanta, thazki ama Mariaman hamuq, mizkaq sipaskunamanta tasakta chazkiqchu kanki?

6. Do you receive tax from women, widows, girls younger than Maria's age at the time of the Annunciation and girls who are precociously in the full bloom of youth?

7. Machu runakunamanta, pichqa chunka watamanta yalliq runakunamantapas, tasakta chazkiqchu kanki, kayri maqt'a, manaraq chunka puzaqiyuq wataman chayaqkunamanta, unay zukzuq, unquqkunamantawanpas tasakta chazkiqchu kanki? kayri tasamanta ña lluqsiqmanta, chazkiqtaqchu kanki?

7. Do you receive tax from old people or from those over fifty years of age? Do you receive tax from juveniles under the age of eighteen and from the very sick and feeble? Or do you receive tax from those already exempt from tax?

8. Kay hinakunamanta zaranta, china atawallpanta, pullitunta, ima kaqllantapas, runtunta, q'achunta qichuqchu kanki, "tasapaqmi" ñispa? kayri, "tasakta hunt'achinqanpaq, ima kaqpaqpas" ñispa?

8. Do you take away their maize, hens, chickens, whatever they have, their eggs, their fodder, saying that it is for the tax? Or saying that it is for completion of the tax or for something else?

9. "Tasapaqmi" ñispa, vacanta, yapuq vacanta, qillay takllanta, imantapas qichupuqchu kanki? kayri, ña chayaqinta quptin, p'achakta qichuqchu kanki?

9. Do you take away their cows, bullocks, iron ploughs, or anything else, saying that it is for the tax? Or, after they have already given what they had to, do you take away clothing?

10. Runap ñak'aymana tarisqanta, qullqinta, imantapas qichupuqchu kanki? kayri, yunkaman mink'ay tukuspa, chakrakunamanpas rispa, tarisqanta qichupuqtaqchu kanki? kayri, q'ipi apasqanmanta, pampa tiyaykuq risqanmanta, "tasapaqmi" ñispa, qampaqchakuspaña, hillupuqchu kanki? kayri, kayhina llamk'aykunapi tarisqanmanta, "as inka quway" ñispa, kamachiqchu kanki, mañaqchu kanki?

10. Do you take away what your people earned by hard work, be it money or something else? Or do you take away what they had earned by hiring themselves out in the lowlands or by going out into the fields? Or do you steal, adding to your possessions, what they earned working as carriers or market vendors, saying that it was for the tax? Or do you order them or ask them to give you a share of what they earned by working this way?

11. Runaykikunamanta qurikta, qullqikta, p'achakta, llamakta, imaymana-hayk'aymanaktapas kallpamanta qichuqchu kanki?

11. Do you take away by force gold, silver, clothing, llamas, or anything else from your men?

12. Waziykikta wazichakuptin, chakraykikta llamk'aptin, huywaykikta michiptin, imapipas runaykikta llamk'achispapas, chayaqinta, hump'in t'uqinta payllapuqchu kanki? kayri manachu?

12. Do you pay your men what they are due for their toil and moil when they build you a house, or till your fields, or graze your cattle, or do any work by your order? Or do you not?

13. Runaykip tasanta huñuspa, chayaqinmanta astawan mañapuqchu kanki? kayri, tasakta mirachiqchu kanki? chay mirayninta, puchunta qampaq, "ña apakusaq" ñispa?

13. Collecting tax from your Indians, do you ask them to pay more than they are obliged to? Or do you increase the tax? Do you decide to take the excess, the profit for yourself?

14. Qamman chapachisqa runakta kamachiqchu kanki, "quri, qullqikta, imaktapas kamaripuway" ñispa?

14. Do you order the men who were brought into your possession to bring you gold, silver, or anything else?

15. Hukpa chiqanpi kuraka kanqanta llulla ñinakuywan qichupurqankichu, kay huchapaq runap qullqinta tantachispataq? kayri yayayki, machuyki, Inqa pachamanta kurakachu karqan? hinaspa rantinpi qamchu kuraka sayanki?

15. Did you take the position of a *kuraka* from somebody who must rightfully be a *kuraka*, by unfair claim, collecting people's money under that pretense? Or was your father or grandfather a *kuraka* from the times of the Incas? And so it is you who stands in his place?

16. Chakraykikta llamk'aq chakrachakuq runa, llamaykikta michiqpas, Inqa pachamanta, mit'akuqiykipaq kamachisqachu? kayri visitadorpa, "mana" ñispa, mayqan apuppas kamachisqanchu? kayri kallpamanta llamk'achisqaykichu?

16. Have the men who work in your fields or graze your llamas been ordered to work there by turns since the times of the Incas? Or were they ordered to do so by an inspector or another official? Or do you make them work for you by force?

17. Chakraykiri machuykimanta, yayaykimanta kaqchu? kayri runakunamanta, payakunamanta hillusqaykichu? kayri má, mana runa maziyuqña, ña wañuqkunap haqisqan kanchu? kayri pampa, sapsi ñisqa, chakraktachu kikiykipaqña tarpukunkichu?

17. And [regarding] your fields, do you have them from your father or grandfather? Or do you steal them from the people or old women? Or tell me, were they left from deceased people who did not have relatives? Or do you sow the fields which are communal property for yourself?

18. Qullqi, quri q'uyaman runakunakta kachaqchu kanki, "quri, qullqikta apamuway" ñispa, mana imallaktapas llamk'achisqaykirayku qupuspa?

18. Do you order the men whom you send to the gold or silver mines to bring you gold or silver from there, without giving them anything for the work they did for you?

19. Wiraquchakunap kayri mayqanpa qullqi (q'ipi apaq runap, kayman chayman chaqnaqkunapaq, llamakta michiqpaq, kaqninpi llamk'aqkunapaqwanpas) qusqanta wanllaqchu kanki? llapallanta kayri wakinninta qichupuspa? kayri tampupipas runakunap kamarisqanmanta qullqi urmaqta qampaqñachu apakuq kanki? kayri kay qullqikta aychaspa, rakispa, as inkanwan qampaqchakuqchu kanki?

19. Do you steal the money given by Spaniards or somebody else for the carriers, the mule drivers, the herdsmen, or the estate workers? Do you take everything or part of it by force? Or do you take the money left to the people in road inns for their services? Or when you divide up and split this money, do you add a small part of it to your possessions?

20. Runaykikunamanta qullqikta huñuchiqchu kanki, mana kamanta kama, llulla ñinakuypaq? kayri padre corregidorwanpas ñinakunqaykipaq? hayk'a kutim? hayk'a chikataq?

20. Do you collect money from your people not for a just purpose, but for a false claim? Or in order to enter into a dispute with the priest or the *corregidor*? How many times [have you done that]? How much [have you collected]?

21. Qullqi, quri, chakraman yunkamanpas kachasqayki runa wañuqchu? kayri ancha wañuq pacha k'itiman runakta kachaqchu kanki?

21. Have any of the men died whom you sent to the gold or silver mines, or to the lowlands? Or do you send people to life-threatening places?

22. Wak'a much'aqkuna sallayuqkuna, "ama rikhurichunchu" ñispa, pakachiqchu kanki? kaykunap huchanta yachachkaspa, mana yachaq tukuqchu kanki? ima lluk'i payllaytapas chazkiqchu kanki, lluk'ikuqchu kanki, mana anyasqa wanachisqa kanqanpaq?

22. Do you order the concealment of idolaters and adulterers, so that nobody will see them? Do you pretend to be ignorant, while being aware of their sins? What bribe do you get and then conceal, so that they will remain blameless and impenitent?

23. Llaqtaykipi, chakraykipi, ima k'itipipas, wak'akunakta waqaychaqchu kanki? layqa umukunaktawanpas? imamanta muchuspa, chay wak'akta much'aqchu rinki? ima muchusqaykimanta, hayk'a huchamantawanpas, "yanapawaychik" ñispa?

23. Do you keep any *wak'as* in your village, in your fields, or in other places? Or do you harbor shamans and sorcerers? If you experience any trouble, do you go to worship these *wak'as*? For what troubles or what necessities do you approach *wa'kas*, asking them to help you?

24. Sut'i pakallapipas runakunawan tantalla upyaspa, machaspa, ñawpaq machuykikunap paqarisqan takiyta takiqchu kanki? qhachwaqchu kanki? kayri ima huchaktapas rurachiqchu kanki?

24. Do you perform *taki*, which were customary for your ancestors, while drinking and getting drunk together with your people, either openly or secretly? Do you take part in *qhachwa*? Or do you make [the people] commit any [such] sins?

25. Padrekta llaqtaykimanta, "qarquchisaq" ñispa, ch'usaqmanta ch'atachiqchu kanki? kayri qazillamanta tumpaqchu kanki? ima mana allimanmi chayachirqanki, qampa tumpasqaykimanta, tumpachisqaykimantawanpas?

25. Do you make false accusations against the priest, intending to expel him from your village? Or do you slander [him]? Did you cause [him] any harm, or was harm done [to him] because of your slander, or because you encouraged somebody to slander [him]?

26. Runaykikta llamk'achispa, imaman chapachispapas, padrep, corregidorpa alliyninpaq, "piktapas kusichisaqmi" ñispapas, "imallaktapas quwanman" yuyaspapas, Domingo fiestakunapi misakta Doctrinakta pazuchiqchu kanki?

26. Do you cause your people to miss Christian teachings and masses on Sundays and holidays, making them work or occupying them in something for the benefit of a priest or *corregidor*, bearing in mind that if you make him happy, he will also give you something [in return]?

27. Runaykip ususinta yanachakuspa, "allquchasaq" ñiqchu kanki? kayri kaykunawan sallayakuqchu kanki,

27. Do you make your peoples' daughters your lovers, intending to mess around[22] with them? Or do you commit adultery

22 The phrase in Quechua literally means 'to mess about with' and it can have the same sexual connotation as 'to mess around with' in English.

hayk'aktam kay hinakta hat'allinki?

with them? How many did you take advantage of?

28. Pi qhari warmiktapas kallpamanta warmiyachiq kayri quzayachiq kanki? quzayakuyta munaqtari "ama" ñiqchu kanki, sipasiykipaq kaykunakta munaspa? hayk'a mit'am casarakunqanta qulluchirqanki?

28. Do you make any man or woman marry by force? Do you impede girls who want to marry, because you want them to become your mistresses? How many times did you break their engagements?

29. Tasaman tumpa runap qullqinta tantachiqchu kanki? kay qullqiwanri kikiykipaq mirachikuqchu kanki? pampa qullqikta qampaq apaqchu kanki?

29. Do you allegedly collect people's money for the tax and instead enrich yourself with this money? Do you take the communal money for yourself?

30. Unquqkunakta, usurikunakta, tasa mana qunqanta, quchiqchu kanki, "waziyuq chakrayuqmi kanki" ñispa? mayninpiri, tasakta iskay mit'apas chazkiqchu palltaqchu kanki, "manaraqmi qunkichu" ñispa?

30. Do you collect tax from the sick and the disabled, who are not obliged to pay tax, saying that they still have homes and fields? Do you sometimes collect or demand that tax be paid twice, saying that [the taxpayers] have not yet paid?

31. Yupasqa, yupturasqa runakta, mayqannin runaktapas pakaqchu kanki, tasa quqiykipaq, yanayki kanqanpaqpas?

31. Do you conceal any people who are counted and registered by authorities, so that they will pay tax only to you and become your serfs?

32. Runaykimanta mit'akuchiqchu kanki? llamanwan, q'achunwan, yamt'anwan, imallanwanpas mana mit'anan kaptin?

32. Do you make your people give you *mit'a*? [Do you make them give you *mit'a*] with their llamas, fodder, wool, or anything else when they do not have to give you *mit'a*?

33. Iglesiap, cofradiap qullqinta imantapas qichuqchu kanki, kamaykiman yachakuchispa? kayri Iglesiapaq cofradiapaqpas chakrachakusqanpa qullqinta zuwaqchu kanki? kayri má? chay qullqiwan mirachikuqchu kanki, qampaq?

33. Do you take money or anything else that belongs to the Church or the confraternities, using it for your own needs? Or do you steal the money gained from the fields of the Church or the confraternities? Or do you enrich yourself with that money?

The *Ritual formulario e institución de curas*[23] was written by the Franciscan cleric Juan Pérez Bocanegra, who lived and worked in colonial Peru in the first half of the seventeenth century. At the time of the publication of his writing, Pérez Bocanegra was a parish priest in Andahuaylillas, a town near the

23 The full title is *Ritual formulario e institución de curas, para administrar a los naturales de este reino los santos Sacramentos del Bautismo, Confirmación, Eucaristía y Viático, Penitencia, Extremaunción y Matrimonio, con advertencias muy necesarias.*

city of Cuzco. The *Ritual formulario* is a work of immense size, containing more than 720 pages of text in Spanish and Quechua, which makes it the most extensive compilation of Quechua missionary literature of the colonial period. It is primarily designed to instruct clerics how to administer the holy sacraments of the Catholic Church among the native Andean population; thus, the Spanish text of the *Ritual formulario* is largely addressed to the clergy, while the parts in Quechua show how a priest should translate the canon and explain the rituals to indigenous neophytes.

More than half of the *Ritual formulario* is dedicated to the sacrament of penance, and to the ritual of confession in particular. Given the multiple differences that exist between the traditional Andean moral code and the Catholic vision of sin and virtue, it is not surprising that Pérez Bocanegra considered this part the most important. In addition to general reprehensions against mortal sins and against those who commit them and violate the holy commandments, the chapter on penance contains a long series of questions that priests direct to confessants. With these questions, the author tried to embrace virtually all of the aspects of social life in contemporary Peru, taking care that any mundane situation that could serve as a ground for sinning would not be left unexamined. Thus, Pérez Bocanegra could not help but refer to many traditional economic, social, and religious practices of the indigenous people of the Andes that were considered sinful or at least deserving of the Church's attention. Therefore, the confessors' questions themselves contain valuable information about native Andean customs, both before and under colonial rule, including a vast number of terms from the preconquest cultural lexicon of the region, some of which are not commonly mentioned, if at all, in other sources.

Although the questions are written in two languages, the Quechua version sometimes differs considerably from the Spanish one. Pérez Bocanegra was highly proficient in what was then termed "the general language of the Incas"—that is, the variety of Quechua spoken in the highlands of Southern Peru. He sought to use all the lexical and morphosyntactic richness of the language (which was not typical for those who wrote ecclesiastical texts in Quechua prior to Pérez Bocanegra), so it is common to find the Quechua version of a given fragment more verbose and even more exquisite than its Spanish equivalent.

The fragment presented in this chapter is only an excerpt from the questions asked of confessants in order to ascertain whether they have broken the Seventh and Tenth Commandments, "Thou shalt not steal" and "Thou shalt not covet." In addition to those posed to *kurakas* and *mandones* 'overseers', there are questions addressed to representatives of a number of other professions that indigenous people practiced at that time. The "Questions to *Kurakas*" immediately follow the first general set of questions, probably because *kuraka* was the highest social position that an indigenous person could occupy in colonial Peru.

Kuraka originally was a local indigenous leader, whose authority could either extend over a whole region or encompass a single village. Notwithstanding, in the time of the colony the Spanish often used the term to refer to any indigenous leader, ignoring the complexity of the Inca social and political system. The etymology of the word *kuraka* is not entirely clear. It could be paronymous with *kuraq* 'elder [son/daughter]' in Quechua (Gonzalez Holguín 1952 [1608]: 56), but in this case the last syllable *ka* should be considered a derivational suffix, the function of which is uncertain. The possibility that *kuraka* might originally come from another language, not of the Quechua family, cannot be ruled out.

In the days of the Inca empire *kurakas* were subordinated to imperial authorities but were not appointed by them; the Inca rulers, when conquering new lands, usually did not attempt to destroy local chiefdoms, solely demanding that their *kurakas* become loyal subjects of the empire and profess the Sun as the principal deity (Inca Garcilaso de la Vega 2009 [1609]: 145). Spanish colonial authorities in effect borrowed this pattern, only now *kurakas* had to become Christians in order to retain their rule, and they now answered to Spanish officials as they had earlier answered to inspectors and accountants sent to their land by the Incas.

According to the analyzed fragment, it was necessary for an interrogator to find out if a respondent inherited his *curacazgo* (the title and possessions of a *kuraka*) legally or if he received it as a result of an 'unfair dispute' *llulla ñinakuy*.[24] If the father (*yaya*) or grandfather (*machu*) of a confessing *kuraka* were themselves *kurakas* before the Spanish conquest, a respondent was considered a lawful holder of his position; even if traditionally there were other legitimate ways to obtain *kuraka* leadership, the colonial authorities did not recognize them. Pérez Bocanegra then uses the following phrase: "And so you stand in his place [as] kuraka?"

---

24 Here the Quechua expression is actually a calque from Spanish: *llulla* means 'false' or 'lying', while *ñi-na-ku-y* means 'to say something to each other', which could also mean 'conversation' or 'discussion', but not 'lawsuit', to which *pleito* in the parallel Spanish text corresponds.

hinaspa	*rantimpi*	*camchu*	*curaca*	*sayanqui?*
hinaspa	ranti-n-pi	qam-chu	kuraka	saya-nki?
and so	substitute–3POSS-LOC	you-INT	kuraka	stand–2SG.SUBJ

The verbal root *saya* generally means 'to stand' or 'to rise' in a physical sense, and here we can assume that *rantinpi kuraka saya-* was a stable expression, denoting the succession of leadership.

We encounter another word related to traditional elite terminology, namely *apu*, in the phrase from the following section: "or [was it] ordered by some lord?"

maycan,	*apuppas*	*camachiscanchu*
mayqan	apu-p-pas	kamachi-sqa-n-chu
any	lord-GEN-AD	order-PP–3POSS-INT

In the preconquest Inca hierarchy, the *apu* represented the highest stratum of elites. They were military leaders or they occupied central positions in the imperial administration and usually were related to the Inca himself. However, in this particular excerpt *apu* is used to denote a colonial official, whose authority was higher than that of an indigenous leader, following the same pattern as during the rule of the Incas, in which *apu* were mightier than *kurakas*. In the *Ritual formulario, apu* could mean, for example, a *visitador* 'royal inspector', who regularly came to examine the state of affairs in the village(s) controlled by a *kuraka* and had the authority to interfere in these affairs. Thus, the traditional terminology eventually came to serve the new order and its new hierarchy.

In the studied fragment we also find a number of terms corresponding to different degrees of subordination of the common indigenous population to *kurakas*, as evidenced in that period. First, it is the word *kamachisqa*, a passive participle from the verb *kamachi-* 'to rule' or 'to command,' literally 'under control'. Any person, who lived in the territory possessed by a *kuraka* fell into this category. These were people who were obliged to pay taxes, to or through the *kuraka*, and on whom a *kuraka* also could rely in the case of necessity, since together they formed one ethnocultural entity. There is another term, *chapachisqa*, a passive participle from the verb *chapachi*, that is found in the following phrase: "Do you give orders to the people who were made your possession?"

Cammâ	*chapachisca*	*runacta,*	*camachecchu*	*canqui*
Qam-man	chapa-chi-sqa	runa-kta	kamachi-q-chu	ka-nki
you-ALL	possess-CAUS-PP	people-ACC	order-AG-INT	be–2SG.SUBJ

Chapachi- actually means 'transfer to someone's possession', and it is mentioned that the people were transferred to a *kuraka*'s ownership. If in fact people could be transferred from one owner to another, *chapachisqa* may represent another, stronger type of subordination than *kamachisqa*. *Chapachisqa runa* could be in fact *yanakuna* (*yana* 'black', *kuna* [plural]), people who practically had the status of serfs. The institution of *yanakuna* existed in the central Andes long before the arrival of Europeans and their system of *encomiendas*. In the cited fragment there is no direct reference to *yanakuna*, but there is the paronymous word, *yanachakuspa* 'turning somebody into *yana*'. However, since it is mentioned with respect to the daughters of the people under a *kuraka*'s rule in the context of sexual relations, *yana* here may well correspond not to 'serf' but to its second meaning, 'lover', attested in the Quechua varieties of Southern Peru and Bolivia (Cerrón-Palomino 1994: 84; Laime-Ajacopa 2007: 138). The term *mit'akuq* also denotes a type of subordination specific to the central Andes, *mit'a*. In the Inca period, or perhaps even earlier, *mit'a* was labor or tribute in material goods, carried out in turns for the imperial or local authorities; those who did *mit'a* could expect various benefits in return for their contribution. During the colonial period, *mit'a* lost its initial meaning and became the name for the system of cheap, forced labor, by which the indigenous population could be massively recruited for work in the mines far away from their native region, often without the possibility of returning. Interestingly, in this fragment of the *Ritual formulario*, *mit'akuq* (a *mit'a* worker) is used in its original sense, as someone who has to provide *mit'a* for a *kuraka* as arranged from the days of the Incas.

In the end, it is worth mentioning that although the "Questions to be Directed to *Kurakas*" are related to the Seventh Commandment, there are also sections in which a priest tries to find out more information about the involvement of a *kuraka* in "pagan" rituals (23, 24), in his relations with women (27, 28), or for example, if a *kuraka* brought false accusations against a priest (25). In the parts dedicated to such commandments as "Thou shalt have no other gods" or "Thou shalt not commit adultery" there are separate sets of questions to be directed to *kurakas*. We can assume that this large concentration of multiple types of questions for *kurakas* was made for the convenience of a confessor. Since the *kurakas* stood out from the indigenous masses, they required a special approach on the part of the Church, and for this reason, special tactics of confession were applied in their case.

DOCUMENT 35

Ritual formulario e institución de curas of Juan Pérez Bocanegra, 1631

Confession of Indigenous Notaries

JAN SZEMIŃSKI

ENGLISH TRANSLATION OF THE SPANISH TEXT

[p. 277]

PREGVNTAS QVE ſe an de hazer a los Indios eſcriuanos.	*Questions that the Indian notaries should be asked*
1 As hecho algun teſtamento falſo? hiziſtelo por que te lo mandò el Padre, S 3 ó el [p. 278] ò el Corregidor, ó el Curaca, el marido, ó la muger del enfermo, ó otra perſona? que te dieron porque lo hizieſſes falſamente?	1. Have you written any false wills? Have you written it by order of the priest (*padre*), the *corregidor*, or the *kuraka,* or the husband, or the ill person's wife, or someone else? What did they give you for writing it falsely?
2 En los teſtamêtos que as hecho, as pueſto mas, ò menos, de lo que dixo, ò mandò el que haze el teſtamento?	2. In the wills that you have written, have you added or deleted anything from what the person who made the will ordered?
3 As trasladado el teſtamento, deſpues de auer muerto, el que teſtò, quitâdo, ò poniendo lo que te pareció? quitaſte delas Miſſas, ò poſſas, ò otras qualeſquier mandas pias, parte, ò algo desto? ó algunas deudas, que deuieſſe, o reſtituciones, q' mandaſſe hazer?	3. Have you rewritten the will after the testator's death, removing or adding or writing whatever you considered appropriate? Have you reduced the masses and peals of bells, or any other pious bequests, writing only a portion or part of them? Or some debts that he or she had, or restitutions he or she ordered made?

DOI: 10.5876/9781607328346.c035

4 As aconſejado al enfermo, que no dexe nada para ſu alma? ó que no ponga enel teſtamento, lo que le deuen, ò el deue?

4. Have you counseled the ill person not to leave anything for his or her soul? Or not to mention in the will what people owe him or her, or what he or she owes?

5 A quitado por conſejo tuyo, el padre, ò la madre, lo que le venia de derecho, a ſu hijo, ó hija? ò el marido a la muger ò a quitado el hijo, ó hija, lo que de derecho le venia a ſu padre, ò madre, por conſejo tuyo?

5. Because of your counsel, has a father or a mother removed what was due to his or her son or daughter? Or the husband to his wife? Or has a son or daughter removed what was due to his or her father or mother, because of your counsel?

6 as aconſejado, ò perſuadido al enfermo, que te dexe a ti ſu hazienda, teniêdo padre, ó madre, hijos, ó deudos? ò que dexe al Padre, ó al Curaca ſu hazienda, ó otras perſonas? ò q' no pague, ò no cobre ſus deudas?

6. Have you counseled or persuaded an ill person to leave his or her possessions to you, even though he or she has a father, a mother, children, and relatives? Or to leave his or her possessions to the priest, or to the *kuraka*, or to anyone else? Or not to pay his or her debts, or not to collect them.

7 Puſiſte mas Miſſas, ó mas poſſas, mas Vigilias, ò mas ofrêdas de las que mâda el teſtador? ò las MIſſas q' manda q' ſean rezadas, puſiſtelas por cantadas? ò las Miſſas câtadas, por rezadas todo por dar contento al Cura, ò porque te dio algo? Que te dio? quantas vezes as hecho eſto?

7. Did you write down more masses, more peals, or more offerings than what was ordered by the testator? Or did you write that masses ordered recited should instead be chanted, or that chanted masses should instead be recited, in order to make the priest happy, or because he gave you something? What did he give you? How many times have you done such things?

Eſcreuiſte

[p. 279]

8 Eſcreuiſte demanera el teſtamento, que por no lo ſaber eſcreuir, ó por no ſaber eſcreuir lo que el teſtador dezia, ſe ſiguieron algunos pleytos, en q' gaſtaron los herederos ſu plata, ò les vino algun daño? quâtos teſtamêtos hiziſte deſta suerte? a quantos hiziſte gaſtar deſta manera ſu hazienda, que tâta gaſtaron? que daño les vino?

8. Did you write any wills in such a way that any lawsuits arose in which the heirs spent their money, or suffered damages, either because you don't know to write wills or because you did not know to write what the testator said? How many wills like this have you written? How many people have you caused to spend their resources in such a way? How much did they spend? What damage did they suffer?

9 Eſtando ſin juyzio el enfermo, hiziſte que hizieſſe teſtamento, como ſi eſtuuieſſe en ſu entero juyzio? ò as hecho algun teſtamento deſpuesde ya muerto el enfermo?

9. When an ill person was not of sound mind, did you write the will as if he or she was in complete possession of his or her faculties? Or have you written a will after the sick person was already dead?

10 Pagandote tu taſſa la comunidad, ó estando reſeruado de taſſa, ó de ſeruicios perſonales, por ſolo que acudas a hazer los teſtamentos, ó porque eſcriuas otras coſas tocantes al pueblo, ò Cofradias as lleuado dineros, ropa, carneros, ò otras coſas?

10. When the whole community has paid your tax, or when you were exempted from tax or forced labor so that you could be free to write wills, or so that you could write other things concerning the town or the confraternities, have you recieved money, clothing, llamas, or anything else?

11 Que tanto te an dado? ó que tanto les as lleuado, ò quitado? a quâtas perſonas? que tantas vezes?

11. How much have they given you? Or how much have you received or taken? From how many people? How many times?

12 As pueſto en algun teſtamento, vna coſa por otra, porque te cohecharon? Que te mandò el teſtador que eſcriuieſſes? y que eſcriuiſte tu? A quien vino eſſe daño? en que câtidad? As hecho eſto muchas vezes? que tantas? en quantos teſtamentos as hecho eſſo?

12. Did you substitute one thing for another in a will because someone bribed you? What did the testator order you to write? And what did you write? Who was hurt by that? How much money was the damage? Have you done this many times? How many? In how many wills you have done these things?

13 Siendo tu eſcriuano del pueblo, y ſiêdo reſeruado para hazer eſte oficio, llamandote para hazer algun teſtamêto, as dexado de ir, deſuerte, que murieſſe algun Indio, ó India, ſin ordenar ſu teſtamêto por culpa tuya?

S 4 As

13. Given that you are a town notary, and that you have been exempted from other duties, have you ever been summoned to write a will, refused to go, and as a result, has an Indian man or woman died without ordering his will, and you are to blame?

[p. 280]

14 As eſcondido algun teſtamento, ò as lo roto, y por eſto dexo alguno de auer lo que heredaua? ó dexaron de cumplirſe algunas mâdas pias, ó pagarſe algunas deudas?

14. Have you hidden or torn up any will so that, as a result, someone did not gain his or her inheritance? Or some pious bequests were not fulfilled, or debts were not paid?

The *Ritual formulario e institución de curas* was written in both Spanish and Quechua. The original Spanish text and its English translation above can be compared with the original Quechua text and its translation below. Certainly, the translator adapted his Quechua translation to the necessities of his Quechua-speaking brethren, but the Spanish original was itself adapted to specific, local conditions, so it conceivably corresponded better to what the sins of a *kuraka*, an Andean administrator, might well have been, including his opportunities to steal and to force his subjects to serve him in ways not permitted by law or by Christian morals.[1]

1 See Document 34.

TWO ORTHOGRAPHIC VERSIONS OF THE QUECHUA TEXT

We have chosen to provide two orthographic versions of the Quechua text below because we wish to call attention to the problems faced by researchers who must reconstruct the phonemes in Quechua texts in order to understand the meanings correctly.

[p. 317]

A LOS INDIOS EScriuanos

1 Llulla *tesʃtamento*cta, quellcacchucanqui? *Padre*p, patachacpa, Curacap, camachijninmantachu, quellcarcanqui? oncoc huarmip coçampa camachijninmantachu? cairi oncoc carip huarmimpa, camachijninmantachu, quellcarcanqui? cairi, maicampa camachijninmantachu? cai hina llullacta, quellcancaiquipac, imactam chazquircanqui

1. ¿Llulla testamentokta qillqaqchu kanki? ¿Padrep, p'atachaqpa, kurakap kamachiyninmantachu qillqarqanki? ¿Unquq warmip quzanpa kamachiyninmantachu? ¿Kayri unquq qharip warminpa kamachiyninmantachu qillqarqanki? ¿Kayri mayqanpa kamachiyninmantachu? ¿Kay hina llullakta qillqanqaykipaq imaktam chazkirqanki?

2 *Teʃtamento* quellcaʃcaiquipi, *teʃtamento*cta quellcachecpa camachijninmanta yallichecchu, cairi piʃʃipachecchu canqui?

2. ¿Testamento qillqasqaykipi testamentokta qillqachiqpa kamachiyninmanta yallichiqchu, kayri pisipachiqchu kanki?

3 *Teʃtamento*cta quellcachec, ña huañuptin, *teʃtamento*cta, hucmanchacchu canqui, huañocpa camachijninmanta, munainijqui raiculla, imallactapas yapaʃpa: piʃʃipachiʃpapas? cairi *Miʃʃa*cunamanta, çamachinamanta, ima alli camachiʃcanmanta, maicantapas, piʃʃipichu quellcarcanqui maicanllanta, asllantapas, quellcaʃpa? manucaʃcantari, manachu quellcarcanqui? cairi, ma? hiticaʃcaita, cutichipuiñiʃcanta, manatacchu quellcarcanqui? cairi *teʃtamento*manta picharcanquichu?

3.¿Testamentokta qillqachiq ña wañuptin testamentocta hukmanchaqchu kanki wañuqpa kamachiyninmanta munayniyki raykulla imallaktapas yapaspa pisipachispapas? ¿Kayri misakunamanta, zamachinamanta, ima alli kamachisqanmanta mayqantapas pisipichu qillqarqanki mayqanllanta asllantapas qillqaspa? ¿Manusqantari manachu qillqarqanki? ¿Kayri ma? ¿"Hitikasqayta kutichipuy" ñisqanta manataqchu qillqarqanki? ¿Kayri testamentomanta picharqankichu?

4 *Teʃtamento*cta quellcaʃpa, oncocta cunac, villacchu canqui ama *anima*iquipac, imallactapas, haqueichu ñiʃpa? ama manuʃcaiquicta, manuiquictapas, quellcachijchu ñiʃpa, villacchu canqui?

4. ¿Testamentokta qillqaspa unquqta kunaq willaqchu kanki "ama animaykipaq imallaktapas haqiychu" ñispa? ¿"Ama manusqaykikta manuykiktapas qillqachiychu" ñispa willaqchu kanki?

Mai-

[p. 318]

5 Maican cari, huarmipas, churimpa checa chayaquenta, huahuampa, checa chayaquentapas, cairi, huarmimpa, checa chayaquenta, coçampa chayaquentapas, quechurcâchu *teſtamento*mpi, campa villacuiñijquimanta? cairi, yayampa mamampa chayaquenta, maicâ cari, huarmipas, quechocchu *teſtamento*mpi campa cunacuiñijquimanta?

5. ¿Mayqan qhari warmipas churinpa chiqa chayaqinta wawanpa chiqa chayaqintapas, kayri warminpa chiqa chayaqinta quzanpa chayaqintapas qichurqanchu testamentonpi qampa willakuyñiykimanta? ¿Kayri, yayanpa mamanpa chayaqinta mayqan qhari warmipas qichuqchu testamentonpi qampa kunakuyñiykimanta?

6 Oncocta villapayacchu, cunacchucanqui, ñocapac ima haicaiquicta haquehuai ñiſpa, yayayoc, mamayoc, churiyoc, runamaciyoc captintac? cairi *padre*pac curacapac, pipacpas, ima haicaiquicta haquei ñiſpa villacchu canqui? cairi, ama manuiquicta, puchucaichu manuſcaiquictapas, ama chazquijchu ñiſpa villac, cunactacchu canqui?

6. ¿Unquqta willapayaqchu kunaqchu kanki "ñuqapaq ima hayk'aykikta haqiway" ñispa, yayayuq mamayuq churiyuq runa maziyuq kaptintaq? ¿Kayri, "padrepaq kurakapaq pipaqpas ima hayk'aykikta haqiy" ñispa willaqchu kanki? ¿Kayri, "ama manuykikta p'uchukaychu, manusqaykiktapas ama chazkiychu" ñispa willaq kunaqtaqchu kanki?

7 *Teſtamento*cta quellcachecpa camachijninmanta, yallin ashuan *Miſſa*cta, camachinacta,[2] *vigilia*cta, ima cocui *offrenda*ctapas, quellcarcâquichu? cairi, *rezada Miſſa*cta *cantada*man ñachu, quellcac canqui? *cantada*ctapas, *rezada*manña quellcac canqui, munaininta mana yupaſpa, *padre*cta cuſſichincaiquipac? cairi imallactapas paimanta chazquiſcaiquimantachu? villahuai ari, imactam coſſunqui, haica mittatac cai hinacta rurarcanqui?

7. ¿Testamentokta qillqachiqpa kamachiyninmanta yallin aswan misakta zamachinakta vigiliakta ima qukuy ofrendaktapas qillqarqankichu? ¿Kayri rezada misakta kantadamanñachu qillqaq kanki, cantadaktapas rezadamanña qillqaq kanki munayninta mana yupaspa padrekta kusichinqaykipaq, kayri imallaktapas paymanta chazkisqaykimantachu? Willaway-ari, ¿imaktam qusunki? ¿Hayk'a mit'ataq kay hinakta rurarqanki?

8 *Teſtamento*cta, manalli quellcaita yachaſcaiquimanta, cairi, *teſtamento* quellcachecpa, munainin, mana chaicama quellcaſscaiquimanta, ima huchapas hatarircanchu, checan chazqueccunacacnin

8. Testamentokta mana alli qillqayta yachasqaykimanta, kayri testamento qillqachiqpa munaynin mana chay kama qillqasqaykimanta ima huchapas hatarirqanchu chiqan chazkiqkuna kaqninta

2 Typesetting error for *çamachinacta.*

ta

[p. 319] ta vçuchincâcupac haica *teſtamento*ctam, cai hinacta quellcarcanqui, haica runap cacnintam, vçuchircanqui? haicacta ñatacmi, vcuchircancu?[3] ima manallimanmi, chayarcâcu?	uzuchinqankupaq. ¿Hayk'a testamentoktam kay hinakta qillqarqanki? ¿Hayk'aktañataqmi uzuchirqanku? ¿Ima mana allimanmi chayarqanku?
9 Oncoc yuyannac ñacaptin, yuyayniyoc hinactachu, *teſtamento*cta quellcarcanqui? cairi, ña huañuptintac, *teſtamento*cta quellcacchu câqui, cauçachcaptin racmi, quellcarcani ñiſspa?	9. ¿Unquq yuyannaqña kaptin yuyayniyuq hinaktachu testamentokta qillqarqanki? ¿Kayri, ña wañuptintaq testamentokta qillqaqchu kanki "Kawzachkaptinraqmi qillqarqani" ñispa?
10 Llactâtin *taſſa*iquicta coptin, cairi, *taſſa*mâta, horcoſca captijquipas, chunca chaimanta, yupacuimanta horcoſca captijquitac *teſtamêto*cunacta, quellcâcaiquipac, cairi, llactap, ima huchantapas quellcancaiquipac, *cofradia*cunapacpas, collquecta, pachacta llamacta, imallactapas, apachcu mañacchu canqui?	10. ¿Llaqtantin tasaykikta quptin, kayri, tasamanta hurqusqa kaptiykipas, chunkachaymanta yupakuymanta hurqusqa kaptiykitaq testamentokunakta qillqanqaykipaq, kayri, llaqtap ima huchantapas qillqanqaykipaq cofradiakunapaqpas, qullqikta, p'achakta, llamakta, imallaktapas apaqchu mañaqchu kanki?
11 Haicactam coſſunqui? camri cana, haicactam hillupurcanqui, quechupurcanqui? haica runactam hinarcanqui? haica çutiñatac?	11. ¿Hayk'aktam qusunki? ¿Qamri kana[4] hayk'aktam hillupurqanki qichupurqqanki? ¿Hayk'a runaktam hinarqanki? ¿Hayk'a kutiñataq?
12 *Teſtamêto*cta quellcaſpa, hucta churanaiquipichu, hucta ñatac churarcanqui, lluquipaillai raycu? *teſtamento*cta quellcachec, imactam quellcai ñiſpa, camachiſſurcâqui? camri cana, imactam quellcarcanqui? pantacta quellcaſcaiqui raicu, pictam raicurcanqui? haica chicapim? achca cutitacchu caita rurarcanqui? haica mitam? haica *teſtamêto*pitac, chaicunacta rurarcanqui?	12. Testamentokta qillqaspa hukta churanaykipichu huktañataq churarqanki lluk'ipayllay rayku? ¿Testamentokta qillqachiq imaktam "qillqay" ñispa kamachisurqanki? ¿Qamri kana[5] imaktam qillqarqanki? ¿Pantakta qillqasqayki rayku piktam raykurqanki? ¿Hayk'a chikapim? ¿Achkha kutitaqchu kayta rurarqanki? ¿Hayk'a mit'am? ¿Hayk'a testamentopitaq chaykunata rurarqanki?
13 Llactap quellcacamayoquen caſpa quellcacllapac, horcoſca caſpatac, *teſtamneto*cta quellcacpac huacyaſca caſpa, ma-	13. ¿Llaqtap qillqa kamayuqin kaspa, qillqaqllapaq hurqusqa kaspataq, testamentokta qillqaqpaq waqyasqa kaspa "Ma-

3 Typesetting error for *vçuchircancu.*

4 Provisional phonemic reconstruction. Aymara data suggest *qhana: qhana* (*'expresado sin embozo; evidente, claro, obvio; notoriamente, de modo notorio'*); *qhanaki* (*'abiertamente, sin reserva, claramente; francamente, con franqueza'*) (De Lucca 1983: 238).

5 See footnote 4.

nam

[p. 320] nam ñechu canqui?. oncoc cari, harmipas, *teſtamento*nnacchu, huañurcancu, manariſcaiquimanta?

nam" ñiqchu kanki? ¿Unquq qhari warmipas teſtamentonnaqchu wañurqanku mana risqaykimanta?

14 Maican *teſtamento*ctapas, pacacchu, lliquecchu canqui? cai hinaſcaiquimanta, pipas chayaquêta, mana chazquicuncampac? cairi, ima allin camachiſca caccunacta, mana puchucaſca cancampac ima manucacpas, mana cutichiſca cancampac?

14. ¿Mayqan testamentoktapas pakaqchu llik'iqchu kanki kay hinasqaykimanta pipas chayaqinta mana chazkikunqanpaq, kayri, ima allin kamachisqa kaqkunakta mana p'uchukasqa kanqanpaq, ima manu kaqpas mana kutichisqa kanqanpaq?

ENGLISH TRANSLATION OF THE QUECHUA QUESTIONS

1. ¿Llulla testamentokta qillqaqchu kanki? ¿Padrep, p'atachaqpa, kurakap kamachiyninmantachu qillqarqanki? ¿Unquq warmip quzanpa kamachiyninmantachu? ¿Kayri unquq qharip warminpa kamachiyninmantachu qillqarqanki? ¿Kayri mayqanpa kamachiyninmantachu? ¿Kay hina llullakta qillqanqaykipaq imaktam chazkirqanki?

1. Do you write false wills? Have you written them by order of a priest (*padre*), a judge, or a *cacique*? Or by order of an ill wife's husband? Or did you write it by order of an ill husband's wife? Or by anyone else's order? What did you receive for writing it falsely in such a way?

2. ¿Testamento qillqasqaykipi testamentokta qillqachiqpa kamachiyninmanta yallichiqchu, kayri pisipachiqchu kanki?

2. In the wills that you write do you add or delete anything from the orders of the person who made you write it?

3.¿Testamentokta qillqachiq ña wañuptin testamentocta hukmanchaqchu kanki wañuqpa kamachiyninmanta munayniyki raykulla imallaktapas yapaspa pisipachispapas? ¿Kayri misakunamanta, zamachinamanta, ima alli kamachisqanmanta mayqantapas pisipichu qillqarqanki mayqanllanta asllantapas qillqaspa? ¿Manusqantari manachu qillqarqanki? ¿Kayri ma? ¿"Hitikasqayta kutichipuy" ñisqanta manataqchu qillqarqanki? ¿Kayri testamentomanta picharqankichu?

3. When the person who ordered the will written is already dead, do you rewrite it, adding or removing anything from the dead person's orders just according to your own interests? Or did you write less [than what was stipulated] regarding masses and the pealing [of bells][6] or any other of his or her appropriate orders, writing only a part them? Or did you not write down his or her debts? Or let us see what else. If he or she said, "Give back to him what I have squandered," did you not write it down? Or did you erase it from the will?

6 Bells that that are rung for the dead.

4. ¿Testamentokta qillqaspa unquqta kunaq willaqchu kanki "ama animaykipaq imallaktapas haqiychu" ñispa? ¿"Ama manusqaykikta manuykiktapas qillqachiychu" ñispa willaqchu kanki?

4. When you write the will, do you counsel the ill person, saying to him or her, "Don't leave anything for [the care of] your soul"? Do you tell him or her, "Do not order your debts written down nor the persons to whom you are in debt"?

5. ¿Mayqan qhari warmipas churinpa chiqa chayaqinta wawanpa chiqa chayaqintapas, kayri warminpa chiqa chayaqinta quzanpa chayaqintapas qichurqanchu testamentonpi qampa willakuyñiykimanta? ¿Kayri, yayanpa mamanpa chayaqinta mayqan qhari warmipas qichuqchu testamentonpi qampa kunakuyñiykimanta?

5. Has any man or woman removed from his or her will what is truly due to his or her children, or to his wife, or to her husband, because of something you have said? Or has any man or woman removed from his or her will what is due to his or her father or mother, because of your counsel?

6. ¿Unquqta willapayaqchu kunaqchu kanki "ñuqapaq ima hayk'aykikta haqiway" ñispa, yayayuq mamayuq churiyuq runa maziyuq kaptintaq? ¿Kayri, "padrepaq kurakapaq pipaqpas ima hayk'aykikta haqiy" ñispa willaqchu kanki? ¿Kayri, "ama manuykikta p'uchukaychu, manusqaykiktapas ama chazkiychu" ñispa willaq kunaqtaqchu kanki?

6. Have you repeatedly counseled an ill person, saying, "Leave everything to me," even though he or she has a father, a mother, children, and relatives? Or do you say, "Leave everything for the priest, for the *cacique*, or for anyone else"? Or do you give counsel, saying, "Don't demand restitution from your borrowers, and don't acknowledge your debts"?

7. ¿Testamentokta qillqachiqpa kamachiyninmanta yallin aswan misakta zamachinakta vigiliakta ima qukuy ofrendaktapas qillqarqankichu? ¿Kayri rezada misakta kantadamanñachu qillqaq kanki, cantadaktapas rezadamanña qillqaq kanki munayninta mana yupaspa padrekta kusichinqaykipaq, kayri imallaktapas paymanta chazkisqaykimantachu? Willaway-ari, ¿imaktam qusunki? ¿Hayk'a mit'ataq kay hinakta rurarqanki?

7. Did you write down more masses, pealing of bells, vigils, or any kind of sacrifices and offerings [than were actually stipulated]? Or do you write a chanted mass instead of a recited mass, or do you write a recited mass instead of a chanted mass, without respecting what the person wants, in order to make the priest happy, or because you have received something from him? So tell me, what has he given to you? How many times did you do such things?

8. Testamentokta mana alli qillqayta yachasqaykimanta, kayri testamento qillqachiqpa munaynin mana chay kama qillqasqaykimanta ima huchapas hatarirqanchu chiqan chazkiqkuna kaqninta uzuchinqankupaq. ¿Hayk'a testamentoktam kay hinakta qillqarqanki? ¿Hayk'aktañataqmi uzuchirqanku? ¿Ima mana allimanmi chayarqanku?

8. Did any lawsuits arise obliging [a will's] true beneficiaries to expend their property, either because you don't know to write wills well or because you did not write it according to the testator's wishes? How many wills like this have you written? How much did [the heirs] expend? What was the extent of the wrong [that came about]?

9. ¿Unquq yuyannaqña kaptin yuyayniyuq hinaktachu testamentokta

9. When an ill person was no longer in possession of his or her faculties, did you

qillqarqanki? ¿Kayri, ña wañuptintaq testamentokta qillqaqchu kanki "Kawzachkaptinraqmi qillqarqani" ñispa?

falsify the writing of the will? Or, when he or she is already dead, do you write the wills, saying, "I have written it when he or she was still alive"?

10. ¿Llaqtantin tasaykikta quptin, kayri, tasamanta hurqusqa kaptiykipas, chunkachaymanta yupakuymanta hurqusqa kaptiykitaq testamentokunakta qillqanqaykipaq, kayri, llaqtap ima huchantapas qillqanqaykipaq cofradiakunapaqpas, qullqikta, p'achakta, llamakta, imallaktapas apaqchu mañaqchu kanki?

10. When the whole town provided your taxes, or when you were exempted from taxes, or when you were exempted from work-force calculations so that you would write wills, or so that you would record any lawsuits for the town or for the brotherhoods, did you take or demand money, clothing, llamas, or anything?

11. ¿Hayk'aktam qusunki? ¿Qamri kana[7] hayk'aktam hillupurqanki qichupurqqanki? ¿Hayk'a runaktam hinarqanki? ¿Hayk'a kutiñataq?

11. How much did they give you? And obviously, how much food did you pillage from them and [how many] things did you steal from them? How many persons have you treated like this? How many times?

12. Testamentokta qillqaspa hukta churanaykipichu huktañataq churarqanki lluk'ipayllay rayku? ¿Testamentokta qillqachiq imaktam "qillqay" ñispa kamachisurqanki? ¿Qamri kana[8] imaktam qillqarqanki? ¿Pantakta qillqasqayki rayku piktam raykurqanki? ¿Hayk'a chikapim? ¿Achkha kutitaqchu kayta rurarqanki? ¿Hayk'a mit'am? ¿Hayk'a testamentopitaq chaykunata rurarqanki?

12. While writing a will, have you put anything down other than what you should have, just because of your bribe? What did the testator order you [to do], saying, "Write it"? And obviously, what have you written? Because you wrote erroneously, whom did you hurt? On how many occasions? Did you do it many times? How many? In how many wills you have done these things?

13. ¿Llaqtap qillqa kamayuqin kaspa, qillqaqllapaq hurqusqa kaspataq, testamentokta qillqaqpaq waqyasqa kaspa "Manam" ñiqchu kanki? ¿Unquq qhari warmipas teſtamentonnaqchu wañurqanku mana risqaykimanta?

13. Given that you are a town notary, and that you have been exempted from other duties, so that you may be a scribe, when you are called to write a will, do you [ever] answer, "No"? Did an ill man or woman [ever] die without a will because you did not come to him or her?

14. ¿Mayqan testamentoktapas pakaqchu llik'iqchu kanki kay hinasqaykimanta pipas chayaqinta mana chazkikunqanpaq, kayri, ima allin kamachisqa kaqkunakta mana p'uchukasqa kanqanpaq, ima manu kaqpas mana kutichisqa kanqanpaq?

14. Have you hidden or torn up any will so that, as a result of this deed of yours, someone would not receive his or her due, or so that he or she would not [have to] fulfill any appropriately ordered things, or so that a debt would not be paid?

7 See footnote 4.

8 See footnote 4.

Just as with the *kurakas*, the questions that notaries had to answer in the confessional were added to the list pertaining to the Seventh Commandment ("Thou shalt not steal"). According to the way that the confessor asks the confessant about his sins, the notaries appear as if they were a group of criminals who falsified wills, received bribes, stole goods, and caused conflicts. The questions in Quechua appear under a formal title, *llaqtap qillqa kamayuqnin* 'the person in the town responsible for writings.' *Llaqta* 'town' refers in this case to a *reducción*, a resettlement town in which there was a church and a parish, a priest, and a municipal council. Since Spanish governors resettled many little villages into a resettlement town, it commonly had more than one cacique. In this case, one of them received the rank and title of *cacique gobernador* of the town or of a larger region, depending on the rank of his family in the provincial preconquest hierarchy. The notary answered to the priest, to the Spanish governor (referred to in the text as *p'atachaq*, probably a Quechua version of *corregidor*) and to the local *kuraka*.

Just as in Document 34, here too we publish the text three times in two columns. First the Spanish original with an English translation, then the Quechua text with a parallel phonemic transcription and lastly a phonemic transcription accompanied by an English translation from the Quechua.

A typical notary knew how to read and write in Spanish. However, the questions suggest that sometimes his knowledge of Spanish might not have been good enough to permit him to write wills using the Spanish legal terms that correspond to the testator's Quechua expressions. The priest Juan Pérez Bocanegra does not offer any example of a legal expression. He himself did not translate church expressions referring to kinds of masses into Quechua. So, at this time in the new post-conquest society, the problem of translation was common both to Spaniards and natives, meeting in the context of the confessional a hundred years after the beginning of the conquest.

If we compare other kinds of data with the examples of wills dictated by different individuals, we can confirm that the group of people who, like the native nobility, served as intermediaries between Spanish colonial society and Andeans, was not very numerous. But notaries were not exempt from taxes and obligatory labor and were not noblemen in the eyes of the Spanish administrators. They achieved their status by their own effort, through learning Spanish and writing. By 1631, the most likely places to learn oral and written Spanish could be either a parish school, where the parish priest should have taught and sometimes actually did teach, or a period of training in a city like Cuzco, Potosí, or Lima. A notary took payment for his legal or illegal services: money, textiles, llamas, "or anything else." His domestic economy combined traditional bartering with some market practices and the use of money. Notaries had to create their own archives, just like Spanish notaries. At the same time it seems that the notaries, apparently good Catholics, to some extent kept with their ancestors and their traditional Andean beliefs. This is suggested by the fact that confessant notaries should be asked if they ever counseled a testator, “Don’t leave anything for your soul.” The word used for soul is *anima*, a Spanish word. Pious Catholics should leave money for masses and prayers for their soul. But good Andeans did not have a soul (*anima*). Their descendants should feed their mummy and seek its protection.

The language of the questions shows that great care was taken to use clear Quechua terminology for family members. The author clearly distinguishes the children of a woman (*wawa*) from the children of a man (*churi*). Sometimes his zeal to name everything he can in good Quechua gives new meanings to Quechua words. For example, *zamana* ‘a rest’ is used to refer to an obligatory pause in a funeral procession during the pealing of the church bells, and *alli kamachisqa kaq* ‘a well ordered thing’ denotes “pious deeds” (*obras pías*).

Glossary

A. = Aymara
E. = English
L. = Latin
N. = Nahuatl
Q. = Quechua
S. = Spanish

Original	*English text form*	*Commentary*
achacallas	*acha qalla*	Q. 'The one who begins to multiply', a class of demons or ancestor gods.
ahijada	*ahijada*	S. Goddaughter, an adopted girl or a girl in a foster family.
ahijado	*ahijado*	S. Godson, an adopted boy or a boy in a foster family.
alcalde ordinario	*alcalde ordinario*	S. Town mayor.
alcalde mayor		S. First or principal mayor (usually there were two).
alguacil	*alguacil*	S. Policeman/constable, who in native villages accompanies the alcalde.
almud	*almud*	S. Dry measure, one-half of a fanega/hanega.
altepetl	*altepetl*	N. Indigenous state, often identified with a head town in the colonial period.
anaco	*anaku*	Q. Female shirt.

DOI: 10.5876/9781607328346.c036

Original	English text form	Commentary
apo tampo	*Apu Tampu*	Q. 'Store of Lords', identified as a forefather of the Inca dynasty in Cuzco.
asvana	*azwana*	Q. Large clay vat for making corn beer.
audiencia	*audiencia*	S. The highest court; court of second instance, or in the case of natives, court of third instance; in the sixteenth and seventeenth centuries there were three audiencias in the Viceroyalty of New Spain (Mexico and Central America], and six in the colonial Viceroyalty of Peru (Panama, Colombia, Ecuador, Peru, Bolivia, and Chile).
avasca	*awasqa*	Q. Home-woven common textile used by ordinary natives.
ayllo	*ayllu*	Q. Lineage, a group of real or supposed descendants of a pair of primogenitors.
cabildo	*cabildo*	S. Municipal town council.
cacique	*cacique*	S. from the Taino language, a Spanish legal term for any local leader.
calpolli, calpulli	*calpolli*	N. 'Big house', usually a constituent part or a subunit of a preconquest altepetl headed by a leader called a teuctlahtoani, and embracing either commoner farmers or specialized professional groups (especially in large cities such as Tenochtitlan). Much of its structure and functions survived into the early colonial period, gradually becoming part of the colonial sociopolitical organization of towns and partly adjusting its land-holding practices to the Spanish system.
camachico	*kamachikuq*	Q. Leader of a workers' group.
ccallac pacha	*qallaq pacha*	Q. 'Epoch that begins', present humanity's time of creation.
coco	*quku*	Q. Cup; may be a local name for ceremonial silver cups, called akilla in Cuzco, used in ceremonial libations; perhaps the word comes from qu-ku-q 'the one who makes an offering'.
colla suyos	*Qulla Suyu*	Q. One of the "four quarters of the civilized world" in the Inca empire; in the sixteenth century it included lands in the southern portion of modern Peru, Bolivia, northern Chile, and part of northwest Argentina.
comadre	*comadre*	S. Godmother of a child in any rite of passage, and a close friend of the child's parents.

Original	*English text form*	*Commentary*
compadre	*compadre*	S. Godfather of a child in any rite of passage, and a close friend of the child's parents.
corregidor	*corregidor*	S. Governor of a province, who is responsible for taxing the indigenous people.
corregimiento	*corregimiento*	S. Area under a corregidor's jurisdiction.
costumbre	*costumbre*	S. Custom, in the Andes; it denotes local religious ceremonies as distinct from official Catholic ceremonies usually referred to as "religion."
cuartilla	*cuartilla*	S. Measure of weight; one-fourth of an arroba.
don	*Don*	S. Title preceding an indigenous male's name and indicating (usually high) nobility.
doña	*Doña*	S. Title preceding an indigenous female's name and indicating (usually high) nobility.
encomendero	*encomendero*	S. In America, a person who received an encomienda grant.
encomienda	*encomienda*	S. A grant of a group of indigenous people, together with its proper authorities and land, to a Spaniard (exceptionally to a native person) for his merits in conquering the land or in maintaining order, usually for one lifetime (generation); the Spaniard received the benefits of native labor and had to organize the religious conversion of the natives; over time, the encomiendas were converted into an income, paid to the encomendero from the local treasury.
fanegada	*fanegada*	S. See *hanega*.
fiscal	*fiscal*	S. Court prosecutor; in colonial Mexico, an indigenous town's main church official, usually a member of the local noble class; in some areas such as Puebla, this important indigenous office survives today.
guauya	*wawya*	Q. Probably an agricultural tool for winnowing cereals; or a fan.
hanega	*hanega*	S. Dry measure, a bushel; today in Castile 55 liters, but in each province the capacity was different.
happi ñuños	*hap'i ñuñu*	Q. 'The one who catches and sucks'; cannibal demons or gods.

Original	*English text form*	*Commentary*
gobernador	*gobernador*	S. 1. One of the titles given to the Spanish governor of a province; 2. native nobleman governor of an indigenous province.
insolidum	*in solidum*	L. Jointly, so as to be answerable to the whole.
khipu	*khipu*	Q. Knot record, which contained numeric and other data.
kuraka	*kuraka*	Q. 'The elder one', a low-ranking leader of a local group; later, a title given to any kind of native leaders in the Viceroyalty of Peru.
kusma	*kusma*	Q. An indigenous tunic, usually of cotton and without embroidery.
lampa	*lampa*	Q. Shovel.
llama	*llama*	Q. Llama (*Lama glama*).
lliclla	*lliklla*	Q. Women's blanket.
macehualli, maceualli	*macehualli*	N. Commoner in Nahua society; toward the later part of the sixteenth century, the term began to be used to denote indigenous people in general and this meaning survives in modern Nahuatl.
macehualtin	*macehualtin*	N. Plural form of *macehualli*.
macma	*maqma*	Q. Large jar.
mandas forçossas	*mandas forzosas*	S. Obligatory pious bequests.
mate	*mati*	Q. Gourd (*Lagenaria siceraria*) or gourd plates and bowls.
mates de madera pintada	*mates de madera pintada*	S. Adorned wooden cups used in ceremonies; known as *qiru* in Quechua.
maitl	*maitl*	N. 'Hand/arm', a native unit of land measurement.
mecatl	*mecatl*	N. 'Rope', a native unit of land measurement.
medio	*medio*	S. Unit of currency, a coin equivalent to one half of a real.
nehuitzantli	*nehuitzantli*	N. Native unit of land measurement based on the distance from the foot to the upstretched hand.
obraje	*obraje*	S. Workshop employing either native forced labor assigned by the Spanish provincial authorities or condemned persons.
oidores	*oidores*	S. Audiencia judges, usually five.
onsa	*onza*	S. Measure of weight, an ounce, equivalent to one sixteenth of a libra.

Original	*English text form*	*Commentary*
ordenanzas reales	*ordenanzas reales*	S. Royal ordinances.
pallar	*pallar*	Q. Lima beans (*Phaseolus luntus*).
partiana	*partiana*	Meaning unknown.
patacon *pataqon*	*patacón*	S. Unit of currency, a coin equivalent to eight reales; see peso.
patacon de a nueve	*patacón de a nueve*	S. Unit of currency, a coin exceeding the prescribed weight and equivalent to nine reales.
peso	*peso*	S. Unit of currency, a coin worth eight reales.
peso de a ocho	*peso de a ocho*	S. See peso.
peso de a ocho reales	*peso de a ocho reales*	S. See peso.
pilli	*pilli*	N. Nobleman, usually claimed to descend from a royal ancestor.
purun pacha	*purun pacha*	Q. Barbarian times before the Inca's coming, characterized by social and cosmic disorder.
purun pacharac captin	*purun pacharaq kaptin*	Q. 'When it was still the barbarian epoch'.
p'urutu	*p'urutu*	Q. Beans (*Phaseolus vulgaris*).
qiru	*qiru*	Q. Ceremonial wooden cup produced and used always in pairs, usually adorned with scenes and t'uqapu signs.
quahuitl	*quahuitl*	N. 'Stick', a native unit of land measurement.
quarta	*cuarta*	S. Unit of land measurement, equivalent to one-fourth of a vara; 'a quarter', 'a palm'.
quartillo	*cuartillo*	S. Dry measure, equivalent to one-fourth of an *hanega* or one-fourth of a *celemín* (see *selemin*).
quingua	*kinwa*	Q. Quinoa (*Chenopodium quinoa*).
real	*real*	S. Unit of currency, a coin worth one-eighth of a peso.
real de a ocho	*real de a ocho*	S. See peso.
reducción	*reducción*	S. A new indigenous town formed by the forced resettlement of several villages, with a Spanish-style urban layout and government; implemented in the Viceroyalty of Peru for better control of the indigenous population.
regidor mayor	*regidor mayor*	S. Leading member of the municipal council.
ruan	*ruán*	S. Linen textile, name taken from the French city of Rouen, famous for its linen textiles.

Original	*English text form*	*Commentary*
selemin	*celemín*	S. Dry measure, equivalent to one-twelfth of an *hanega*; 'a peck'.
sora	*sura*	Q. Germinating maize for brewing corn beer.
suysuna	*suysuna*	Q. Strainer, sieve.
tara paca Vira cocham pachayachip Cachan o pachacan	*Tara Paka Wira Quchan Pacha Yachachip kachan o pachak'an*	Q. 'Envoy' or 'servant' of 'the one who conceals ancestor pairs', 'Nursery of Identities', and 'The one who causes the cosmos to become'. *Tara Paka* 'The one who conceals ancestor pairs' is an image of God as the one in whom ancestors of all beings are hidden, since, according to the Andean religion, the ancestors must be a pair composed of a male and a female. *Wira Quchan* 'Nursery of Identities or of Life' is an image of God as the one who contains in itself the potential existence of all beings. 'The one who causes the cosmos to become' may be a writer's error: *pachayachi* may have been mistakenly written instead of *pacha yachachi*, meaning 'The one who gives the world vital force' or 'The one who peoples or teaches the cosmos'. *Pacha Yachachi* is a very frequent name for God in sixteenth century Cuzco sources, while *Pachayachi* does not occur.
tauantin suyu *tabantin suyu*	*Tawantin Suyu*	Q. 'Four United Parts', the civilized world under the Sun, the Inca empire, and the Viceroyalty of Peru.
taure	*tawri, tarwi*	Q. Andean lupin (*Lupinus mutabilis*).
teccalli/tecalli	*teccalli*	N. 'Lordly house', a unit of organization within an *altepetl*, with rights to specific lands, headed by a *teuctli*, or lord, and including noble kin and dependents, *teixhuihuan*, and commoners (*macehualtin*); depending on the region, it is also known as *tecpan*.
tecpan	*tecpan*	N. 'Lordly house', a unit of organization within an *altepetl*, with rights to specific lands, headed by a *teuctli*, or lord, and including noble kin and dependents, *teixhuihuan*, and commoners (*macehualtin*); depending on the region, also known as *teccalli*.
tecuhtli, teuctli	*teuctli*	N. 'Lord', head of a lordly or noble house (*tecpan* or *teccalli*).

Original	English text form	Commentary
teixhuihuan	*teixhuihuan*	N. 'One's grandchildren'; a particular group of dependents bound to the *teccalli* and probably usually claiming some remote form of kinship with a founder of a *teccalli/tecpan*, but considered a lower category than the nobles proper (*pipiltin*). They could own land but were obliged to fulfill tribute duties.
tetecuhtin, teteuctin	*teteuctin*	N. Plural form of *teuctli*; 'lords'; also sometimes employed in a collective reference to municipal officials.
taqui	*taki*	Q. A song and a dance executed together and recounting a myth or a story; the word is actually the verb 'to sing the truth'.
tlatoque	*tlahtohqueh*	N. Plural form of *tlahtoani* (see *tlahtoani*) 'rulers'; also sometimes employed in a collective reference to municipal officials.
tlatoani	*tlahtoani*	N. 'He who speaks', the dynastic ruler of an *altepetl*.
tomin	*tomin*	S. Unit of currency, a coin worth one-eighth of a peso, equivalent to a real.
tompina	*tupina*	S. Tompina has been written in error for tupina, which can mean a small tupu pin.
tonapa *thonapa*	*T'unapa*	A. 'The Crumbler, the Destroyer', an image of the Creator God as the one who punishes and destroys sinners and teaches a new way of life.
Vira cochampa cachan	*Wira Quchanpa kachan*	Q. 'Envoy of the Nursery of Identities or of Life'.
topo	*tupu*	Q. Large silver pin used by women.
tutayac pacha	*tutayaq pacha*	Q. 'Epoch of darkness', before the creation of the Sun, the Moon, and the stars.
t'uqapu	*t'uqapu*	Q. A. Rectangular, mostly abstract signs on textiles and ceremonial wooden cups.
unku	*unku*	Q. Ceremonial embroidered tunic with signs of rank and lineage.
vara	*vara*	S. Measure of length, always equal to three feet as locally used.
visitador	*visitador*	S. Inspector sent either by the Spanish Crown to handle specific issues in the colonies, or by an audiencia to deal with local problems in a province.
wayaw	*wayaw*	Q. Willow (*Salix humboldtiana*).

Original	*English text form*	*Commentary*
ybicchhay camayoc. cunacuy camayoc	*iwich'ay kamayuq, kunakuy kamayuq*	Q. Professional adviser and ritual practitioner, whose participation is obligatory during rites of passage.
ychocan	*ichuqan*	Q. 'The one on the left'; this constitutes clear evidence that the traditional organization of lineages in moieties had existed and perhaps even still existed in Ambar.

References

Acosta, Joseph. 1979 [1590]. *Historia Natural y Moral de Las Indias en que se tratan las cosas notables del cielo/elementos/metales/plantas y animales dellas y los ritos/y ceremonias/leyes y gobierno de los indios, compuesto por el Padre . . . , religioso de la Compañía de Jesús*. Edición preparada por Edmundo O'Gorman con un prólogo, tres apéndices y un índice de materias. Mexico: Fondo de Cultura Económica.

Adorno, Rolena, and Ivan Boserup, eds. 2015. *Unlocking the Doors to the World of Guaman Poma and His Nueva Corónica*. Copenhagen: The Royal Library, Museum Tusculanum Press.

Aguilar Rodríguez, Sergio H. 2000. "Registro de la perdiz veracruzana o Chivizcoyo (*Dendrortyx barbatus Gould*) en la sierra norte de Oaxaca." *MéxicoHuitzil: Revista Mexicana de Ornitología*, no. 1. http://www.redalyc.org/articulo.oad?id=75610101.

Alva Ixtlilxochitl, Fernando de. 2000. *Historia de la nación chichimeca*. Madrid: DASTIN Historia.

Alvarado Tezozomoc, Fernando. 1949. *Cronica Mexicayotl*. México: Imprenta Universitaria.

Alvarado Tezozomoc, Fernando. 1943. *Cronica Mexicana*. México: Universidad Nacional Autónoma de México.

Amado, Donato. 2002. "El alférez real de los incas: Resistencia, cambios y continuidad de la identidad indígena." *Incas e indios cristianos: Élites indígenas e identidades cristianas en los Andes coloniales*, ed. J. J. Decoster. Cusco: Centro Bartolomé de las Casas, Asociación Kuraka, Instituto Francés de Estudios Andinos.

Anders, Ferdinand, Maarten Jansen, and Luis Reyes García. 1993. *Los templos del cielo y de la oscuridad: Oráculos y liturgia; Libro explicativo del llamado Códice Borgia*. Madrid: Sociedad Estatal Quinto Centenario; Graz: ADEVA; México: FCE.

DOI: 10.5876/9781607328346.c037

Anderson, Arthur J. O., Frances Berdan, and James Lockhart 1976. *Beyond the Codices*. Berkeley: University of California Press.

Anderson, Greg. 2015. "Retrieving the Lost Worlds of the Past: The Case for an Ontological Turn." *American Historical Review* 120 (3): 787–810.

Arguedas, José María. 1956. *Puquio, una cultura en proceso de cambio*. Lima: Instituto de Estudios Etnológicos.

Ayala Falcón, Maricela 2002. *El bulto ritual de Mundo Perdido, Tikal*. Instituto de Investigaciones Filológicas. México: Universidad Nacional Autónoma de México.

Baber, Jovita R. 2010. "Empire, Indians, and the Negotiation for Status in the City of Tlaxcala, 1521–1550." In *Negotiation with Domination: Colonial New Spain's Indian Pueblos Confront the Spanish State*, ed. E. Ruíz Medrano and S. Kellogg, 19–44. Denver: University Press of Colorado.

Campbell, R. Joe. in preparation. *A Comprehensive Dictionary of Classical Nahuatl*. Combining original and standardized spellings along with morphological analyses for all lexical items from Molina's three dictionaries and from Sahagun's Florentine Codex.

Berdan, Frances F. 1996. "The Tributary Provinces." In *Aztec Imperial Strategies*, ed.Frances Berdan et al., 115–135. Washington, DC: Dumbarton Oaks Research Library and Collection.

Berdan, Frances F. 2006. "The Role of Provincial Elites in the Aztec Empire." In *Pre-Columbian States and Empires*, ed. Christina Elson and R. Alan Covey, 154–165. Tucson: University of Arizona Press.

Berdan, Frances F. 2007. "Continuity and Change in Aztec Culture: From Imperial Lords to Royal Subjects." In *Globalization and Change in Fifteen Cultures*, ed. George Spindler and Janice Stockard, 1–23. Belmont, CA: Wadsworth.

Berdan, Frances F., and Michael E. Smith. 1996. "Imperial Strategies and Core-Periphery Relations." In *Aztec Imperial Strategies*, ed. Frances Berdan, et al., 209–217. Washington, DC: Dumbarton Oaks Research Library and Collection.

Berdan, Frances F., and Michael E. Smith. 2003. "The Aztec Empire." In *The Postclassic Mesoamerican World*, ed. Michael E. Smith and Frances F. Berdan, 67–72. Salt Lake City: University of Utah Press.

Borah, Woodrow Wilson. 1983. *Justice by Insurance: The General Indian Court of Colonial Mexico and the Legal Aides of the Half-Real*. Berkeley: University of California Press.

Burkhart, Louise. 1989. *The Slippery Earth: Nahua-Christian Moral Dialogue in Sixteenth-Century Mexico*. Tucson: University of Arizona Press.

Burkhart, Louise. 2001. *Before Guadalupe: The Virgin Mary in Early Colonial Nahua Literature*. Albany: State University of New York.

Campos Carlés de Peña, María 2013. *Un legado que pervive en Hispanoamérica: El mobiliario del Virreinato del Perú de los siglos XVII y XVIII*. Madrid: Ediciones el Viso.

Carrasco, Pedro. 2011. *The Tenochca Empire of Ancient Mexico: The Triple Alliance of Tenochtitlan, Tetzcoco, and Tlacopan*. The Civilization of the American Indian Series. Norman: University of Oklahoma Press.

Castañeda de la Paz, María 2009. "Central Mexican Indigenous Coats of Arms and the Conquest of Mesoamerica," *Ethnohistory* 56 (1): 125–161.

Castañeda de la Paz, María. 2013a. *Conflictos y alianzas en tiempos de cambio: Azcapotzalco, Tlacopan, Tenochtitlan y Tlatelolco (siglos XII al XVI)*. Instituto de Investigaciones Antropológicas. México: Universidad Nacional Autónoma de México.

Castañeda de la Paz, María. 2013b. "Dos parcialidades étnicas en Azcapotzalco: Mexicapan y Tepanecapan." *Estudios de Cultura Nahuatl* 46: 223–248.

Castañeda de la Paz, María. 2015. "La nobleza del centro de México ante la amenaza a sus bultos sagrados." In *Identidad en palabras: Nobleza indígena novohispana colonial*, ed. Patrick Lesbre and Katarzina Mikulska. Instituto de Investigaciones Antropológicas/Centro de Estudios Ibéricos e Iberoamericanos. México: Universidad Autónoma Nacional de México; Warsaw: University of Warsaw.

Castillo Farreras, Victor Manuel. 1972. "Unidades Nahuas de Medida," *Estudios de Cultura Náhuatl* 10: 195–223.

Castro Vásquez, Aquilino 2005. Teresa Apolaya: La muy poderosa Señora Catalina Huanca. Chupaca/Junin: Imprenta Ríos.

Catálogo de documentos escritos en náhuatl siglo XVI. 2013. Vol. 1. Coordinación de la serie: Yolanda Ramos Galicia. Tlaxcala: Gobierno del Estado de Tlaxcala.

Cerrón-Palomino, Rodolfo. 1994. *Quechua sureño: Diccionario unificado*. Lima: Biblioteca Nacional del Perú.

Charney, Paul 2012. "For My Necessities": The Wills of Andean Commoners and Nobles in the Valley of Lima, 1596–1607." *Ethnohistory* 59 (2): 323–351.

Chavez Hayhoe, Arturo. 1991. *Guadalajara en el siglo XVI*, vol. 2. Guadalajara, México: Ayuntamiento de Guadalajara.

Chimalpahin Cuauhtlehuanitzin, Domingo Francisco de San Antón Muñón. 1997. *Codex Chimalpahin: Society and politics in Mexico Tenochtitlan, Tlatelolco, Texcoco, Culhuacan, and other Nahua altepetl in Central Mexico*. 2 vols. Ed. and trans. S. Schroeder and A.J.O. Anderson. Norman: University of Oklahoma Press.

Chimalpahin Cuauhtlehuanitzin, Domingo Francisco de San Antón Muñón. 2003. *Las ocho relaciones y el Memorial de Colhuacan*. Ed. and trans. Rafael Tena. Mexico: Conaculta.

Chimalpahin Cuauhtlehuanitzin, Domingo Francisco de San Antón Muñón. 2006. *Annals of His Time*. Ed. and trans. by J. Lockhart, S. Schroeder, and D. Namala. Stanford, CA: Stanford University Press.

Christensen, Mark Z. 2010. "The Tales of Two Cultures: Ecclesiastical Texts and Nahua and Maya Catholicisms." *The Americas* 66 (3): 353–377.

Christensen, Mark Z. 2012. "The Use of Nahuatl in Evangelization and the Ministry of Sebastian." *Ethnohistory* 59 (4): 691–712.

Chuchiak, John F. IV. 2010. "Writing as Resistance: Maya Graphic Pluralism and Indigenous Elite Strategies for Survival in Colonial Yucatan, 1550–1750." *Ethnohistory* 57: 87–116.

Cline, Sarah L. 1986. *Colonial Culhuacan, 1580–1600: A Social History of an Aztec Town*. Albuquerque: University of New Mexico Press.

Cline, Sarah. 1993. *The Book of Tributes: Early Sixteenth-Century Nahuatl Censuses from Morelos Mexico*. Los Angeles, CA: UCLA Latin American Center Publications.

Cline, Sarah. 1998. "Fray Alonso de Molina's Model Testament and Antecedents to Indigenous Wills in Spanish America." In *Dead Giveaways: Indigenous Testaments of Colonial Mesoamerica and the Andes*, ed. S. Kellogg and M. Restall, 13–33. Salt Lake City: University of Utah Press.

Cline, Sarah L., and Miguel León-Portilla. 1984. *The Testaments of Culhuacan*. Los Angeles, CA: UCLA Latin America Center Publications.

Cook, Nobel David. 1998. *Born to Die: Disease and New World Conquest, 1492–1650*. New Approaches to the Americas. New York: Cambridge University Press.

Correa Valdivia, Paulo 2014. "In toptli in petlacalli, in piyalli in nelpilli: Contener y revelar el poder divino. Los envoltorios sagrados en los códices del centro de México." MA thesis, Facultad de Filosofía y Letras, Instituto de Investigaciones Antropológicas, Universidad Nacional Autónoma de México, México.

Crosby, Alfred W. 1972. *The Columbian Exchange: Biological and Cultural Consequences of 1492*. Westport, CT: Greenwood Press.

Crosby, Alfred W. 1994. *Germs, Seeds and Animals: Studies in Ecological History*. New York: M.E. Sharpe.

Curatola Petrocchi, Marco, and Carlos de la Puente Luna, eds. 2013. *El quipu colonial: Estudios y materiales*. Lima: Fondo editorial, Pontificia Universidad Católica del Perú.

Curcio-Nagy, Linda A. 2004. *The Great Festivals of Colonial Mexico City: Performing Power and Identity*. Albuquerque: University of New Mexico Press.

Cusihuaman, Antonio. 1976. *Gramática quechua: Cuzco-Collao*. Lima: Ministerio de Educación, Instituto de Estudios Peruanos.

Dakin, Karen, and Christopher Lutz. 1996. *Nuestro pesar, nuestra afliccion: Memorias en lengua nahuatl enviadas a Felipe II por indigenas del Valle de Guatemala hacia 1572*. Mexico City: Universidad Nacional Autonoma de México and Centro de Investigaciones Regionales de Mesoameric

De la Peña, Benito. 1970. "Testimonio dado por Benito de la Peña escribano de esta ciudad del Cuzco en 22 de abril de 1552 de las diligencias practicadas, en virtud de Real Provisión de la Real Audiencia de Lima, expedida en 20 de octubre de 1550 sobre la averiguación que se hizo de los indios que tenían el valle de Yucay, y que tierras, casas, y haciendas eran de los Incas, señores que fueron del Perú, y tenían dedicadas al Sol y quien las poseía desde la conquista de los españoles, en cuyo cumplimiento se calificó la extensión de dicho valle, tierras que fueron de Huayna Capac, sus mujeres, y de otros Incas reyes gentiles del Perú, con todo lo demás que resulta en la representación según el mapa que formaron y acompaña." *Revista del Archivo Histórico del Cuzco* 13: 21–54.

Diccionario de autoridades. 2002 [1737]. 3 vols. Real Academia Española. Madrid: Editorial Gredos.

Doctrina Christiana. 1548(1944). *Doctrina Christiana en lengua Española y Mexicana por los Religiosos de la Orden de Santo Domingo, Juan Pablos, Mexico*. Colleción de Incunables Americanos Siglo XVI. Madrid: Ediciones Culutra Hispanica.

Doesburg, Sebastian van. 2002. *Documentos Antiguos de San Miguel Tequixtepec, Oaxaca: Los primeros cien años de la Colonia (1533–1617)*. CNWS Publications, vol. 112. Leiden: Leiden University.

Duranti, Alessandro. 2001. "Performance and Encoding of Agency in Historical-Natural Languages." *Texas Linguistic Forum* 44: 266–287.

Eire, Carlos M. N. 1995. *From Madrid to Purgatory: The Art and Craft of Dying in Sixteenth Century Spain*. Cambridge: Cambridge University Press.

Escalante Gutiérrez de Valderrama, Carmen, and Ricardo Valderrama Fernández. 2013. "Las Rivalidades entre descendientes de Incas y la Rebelión de José Gabriel Tupa Amaru: Documentos inéditos de los Tupa Guamanrimachi Ynga. Cusco 1776–1825." In *Tupac Amaru: La Revolución precursora de la Emancipación Continental*, ed. Jorge Cornejo Bouroncle. Cusco: Universidad Nacional de San Antonio Abad del Cusco.

Estenssoro Fuchs, Juan Carlos. 1998. *Del paganismo a la santidad: la incorporación de los indios del Perú al catolicismo, 1532–1750*. Trans. Gabriela Ramos. Lima: Instituto Francés de Estudios Andinos.

Estenssoro Fuchs, Juan Carlos. 2003. *Del paganismo a la santidad: La incorporación de los indios del Perú al catolicismo 1532–1750*. Lima: Fondo Editorial, Pontificia Universidad Católica del Perú, Instituto Francés de Estudios Andinos.

Estenssoro Fuchs, Juan Carlos. 2005. "Construyendo la memoria: la figura del inca y el reino del Perú, de la conquista a Túpac Amaru II." In *Los incas, reyes del Perú*, ed. Tom Cummins and Thomas Bitting Foster. Lima: Banco de Crédito.

Fernández de Recas, Guillermo S. 1961. *Cacicazgos y nobiliario indígena de la Nueva España*. Mexico: Instituto Bibliográfico Mexicano.

Gibson, Charles 1952. *Tlaxcala in the Sixteenth Century*. New Haven, CT: Yale University Press.

Gibson, Charles. 1960. "The Aztec Aristocracy in Colonial Mexico." *Comparative Studies in Society and History* 2 (2): 169–196.

Gibson, Charles. 1964. *The Aztecs under Spanish Rule: A History of the Indians of the Valley of Mexico 1519–1810*. Stanford, CA: Stanford University Press.

Glave, Luís Miguel. 1999. "The 'Republic of Indians' in Revolt (c. 1690–1790)." In *The Cambridge History of the Native Peoples of the Americas*, Vol. 3, *South America*, Part 2, 502–557. Cambridge: Cambridge University Press.

Gonçález Holguín, Diego. 1952 [1608]. *Vocabulario de la Lengua General de todo el Peru llamada Lengua Qquichua o del Inca*. Lima: Imprenta Santa Maria.

Gonzales, Odi. 2014. *Elegía Apu Inka Awawallpaman: Primer documento de la resistencia Inka (siglo XVI)*. Biblioteca Qillqakuna N°8. Cuzco: Editorial Pakarina.

Graubart, B. Karen. 2007. *With Our Labor and Sweat: Indigenous Women and the Formation of Colonial Society in Peru*. Stanford, CA: Stanford University Press.

Greenleaf, Richard E. 1988. *Zumárraga y la inquisición mexicana, 1536–1543*. México: Fondo de Cultura Económica.

Guaman Poma de Ayala, Phelipe. 1615. *EL primer nueua corónica y buen gobierno*. Biblioteca Real de Dinamarca, Copenhague, manuscrito GkS 2232, 4to. http://www.kb.dk/permalink/2006/poma/info/en/frontpage.htm.

Guillén Guillén, Edmundo. 1981. "Titu Cusi Yupanqui y su tiempo. El estado imperial Inka y su tragico final: 1572." *Historia y Cultura* 13–14: 61–99.

Haimovich, Gregory. 2018. "Identification and Classification of Neologisms in the Early Colonial Quechua Corpus: Considerations on Neology and Cross-Cultural Contact." Unpublished manuscript.

Hampe Martínez, Teodoro. 2010. "Santiago del Cercado el devenir histórico de un espacio doctrinario, educativo y asistencial en Lima." *Arkinka: revista de arquitectura, diseño y construcción* 14 (177): 94–101.

Haskett, Robert. 1985. "A Social History of Indian Town Government in the Colonial Cuernavaca Jurisdiction." PhD dissertation, University of California, Los Angeles.

Haskett, Robert. 1991. *Indigenous Rulers: An Ethnohistory of Town Governments in Colonial Cuernavaca*. Albuquerque: University of New Mexico Press.

Haskett, Robert. 1996. "Paper Shields: The Ideology of Coats of Arms in Colonial Mexican Primordial Titles," *Ethnohistory* 42 (1): 99–126.

Hermann, Manuel A. 2008. "Religiosidad y bultos sagrados en la Mixteca prehispánica." Desacatos 27: 75–94.

Hernandez de León-Portilla, Ascensión. 2010. "Una carta en náhuatl desde el Sosonusco, siglo XVI." *Estudios de Cultura Náhuatl* 31: 237–258.

Hassig, Ross. 1988. *Aztec Warfare: Imperial Expansion and Political Control*. Norman: University of Oklahoma Pres.

Hicks, Frederic. 1999. "The Middle Class in Ancient Central Mexico." *Journal of Anthropological Research* 55: 409–427.

Horn, Rebecca. 1997. *Postconquest Coyoacan: Nahua-Spanish Relations in Central Mexico, 1519–1650*. Stanford, CA: Stanford University Press.

Hosselkus, Erika. 2011. "Noble Nahuas, Faith, and Death: How the Indigenous Elite of the Colonial Puebla-Tlaxcala Valley Prepared to Perish." In *Death and Dying in Colonial Spanish America*, ed. Martina Will de Chaparro and Miruna Achim, 28–52. Tucson: University of Arizona Press.

Husson, Jean-Phelippe, ed. and trans. 2001. *La Mort d'Ataw Wallpa ou La fin de l'Empire des Incas: Tragédie anonyme en langue quechua du milieu du XVIe siècle*, Edition critique trilingue quechua-espagnol-français. Avant-propos de Nathan Wachtel. Genève: Patiño.

Husson, Jean-Phelippe, ed. 2005. *Entre tradición e innovación: Cinco siglos de la ulioture amerindia: Actas del simposio "Fondo autóctono y aportes europeos en las literaturas amerindias; Aspectos metodológicos y filológicos" (50º Congreso internacional de Americanistas, Varsovia, julio de 2000)*. Lima: Pontificia Universidad Católica del Perú, Fondo Editorial.

Ibarra Grasso, Dick Edgar. 1953. *La Escritura Indígena Andina*. Biblioteca Paceña, Alcaldía Municipal.

Kalyuta, Anastasia V. 2011. "El arte de acomodarse a dos mundos." *Revista Española de Antropología Americana* 41 (2): 471–500.

Karttunen, Frances. 1992. *An Analytical Dictionary of Nahuatl*. Norman: University of Oklahoma Press.

Karttunen, Frances, and James Lockhart. 1976. *Nahuatl in the Middle Years: Language Contact Phenomena in Texts of the Colonial Period*. Los Angeles: University of California Press.

Karttunen, Frances, and James Lockhart, eds. 1987. *The Art of Nahuatl Speech: The Bancroft Dialogues*. UCLA Latin American Studies, Vol. 65. Los Angeles: University of California.

Kellogg, Susan M. 1986. "Kinship and Social Organization in Early Colonial Tenochtitlan." In *Supplement to HMAI, Ethnohistory*, ed. R. Spores, 103–121. Austin: University of Texas Press.

Kellogg, Susan. 1995. *Law and Transformation of Aztec Culture, 1500–1700*. Norman: University of Oklahoma Press.

Kellogg, Susan. 1999. "From Parallel and Equivalent to Separate but Unequal: Tenochca Mexica Women, 1500–1700." In *Indian Women of Early Mexico*, ed. Susan Schroeder, Stephanie Wood, and Robert Haskett, 123–143. Norman and London: University of Oklahoma Press.

Kranz, Travis Barton. 2007. "Sixteenth-Century Tlaxcalan Pictorial Documents on the Conquest of Mexico." In *Sources and Methods for the Study of Postconquest Mesoamerican Ethnohistory, Provisional Version*, ed. James Lockhart, Lisa Sousa, and

Stephanie Wood. Wired Humanities Projects. Eugene: University of Oregon. http://whp.uoregon.edu/Lockhart/index.html.

Lamana, Gonzalo. 2001. "Definir y dominar. Los lugares grises en el Cuzco hacia 1540." *Colonial Latin American Review* 10 (1): 25–48.

Lamana, Gonzalo. 2008. *Domination without Dominance: Inca-Spanish Encounters in Early Colonial Peru*. Durham, NC: Duke University Press.

León Gómez 2002. *Paños e hidalguía: Encomenderos y sociedad colonial en Huánuco*. Lima: Instituto de Estudios Peruanos.

León Rivera, Jorge de 1997. "Códice Miguel León-Portilla. Los dioses del Templo Mayor de la ciudad de México-Tenochtitlan custodiados en el Cerro de la Estrella de Iztapalapa." In Códices y documentos sobre México: Segundo Simposio, ed. Salvador Rueda Smithers, Constanza Vega Sosa, and Rodrigo Martínez Baracs, 111–127. 2 vols. México: Instituto Nacional de Antropología e Historia/Consejo Nacional para la Cultura y las Artes.

León-Portilla, Miguel. 1959. *Visión de los vencidos: relaciones indígenas de la conquista*. Mexico: Universidad Nacional Autónoma de México.

Lewin, Boleslao. 1943. *La rebelión de Túpac Amaru y los órigenes de la independencia de Hispanoamérica*. Tercera edición ampliada. Buenos Aires: Sociedad Editoria Latinoamericana SELA.

Lockhart, James. 1991. *Nahuas and Spaniards: Postconquest Central Mexican History and Philology*. Stanford, CA: Stanford University Press; Los Angeles: UCLA Latin American Center Publications, University of California.

Lockhart, James. 1992. *The Nahuas after the Conquest: A Social and Cultural History of the Indians of Central Mexico, Sixteenth through Eighteenth Centuries*. Stanford, CA: Stanford University Press.

Lockhart, James. 1998. "Three Experiences of Culture Contact: Nahua, Maya, and Quechua." In *Native Traditions in the Postconquest World*, ed. Elisabeth H. Boone and Tim Cummins, 31–53. Washington, DC: Dumbarton Oaks Research Library and Collection.

Lockhart, James 2001. *Nahuatl as Written: Lessons in Older Written Nahuatl, with Copious Examples and Texts*. Los Angeles, CA: UCLA Latin American Center Publications; Stanford, CA: Stanford University Press.

Lockhart, James. 2007. "Background and Course of the New Philology." In *Sources and Methods for the Study of Postconquest Mesoamerican Ethnohistory*. Provisional Version hosted by the Wired Humanities Project at the University of Oregon.

Lockhart, James, Frances Berdan, and Arthur J. O. Anderson. 1986. *The Tlaxcalan Actas: A Compendium of the Records of the Cabildo of Tlaxcala (1545–1627)*. Salt Lake City: University of Utah Press.

Lopes Don, Patricia. 2010. *Bonfires of Culture: Franciscans, Indigenous Leaders, and Inquisition in Early Mexico, 1524–1540*. Norman: University of Oklahoma Press.

López Lujan, Leonardo, and Alfredo López Austin. 2007. "Los mexicas en Tula y Tula en Mexico-Tenochtitlan." *Estudios de la cultura nahuatl* 38: 33–83.

Madajczak, Julia. 2015. "Nahuatl Kinship Terminology as Reflected in Colonial Written Sources from Colonial Mexico: A System of Classification." PhD dissertation, University of Warsaw, Faculty of "Artes Liberales."

Madajczak, Julia, and Justyna Olko. 2015. "Diálogo con Europa, diálogo con el pasado: Antepasados y tradición entre la nobleza colonial nahua." *Revista Española de Antropología Americana* 45 (1): 57–74.

Mannheim, Bruce. 1991. *The Language of the Inka since the European Invasion*. Austin: University of Texas Press.

Martínez Baracs, Andrea. 2008. *Un gobierno de indios: Tlaxcala, 1519–1750*. Mexico: Fondo de Cultura Económica.

Martínez Cereceda, José Luís. 1995. *Autoridades en los Andes, los atributos del Señor*. Lima: Pontificia Universidad Católic del Perú, Fondo Editorial.

Matthew, Laura E., and Michel R. Oudijk□□. 2014. *Indian Conquistadors: Indigenous Allies in the Conquest of Mesoamerica*. Norman: University of Oklahoma Press.

McDonough, Kelly S. 2014. *The Learned Ones: Nahua Intellectuals in Postconquest Mexico*. Tucson: University of Arizona Press.

Melton-Villanueva, Miriam. 2012. "The Nahuas at Independence: Indigenous Communities of the Metepec Area (Toluca Valley) in the First Decades of the Nineteenth Century." A dissertation submitted in partial satisfaction of the requirements for the degree Doctor of Philosophy in History, University of California, Los Angeles.

Melton-Villanueva, Miriam, 2016. *The Aztecs at Independence: Nahua Culture Makers in Central Mexico, 1799–1832*. Tucson: The University of Arizona Press.

Miller, Mary, and Karl Taube. 1993. *The Gods and Symbols of Ancient Mexico and the Maya: An Illustrated Dictionary of Mesoamerican Religion*. London: Thames and Hudson.

Millones, Luís, ed. 1990. *El retorno de las Huacas: Estudios y documentos sobre el Taki Onqoy, Siglo XVI*. Lima: Instituto de Estudios Peruanos, Sociedad peruana de Psicoanálisis.

Miranda M., Juan. 1988. *Catecismo: Diuswan Munanakuypi kawsanapaj*. Sucre, Bolivia: Talleres Gráficos "Túpac Katari."

Molina, fray Alonso de. [1977] 2001. *Vocabulario en lengua castellana y mexicana y mexicana y castellana*. 2 vols. Mexico: Editorial Porrua.

Molina, fray Alonso de. 1569. *Confessionario mayor, en la lengua Mexicana y Castellana*. Mexico: Casa de Antonio de Espinosa.

Molina, Christoual de. 1575? *Relación de las Fábulas y Ritos de los Ingas*. Manuscript 3169, folios 2–36. Madrid: Biblioteca Nacional.

Murra, John Victor, 1983. *La organización económica del estado inca*. Lima: Siglo veintiuno, Instituto de Estudios Peruanos.

Navarro Gala, Rosario. 2015. *El primer notario indígena y su libro de protocolo (Cuzco, siglo XVI): Cuestiones filológicas, discursivas y de contacto de lenguas*. Madrid: Iberoamericana; Frankfurt/Main: Vervuert.

Nowack, Kerstin 2006. "Como cristiano que soy: Testamentos de la elite indígena en el Perú del siglo XVI." *Indiana* 23: 51–77.

Nutini, Hugo D., and Barry L. Isaac. 2009. *Social Stratification in Central Mexico, 1500–2000*. Austin: University of Texas Press.

Obregón, L. González, ed. 1912. *Procesos de indios idólatras y hechiceros*. Mexico: Publicaciones de la Comisión Reorganizadora del Archivo General y Público de la Nación, vol. 3.

Offner, Jerome A. 1983. *Law and Politics in Aztec Texcoco*. Cambridge: Cambridge University Press.

Olivier, Guilhem. 1995. "Les paquets sacrés en Mésoamérique ou la mémoire cachée des Indiens du Mexique central (XVe–XVIe siècles)." *Journal de la Société des Américanistes* 81: 97–133.

Olivier, Guilhem. 2007. "Sacred Bundles, Arrows and New Fire. Foundation and Power in the Mapa de Cuauhtinchan No. 2." Trans. by Scott Sessions. In *Cave, City, and Eagle's Nest: An Interpretive Journey through the Mapa de Cuauhtinchan No. 2*, ed. David Carrasco and Scott Sessions, 281–313. Alburquerque: University of New Mexico Press.

Olivier, Guilhem. 2010. "Los bultos sagrados: Identidad fundadora de los pueblos mesoamericanos." *Arqueología Mexicana* 18 (106): 53–59.

Olko, Justyna. 2011. "Supervivencia de los objetos de rango prehispánicos entre la nobleza colonial nahua." *Revista Española de Antropología Americana* 41 (2): 455–469.

Olko, Justyna. 2014a. *The Insignia of Rank in the Nahua World: From the Fifteenth to Seventeenth Centuries*. Boulder: University Press of Colorado.

Olko, Justyna. 2014b. "El 'otro' y los estereotipos étnicos en el mundo nahua." *Estudios de Cultura Náhuatl* 44: 165–198.

Olko, Justyna. 2014c. "Alphabetic Writing in the Hands of the Colonial Nahua Nobility." *Contributions in New World Archaeology* 7: 165–185.

Olko, Justyna. 2018. *A System at Risk? Animacy and Noun Pluralization in Colonial and Modern Nahuatl*. A conference paper presented on 12.05.2018 at the conference of the Northeastern Group of Nahuatl Scholars. New Haven: Yale University.

Olko, Justyna, and John Sullivan. 2014. "Toward a Comprehensive Model for Nahuatl Language Research and Revitalization." *Proceedings of the Fortieth Annual Meeting of the Berkeley Linguistics Society* 40: 369–397.

Olmos, fray Andrés. 1993 [1547]. *Arte de la lengua mexicana y vocabulario (1547)*. Introduction and transliteration by A. León-Portilla and M. León-Portilla. Madrid: Ediciones de Cultura Hispánica.

Oudijk, Michel R. 2000. *Historiography of the Bènizàa: The Postclassic and Early Colonial Periods (1000–1600 AD)*. Leiden, Netherlands: CNWS.

Pachacuti Yamqui Salcamaygua, Joan. n.d. *Relación de antigüedades deste Reyno del Pirú*. Madrid: Biblioteca Nacional, manuscript 3169, folios 131 [1] etseqq.

Padden, R. C. 1967. *The Hummingbird and the Hawk: Conquest and Sovereignty in the Valley of Mexico, 1503–1541*. Columbus: Harper Colophon Books/Ohio State University Press.

Pärssinen, Martti, and Jukka Kiviharju. [2004] 2010. *Textos andinos: Corpus de textos khipu incaicos y colonials*. Vols. 1–2. Madrid: Acta Ibero-Americana Fennica, Instituto Iberoamericano de Finlandia and Departamento de Filología Española; Facultad de Filología, Universidad Complutense de Madrid.

Paso y Troncoso, Francisco del. 1942. *Epistolario de la Nueva España*. Vol. 16. Mexico: Antigua Librería Robredo, de José Porrúa e Hijos.

Perace, Sarah. 2007. "Translating for Ptolemy: Patriotism and Politics in the Greek Pentateuch?" In *Jewish Perspectives on Hellenistic Rulers*, ed. T. Rajak, S. Pearce, J. Aitken, and J. Dines, 165–189. Berkeley: University of California Press.

Pérez Bocanegra, Juan. 1631. *Ritual formulario e instrucción de curas*. Lima: Gerónimo de Contreras, El Convento de Santo Domingo.

Pérez-Rocha, Emma, and Rafael Tena 2000. *La nobleza indígena del centro de México después de la conquista*. Mexico: Instituto Nacional de Antropología e Historia.

Pizarro, Pedro. [1571] 1978. *Relación del descubrimiento y conquista del Perú*. Edición, Consideraciones Preliminares Guillermo Lohmann Villena y Nota Pierre Duviols, Lima: Pontificia Universidad Católica del Perú, Fondo Editorial.

Pizzigoni, Caterina. 2007. *Testaments of Toluca*. Stanford, CA: Stanford University Press; Los Angeles, CA: UCLA Latin American Center Publications.

Pizzigoni, Caterina. 2012. *The Life Within. Local Indigenous Society in Mexico's Toluca Valley, 1650–1800*. Stanford, California: Stanford University Press.

Prem, Hanns J. 1997. *The Ancient Americas: A Brief History and Guide to Research*. Trans. Kornelia Kurbjuhn. Salt Lake City: University of Utah Press.

Prządka-Giersz, Patrycja. 2014. "Ajuar personal: las mujeres de la élite wari y su atuendo." In *Castillo de Huarmey: El mausoleo imperial Wari*, ed. M. Giersz and C. Pardo, 100–127. Lima: Museo de Arte de Lima – MALI.

Puente Luna, José Carlos de la. 2016. "'En lengua de indios y en lengua española': cabildos de naturales y escritura alfabética en el Perú colonial." In *Visiones del pasado: Reflexiones para escribir la historia de los pueblos indígenas de América*, ed. A.L. Izquierdo, 51–113. Mexico, DF: Universidad Nacional Autónoma de México.

Ramírez, Susan E. 1998. "Rich Man, Beggar Man, or Chief: Material Wealth as a Basis of Power in Sixteenth Century Peru." In *Dead Giveaways: Indigenous Testaments of Colonial Mesoamerica and the Andes*, ed. S. Kellog and M. Restall, 215–248. Salt Lake City: University of Utah Press.

Ramos, Gabriela, and Yannakakis, Yanna. 2014. *Indigenous Intellectuals: Knowledge, Power, and Colonial Culture in Mexico and the Andes*. Durham, NC: Duke University Press.

Restall, Mathew. 1995. *Life and Death in a Maya Community: The Ixil Testaments of the 1760s*. Lancaster, CA: Labyrinthos.

Restall, Mathew. 2003. *Seven Myths of the Spanish Conquest*. New York: Oxford University Press.

Restall, Mathew. 2003. "A History of the New Philology and the New Philology in History." *Latin American Research Review* 38 (1): 113–134.

Restall, Matthew. 2012. "The New Conquest History." *History Compass* 10: 151–160.

Restall, Mathew, and Florine Asselbergs. 2007. *Invading Guatemala: Spanish, Nahua, and Maya Accounts of the Conquest Wars*. Latin American Originals, 2. University Park: Penn State University Press.

Restall, Mathew, and Michel Oudijk. 2014. *Conquista de Buenas Palabras y de Guerra: Una visión indígena de la conquista*. Mexico City: UNAM.

Restall, Matthew, Lisa Sousa, and Kevin Terraciano 2005. *Mesoamerican Voices: Colonial Mexico, Oaxaca, Yucatan, and Guatemala*. Cambridge: Cambridge University Press.

Reyes García, Luis. 1972. "Ordenanzas para el gobierno de Cuauhtinchan, año 1559." *Estudios de cultura náhuatl* 10: 245–313.

Reyes García, Luis, ed. 1988a. *Documentos sobre tierras y señoríos en Cuauhtinchan*. Mexico-Puebla, FCE, CIESAS y el Gobierno del Estado de Puebla. Colección Puebla.

Reyes García, Luis. 1988b. *Cuauhtinchan del Siglo XII al XVI*. Mexico: CIESAS.

Reyes García, Luis, ed. 2001. Cómo te confundes? acaso no somos conquistados? Anales de Juan Bautista. Mexico: Biblioteca Lorenzo Boturini, Insigne y Nacional Basílica de Guadalupe.

Reyes García, Luis et al., eds. 1996. *Documentos nauas de la Ciudad de Mexico*. Mexico: CIESAS and Archivo General de la Nación.

Rojas, José Luis de. 2010. *Cambiar para que yo no cambie: La nobleza indígena en la Nueva España*. Buenos Aires: Editorial SB.

Rojas Rabiela, Teresa, Elsa Leticia Rea López, and Constantino Medina Lima, eds. 1999. *Vidas y bienes olvidados: testamentos indígenas novohispanos*, Vol. I, *Testamentos en castellanos del siglo XVI y en náhuatl y castellano de Ocotelulco de los siglos XVI y XVII*. Mexico: Centro de Investigaciones y Estudios Superiores en Antropología Social.

Rostworowski, Maria, and Craig Morris. 1999. "The Fourfold Domain: Inka Power and Its Social Foundations." *The Cambridge History of the Native Peoples of the Americas*, Vol. 3, *South America*, Part 1, 769–863. Cambridge: Cambridge University Press.

Rowe, John Howlland. 1955. "El movimiento nacional inca del siglo XVIII." *Revista Universitaria del Cuzco* 107 (2).

Rowe, John Howlland. 2003. *Los Incas del Cuzco: Siglos XVI–XVII–XVIII*. Cuzco: Instituto Nacional de Cultura, Región Cusco.

Roy, Hélène. 2013. *La résistance néo-inca de Vilcabamba (1537–1572) et son héritage dans le Pérou actuel: Étude historique et anthropologique*. Thèse pour obtenir le grade de docteur de l'Université de Poitiers.

Ruiz Medrano, Ethelia, and Susan Kellogg. 2016. *Negotiation within Domination: New Spain's Indian Pueblos Confront the Spanish State*. Boulder: University Press of Colorado.

Ruz Barrio, Miguel Ángel. 2007. "La embriagadez indígena en la nueva España." In *Ocio y vida cotidiana en el mundo hispánico moderno*, ed. F. Núñez Roldán, 595–604. Sevilla: Universidad de Sevilla, Secretariado de Publicaciones.

Sahagún, fray Bernardino de. 1950–1969. *The Florentine Codex: General History of the Things of New Spain*, ed. and trans. Ch. E. Dibble and A.J.O. Anderson. 12 vols. Santa Fe: The School of American Research and the University of Utah.

Saignes, Thierry. 1999. "The Colonial Condition in the Quechua-Aymara Heartland." *The Cambridge History of the Native Peoples of the Americas*, Vol. 3, *South America*, Part 2, 59–137. Cambridge: Cambridge University Press.

Salomon, Frank 1988. "Indian Women of Early Colonial Quito as Seen through Their Testaments." *The Americas* 44 (3): 325–341.

Salomon, Frank, and George L. Urioste, translation from Quechua. 1991. *The Huarochirí Manuscript: A Testament of Ancient and Colonial Andean Religion*. Annotations and introductory essay by Frank Salomon, transcription by George L. Urioste. Austin: University of Texas Press.

Sánchez C. Walter and Ramón Sanzetenea R. 2000. "Rogativas Andinas." *Boletín del INIAN-Museo, Serie antropología boliviana* 8.

Schroeder, Susan. 1991. *Chimalpahin and the Kingdoms of Chalco*. Tucson: University of Arizona Press.

Schroeder, Susan, ed. 2010a. *The Conquest All Over Again: Nahuas and Zapotecs Thinking, Writing, and Painting Spanish Colonialism*. Brighton, UK: Sussex Academic Press.

Schroeder, Susan. 2010b. "Chimalpahin Rewrites the Conquest: Yet Another Epic History?" In *The Conquest All Over Again: Nahuas and Zapotecs Thinking, Writing, and Painting Spanish Colonialism*, ed. Susan Schroeder, 101–123. Brighton, UK: Sussex Academic Press.

Schwaller, John F. 2012. "The Expansion of Nahuatl as a Lingua Franca among Priests in Sixteenth-Century Mexico." *Ethnohistory* 59 (4): 675–690.

Schwaller, John F., and Barry Sell, eds. 1999. *A Guide to Confession Large and Small in the Mexican Language (1634)*. Norman: University of Oklahoma Press.

Sell, Barry D. 1993. "Friars, Nahuas, and Books: Language and Expression in Colonial Nahuatl Publications." PhD dissertation, University of California, Los Angeles.

Smith, Michael E. 2003. "Economic Change in Morelos Households." In *The Postclassic Mesoamerican World*, ed. Michael E. Smith and Frances F. Berdan, 249–258. Salt Lake City: University of Utah Press.

Smith, Michael E. 2005. "Life in the Provinces of the Aztec Empire." *Scientific American* 15: 90–97.

Smith, Michael E. 2008. *Aztec City-State Capitals*. Gainesville: University Press of Florida.

Solís, Eustaquio Celestino Armando Valencia R., and Constantino Medina Lima. 1985. *Actas de cabildo de Tlaxcala, 1547–1567*. México, DF: Archivo General de la Nación; Tlaxcala: Instituto Tlaxcalteca de la Cultura.

Spalding, Karen. 1999. "The Crisis and Transformations of Invaded Societies: Andean Area (1500–1580)." *The Cambridge History of the Native Peoples of the Americas*, Vol. 3, *South America*, Part 1, 904–972. Cambridge: Cambridge University Press.

Spores, Ronald. 1993. "Spanish Penetration and Cultural Change in Early Colonial Mexico." In *The Indian in Latin American History: Resistance, Resilience, and Acculturation*, ed. John E. Kicza, 88–107. Wilmington, DE: Scholarly Resources.

Stevens, J. 1706. "A new Spanish and English dictionary: collected from the best Spanish authors, both ancient and modern . . . to which is added, a copious English and Spanish dictionary, likewise a spanish grammar . . . wherein the Spanish dialogues that have been publish'd are put into proper English / the whole by John Stevens. Londres. Viñaza, C. de la (1893): Biblioteca histórica de la filología castellana." Madrid. [Ed. facsímil, 3 vols., Madrid: Atlas, 1978.]

Sullivan, John. 2003. *Ytechcopa Timoteilhuia Yn Tobicario: Acusamos a Nuestro Vicario; Pleito Entre Los Naturales de Jalostotitlán y Su Sacerdote, 1618*. Zapopan: El Colegio de Jalisco.

Sullivan, John, Eduardo de la Cruz Cruz, Abelardo de la Cruz de la Cruz, Delfina de la Cruz de la Cruz, Victoriano de la Cruz Cruz, Sabina Cruz de la Cruz, Ofelia Cruz Morales, Catalina Cruz de la Cruz, and Manuel de la Cruz Cruz. 2016. *Tlahtolxitlauhcayotl: Chicontepec*. Warsaw: Universidad de Varsovia, Facultad de "Artes Liberales"; Instituto de Docencia e Investigación Etnológica de Zacatecas.

Sullivan, Thelma. 1976. *Compendio de la grammática náhuatl*. Instituto de Investigaciones Históricas. México: Universidad Nacional Autónoma de México.

Sullivan, Thelma. 1987. Documentos tlaxcaltecas del siglo XVI en lengua náhuatl. Mexico, UNAM.

Szemiński, Jan 1993a. *La utopia tupamarista*. Segunda edición. Lima: Pontificia Universidad Católica del Perú, Fondo Editorial.

Szemiński, Jan 1993b. "The Last Time the Inca Came Back: Messianism and Nationalism in the Great Rebellion of 1780–1783." In *South and Meso-American Native Spirituality: From the Cult of the Feathered Serpent to the Theology of Liberation*, ed. Gary H. Gossen in collaboration with Miguel León-Portilla, 279–302. World Spirituality. An Encyclopedic History of the Religious Quest, Vol. 4. New York: Crossroad.

Szemiński, Jan. 1997. *Wira Quchan y sus obras: Teología andina y lenguaje, 1550–1662*. Lima: Instituto de Estudios Peruanos, Banco Central de Reserva del Perú.

Szemiński, Jan. 2016. *De las vidas del Inka Manqu Qhapaq: Manqu Qhapaq Inkap Kawsasqankunamanta*. Segunda edición aumentada y corregida. Arequipa: Ediciones El Lector S.R.L.

Szemiński, Jan. 2017 "Apukunap yachaynin." Research in progress.

Sztompka Piotr. 1991. *Society in Action: The Theory of Social Becoming*. Chicago, IL: University of Chicago Press.

Tavárez, David. 2013. "Nahua Intellectuals, Franciscan Scholars, and the *Devotio Moderna* in Colonial Mexico." *The Americas* 70 (2): 203–235.

Tomicki, Ryszard. 2003. "El problema de quauh- en quauhpilli, quauhtlatoani y palabras parecidas." *Anales de Antropologia* 2003: 241–258.

Townsend, Camilla. 2010. Here in This Year: Seventeenth-Century Nahuatl Annals of the Tlaxcala-Puebla Valley. Stanford, CA: Stanford University Press.

Townsend, Camilla. 2016. *Annals of Native America: How the Nahuas of Colonial Mexico Kept Their History Alive*. Oxford: Oxford University Press.

Trelles Arestegui, Efraín. 1982. *Lucas Martínez Vegazo: Funcionamiento de una Encomienda Peruana Inicial*. Lima: Pontificia Universidad Católica del Perú, Fondo Editorial.

Urton, Gary. 2003. *Signs of the Inka Khipu: Binary Coding in the Andean Knotted-String Records*. Austin: University of Texas Press.

Varón Gabai, Rafael. 1980. *Curacas y encomenderos, acomodamiento nativo en Huaraz siglos XVI–XVII*. Lima: P. L. Villanueva.

Vega, Juan José. 1963. *La guerra de los viracochas: Resumen de la conquista del Perú: Con apuntes sobre la Conquista de Ecuador, Bolivia, Chile y Argentina*. Lima: Populibros.

Villella, Peter B. 2016. *Indigenous Elites and Creole Identity in Colonial Mexico, 1500–1800*. Cambridge: Cambridge University Press.

Wachtel, Nathan. 1971. *La Vision des Vaincus: Les Indiens du Pérou devant la Conquête Espagnole (1530–1570)*. Paris: Gallimard.

White, Richard. 1991. *The Middle Ground: Indians, Empires, and Republics in the Great Lakes Region, 1650–1815*. Cambridge Studies in North American Indian History. Cambridge: Cambridge University Press.

Wood, Stephanie. 1991. "The Cosmic Conquest: Late-Colonial Views of the Sword and Cross in Central Mexican Títulos." *Ethnohistory* 38 (2): 176–195.

Wood, Stephanie. 1997. "Matters of Life and Death: Nahuatl Testaments of Rural Women, 1589–1801." In *Indian Women of Early Mexico*, ed. S. Schroeder, S. Wood, and R. Haskett, 165–184. Norman: University of Oklahoma Press.

Wood, Stephanie. 1998. "The Social vs. Legal context of Nahuatl Títulos." In *Native Traditions in the Postconquest World*, ed. Elizabeth H. Boone and Tom Cummins, 201–231. Washington, DC: Dumbarton Oaks.

Zapata y Mendoza, Juan Buenaventura. 1995. *Historia cronólogica de la Noble Ciudad de Tlaxcala*. Transcripción paleográfica, traducción y notas, Luis Reyes García y Andrea Martínez Baracs. Tlaxcala: Universidad Nacional Autónoma de Tlaxcala, CIESAS.

Ziółkowski, Mariusz S., Jarosław Arabas, and Jan Szemiński. 2008. "La Historia en los *Queros*: Apuntes acerca de la Relación entre las Representaciones Figurativas y los Signos *Tocapus*." In *Lenguajes Visuales de los Incas*, ed. Paola González Carvajal and Tamara L. Bray, 163–176. BAR International Series 1848. Oxford: British Archaeological Reports.

Index